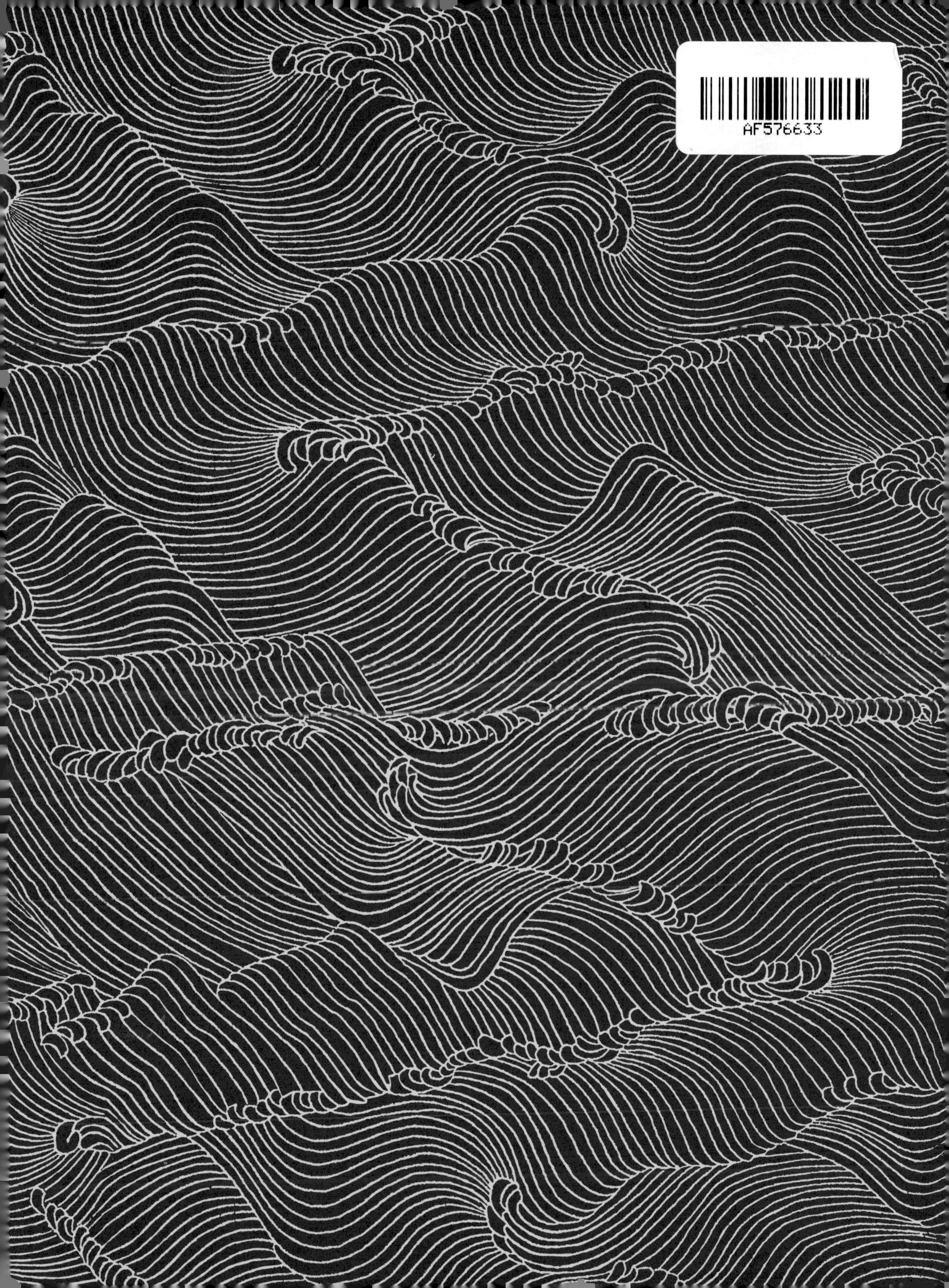

COLLECTING MODERN JAPANESE PRINTS THEN & NOW

(Frontispiece). Yoshida Hiroshi (1876–1950). Titled in the left margin in Japanese *Yamanaka Mura* (Yamanaka Village), titled in English *Fuji-san from Yamanaka.* Also in the left margin in Japanese *jizuri* (self-printed), *Showa juni-nen* (Showa 12 [1937]), woodblock, 25x37.8 cm. Signed Hiroshi Yoshida, sealed in kanji Hiroshi.

From a wide world of outstanding artists with an extensive range of techniques and subject matter, it is difficult to select one to set the tone for a book. We felt, however, that Yoshida Hiroshi would be eminently suitable.

Yoshida is a pivotal figure between the eras of *ukiyo-e* (Japan's antique woodblock prints) and modern creative prints, having had a foot in both worlds. Like the older generation of *ukiyo-e* artists, he chose to emphasize the medium of the woodblock and follow the convention of having an artisan carver and printer to effect his designs. Also like the earlier artists, he often used landscapes as subject matter. From the creative-print artists at the beginning of the twentieth century he borrowed an interest in the Western art aesthetic, to the extent that he traveled to Europe, Africa, and America twice, where he was influential in arranging exhibitions of works of the *shin-hanga* (new print) movement, of which he was so much a part. This book begins from around the time of his death.

In addition, it is said that no matter what theme or motif a Japanese artist pursues, at some time in his career he inevitably presents his view of Mount Fuji, which has long served as an inspiration for Japanese artists. Mount Fuji is the ultimate symbol of Japan and seems to us to serve well as the proper starting point for a venture into the realm of the Japanese print.

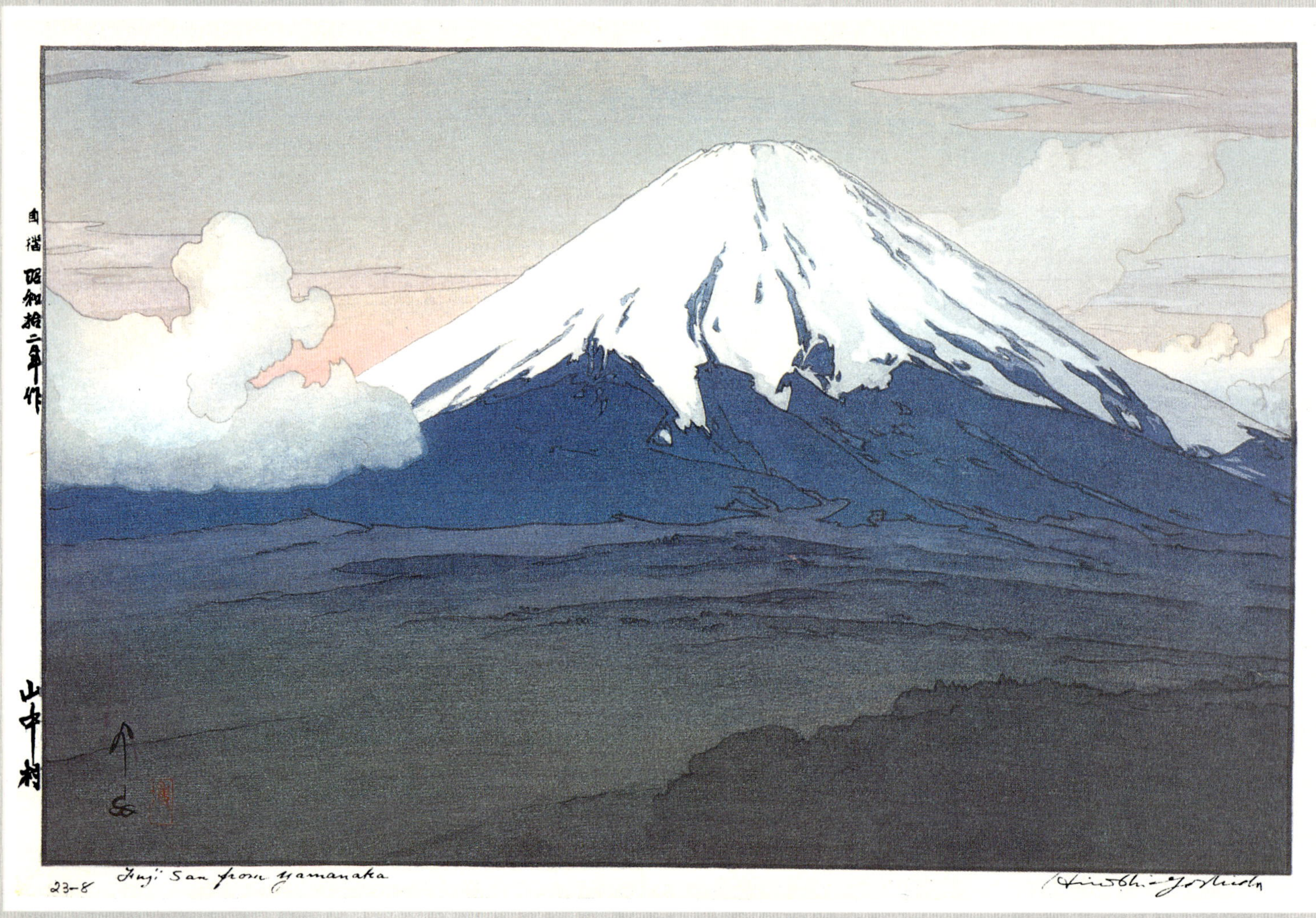
自摺
昭和拾二年作
山中村
23-8
Fuji San from Yamanaka
Hiroshi Yoshida

COLLECTING MODERN JAPANESE PRINTS THEN & NOW

Mary & Norman Tolman

With a Foreword by James Michener

CHARLES E. TUTTLE COMPANY
Rutland, Vermont & Tokyo, Japan

Published by the Charles E. Tuttle Company, Inc.
of Rutland, Vermont & Tokyo, Japan
with editorial offices at
2-6 Suido 1-chome, Bunkyo-ku, Tokyo 112

LCC Card No. 94-60823
ISBN 0-8048-1936-X

First printing, 1994

Printed in Singapore

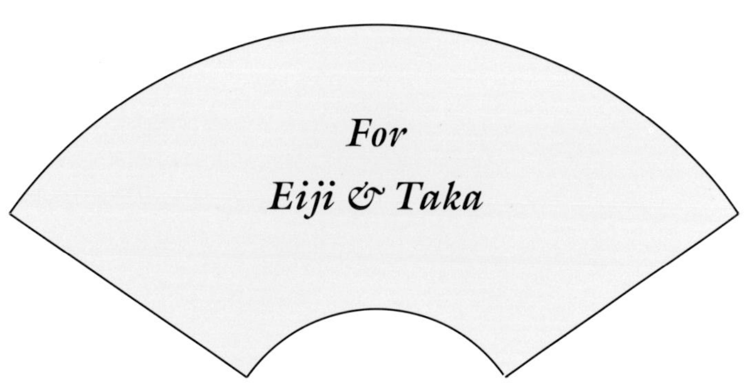
For
Eiji & Taka

Contents

Note: Factual information about each print is found in the caption accompanying the plate. That information includes the author's name and dates; the title or titles of the print; a translation of the Japanese title in parentheses; the edition number; the year; the medium; the image size in centimeters; and particulars concerning the signature and seal.

List of Plates

Acknowledgments

Without the wonderful artists whose works and selves have enriched our lives in every possible way, we would have nothing to write about, so it seems natural to thank them first and we do so from the bottom of our hearts.

Our interest in contemporary Japanese prints was first captured by the writings of James Michener and Oliver Statler, both of whom were pioneers in introducing these wonders to the Western world. Naturally we were ecstatic when Mr. Michener kindly agreed to write the foreword to our book. We extend profound thanks to him.

While compiling the factual information about the artists, exhibitions, and collections, we turned to several sources to whom we remain very grateful for their cooperation. For providing detailed information we are indebted first of all to the artists and their families. Also of particular help were staff members of the Yoseido, Franell, Kato, Nantenshi, Bancho, Print Art Center, and Akira Ikeda galleries in Tokyo; the Yamada Gallery in Kyoto; the M&Y Office of Masuo Ikeda and Sato Yoko in Tokyo; the Hiratsuka Museum in Suzaka City; and the Striped House Museum in Tokyo. We also wish to thank the magazines *Hanga Geijutsu* and *21 Seiki Hanga* for special assistance in tracking down obscure information. Everyone provided cheerful and unstinting responses to our many phone calls concerning who did what when.

Very special thanks must be extended to Ushizawa Fujio of the Yoseido Gallery and Kato Tatsuo of the Kato Gallery. Both have been dear friends all along the way, first as helpful advisors when we began collecting, then as willing consultants when we started our business, and later as steadfast supporters when we became business associates and friendly competitors. Perhaps our first real feelings of success as gallerists can be traced to our first sales to Yoseido and Kato, from whom we had bought so many prints over the years. We must thank them both for serving as sounding boards as to which prints by which artists should be included in this book. We are truly sorry that we could not include every one, but the final choices were ours.

A special debt of gratitude is owed to Terajima Teruo, who is responsible for the photographs of the prints in the book and our photo on the back jacket. We have long appreciated his efficiency, speed, availability, and, of course, his talent. His many years of expertise in art photography will be obvious to everyone.

Our deepest gratitude goes to the two to whom this book is dedicated, Eiji and Taka, who have been indispensable in helping the Tolman Collection achieve the respected status it has today as a major purveyor of contemporary Japanese art throughout the world.

Nagao Eiji, our gallery manager, began on a part-time basis while he was finishing his studies at Meiji University. That was in 1980, and he has been our right-hand man ever since. The many difficulties we have faced as gallery operators have been greatly eased by Eiji, who has actually become a fixture at the Tolman Collection, Tokyo. Starting with virtually no knowledge of prints, under our tutelage Eiji has come to know more about the world of contemporary Japanese prints than anyone else his age because of the active role our gallery has played with the artists themselves.

Yamamoto Nobutaka, our gallery assistant manager, came a few years later, in 1984. Together Eiji and Taka have formed a warm working relationship that has been instrumental in the smooth operation of our gallery. They have endeared themselves to our many clients from all over the world, and when they accompany us on international trips they bring their charm with them. Everyone knows them as Eiji and Taka of the Tolman Collection.

Here we want to thank them for their many years of devotion to our aim of promoting contemporary Japanese prints and, in particular, for their extra hard work during the writing of this book. It is they we must thank for their diligent labor in compiling the biographical data on the artists, much of which was available only in Japanese. We are happy to say that we feel fortunate in having "two Japanese sons" to help our two American daughters in all our ventures.

The Charles E. Tuttle Publishing Company deserves a multitude of thanks, which we wholeheartedly give. Beginning with the books by Michener and Statler, Tuttle has consistently sought out authors who have held a special affection not only for the art but also for the artists who make prints. No words can describe our feeling when we were invited by Nicholas Ingleton, president of Tuttle, to write this book. By placing us in such company he has asserted his confidence in our ability in a most positive way, and we humbly hope that we have met his expectations. In addition, we are grateful to Nick and his staff for help in editing, designing, and laying out this book.

Foreword

by James A. Michener

One of the most rewarding adventures I've had in the world of art occurred when I was a correspondent in the Korean War. On frequent leaves for R & R, rest and recuperation, I scurried over to Japan, where I met an extraordinary young man. Oliver Statler, from a suburb of Chicago, had remained in Tokyo after World War II as a member of General Douglas MacArthur's Occupation team. With both skill and an aptitude for making friends among the Japanese, he accumulated the rich materials he would later use in writing his international bestseller *Japanese Inn*.

In the course of his researches, which reached back to 1945 when he landed in Japan along with MacArthur, Statler, who had wide experience in the arts, had become acquainted with a group of Japanese woodblock artists who were remaking the traditions of that ingratiating art form, the *ukiyo-e* print. Those prints dealt with the "floating" or underground world of geishas, samurais, and sumo wrestlers and was made famous by world-class artists like Masanobu, Harunobu, Kiyonaga, Utamaro, Sharaku, and especially Hokusai and Hiroshige. Their prints won worldwide approval, with major collections assembled in Paris, in London, and notably in Boston.

But the classic *ukiyo-e* print, of which I would collect some six thousand, had become typecast, offering mainly scenes of Japanese life, portraits of famous geishas, and landscapes of Mount Fuji. The younger artists of Statler's day longed to become not Japanese artists bound by the old clichés but artists in the worldwide sense, free to use any subject matter that inspired fellow artists in Paris, New York, or Vienna. They rejected the designation *ukiyo-e* artists, preferring the term *hanga* artists, and this handsome book portrays their art and the revolution they engineered.

Statler was so impressed with their work that by the time I reached him he had already assembled a huge collection of their best work, and in time he would have one of the world's best collections of the modern Japanese print. He was so excited by his discoveries that he launched me on an exploration of the field, and this present volume reproduces work by some three dozen artists I collected at that time. Before long I became an aficionado, and even formed fast friendships with several of the artists and carvers whose work I admired.

In those exciting days, when each visit to Tokyo brought

new discoveries, the field was dominated by four artists, three of whom are not represented in this publication because their work antedated the time period covered by this book. Hashiguchi Goyo had produced ravishingly beautiful portraits of women from everyday Japanese life, but he had little effect on the larger movement. Munakata Shiko composed wonderful designs in bold black and white, while Onchi Koshiro, with a European taste welded to a strong Japanese tradition, did captivating prints that could have been done by Klee, Miro, or Schwitters, had they been Japanese. He would exert a powerful force on the printmaking of his day.

The fourth dominant figure in this early postwar period was Saito Kiyoshi, who is handsomely represented here (plates 2, 58). Many American and European collectors started their gathering with two or three Saitos, and his works still command attention.

My affection goes to the work of two men I knew well. Azechi Umetaro (plate 14) was a rugged little fellow who excelled in mountaineering and whose prints reflected that obsession. Hiratsuka Un'ichi (plates 5, 76) was a handsome old man when I knew him as a family friend, and I marvel at his continued productivity as he nears the age of one hundred. I love his bold use of black and the effectiveness of his depiction of Japanese architecture.

Since this excellent book is divided into three parts—"Then," "Between Then and Now," "Now"—it is obvious that most of the artists whose work I knew well and collected will fall in the first segment, and seeing them again gladdens my heart. How bold are the two Sasajima Kiheis (plates 4, 91), how delightful to see again an architectural print by Hashimoto Okiie (plate 6). I once bought several strong ones from him as we talked in his studio.

I break into laughter when I see Mori Yoshitoshi's three wild rickshaw pullers (plate 8), and Inagaki Tomoo's *Long Tail Cat* (plate 11) demonstrates how the artist can utilize traditional line to depict a radically new type of subject matter.

I recommend enthusiastically the final portion of the Tolmans' book, for it gives affectionate accounts of experiences the couple has had as collectors. Each story is different, each is instructive as to how amateur aficionados matured into sophisticated operators of a modern-print gallery that often commissions specific artists to produce prints typical of their best work. This means that this book is in some ways an advertisement for the prints they have on sale, but this emphasis can be forgiven because of the very high quality of the work they sponsor.

Were I still on the scene and collecting—the collection my wife and I did make has been given to the Honolulu Academy of Arts—I am sure I would want to add the following prints: Iwami Reika's elegant *Silver Waterfall* (plate 27) because of its imaginative use of texture; Kinoshita Tomio's delightful *Gray-Colored People* (plate 51) because of its amazing sense of being an actual woodblock; Mori Yoshitoshi's warmhearted *Tsukiji Fish Market* (plate 50) because it recalls old-style works that featured many human beings; and Nakayama Tadashi's *Running Horses* (plate 44) because it represents the joyous freedom with which these newer artists work.

There remains one other print whose artist I had not heard of, and a special case he is. Clifton Karhu is an American of Finnish ancestry and is thus a prominent example of the recent phenomenon in which foreign artists have come to Japan to learn the business of making prints and have succeeded. But I would want this print (plate 52) for another reason. It depicts the kind of Japanese house with which I was familiar in the postwar days. In the inland town of Morioka, north of Tokyo, I lived in such a house during my earliest days in Japan, and seeing this print evokes a world of nostalgia.

I believe that anyone with a love of art and the mysterious miracles it can perform would find in postwar prints one or two examples of this exquisite art that would give her or him great pleasure and understanding. How about six that came to me as a complete surprise: plate 55 (Watanabe Sadao) because of its use of Western legend; plate 56 (Takahashi Hiromitsu) because of its use of very old Japanese legend; plate 59 (Sekino Jun'ichiro) because it exhibits the marvelous accuracy of Japanese carving; plate 60 (Maki Haku) because of its stark Japanese simplicity and design; plate 65 (Miyashita Tokio) because of its Klee-like exuberance; and plate 79 (Shinoda Toko), the mistress of the lot for two strong reasons: it was done by a woman artist, a rarity, and it bespeaks the soaring simplicity of much of the best postwar work.

Austin, Texas

Preface

It is reported that when asked their occupation, some 70,000 Japanese listed it specifically as "artist." One can realize then the impossibility of including more than a handful in this book, even though we are concentrating only on the modern print. Our purpose is to tell the story of contemporary prints from a position of our own close involvement for more than a quarter of a century, starting as poor students, continuing as diplomats (still poor but with better connections), and moving through the period of beginning, evolving, maturing, and finally becoming successful art dealers and avid collectors for whom, at present, finding has become more of a challenge than acquiring.

Our point of view is necessarily a particular one from which we hope to lead new collectors along a path we have already trod, minus the pitfalls. Naturally we have written about those artists whom we have come to know best personally.

This book contains several bodies of information. An introductory essay puts Japanese prints into historical perspective and gives a brief outline of techniques. The second section, "Then," illustrated with prints by the older masters of the twentieth century, seeks to describe how we went about putting together our collection. There should not be many surprises here since these artists, many in their seventies, eighties, and nineties, will be known and easily recognized by anyone who has even a minor interest in modern Japanese prints. These artists have been written about at great length elsewhere, though not perhaps from our unique viewpoint as collectors and dealers.

The following section, "Between Then and Now," is a lengthy essay meant to be amusing. In this book about collecting, this essay gives a play-by-play description of a collector and his determined search for a specific print. It was not intended to be the ultimate in name-dropping, but was included to indicate the esteem and admiration that Japanese prints command abroad.

The last section, "Now," using fifty artists with fifty illustrations to explain specific points about print collecting, gives not only objective facts about each artist and his work but also includes anecdotes that may help a collector better recognize and remember them. Some of these artists have already been briefly mentioned in the "Then" section. We wish to state that not all of the artists talked about are artists whom we handle in our gallery; we also hasten to point out that all of the artists whom we do carry are, of course, included here.

We have presented all of the prints in full color, in as large a format as possible, so that the art lover can savor the details of each work. We sell prints every day and have attempted to write the text in a rather breezy manner, in much the same way we deliver our presentation to clients from more than thirty-five nations. Since we have been doing this for twenty years, we have come to realize what sort of information people are looking for to make a print come alive for them.

During the gathering of the prints in the "Then" section, we were young students and following that, diplomats. There was never a single purchase that did not require a sacrifice since, as everyone knows, neither students nor diplomats are noted for voluminous amounts of disposable income. Nevertheless, we found that our involvement with prints came to be one of the most absorbing and satisfying aspects of our lives. We continued to search for the works we read about, saw illustrated, yearned over at galleries and museums, or simply stumbled across in unlikely places. Needless to say, this hobby cramped us monetarily for years.

After a while, when we found our original occupation to be less and less rewarding both emotionally and financially, we decided to make a change and become art dealers, a decision we have never regretted. This did not happen overnight. During the years Norman worked in the Cultural Office (USIS) of the American Embassy in Tokyo and in its various branches throughout Japan, quite a bit of time was given to visiting divers artists, escorting state visitors to interesting ateliers, helping artists with little English-language ability answer their overseas correspondence, arranging the presence of artists at ambassadorial dinners or other embassy functions, and, in general, having a great deal of contact with the Japanese art scene.

It does not occur to most people that one cannot actually go to school and take a few courses to learn how to be an art dealer. On-the-job training seems to be the only road to knowledge in this area. But our very strong interest and heavy private involvement provided an inestimable background and a certain amount of preparation for our new career.

Being young and idealistic, we were also quite ignorant in not realizing what it would be like to start a business from zero with 1) no business experience, 2) insufficient capital, and 3) no known clients. What we did have in our favor was unquenchable enthusiasm and a deep and total sense of adventure to spur us on, along with two small daughters who enjoyed their three square meals a day. As they say nowadays, it's the bottom line that counts. After the usual amount of trial and error and occasional success, with a certain amount of good luck usually measurable in direct proportion to the hard work entailed, we eventually managed to evolve a formula of doing business that has enabled us to have a life filled with encounters with artists, with the prints we love, and with our clients, who obviously enjoy our enthusiasm for this aspect of Japanese culture. But hard work it was, harder than we thought we were capable of—even more arduous than the years we had spent learning to speak, read, and write Japanese.

Japanese etiquette requires that people apologize in advance for situations and circumstances in which Westerners would not necessarily feel a need. Having lived here for a long time, we know that we must extend our expressions of regret to the many outstanding artists whom we could not include in this book.

As we have mentioned, writing a personal book means having the prerogative to draw on specific prints and on particular contacts with certain people. Naturally we have chosen the ones we know and like best but at the same time feel that they present a very good picture of the print world from the late 1950s to the early 1990s, as witnessed by us during the two separate phases of our encounter, first as collectors and later as dealers. We hope that readers will begin to learn about and to recognize the works of the various artists and will come to enjoy and understand to some extent the breadth and depth of the contemporary Japanese print world.

Since this is not intended to be a scholarly work, we hope readers will approach it with the idea of enjoying our experiences as we have lived them, and perhaps finding relevance in their own quests as collectors.

Introduction

Historical Background

It does not seem fair to hurl an interested reader directly into the twentieth-century world of contemporary Japanese prints without providing a few historical signposts along the way. The complex journey of Japanese prints from "then" to "now" extends back at least to the eighth century, and we would like briefly to mention some of the crossroads.

The importation of Buddhism to Japan from China through Korea in the sixth century created the necessity for devotional images. The missionaries brought, along with their philosophy, the art of woodblock printing. Circa A.D. 765 Japan's Empress Shotoku, who was an avid follower of the new religion, decided that everyone else should be too. She ordered millions of sutras, amulets, images, and prayers to be printed for dissemination among the temples and the populace. The new religion (unlike the indigenous Shinto religion, which had little iconography) required representational art to portray its extensive pantheon. This art had to be quickly produced in multiple copies, and for that purpose the woodblock medium was well suited. During the following centuries woodblock prints associated with Buddhism were produced with an ever-increasing degree of technical expertise.

In the late fifteenth century Portuguese and Spanish trading vessels came to Japan, introducing Christianity as well as the art of copperplate etching and other Occidental methods of drawing and printing. However, due to the strict ban on Christianity officially imposed by the shogunate in 1637, the learning of these techniques was discouraged because of their foreign and religious associations.

Until the middle of the seventeenth century, fine art, especially painting, had been the province of the elite classes—samurai, nobility, and priests. After Tokugawa Ieyasu set up the shogunate in Edo (now Tokyo) in 1603, a new class began to arise—merchants and townsmen—with its own demands for popular mass art. Woodblock prints began to be churned out as book illustrations, as broadsheets and advertisements, as albums of erotica and novels, as wall decorations and souvenirs of travels, and as simple scenes depicting contemporary manners and customs.

The heyday of this genre occurred from the seventeenth to the nineteenth centuries, and the prints are known as *ukiyo-e* (Japan's antique woodblock prints, literally pictures of the fleeting world). Japan was still an isolated country much turned in upon itself, but the class of society that had recently come to the fore created a demand for mass-produced art. *Ukiyo-e* were definitely a product of the rapid social changes occurring among newly affluent city dwellers.

These woodblock prints of colorfully bedecked courtesans, flamboyantly dramatic Kabuki actors, and dramatically presented landscapes (especially those of Hiroshige and Hokusai) have been Japan's cultural ambassadors for decades. Even as recently as twenty years ago, when the Japanese government or the Cultural Affairs Agency was asked to mount a show of Japanese prints overseas, it invariably trotted out *ukiyo-e* as representatives of Japanese print art. Frankly these works, no matter how lovely one may consider them, have been the bane of our existence as dealers in contemporary Japanese prints. Not only have they convinced Western minds that coy geisha and grimacing actors are the symbols of Japan, but they have also come to be regarded everywhere as the sole representatives of Japan as "the land of the woodblock print." In the meantime, Japanese artists have moved far ahead, anticipating the twenty-first century, and these old cultural icons are no longer fitting to represent the Japanese print world. It is true, of course, that Japan has long been renowned for its artists' expertise in woodblock printing, but not to the exclusion of the multitudinous other techniques currently being used in the print world.

We will make the point numerous times, but this might as well be the first mention: the Japanese excel at what they choose to do. They have borrowed many things from other cultures, both Asian and Western, perfecting them and making them their own. Everything is grist for the collective national mind in every field of endeavor, and art is no exception.

The *ukiyo-e* print, in particular, which has made a worldwide impression, was the product of several people: an artist, a carver, a printer, and a publisher. The collaboration worked well. The artist provided the design (quite often suggested by the publisher, who was usually not only educated but also astute as to what would please the public); the carver pasted the design on the block and did the appropriate carving; the printer pulled the proofs; the publisher handled distribution. *Ukiyo-e* were extremely popular with the general Japanese public, but the formal art establishment regarded them simply as multiply reproduced pictures for the mass market and therefore not worthy of serious consideration. The editions were not numbered and even today it is guesswork to decide exactly how many were made originally.

With the diplomatic opening of Japan to the outside world in 1853 (with the famous "black ships" of Commodore Perry setting the tone) communication began to flow in two directions. Western painting and printing techniques, perspective, and color were of great interest to the heretofore isolated Japanese artist, while the charming and exotic *ukiyo-e* crossed the seas to become a hit in Europe, influencing such important Impressionist artists as Whistler, Degas, Cassatt, Manet, Monet, Van Gogh, and Toulouse-Lautrec. (It is interesting to note that many Japanese who traveled abroad in the twentieth century were immediately attracted to these

European artists, probably because the strong line and perspective they were using reminded them of their own tradition.)

In North America in the early days of the twentieth century, three Americans were fundamentally responsible for the fact that today the Boston Museum of Fine Arts has more than 100,000 *ukiyo-e* among its holdings. Ernest Fenollosa, a native of Massachusetts and a teacher at Tokyo Imperial University, began to collect in great numbers in 1888. He encouraged his friend Dr. William Bigelow, a Boston surgeon, to become interested in *ukiyo-e,* and Bigelow bought thousands. In the 1920s when Frank Lloyd Wright came to Japan to design and build the Imperial Hotel, he also was smitten and raised large amounts of money among Boston art lovers to add to the already phenomenal museum collection.

By the time the Japanese realized that both Europeans and Americans had acquired *ukiyo-e* in enormous numbers and had taken them abroad, there were not so many left in Japan. In addition, the production of *ukiyo-e* had begun to decline since the demand in Japan had disappeared, basically because the society and mores that had been depicted in these prints were no longer in existence. Ironically, Westerners, particularly in Europe, were creating bold, new, colorful compositions in the Japanese style, while the Japanese were eagerly attempting to assimilate the interesting methods of Western-style painting and printmaking.

During the Meiji era (1868–1912) it was clear that the art of *ukiyo-e* was seriously on the wane. For a short while there was a burst of enthusiasm for works portraying the newly arrived foreigners in the ports of Yokohama and Nagasaki, and these enjoyed a certain popularity because of their "exoticism," but the genre itself fell into a decline.

Thereafter Japan fought two wars (with China and with Russia), and in the decade or so following 1894 *ukiyo-e*-style prints of victorious battle scenes were in demand. Along with the importation of Western arts, letters, and science during this period was the introduction of aniline dyes, so one can often distinguish these Meiji era prints by their garish red and purple tones.

In the early twentieth century two differently focused art movements arose at the same time. One produced *shin-hanga* (new prints) and the other *sōsaku-hanga* (creative prints). The only thing they basically had in common was the use of the woodblock technique.

Shin-hanga are connected with the publisher Watanabe Shozaburo (1885–1962), who attempted to breathe new life into the then moribund *ukiyo-e.* Finding sympathetic artists, he encouraged the *ukiyo-e* method of collaboration among artist, carver, printer, and publisher, as well as the traditional *ukiyo-e* imagery of idyllic landscapes and "beauties," stylized portraits of beautiful women.

The three best-known artists of the early twentieth century are Ito Shinsui (1898–1972), Kawase Hasui (1883–1957), and Hashiguchi Goyo (1880–1921). Their prints are softly sentimental and lovely, and they enjoyed great commercial success because they were produced expressly to meet the demand of foreigners who wanted an image of "traditional Japan." They also helped perpetuate the myth of Japan as a land of graceful kimonoed women, continuously falling cherry blossoms, and ruined castles with a moon hanging overhead.

The world of *sōsaku-hanga*, however, with the woodblock technique as its chief medium of work, diverged in several ways important enough to change the course of printmaking in Japan. Through travel and exposure to magazines and art books, Japanese artists gradually became inspired by the artistic revelations coming from Europe, namely, that an artist could design, carve, print, and distribute his work by himself; that prints could be made in small, numbered editions; and, most important of all, that print art was an art form in its own right and not looked down upon as a "reproduction technique."

The *sōsaku-hanga* artists began to gain confidence, enough to enter their works in overseas juried biennials. In 1951 at the First São Paulo Biennial, Japanese sculptures and paintings were passed over, and prizes were awarded to the printmakers Saito Kiyoshi and Komai Tetsuro. The Japanese art establishment was stunned. In 1955 when Munakata Shiko won the Grand Prix at the Third São Paulo Biennial, it became clear in Japan that prints would now have to be considered in a different light—not as mass-produced works by artisans but as creative art in numbered editions. This was the beginning of the new role for prints in the Japanese art world.

The artists who came to prominent attention over the next two decades, especially internationally, were products of the *sōsaku-hanga* movement. They will be discussed in some detail later in this book since they were the liberal, imaginative, and indomitable springboard pointing the way for future generations of printmakers.

General Terms

Some of the terminology used in the book probably needs clarification. For example, we speak of "original prints," which seems a contradiction in terms, but the phrase traditionally means work that has been designed and personally executed by the artist on the block or plate to be handprinted. This is different from a "reproduction," which has been manufactured by mechanical or photographic means. Using the word print in a sentence like "I bought a print of the Mona Lisa when I was in Paris" adds to the confusion. The traveler in Paris may indeed have bought a "print," but that is not the sort of print we are referring to in this book. The word print is loosely bandied about, but we are narrowing the definition to mean a work of fine art made in multiple copies, each of which is an original. There is no "original" from which others have been reproduced by an automatic copier or photomechanical process. The print is a distinct and independent art form.

Over the years there have been several international conferences to try to pin down the meaning of the expression "original print." The convention agreed upon is that at the very least the artist must have been the creator of the idea and the executor on the medium used, whether it be wood, metal, stone, or screen, from which the inked image is then transferred to paper. In addition, the prints should be individually numbered and signed by the artist.

In the early days of the creative-print movement in Japan, the artist wished to do everything himself—create the design, execute it on the block, and do the printing as well. But we must remember that at that time, in the early twentieth century, woodblock prints were the primary form of print art in this country, probably because one needed only a small studio and a few tools to carry out the various processes.

Nowadays, with a preponderance of silkscreen and lithographic prints, it is an accepted international practice to use a professional printer. This has come to be the case in Japan as well. The average artist's biggest stumbling block in this country is lack of space. It is difficult for an aspiring artist in Tokyo, for example, to be able to afford the astronomical price required to buy or even to rent a small studio in which to house a behemoth of a lithographic press—or even to afford the press itself.

The solution is to use an established atelier operated by skilled, professional printers who are completely in tune with the artists for whom they work. An artist often collaborates with only one printer, who understands his special requirements. The printer must have a rapport with the artist so that he can contribute the experience, knowledge, technical expertise, and especially the quality demanded by the artist. Shinoda Toko, for example, has used the same printer, Kimura Kihachi, for thirty years.

There are quite a few professional ateliers in Japan manned by hard-working, conscientious printers who strive for perfection. Their desire to produce work of impeccable quality is part of the Japanese artisan tradition of craftsmanship. Since there are numerous studios, the competition is keen, and artists can shop around until they find the exact one to suit their needs.

The advantages for an artist in having a good printer are many. The most important is that the artist is free to think, to create, to imagine a new work without having to go through the time-consuming process (or drudgery, some would call it) of printing what has already been invented. The printer, who is a professional with a skilled staff, can operate with speed and excellence, printing an entire edition at once and greatly simplifying the life of the art dealer and the public as well, both of whom are waiting in the wings for the new masterpiece to be released. This is the scenario for a great number of silkscreen and lithographic print artists in producing their works.

On the other hand, Japanese woodblock printmakers, for the most part, still prefer to do their own work right through to the completion of printing. One reason may be that they do not need so much room, since they ink each block by hand and print their works without a large press or a studio space of magnificent size. An equally important consideration might be that they actually enjoy the tactile interaction with the handmade paper and the natural wood, and that the carving and printing processes give both a physical and an emotional pleasure. In addition, some artists like to test the water to see whether or not their new print will be popular and saleable. Woodblock print artists, in particular, have the option of printing just a few copies. There is no need to make the whole edition if the first prints do not have a warm reception. Those artists who use printing ateliers are committed to having their entire editions printed at once. Of course, printing an entire edition can be a disadvantage if, for some reason, the work fails to attract an audience.

This self-printing by woodblock makers is common in Japan, but the complete edition of a print is seldom pulled all at once. The artist gets tired or bored and wants to go on to something new. He keeps a journal, however, in which he lists the title of the print and how many copies he eventually intends to produce. If he sets the total edition number at fifty, for example, perhaps he makes ten at first and then goes on to another work. It may even be a few years before he gets out his old blocks and decides to make another ten copies because he happens to be in the mood to work on that particular print.

This pattern was especially common in the early years of the creative-print movement. The artists were basically interested in creating a print, carving it, and printing just a copy or two to see the various results that could be obtained. Many of the earlier print editions have never been pulled in their entirety.

The older *sōsaku-hanga* print artists are notoriously the most individualistic of all. Some of them dated their prints the year they first printed them; others dated them the year the block was carved no matter how much later they may have been printed; and still others refused to date their prints at all. There is a lot of work coming up for the art historian fifty years from now!

When we speak of an "edition," we are referring to the total number of prints to be made from a specific image. "Original prints" are in "limited editions," an order indicated on the bottom of the print, as in 32/50, with 50 meaning the size of the entire run and 32 indicating that particular number among the fifty.

People often ask if a lower number is better than a higher one. Our experience has been that there is seldom any difference. First of all, in Japan (and we are speaking in particular about contemporary Japanese prints, in which nothing less than excellent technical execution would even be considered), the editions are relatively small so it is highly unlikely that the block or plate will get worn down and produce an image of a lesser quality.

Secondly, who knows what is first and what is last? We have been present in an artist's studio as he was preparing to number an edition. He had just spread it all out when his telephone rang. When he returned to begin his numbering, he started at the opposite end to that he had originally chosen!

In addition, when there are many stages in the printing of each color, the artist hangs each print up to dry here and there, not necessarily in the order in which he printed them, so there is bound to be some confusion. Some people feel better if they own a #1, and perhaps that magic number will have some commercial value later on. But it does not necessarily indicate the first print produced, nor does it mean that it was the best printing.

The technical standard of printing in the Japanese print world is very high, but when works of art are pulled by hand there are bound to be small variations. That variety is the beauty of a handmade work as opposed to a photocopied reproduction. Sometimes the first few prints pulled seem the best; sometimes the artist does not get into his stride until he has warmed up and made twenty prints or so. But keep in mind that in Japan technical excellence can be taken for granted, so the real criterion is whether or not you like the print. And with copies of the same print, the one you like is the one for you.

An aesthetic evaluation is subjective. If one has a few copies to choose from, the selection process can sometimes be difficult because the variations are minute. On the other hand, if there is only one copy to look at, comparison is irrelevant. Making an effort to look at prints in galleries and museums adds to one's knowledge and helps develop an eye for knowing what is excellent and what is mediocre. It is important for a budding collector to find a gallery with a good reputation for handling fine work, one whose taste in artists corresponds to that of the collector, and one whose staff is willing to be an educational source as well. There is no substitute for putting in the time simply to "look."

In addition to the works that are strictly numbered in the "limited edition" series, one may come across another notation at the bottom of a print, A.P. or AP for artist proof or E.A. for *épreuve d'artiste*. Originally the term artist proof simply meant a test or trial proof of the different stages in the printing process. Later it came to be called a *bon à tirer,* the artist's notation on the final proof indicating that the printer could then proceed, using that particular proof as the standard for printing the entire edition.

Nowadays the term has evolved to mean that artists by convention are allowed to make ten percent of their edition in the artist-proof category. Some artists number their proofs, as in A.P. 2/5, some use Roman numerals to indicate proofs, but there is no fixed rule. Some artists simply write A.P.

In general, the idea of artist proofs has some merit. The artist has A.P.'s to use as entries in biennials or for other exhibition purposes, to give as gifts, or for a reciprocal exchange with other artists. The temptation to abuse this system exists, however. There are a few artists who, upon discovering that a particular print has been wildly popular, will continue to make A.P.'s for the market as long as the demand lasts. Fortunately this is not a common practice among Japanese artists, but people who are interested in collecting should be aware of it. We find that we look at A.P.'s with a gimlet eye since we view the practice as a basically reprehensible one. Collectors who pay for a limited-edition, numbered print should not have their investment diluted by a plethora of A.P.'s manufactured by the occasional greedy and unscrupulous artist. As a result of this feeling, our gallery policy has been not to traffic in artist proofs at all.

As collectors we must confess that we have occasionally bought an A.P. because we loved the particular print and could not pass it by. Usually this has happened with the older prints of the *sōsaku-hanga* era, when the editions were quite small. As owners, however, we do not sell artist proofs in our galleries.

Along with the edition number at the bottom of the print, one is also likely to find the title and the artist's signature. One cannot generalize about these, however. Sometimes prints are not titled at all; some artists sign their name at the bottom but others use their personal seals; other artists do both, sign and chop.

Generally speaking, the edition number, title, and artist's signature are written in pencil at the bottom of the print. Why pencil? In the case of original prints, it seems to be the tradition worldwide but, of course, there are exceptions. We clearly remember that in the early days Saito Kiyoshi often signed his name in white ink on the image itself.

Another question often asked is why so many Japanese artists title their works in English. (We have noticed that those artists who have studied at the famous French ateliers also like to title their prints in French.) One immediate thought is that perhaps they feel it is exotic or chic. But the answer is more fundamental than that.

The first audience to recognize, love, and appreciate the artistry of Japanese prints has always been foreigners. The Japanese never considered their early *ukiyo-e* prints as "art." Only when the

Impressionists found them a source of inspiration, when Dutch, German, and French collectors began to lavish praise and actually buy them, and when the Americans began to collect seriously for the Boston Museum of Fine Arts did the Japanese begin to pay attention to their own prints.

The reason contemporary prints are almost always titled in Roman letters is related to this phenomenon, and history, not surprisingly, is repeating itself. It is a fact that again today it is foreigners—most galleries would estimate approximately eighty percent—who are the buyers of contemporary Japanese graphic art. Therefore, it is counterproductive for an artist to title his work in Japanese since most of his potential audience may not be able to read it.

Contemporary Japanese prints are still being bought on the international level by private collectors, museums, and galleries as fine examples of the most creative and sophisticated graphic art being produced today. But where are the Japanese buyers? There are a few, of course, who are aware of and appreciate what present-day artists are doing. They are among those whom one would call confident and knowledegable, and they deserve praise for having the courage of their convictions. Unfortunately there are not many of them. The average Japanese may be reluctant to say what he really likes for fear of being laughed at. He would rather go with world opinion for the tried-and-true masters because that view avoids embarrassment.

Great publicity in recent years has been given to those Japanese who have rushed to the various famous auction houses to buy Impressionist paintings at outrageously inflated prices. At the same time another group of Japanese, enjoying their affluence during the "bubble economy," also dashed off to the same auction houses in Europe and the U.S. to buy and bring back their own *ukiyo-e* prints of the eighteenth and nineteenth century, prints that had long charmed the West and had won a loving and appreciative audience there but had been scorned by the Japanese art establishment in the past.

Suddenly these very same prints, which allegedly had once been used as wrapping paper for shipping Japanese porcelain abroad—this story may be true, since the works were produced in enormous quantities—were commanding unheard-of prices in all the art "marts." The Japanese were out there buying everything and bringing it back home.

Printing Techniques

Today's prints are a far cry from the *ukiyo-e* of yore. The diverse and high-tech choices available to printmakers now are almost without limit. An artist can combine any number of other processes with the woodblock, lithograph, silkscreen, and etching techniques, which are the basic types of printmaking media, to produce what is termed a mixed-media print. He can experiment with photographic techniques, lasers, computer graphics, collages of diverse materials built up on a matrix and then printed (collagraphy). In short, the latest scientific printing breakthroughs are the modern print artist's dream. Young Japanese artists enjoy blending all of the new processes with those from their own ancient woodblock and stencil heritage, thereby creating something new and uniquely Japanese.

Each artist responds to the multitude of techniques available in an individualistic way because each technique conveys a different feeling on paper. Artists do not choose printing techniques at random. They use one form or another because it is emotionally or technically satisfying for what they wish to portray: the texture of handmade paper and wood grain in a woodblock print; the painterly effects achievable in a lithograph; the purity of solid color and hard edges characteristic of a silkscreen; the exquisite detail possible in an etching.

Despite the numerous variations available, print techniques can be reduced to some basic forms. We do not want to write a book about the numerous techniques because that information is widely available, but we would like to provide some rudimentary information as a guideline for the general reader.

The relief print includes woodblocks, wood engravings, linocuts, and collagraphs. Knives, gouges, scoops, or chisels are used to cut away the part of the material that will not be included in the image. The raised surface is inked and printed, with a separate carving, inking, and printing of each block for a multicolored print. Since a separate block is used to print each color, the placement of the paper in the exact same spot on the inked block is required for precise color registration throughout the whole printing process. To insure that the color prints in the same place each time, the Japanese artist uses a *kentō* (a small groove about the thickness of the paper that is notched into the block, generally on the lower right corner and along the edge of the left side). The artists slides the paper into the *kentō* notching, thereby insuring that it does not move and that the color registers consistently in the exact area to be printed.

Woodcut print artists almost always use *washi* (handmade Japanese paper), which is dampened, put face down on the inked block to be printed, and then rubbed on the back in a circular motion with a *baren* (a handmade disk of tightly coiled rope within a bamboo sheath). Many woodblock artists make their own *baren* to fit their hand and their personal touch.

Woodblocks are especially suited for delineating strong lines and broad areas of color, and the grain of the wood plank itself can often be found as part of the texture in the final print. If one looks at the reverse side of a woodblock work, the circular rubbing strokes of the *baren* will be apparent where the ink has been absorbed into the paper. In the old days of *ukiyo-e*, cherry wood was employed, a wood that restricted the size of the final print. Today the woodblock artist has access to other choices, including plywood, so woodblock prints can be made in much larger sizes than ever before.

A wood engraving is different from a woodblock because the wood used is taken from the end grain of the block, and the tools used are those of an engraver, allowing the artist to achieve the fine lines and detail of an etching. Wood engraving is a less spontaneous process than woodblock printing and demands contemplation and patience.

The lithographic method of printing images from a flat surface (the planographic process) was invented by a German, Alois Senefelder, in 1798, and is based on the fact that grease and water do not mix. Lithographs are made on a specially ground and polished stone, zinc, or aluminum plate upon which the artist draws his image with a greasy crayon, pencil, or special oily ink. The plate is then chemically "set" with gum arabic and nitric or phosphoric acid. When the plate is dampened and inked for printing, the ink will adhere only to the greasy particles and will be rejected in the undrawn portions.

Lithographs require a press with a sliding bed that moves under a wood and leather scraper that applies the pressure to transfer the image to the paper. A separate plate is made for each color used. Because the artist can draw directly on the plate, he can enjoy spontaneity of gesture and can experiment freely. Sometimes the images resemble paintings, since many textures and tonalities can be achieved, depending on the skill of the artist.

Silkscreen printing (serigraphy) is basically a stencil process requiring a silk, nylon, polyester, or fine wire-mesh screen. The screen is tightly stretched across a wooden or aluminum frame and the areas not to be printed are blocked out by a material like paper, glue, or specially prepared lacquer film. The ink is forced through the screen with a rubber squeegee onto the paper below, where it appears to be lying on the paper's surface. One of the great advantages of silkscreen printing is that the image created on the screen does not have to be prepared in reverse by the artist, as is necessary in all of the other printing processes.

This printing method has its origins in primitive and prehistoric art, probably having been used even as a way of tattooing. In the Orient it has long been employed to create fabric designs. In Japan, as far back as the eleventh century, it was used to decorate samurai leather armor and horse trappings. Today, along with being a method for fine-art printing, silkscreen printing is widely used commercially since it can be applied to just about any surface—paper, vinyl, glass, cloth, ad infinitum.

A unique stencil technique employed in Japan is *kappazuri*, which requires a special matrix made by laminating together several sheets of *washi* with *kakishibu* (persimmon tannin), then smoke-drying the laminated sheet to produce a highly water-resistant and durable stencil. This method has been used for ages for dyeing Okinawan *bingata* textiles, for printing family crests on kimono, and as a supplementary technique in the making of *ukiyo-e*.

The artist affixes his rough sketch to the stencil paper and then cuts away his "key" impression with a small, sharp knife. From this "key" he will proceed to cut individual stencils for each color to be printed. Prior to the printing, a dye-resist paste is applied to the portions of the design to be left blank. Each color process requires an application of resist paste in the places not to be dyed. After the colors are all printed, the "key" stencil is placed over the print and the entire print is covered with the resist paste. The "key" is then removed, and when the paste has completely dried the uncovered "key" lines are printed with India ink. After the ink dries, the resist paste is washed off and the work is complete. One can see why the stencil has to be very strong to withstand all of these processes.

Intaglio (from the Italian meaning cut into or engrave) is a generic term for a variety of etching techniques. Pits or grooves are created on a copper, zinc, aluminum, or steel plate in two ways, either with a sharp tool or by the action of a strong acid solution. Greasy ink is then worked into these depressions and the surface of the plate is wiped clean. Using a press resembling a giant wringer, the artist places his dampened paper on the plate and runs it through the press. The intense pressure forces the paper into the incisions and the image is thus transferred. Intaglio prints are easy to identify because the printing pressure is so great that the plate leaves the image depressed and raises the margins surrounding it.

Basic intaglio processes executed with sharp tools are engraving, drypoint, and mezzotint. In engraving, the artist uses a wedge-shaped or pointed steel instrument called a burin to work directly on the plate, scraping the metal away. The result is a hard, crisp line. In drypoint, a steel needle displaces the metal on the plate, not only incising a line but leaving a burred edge. Both incision and burr hold ink, so the resulting printed line is soft and feathery. Mezzotint is similar to drypoint except that a rough burr is raised all over the plate with a heavy, serrated tool called a rocker, so that the plate will print totally black. Tones are then developed with a burnishing tool. (Hamanishi Katsunori, one of Japan's outstanding young mezzotint artists, says that creating this burred background with a rocker is boring and tedious and he does it while watching TV.)

The most common intaglio processes using acid are etching and aquatint. In an etching, scrapings in the plate are produced by drawing with a needle through an acid-resistant wax base and then immersing the plate in an acid bath that "bites" into the lines. Darker lines are produced by lengthening the immersion time and strengthening the acid. In aquatint, the plate is dusted with rosin particles, which are then melted to adhere them to the plate. The acid in the bath bites around the particles to create a tonal effect. This process is often combined with other intaglio techniques.

Printmaking seems well suited to the Japanese temperament, which prizes excellent and precise workmanship. In oil paintings or watercolors, one can sometimes discern the occasional blurring of a line, a little smudge here or there, and find it unique or charming. But there are no allowances made for any vagaries in the execution of a print. There can be no element of chance when the knife cuts into the wood, no tentativeness in the engraving of a plate. The line is final; there is no going back. Everything is clearly calculated to produce an exact and certain result.

Print artists are always intrigued by the many avenues available to achieve their desired expression. Moreover, it is impressive to see the broad range of imagery, techniques, and combinations that emerges from each new generation of artists. The creative use of these varieties adds to the delight of the collector.

On top of that, we can add that Japanese printmakers in particular have long been noted for their respect and feeling for their materials, for their artistic sensitivity, their single-minded devotion to their work, their eye for composition and color, and their heritage of printing. Japan has changed a great deal, overwhelmingly in just the past two decades, but artistic ideals have remained consistently high.

This bustling country provides an atmosphere rich in contrasts, having jumped from a long, feudal, isolated past into the mainstream of the international economic and political world in just 135 years. The contemporary Japanese artist has a virtual panorama of images to draw on, from quaint temple gardens to the glitzy neon of the Ginza. And now that so many artists are traveling and studying in foreign countries, they are culling additional inspiration from both East and West for a visually exciting and stimulating amalgam of original work.

The art of the print is alive and well in the hands of the Japanese printmaker, who at present, as never before, is enjoying a confident and prominent position on the international art scene. The outpouring of vigorous and exuberant new work is a delight.

The prints illustrated here provide ample visual proof that Japan's new cultural ambassadors have the same appeal and vitality as their *ukiyo-e* predecessors and are a testimony to a continuing tradition of virtuosity and elegance. They are the nation's cultural voice in the international art forum, the couriers of a continuing contribution to the world of print art.

Then

Our collection began with a woodblock print by Saito Kiyoshi called *Clay Image, 1950* (presently on loan to the University of Maryland at College Park and thus not illustrated here). It depicts four *haniwa* (ancient Japanese clay tomb figures), two of them in full face and two in profile, executed in black, white, gray, and terracotta. I saw the print at an exhibition in New York in the fall of 1967 and knew that I had to have it. How can one explain this kind of elemental appeal that a work of art can exert? The faces of the figures were obviously from a primitive culture much like those that had produced the African or pre-Columbian artifacts that had such an enriching influence on many Western artists, including Picasso. Like them, these Japanese figures command a universal fascination because of their simplicity and vitality.

The print in New York was not for sale. "Maybe you could find a copy of it in Japan," said the clerk unfeelingly. Little did she know that a trip to Tokyo was on my schedule, a stopover for embassy consultation en route to my posting at the U.S. Consulate General in Hong Kong. Now after all these years of living in Japan I recall that day still. Imagine having only a thirty-six-hour stopover for official business and spending much of one's free time tramping the pavements looking for a print, with hardly a word of Japanese at one's command. I did not get the print at that time, but I got something even more valuable—Saito Kiyoshi himself—and we still have him as a dear friend after all these years.

I eventually located the Murakami Gallery, which specialized in Saito's work. A lengthy description of the composition was duly given to Mr. Murakami, who racked his brain and with patience and kindness showed me all of the Saito woodblocks he had on hand. They numbered into the hundreds, and though I leafed back and forth for almost three hours, the sought-after print did not appear. Much time had elapsed, and the still polite Mr. Murakami explained that he did not exactly know the print I was looking for and, in fact, seemed to doubt its existence, even though he was Saito's son-in-law and knew the master's works very well.

Since my heart was set on that print only, I thanked him for his time, bought nothing, and dejectedly turned to leave, actually bumping into an older gentleman in the doorway. "Wait!" shouted Mr. Murakami. "It's Saito-*sensei*." The thrill of meeting this famous man who had made such an impressive body of woodblock prints was a memorable experience. We have often wished in retrospect that we had been able to buy one of every work of his available that day.

Yet again, the story of the elusive print was told, with Mr. Murakami translating into Japanese for Saito. I did not speak Japanese at that time, and even today when interpreting between our clients and artists I clearly remember the frustration of not being able to communicate. Saito immediately recalled the print from my description. He said that he thought he had a copy in his studio, and if so it was mine. Lunch was then brought in and a long friendship was launched.

Several weeks later, Mary, on her way to join me in Hong Kong with two small children in tow, went through the "search and find" process—so much of the "charm" of getting around in Tokyo—located the gallery, got the print, paid the bill, and our collection was officially on its way.

We have long enjoyed the pleasure of Saito's friendship. During our time in Hong Kong, reading in the newspaper that he was to stop there on his way back from a sketching trip to India, I immediately phoned my counterpart in the Japanese Consulate General, Kato Koichi, now a well-known Japanese politician and recent chief cabinet secretary, whose response at that time to "Where is Saito Kiyoshi?" was "Who is Saito Kiyoshi?" Never one to give up, I phoned various hotels where Japanese were likely to stay and found him on the third try.

Mary and I quickly organized a large party and presented Saito to the Hong Kong art world. Later, after our transfer to Japan, he was the first artist we contacted, and his personal introduction to other artists, galleries, and personalities in the print world was instrumental in establishing us as serious art lovers and patrons. We have been guests in his home in Kamakura when he lived there, and have also visited him in Aizu Wakamatsu, his old hometown, current residence, and the subject of more than one hundred prints in the *Winter in Aizu* series. He has literally put the snowy scenes of this northern area on the artistic map. We are always invited to the openings of his many shows in Tokyo and make every effort to attend them all, including one on March 23, 1994, at the Odakyu Department Store Museum, taking place just as we are writing this. (We succumbed yet again and added another Saito to our collection.) During a recent opening of his works at the Odakyu Department Store in Shinjuku, Saito started to speak and suddenly stopped, telling the audience in his charming, unaffected manner, "I don't want to be saying the same old things over and over. Besides, there is someone here who knows more about Japanese prints than all of us." To our great surprise, he asked Norman to speak, the ultimate compliment from the master.

And so we begin with "Then" and Saito Kiyoshi, at a time when each purchase was a major decision, whose memory brings to mind an entire gamut of emotions and experiences that seems real even today. In those days Saito was often the first Japanese print artist whose work any foreigner might be expected to encounter. His woodblocks were extremely popular with Americans in postwar Japan, and hundreds found loving homes throughout the U.S. He was already famous when we began to collect, so it was not necessary for us to put our aesthetic feelings on the line by admitting that we loved his work. Everybody loved it. Even *Time* had used his compositions on two covers, portraits of prime ministers Sato Eisaku and Fukuda Takeo. Many museums collected his prints and he had won international acclaim as the first woodblock artist from Japan to capture a prize in the renowned First São Paulo Biennial in 1951. In addition to the technical excellence of the work, we enjoyed the colors, the exotic (to us, as newcomers to Japan) subject matter of *haniwa*, temple courtyards, and thatched-roof villages in wintry Aizu. Each print left a singular impression. After the fortitude required first to find the gallery and then to allocate the money to buy the print, each succeeding acquisition became gradually easier as our fortunes and sense of direction improved.

Saito's works are widely imitated, but to the aware art lover there is never any confusion as to the real thing. No one else uses those specific colors and no one else's work can convey that certain essentially Japanese predilection for texture, simplicity, and pattern epitomized in Saito's works.

Plate 2 *Maiko, Kyoto (S)* is an almost erotic composition showing the back view of a *maiko* (apprentice geisha) with the nape of her neck exposed, which is considered quite sensual in Japan. Saito has depicted her from an unusual angle, getting right to the heart (or neck) of the matter. Her kimono and patterned obi, in which the natural grain of the woodblock has been used to provide texture, are striking. With the understatement that characterizes Japanese prints, Saito has conjured up the entire geisha mystique simply by using four dabs of color—one of brilliant red and three of terra-cotta—to suggest the *maiko*'s decorative hair ornaments. In the same terra-cotta hue, he depicts the neckline of the kimono from an unusual perspective, stirring the imagination and heightening the sensuality of the *maiko*. The beautiful face is not revealed, but is saved for one's imagination. Being able to own and repeatedly look at this print enabled us gradually to come to some understanding of the Japanese appreciation for what is unstated but implied.

In those days of collecting and searching for the "real Japan," Sekino Jun'ichiro seemed a likely artist to pursue. His vignettes of tranquil Kyoto courtyards, undulating tile roofs, and scenic villages presented glimpses of such irresistible charm that one suspected the artist of making them all up. The joy of discovering that the subject was a real place that could actually be visited was a delight almost as
Plate 3 great as finding the print itself. *Keio Hyakka-en* (a place name) is such a print. Who could imagine that this idyllic vista of floral beauty, with its field of luxuriant irises, was not just in the artist's mind but was actually viewable if one got off the train at Keio Tamagawa Station in the suburbs of Tokyo. *Now* it is slightly annoying to find that recent compositions by other artists are often imaginary, but *then* it was different.

I am reminded of an incident that occurred many years after our collection had developed to significant proportions. Although we owned several of Sekino's landscapes, we had neglected a very important aspect of his oeuvre—his skill in portraiture. His depictions of Bunraku and Kabuki actors as well as other famous figures from the art world are well known. One particular portrait haunted us. We had never seen the actual print, but it kept appearing regularly in books, magazines, and catalogues. It was also featured prominently in Oliver Statler's book *Modern Japanese Prints: An Art Reborn*, an invaluable tool to anyone who is at all interested in the early days of the *sōsaku-hanga* movement. This trailblazing book was published in 1959 and reprinted numerous times by the same Tuttle Publishing Company involved in this work. Nine years later James Michener wrote *The Modern Japanese Print: An Appreciation*, also published by Tuttle. These two books were the first important works in English on the early modern print artists and were the proverbial Bibles in our quest for prints. Even now hardly a day goes by when we do not cite them as references.

The Sekino print mentioned above, *Kichiemon, Kabuki Actor*, appeared in 1947. In those days immediately following the war, the creative-print movement itself was in its infancy, paper was scarce, editions were hardly ever pulled in their entirety, and records were sketchy. I despaired of ever finding and owning a copy of this print.

Then one day we were invited to a major retrospective of Sekino's work at the Central Museum Gallery on the Ginza. We all know that hope springs eternal, especially to collectors, and so it was with high spirits that we looked forward to the show. Mary, our gallery manager, Nagao Eiji, and I, converging from different quarters at the agreed hour, planned to meet at the Central Museum Gallery at five o'clock. Eiji and I, having finished our respective appointments early, used the time to drop in at the Yoseido Gallery, for us at that time the main source of *sōsaku-hanga* prints. I inquired in passing, not really expecting an answer, about Sekino's works. The gallery staff had, of course, also been invited to the retrospective and knew of the interest that such an event would engender. "Why, yes," they said, "we do have something that you might be interested in." Out came the portrait of Kichiemon. I still savor the moment.

But there was a catch to this story. The price they quoted was enough to stop even the most dedicated and well-heeled collector in his tracks. The gallery kindly agreed to hold the print overnight. Even they knew that the price required a bit of further consideration and that the print certainly was at the acme of saleability with the retrospective show occurring just down the street.

At five o'clock Eiji and I met Mary at the opening, got in line, congratulated the artist, listened to the speeches, and drank the toast. Then while others dug into the lavish buffet that usually

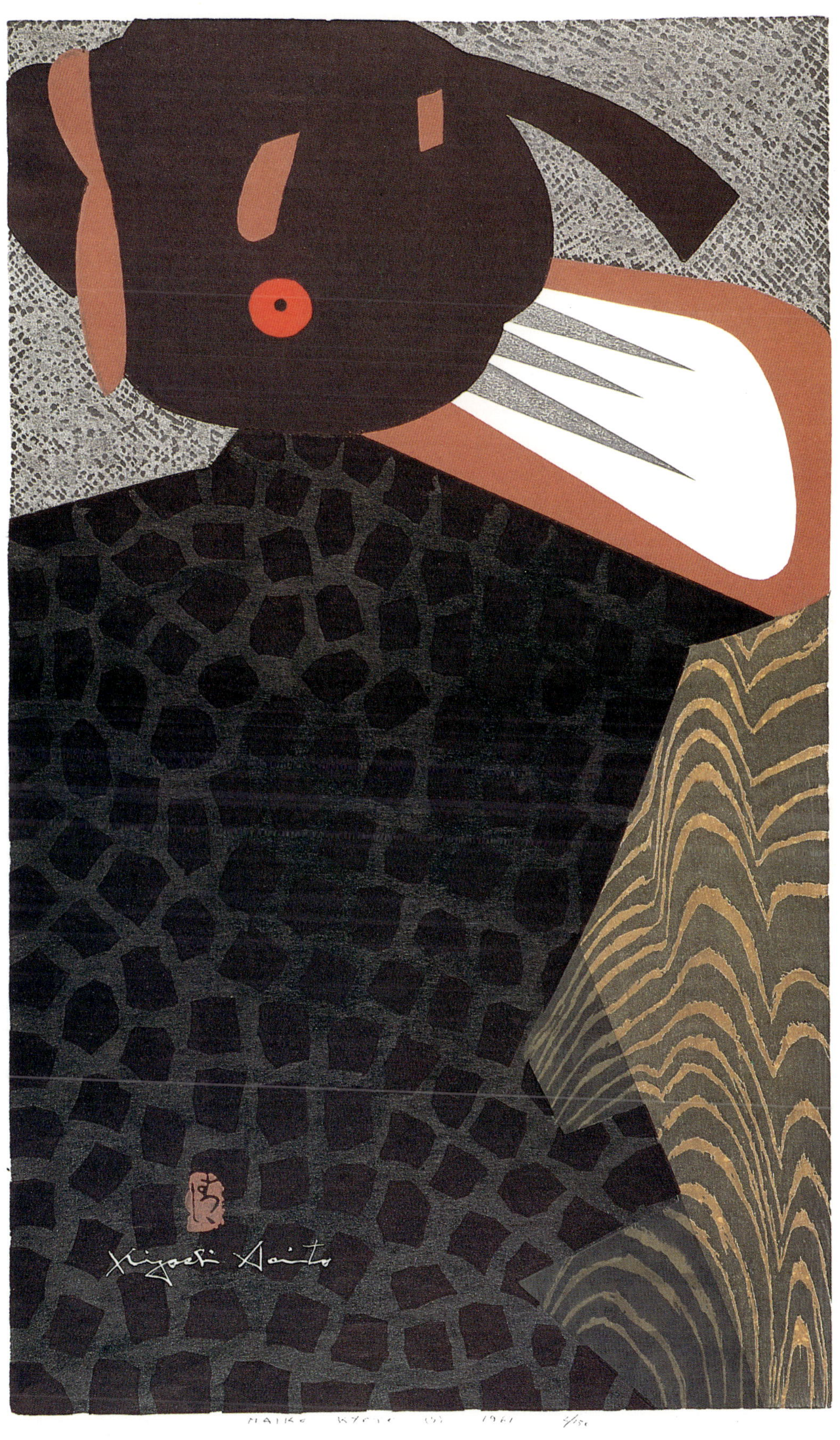

2. Saito Kiyoshi (b. 1907). *Maiko, Kyoto (S),* 2/150, 1961, woodblock, 75.5x44.5 cm. Signed on the image Kiyoshi Saito, sealed in kanji Kiyoshi.

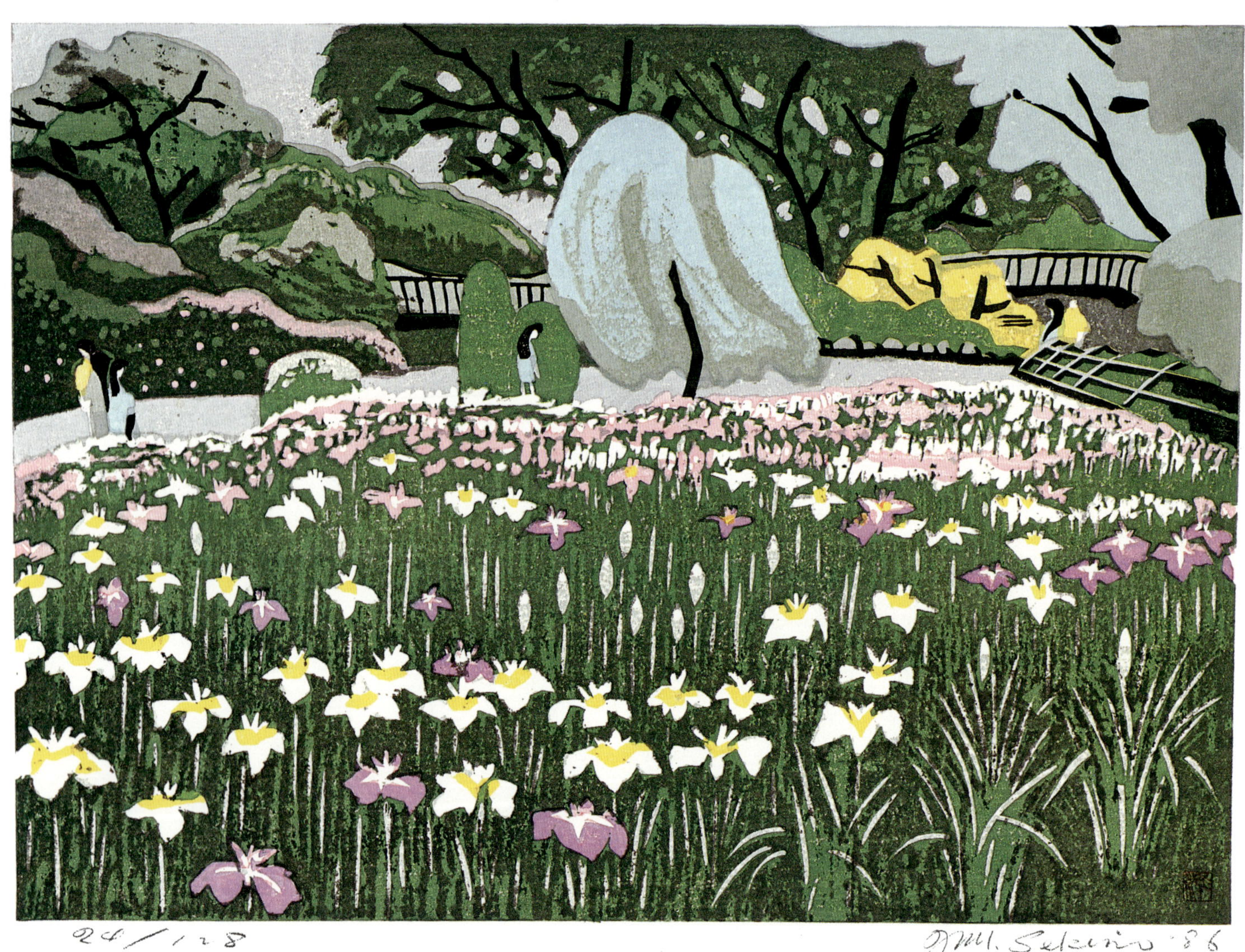

3. Sekino Jun'ichiro (1914–88). Titled in Japanese *Keio Ka Hya-en* (Keio Flower Garden). (The Japanese should be *Keio Hyakka-en* but Sekino was known to transpose characters as well as edition numbers. He normally made editions of 128 but some prints are marked 182.) 24/128, 1986, woodblock, 32.9x45.1 cm. Signed Jun Sekino, sealed in kanji Jun.

accompanies such openings, our little threesome scurried around the show, scanning every piece and especially checking the tags. Considering the status and reputation of the artist, prices were not too high, though certainly not inexpensive. Kichiemon's portrait was not there. I felt it, of course, poignantly beckoning from the "hold drawer" at the Yoseido Gallery, so I knew it was safe at least overnight. We almost decided on several other works to buy, but before that were able to speak with Sekino and ask about the prints in the show. Smoothly (or so I thought) I inquired about his portrait of Kichiemon. "Oh, I think that was one of my very best works," said Sekino. "Of course, it's gone now, but if you ever find one you should have it at any price."

That did it. We quickly excused ourselves, and there are probably people even today who recall Mary being lifted up under each arm by Eiji and me and trundled with alacrity down the Ginza back to Yoseido to retrieve Kichiemon before they closed for the night or changed their minds by morning. Mary regretted having to leave so many beautiful prints back at the retrospective. However, one look at Kichiemon was enough. She gulped at the price, we paid it, and took it home. It is still one of the most expensive prints we have ever bought.

Sekino died in 1988, but the role he played as a teacher and influencer of many artists, including Iwami Reika and Miyashita Tokio, is amply evident in many of the prints in this book.

Since we have had the privilege of living throughout Japan, in Tokyo, Yokohama, Sapporo, Kyoto, and for the past twenty years back in Tokyo again, our collection embodies a certain breadth that our repeated geographic relocation provided. At the start we did not know very much about Japanese history, customs, and culture, but as we continued collecting prints we were able to use our curiosity about them as a tool to learn more. Although many artists live in Tokyo, our postings in other cities put us in close personal touch with those artists who might have been otherwise unavailable or inaccessible to the novice.

It was obvious at the beginning that we would have to learn more about the two major religions of Japan, Shinto and Buddhism, particularly because temples, shrines, and pagodas are everywhere. Sasajima Kihei's Buddhist prints and Hiratsuka Un'ichi's renderings of temple and shrine precincts helped one appreciate not only the architectural accomplishments of Japan's coexisting ancient religions but their influence on a multitude of art forms.

Sasajima passed away last year, and although I was sad to hear the news since we have many of his prints that we count among our favorites, I cannot honestly say that their creator was someone whose company I particularly enjoyed.

Sasajima was a loner. Born in Mashiko, a rural locale known for its *mingei* (folk art) pottery, he came to Tokyo as a school teacher and was first introduced to prints when he happened to take an art class for teachers that was taught by the great Hiratsuka, one of the fathers of the *sōsaku-hanga* print movement. In addition, his hometown friend, a Living Cultural Treasure for pottery, Hamada Shoji, introduced him to Munakata Shiko, another Living Cultural Treasure for prints, and so Sasajima was in good hands with the best teachers and excellent connections. But somehow he never quite fit in, being on really friendly terms with only very few people, such as Saito Kiyoshi, whose warmth embraced everyone.

Knowing of his difficult personality perhaps I should not have been so optimistic when I went to ask him to allow us to sell his work in our fledgling gallery. An unsophisticated man from the countryside, Sasajima made no bones about not intending to take up with a yet unknown gallery (ours) and refused completely, abruptly, and finally.

I attributed his refusal to a major operation he had just had, my bad timing, and his overall poor health. Later I realized that Sasajima was definitely from the old school with a strong feeling for prior loyalties and may have felt that in his weakened condition he might be able to fulfill his commitments only to those galleries with which he already had a connection and obligation.

Our feelings for this artist's works are ones of admiration. His vigorous black-and-white woodblocks of raging mountain brooks, rugged forests, and other facets of the strength of nature are powerful and dynamic. However, that first face-to-face encounter made a disagreeable impression, and I have always remembered Sasajima's tongue as being as sharp and direct as his carving tools.

The uncompromising effect of black and white is this artist's

Plate 4

forte. The untitled print of a Buddhist deity shown here was but one of a myriad of nearly similar compositions that he devoted his time to in his later years. The artist's desire to be a good craftsman is germane to his way of thinking about woodblock prints, and his starkly powerful works reflect this. The multifaced, multiarmed Buddha expresses another aspect of this artist—the importance of his religion. He hoped during his life to accumulate merit, as is the Buddhist belief, by producing thousands of these images, each one a prayer.

Hiratsuka Un'ichi, now aged 99, has lived in Washington, D.C., with his daughter since 1962, so it is hard to believe how much he had already accomplished in the print world in Japan before then. He is acknowledged as one of the stalwarts and a main teacher of *sōsaku-hanga,* having instructed dozens of young artists who went on to great heights. His role in establishing prints as a recognized, bona fide art form in Japan was carved out when most of the artists working today were not yet born. Through his decades of incessant chipping away by teaching, through his own writings, and through his promotion of various magazines specializing in

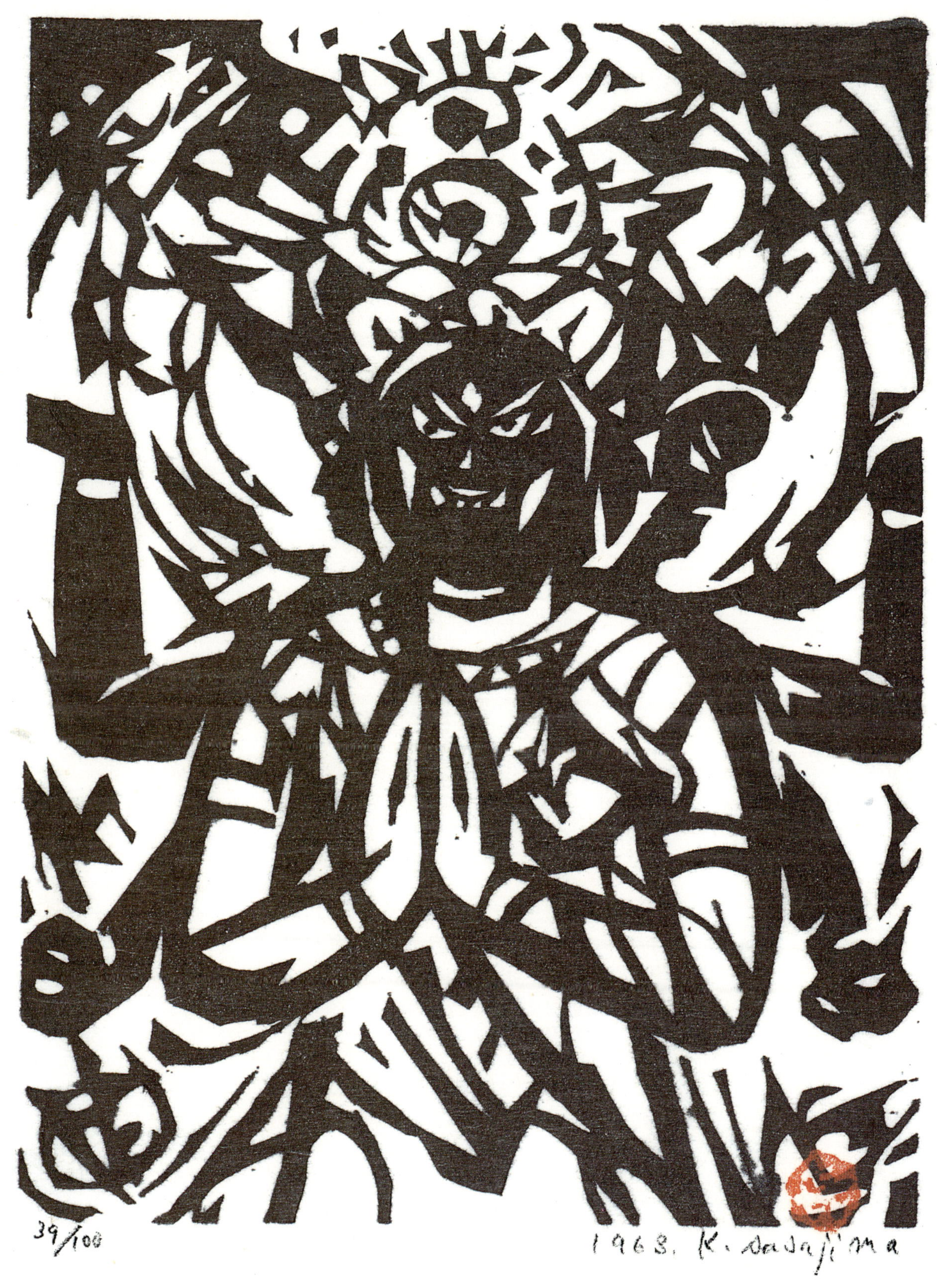

4. Sasajima Kihei (1906–93). Title unlisted but known to be one of a series on the Buddhist deity Fudo, 39/100, 1963, woodblock, 30.5x22.8 cm. Signed K. Sasajima, sealed in kanji Sasa.

print art, he was instrumental in forwarding the aims of the new movement and gave it heart and courage.

Hiratsuka, like Munakata, has been the subject of attention even in English-language materials, so there is not much need to discuss his role at length except to say that it has been an immense one. Since 1962, however, he has worked at his own pace and produces the occasional print of American scenery as the spirit moves him. During our early collecting period, when we had read the few books available, it was obvious that a collection of any significance would have to include his work.

Like all artists of genius, Hiratsuka makes his prints look effortless, but anyone who has ever tried to convey line, mass, tension, and emotion with only black and white will know the
Plate 5 difficulties to be faced. *Uchi Kongō Hyokunji* (a temple name) demonstrates the artist's mastery as well as his devotion to Buddhism. The strong, assured lines make the weighty temple building appear to be a massiveness rooted in the earth, full of power and might. As the artist is the son of a shrine carpenter and the grandson of an architect, it is not surprising that he is especially skilled at reaching so unerringly to the heart of these imposing old structures.

Hashimoto Okiie was another near centenarian who passed away during the writing of this book. He studied seriously to be an artist during a regular four-year liberal arts college course, unlike so many of the early generation who were largely self-taught. He became an art teacher to earn his living, dabbling occasionally in printmaking for his own enjoyment. After retirement he still had several decades of print productivity. Gardens, castles, and other admired historic spots in Japan were his passion, possibly a result of his long friendship with Hiratsuka, who also loved old Japan. Hashimoto had taken one of Hiratsuka's printmaking courses in the early days and they became lifelong friends. To both of these artists we owe a debt for their recordings of historical and traditional Japanese scenes, which spurred us on to learn more about the history of the country.

Plate 6 Hashimoto's *Osaka Castle,* with its somewhat exaggerated scale of height of the moat walls and its clearly delineated stones, conveys the majesty of the stronghold and the esteem the artist felt for this remnant of the colorful samurai past. It is a quiet but masterful print.

Mabuchi Toru (who often spelled his given name Thoru), another of Hiratsuka's students, was also influenced toward things Japanese by his mentor. However, although he used the woodblock medium, his subjects were presented in a form resembling mosaic and pointillist imagery, inspired by his longtime interest in the art of Byzantium and of the French painter Seurat. His work *From the*
Plate 7 *Earth* depicts five *haniwa* that somehow look rather decorative because of the Byzantine coloring and rhythmic design.

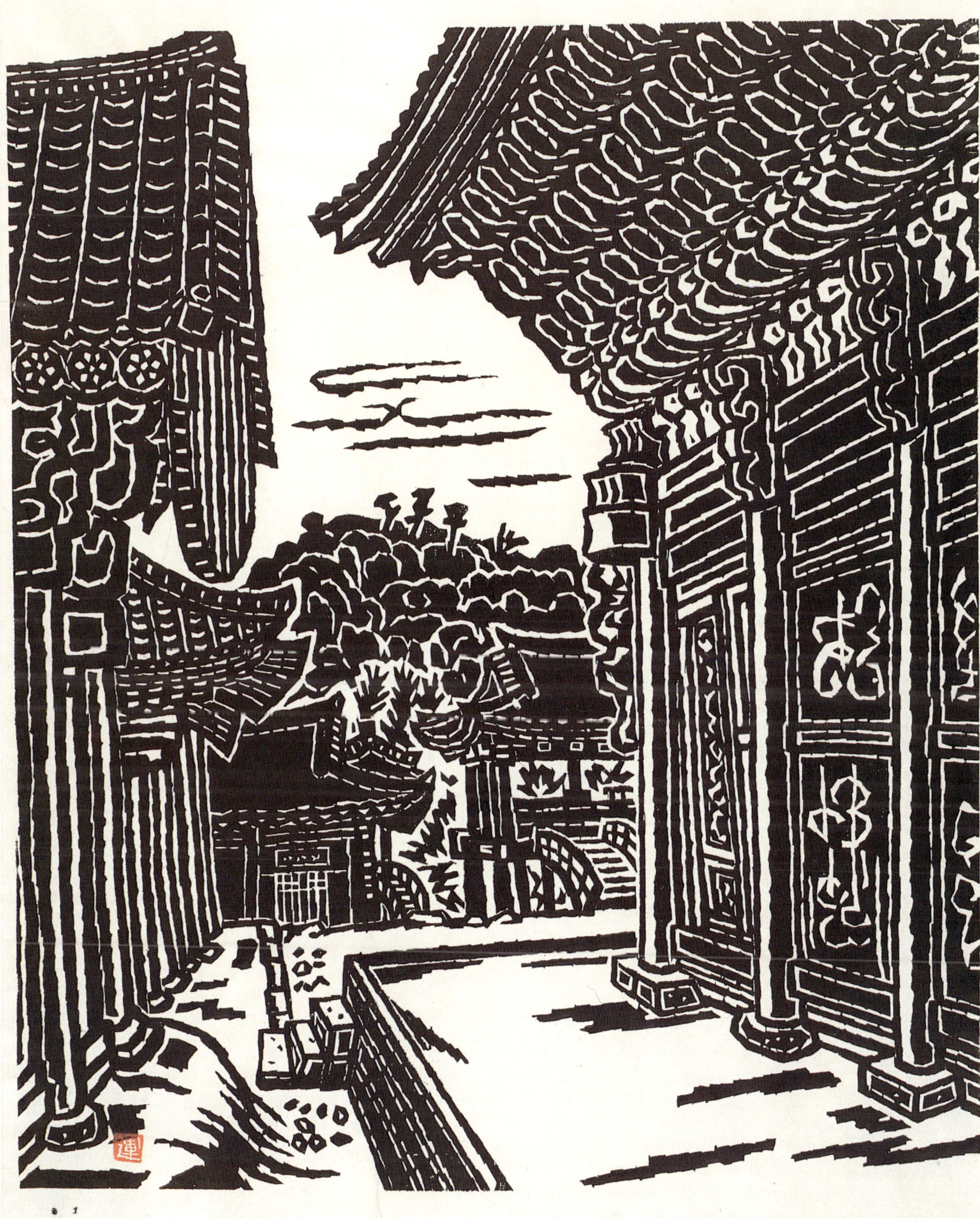

5. Hiratsuka Un'ichi (b. 1895). Titled on the reverse in Japanese *Uchi Kongō Hyokunji* (Inner Precinct of Hyokun Temple), unnumbered, undated, woodblock, 52.5x44 cm. Signed Un-ichi Hiratsuka, sealed on the image in kanji Un, printed in the right margin in kanji Hiratsuka Un'ichi.

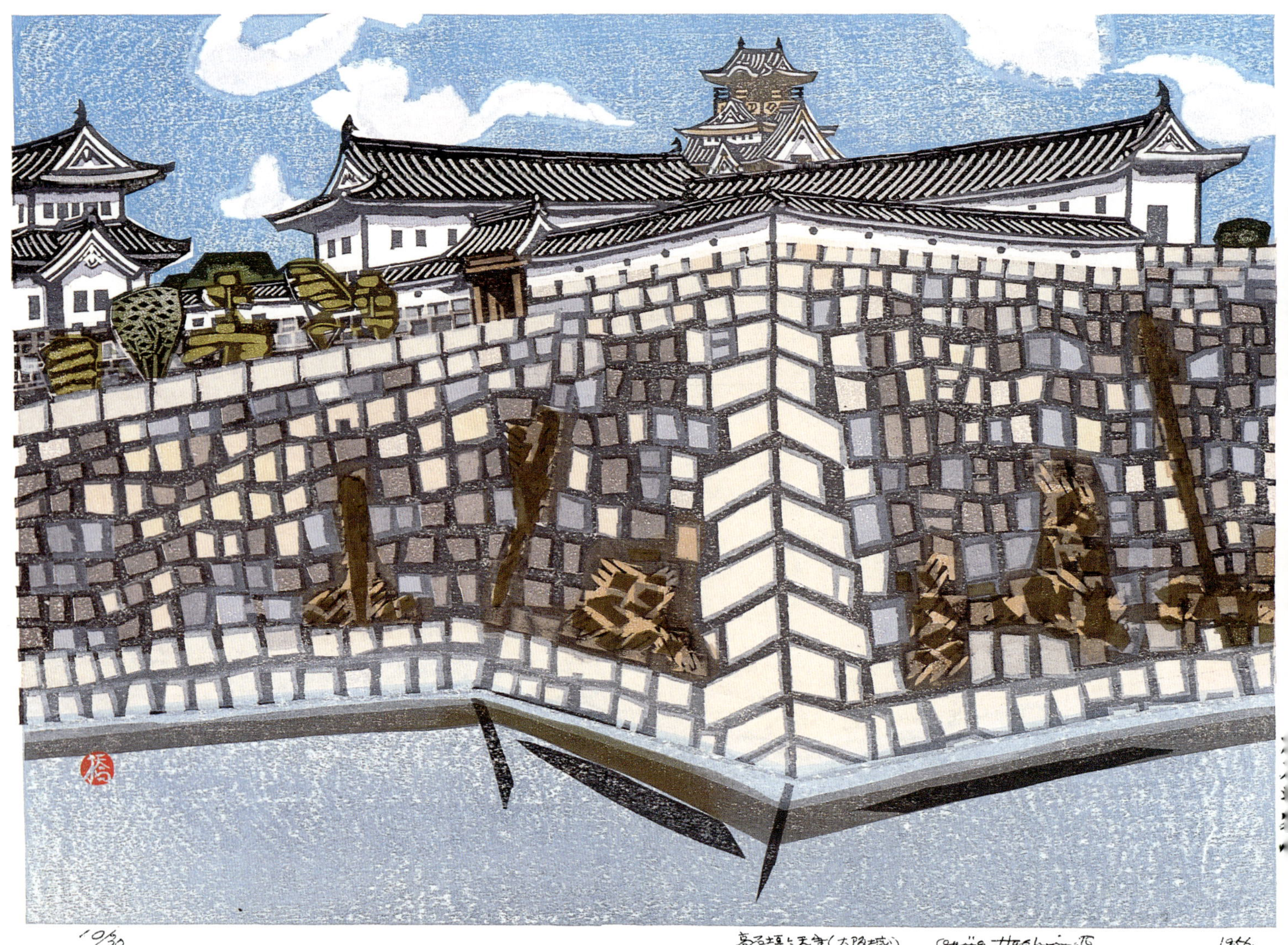

6. Hashimoto Okiie (1899–1993). Titled in Japanese *Taka-ishigaki to Tenshu (Osaka-jō)* (High Stone Wall and Castle Stronghold [Osaka Castle]), 10/30, 1956, woodblock, 39.3x54.2 cm. Signed Okiie Hashimoto, sealed on the image Hashi, in the right margin in kanji Hashimoto Okiie *saku* (made by Hashimoto Okiie).

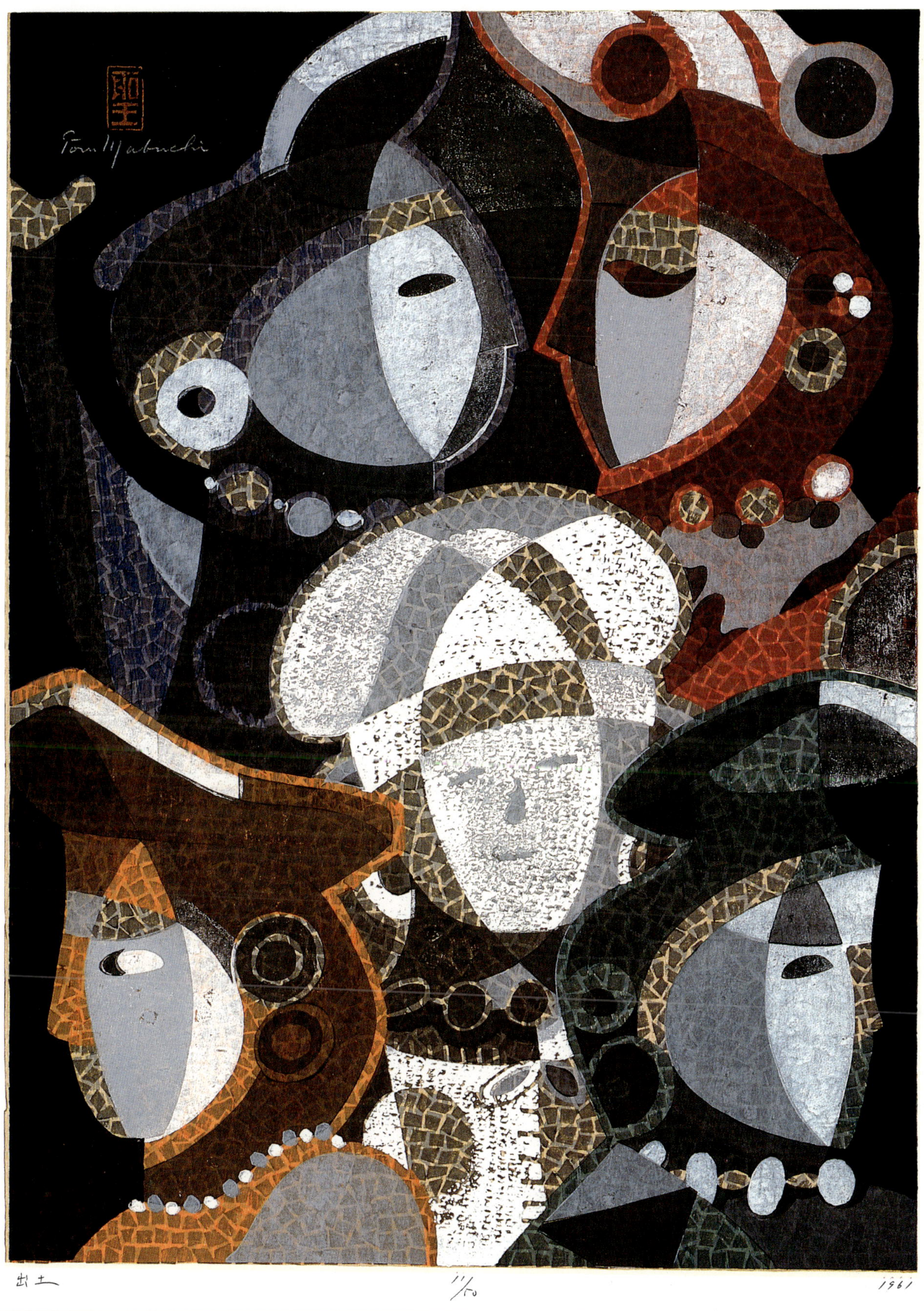

7. Mabuchi Toru (1920–94). Titled in Japanese *Shutsu-do* (From the Earth), 11/50, 1961, woodblock, 56x41 cm. Signed on the image Toru Mabuchi, sealed on the image in kanji Toru.

As was the case with many who set out to collect the *sōsaku-hanga* prints, the works we were particularly fond of were all woodblocks. At that time those prints were the ones that held the most appeal probably because of subject matter. We did not even think particularly about their being woodblock prints; the themes were unfamiliar and captivating and that was their charm for us and for others. Perhaps that charm was a product of our initial response to the wonders of geisha, stylized gardens, Buddhist statues and temples, Shinto shrines, castles, and *haniwa*. All represented the eternal charisma of Japan, and these pioneer artists strongly felt an awareness of their roots in their chosen subject matter, even though they were leaning toward Western perspective and modes of creating in executing their works.

About this time we parted, though only briefly, from the conventional woodblock and entered the inviting worlds of Mori Yoshitoshi's *kappazuri* (stencil prints), of Fukazawa Shiro's silk-screen prints, and of Ouchi Makoto's etchings. These artists also used traditional subjects like the Kabuki theater, legendary figures, folklore, or street markets, but the media employed were different and the subject matter was not quite so realistic. We embarked on an imaginative, thought-provoking journey not only because of the artists' creativity but also because we began to be aware of the different effects that could be achieved on paper with different printing methods. The subtle changes from realism to fanciful ideas and stories from the complicated repertoire of the Kabuki theater also intrigued us. Kabuki provided an inexhaustible source of inspiration for all three artists, and the addition of their prints contributed a new dimension to our collection.

After we met Mori Yoshitoshi, our collection grew by leaps and bounds. Mori seemed like a Japanese grandfather to us, and his passing at age 94 affected us deeply. Our various homes are filled with his works, which we number in the hundreds, and we never look at one of his masterpieces without recalling fondly the warmth and humor that he brought to every encounter. He was our Meiji-era connection and our oldest Japanese friend. During our long acquaintance he was responsible for much of the fun in our lives and enough earthy conversation to fill several books. Just as we became aware that our collection consisted only of woodblock prints he appeared on the scene as a stencil printmaker. Stencils had been used in Japan from time immemorial to produce designs for printing on textiles and Mori, in fact, had worked at this occupation for many years. He was more than 50 years old when he decided to carry this technique over to making works on paper.

Our friend Henry Steiner, a graphic designer whom we met in Hong Kong during our diplomatic posting there, had been much earlier enraptured by Mori's prints and suggested that we call on him in Tokyo when we were transferred, even providing a letter of introduction. We made the visit, unprepared for such a delight. But the greatest of all treats was to go to the Kabuki with Mori. This charming little man, whose entire life was bound up with the down-to-earth mores of Tokyo's *shita-machi* (the old downtown area), where his family had lived for generations, enjoyed with gusto the complex plots of the plays, appreciated the subtleties of the acting, and while not missing a beat of the story would sketch furiously all of the actors' dramatic poses (which he already knew by heart), while still finding time to clue us in on what was happening on stage. Later at his home and atelier, Mori would cut his stencils with breathtaking speed, defying not only the various laws of nature but also of common sense, since the very sharp tools that he used with such rapidity could easily have sliced off a finger.

His prints sometimes seem to border on caricature, conveying *Plate 8* his innate spirit of fun. *Kuruma-hiki, San Kyōdai* (Three Brothers, Carriage Pullers [from the Kabuki play of that name]) is just the sort of humorous scene Mori loved. No amount of devilment was too much for him. He was a practical and canny son of old Edo, and loved wine, women, and song, especially women, whom he liked to draw in all their voluptuousness. Even at the age of 94 his head would turn if a curvaceous woman walked by, and his face would light up even more if she stopped to chat.

Another funster who smashed the stereotype that Japanese are staid and stolid, wear only dark-blue or gray suits, and have an inscrutable expression was Fukazawa Shiro. He dressed like a Japanese gypsy might if there were any: a black velvet wide-brimmed hat with dangling red and yellow balls, holding in place a mane of wild white hair that had a tendency to blow in the breeze. He could always be found in an outrageously bright shirt and black leather pants, quite a novelty in the early 1970s, especially for a man of his age. Mary quite clearly remembers meeting him at the main intersection of the Ginza one day by prearranged appointment to attend a gallery opening. She noticed that they were given a wide berth by the various passersby.

Plate 9 *Sharaku and I* borrows from an early *ukiyo-e* master, again featuring a Kabuki-based theme. The purity of the silkscreen colors and the perfect technical execution were of interest to us in our shift to a third medium. Fukazawa's sense of composition and design was also unusual, with the print giving the viewer just a glimpse of a scene or a face and forcing one to fill in the blanks. It was hard to believe that such a traditional subject could be conveyed in such a modern way.

The third of our Kabuki-inspired artists was also cast from a different mold. Perhaps it is an attribute of those artists who are totally enamored with the flamboyant Kabuki theater to carry its colorful gaiety over into their own lives. And we have often wondered, since so many Japanese artists tend to be a rather

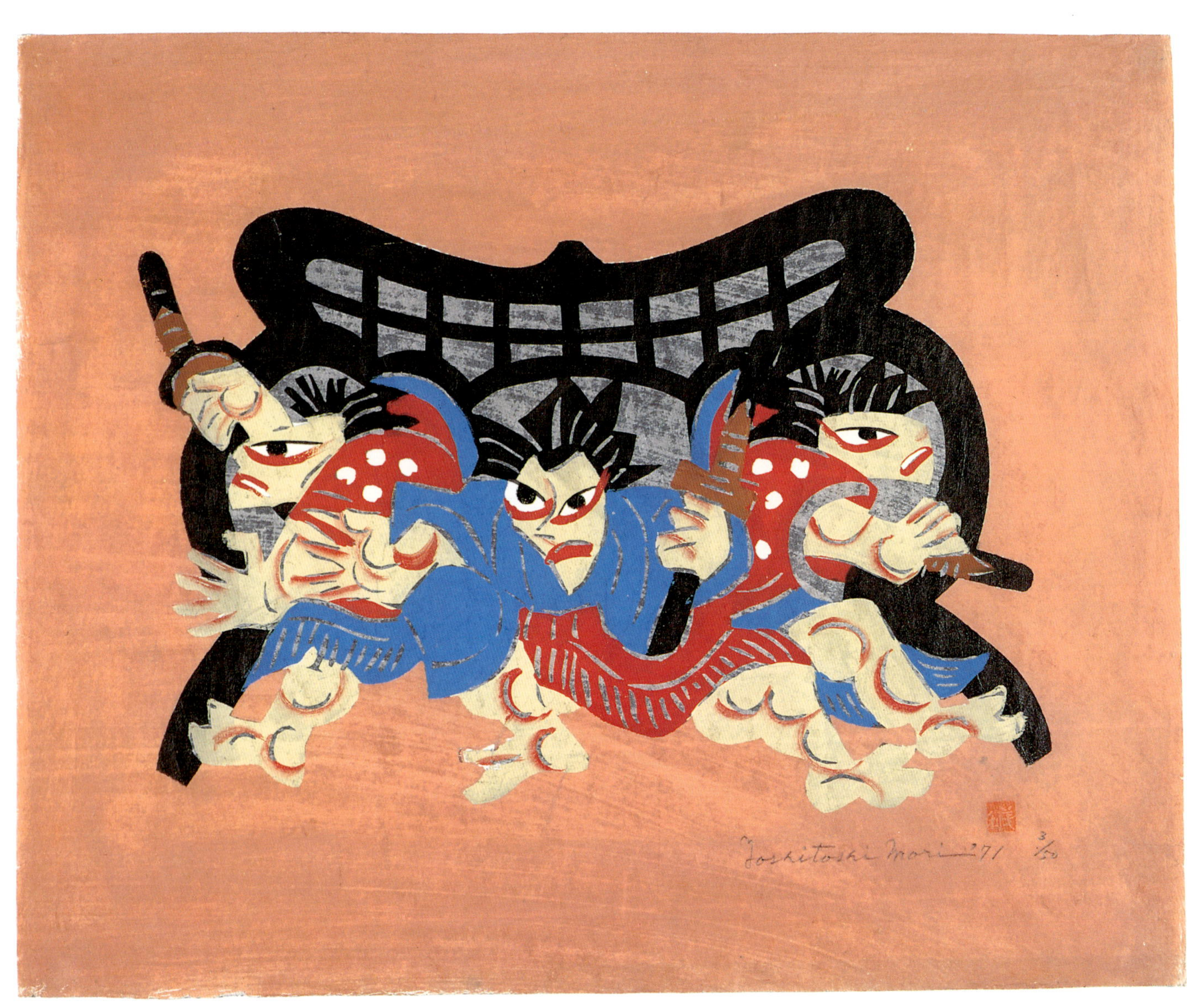

8. Mori Yoshitoshi (1898–1992). Titled on the reverse in Japanese *Kuruma-hiki San Kyōdai* (Rickshaw Pullers, Three Brothers), 3/50, 1971, stencil, 57.5x70.5 cm. Signed Yoshitoshi Mori, sealed on the image in kanji Yoshitoshi.

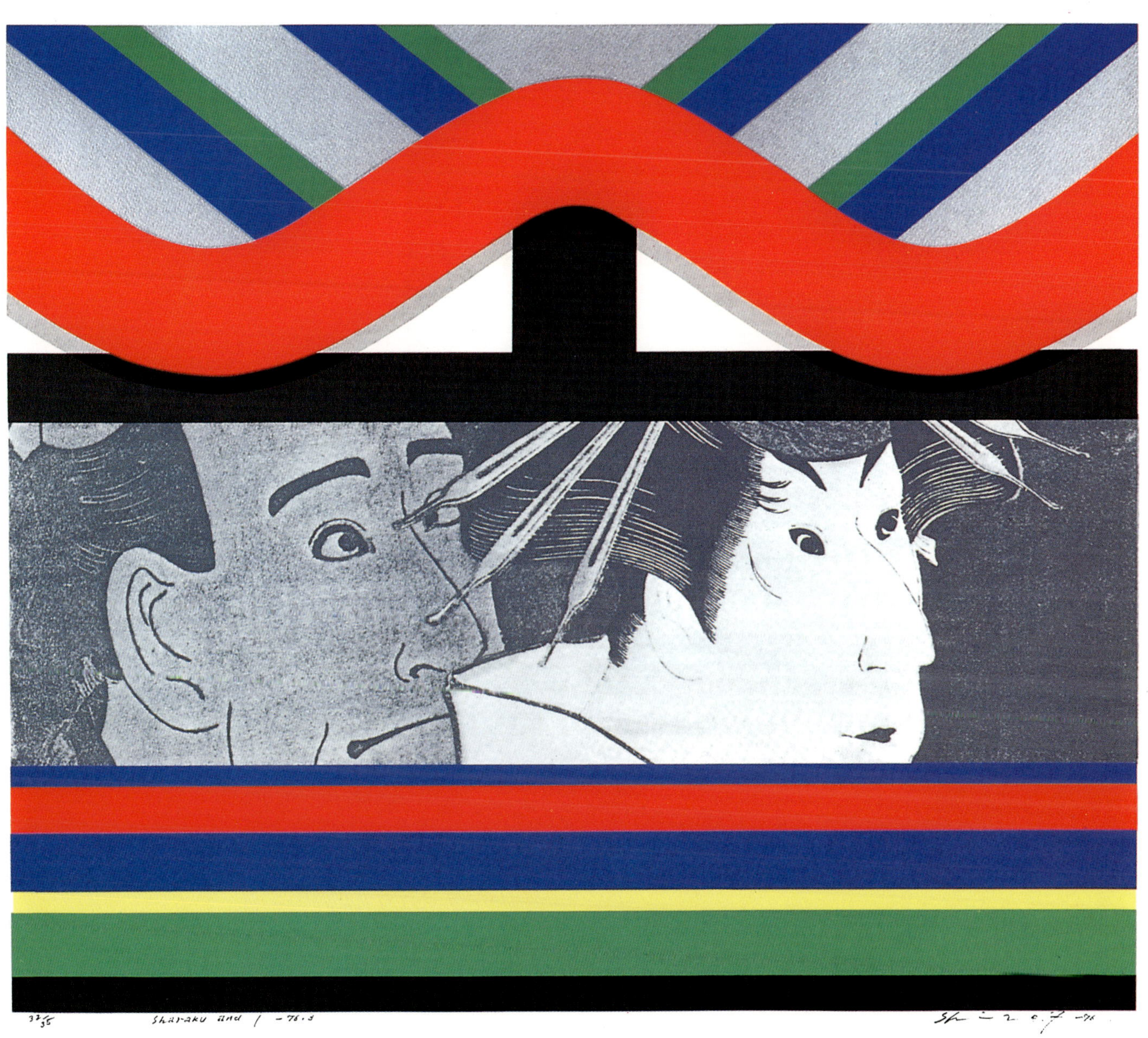

9. Fukazawa Shiro (1907–78). *Sharaku and I*, 32/35, 1976, silkscreen, 60x69 cm. Signed Shiro F.

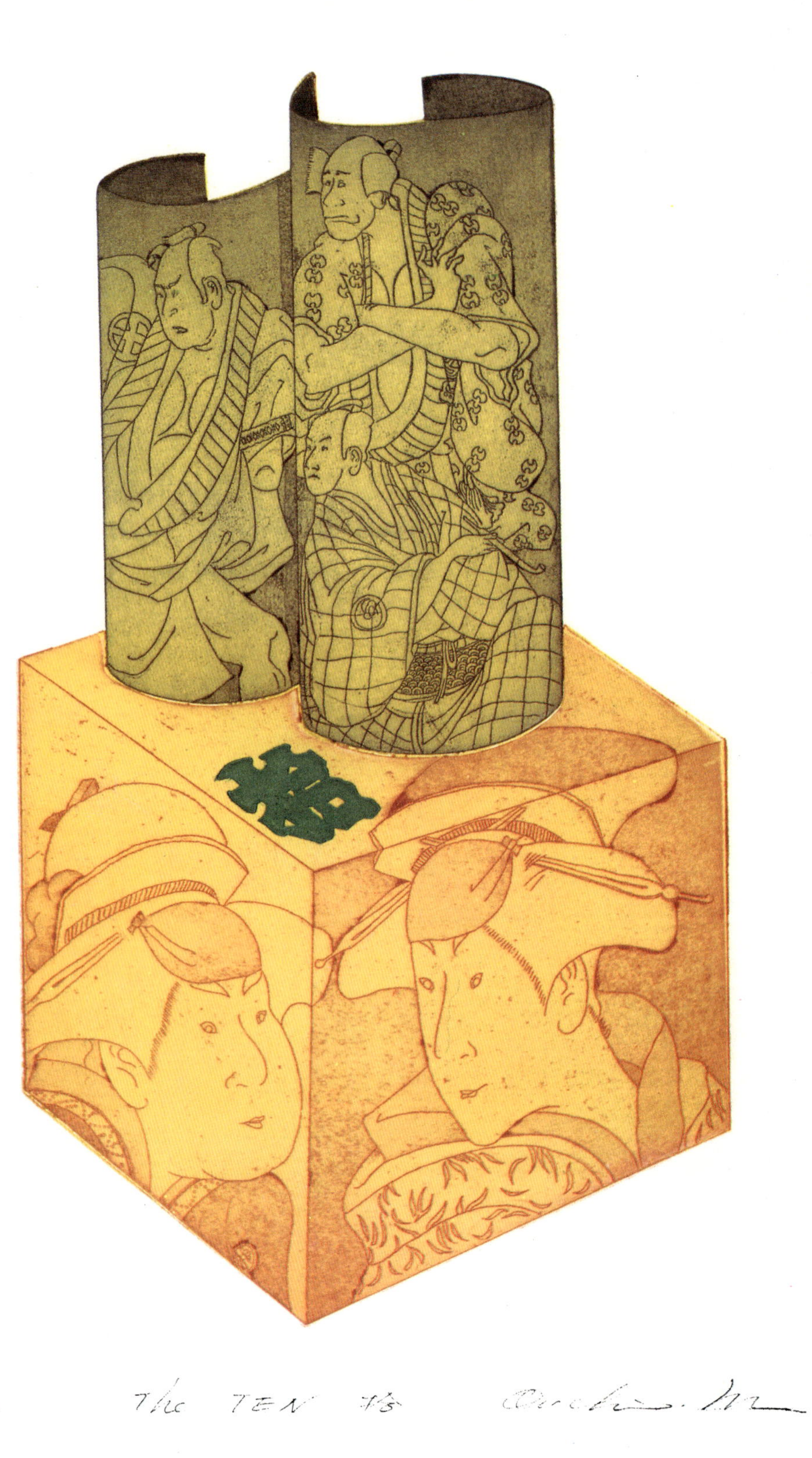

10. Ouchi Makoto (1926–89). Titled in Japanese *Jū*, titled in English *The Ten*, 16/25, 1981, etching, 55x40 cm. Signed Ouchi M. Published by the Tolman Collection, Tokyo.

conventional lot, what the average Japanese thought of such marvels as Mori, Fukazawa, and Ouchi.

We found it remarkable that although *ukiyo-e* employed much Kabuki lore as subject matter, all of the latest prints featuring Kabuki were executed in other media. Ouchi Makoto's etchings were certainly a link with the past, but he felt that *ukiyo-e* were very flat. Wanting his work to be more three-dimensional, he often used cubes and cylinders as compositional devices. He created the print

Plate 10

The Ten to celebrate our gallery's tenth anniversary, which coincided with his twenty-fifth anniversary as an artist. To commemorate that event we compiled a book about him. Ouchi was a diamond-in-the-rough, heart-of-gold, shirt-off-his-back type, but somewhat hard to take when he was in his cups, which he often was, a circumstance that eventually resulted in strained relations between us. Just as we could not love every print to the same degree, we realized we could not enjoy every artist's personality the same way either. And so we devoted our time to artists with whom we had much in common.

Looking back, we recall that our conversations came to be more and more concerned with our hobby. We wondered what people thought since it became increasingly obvious that we were devoting a considerable amount of time and money to this avocation. What to others was an occasional diversion was becoming our main interest. We were building a collection, having a great deal of fun, and finding it effortless to involve ourselves in such an absorbing occupation. Other bonuses were that we began to meet people who had a similar passion and we were learning in depth about the history and culture of Japan.

At this point we became a bit self-conscious about what others might think of the level of our collection. Although we know by now that even among people of independent spirit with supreme good taste and the intellectual means to defend their choices, there is a period when one considers "what others might think." Whether this is expressed verbally or not does not matter. We notice that people do it in our gallery even today. After all these years we can recognize the look of uncertainty and we know the reason. We had it once too.

The notion of creating a collection and making it a focal point in our lives was still a bit hazy, so the matter of justifying our purchases still lurked in the background, encouraging us to turn for a moment to subjects that seemed easy to rationalize. We found that cats were mostly a "safe" item. They were then and they are now a subject that finds a ready audience among cat-o-philes. We have clients who will buy any composition featuring a cat; everyone is familiar with them and even those who do not particularly like real cats find they can tolerate them in art. Compositions with cats can thus be given as presents, along with that other "safe" subject—

trees. Two artists have become famous mainly for using only these objects in their woodblock prints.

Plate 11 *Plate 12* *Long Tail Cat* by Inagaki Tomoo and *Mist* by Hoshi Joichi have universal appeal, and like so many other Japanese printmakers, both artists found their major themes early in their print careers and spent the rest of their lives refining them. Inagaki's cat, with its glittering yellow eyes and insouciantly curled tail, recalls any particularly self-contained cat one may have encountered, with the emphasis on feline sensuality. Hoshi's trees in the mist are clearly recognizable elements, yet the intriguing fog invites one's mind to wander into the unknowable world beyond realism. Hoshi's earlier prints concentrated on star constellations but it is his trees that have made him famous. We bought these prints primarily not because they were by our favorite artists but because they were first praised and collected by others.

Hoshi was the man of the hour in those days, and his prints seemed to be everywhere. It was even said, as a sort of selling point, that Henry Kissinger had bought a few during a trip to Tokyo. As young, rising art dealers we joked about how unusual it was that people who were not so interested in what we had to say about foreign affairs could take Kissinger's purchase as the acme of what was desirable in the modern print world. But, of course, a point was made: many people liked to own a Hoshi print just because Kissinger had one.

Needless to say, Inagaki and Hoshi are celebrated printmakers so they do not need our personal blessing on their work. But we were not so drawn to their prints as to others; we bought them because others recommended them and it seemed the thing to do at the time.

In keeping with the thought that for every action there is an opposite and equal reaction, there then ensued a period when we were determined to be adventurous, follow our eyes and hearts, and trust only our own instincts. We next set out to acquire those compositions especially to our own liking, even if they were works that no one else had ever heard of or particularly appreciated. It was only natural that after years of looking our taste began to change gradually and we became more confident in our selections. The following print falls into that category.

Plate 13 Fukita Fumiaki called his print *Windmills*. It looked then, and it looks now, like umbrellas to us, but that did not really matter. We were attracted by the harmonious colors, the results achievable by a talented artist with a block of wood and a few tools, and most of all by the explosive energy inherent in the work. Choosing this print was one of the first manifestations of our newly acquired assurance. We have since reflected that this is one of the ways artists become known. They all need brave young collectors who are willing to buy their work and support them in their endeavors.

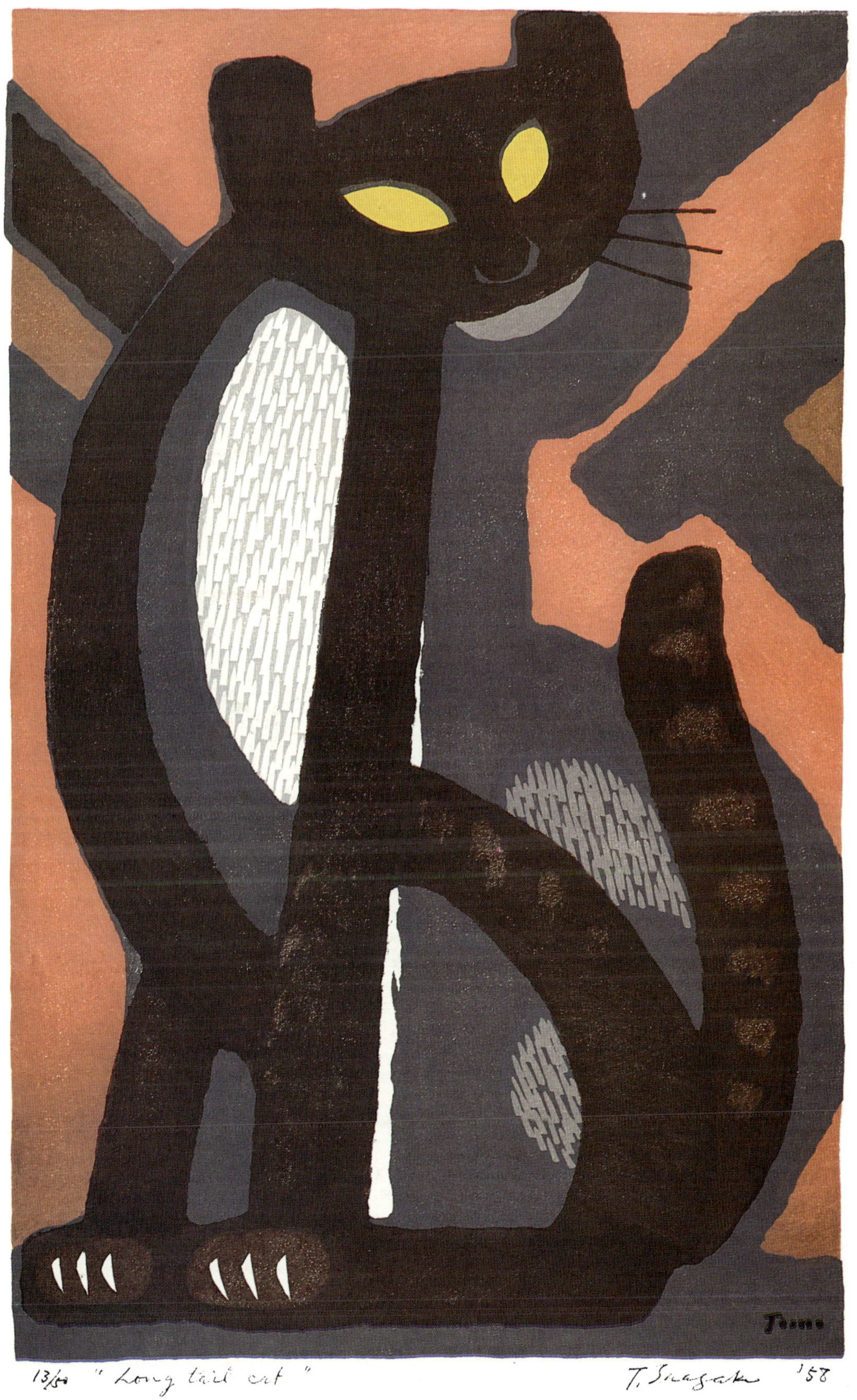

11. Inagaki Tomoo (1902–80). *Long Tail Cat,* 13/50, 1958, woodblock, 53.5x33 cm. Signed T. Inagaki, sealed on the image in English Tomoo.

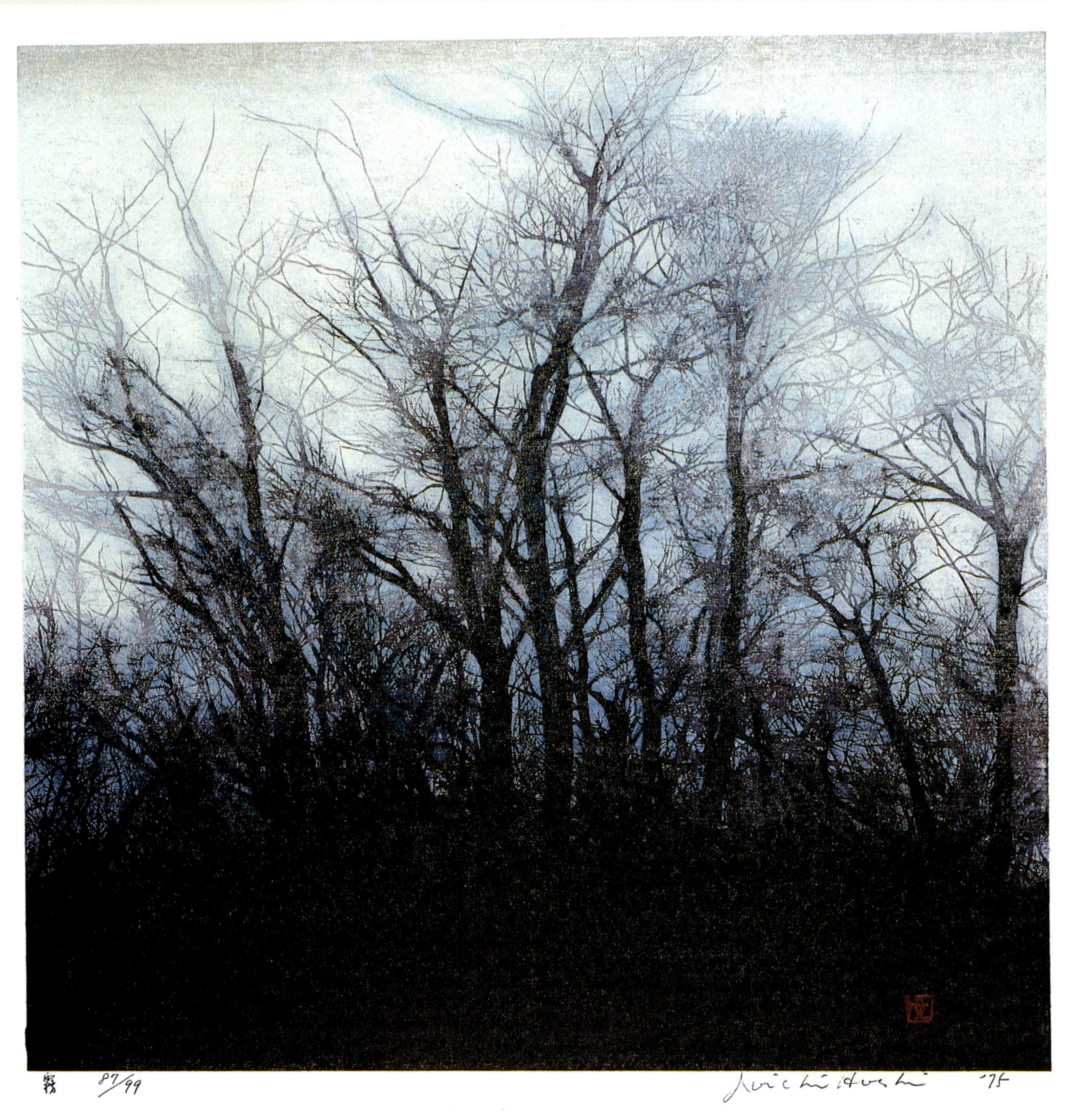

12. Hoshi Joichi (1913–79). Titled in Japanese *Kiri* (Mist), 87/99, 1975, woodblock, 55.5x55.5 cm. Signed Joichi Hoshi, sealed on the image with a personal seal of three trees growing from the earth.

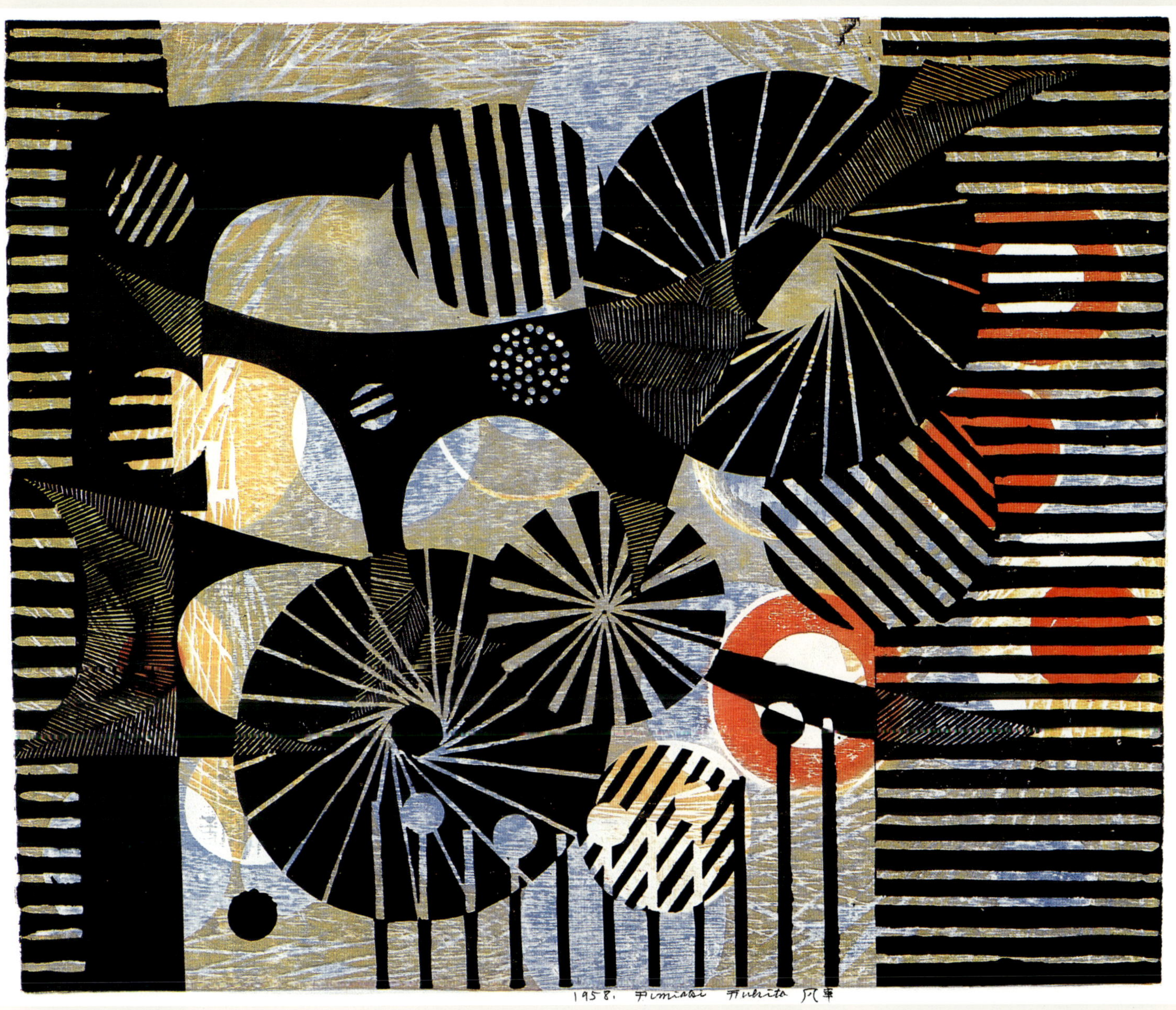

13. Fukita Fumiaki (b. 1926). Titled in Japanese *Fūsha* (Windmills), unnumbered, 1958, woodblock, 60.4x72 cm. Signed Fumiaki Fukita.

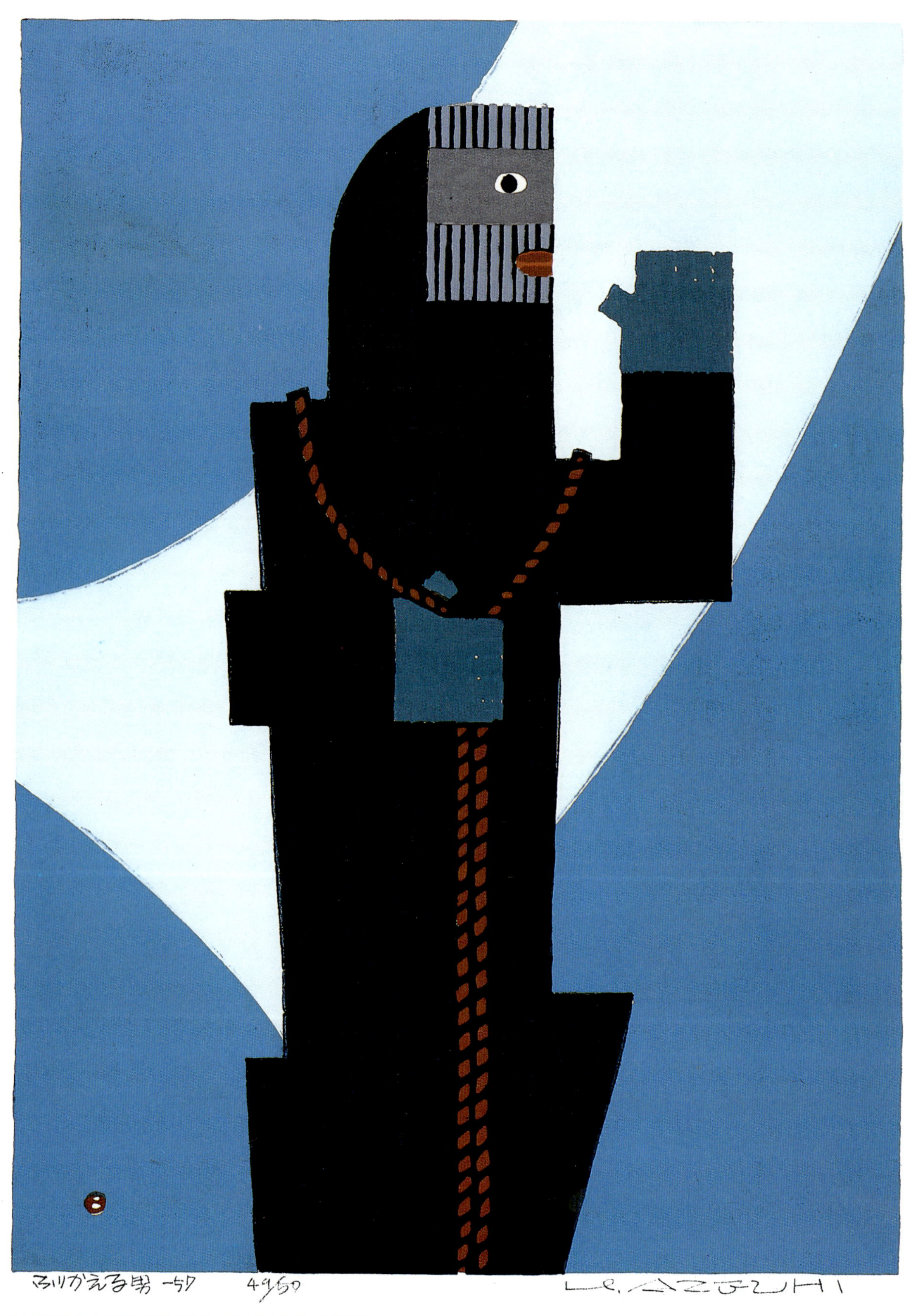

14. Azechi Umetaro (b. 1902). Titled in Japanese *Furikaeru Otoko* (Man Looking Back), 49/50, 1957, woodblock, 61x43.5 cm. Signed U. Azechi, sealed on the image in *hiragana u*.

Although we experimented again and again with buying prints in other media, the appeal of those early woodblock prints was strong. We remember well the excitement of *Man Looking Back* by Azechi Umetaro. The artist, from Ehime Prefecture in Shikoku, grew up with a love of mountains, eventually becoming an accomplished alpinist himself. At 92 he is still active and his prints continue to be as hardy, rugged, and enduring as the mountain men he is so fond of portraying. His depictions are straight and direct with stylized, angular forms. His prints can always be recognized by his use of an inimitable shade of teal blue.

Plate 14

Soon afterward we purchased a pleasing picture of city roofs by Kitaoka Fumio, *Early Summer in Suchow*. It really did not matter if the tile roofs were in a city in China and not in Kyoto, which they seemed to be at first glance. The execution was meticulous, rhythmic, and orderly, with just a casual touch of repaired tile to indicate a real place. Kitaoka is one of the most productive and versatile woodblock artists on the scene and is the master of so many diverse themes that we have developed a private joke. Whenever we come across a woodblock print we love but cannot exactly pin down the artist, one or the other of us says, "It's probably Kitaoka Fumio," and it usually is.

Plate 15

Kitaoka, who actually lived in China, is well traveled and therefore quite comfortable with foreigners, a rarity. For a time he took pupils and was patient enough to give his time to those who wanted to learn how to make woodblock prints. We always admired him, an artist of some stature, for being such a giving person, and his classes provided yet another way for those interested to see an artist at work.

Gallery openings in Tokyo were then and still are among the best ways to meet artists, who are generally pleased to answer questions about their work, of course, usually in Japanese. Galleries too are happy to give information, to the extent of their foreign-language ability, which is usually there if one has the patience to ferret it out. The Tokyo art scene offers countless exhibitions, sadly none of them lasting very long, usually only six days. Of course, exhibitions from abroad sponsored by the major national and prefectural museums stay a bit longer, but in galleries and department stores six days seems to be the custom.

In Japan department stores are major showcases for art and always have a gallery or two, or even three, on the premises. The monumental exertion necessary to mount an exhibition that lasts such a short time is reminiscent of the cherry blossoms, which are awaited with such anticipation all year long and float away on the breeze a few days later. The exhibitions occur back-to-back and never seem to stop. As young collectors we attended every one possible on a regular basis and soon became part of the art scene. After a short time we found that lots of the "guests" at gallery

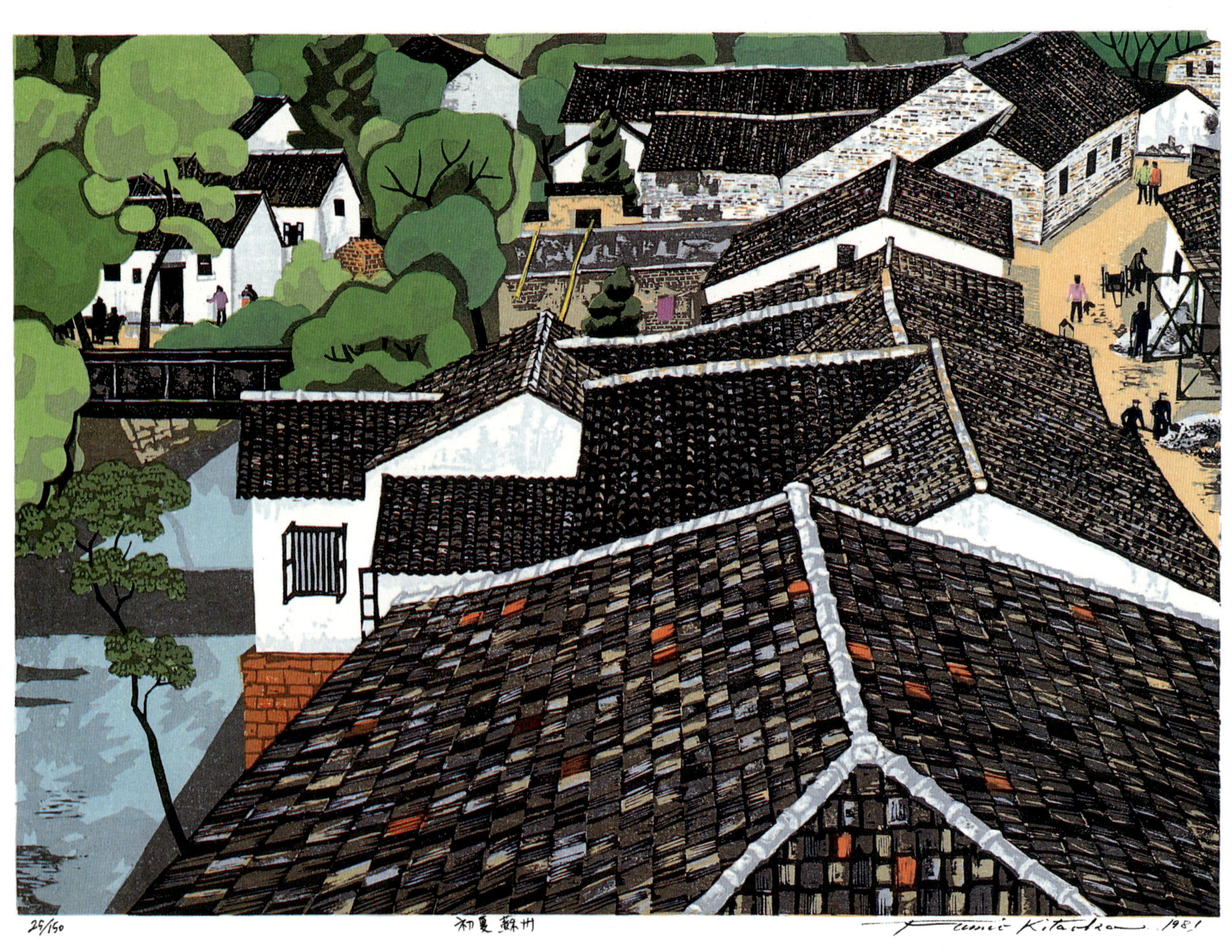

15. Kitaoka Fumio (b. 1918). Titled in Japanese *Shoka Soshu* (Early Summer in Suchow), 25/150, 1981, woodblock, 40x54.8 cm. Signed Fumio Kitaoka.

openings were other artists and their friends, and since we could question them directly about their art, our knowledge grew rapidly.

In other parts of the world, museum and gallery exhibitions are often advertised with posters that themselves become collectibles. In Japan the poster has not played a similar role. Perhaps it is because original prints were not expensive in the first place, and it was possible to contemplate buying a real work rather than settle for a poster. There are exceptions, of course, and in the case of Murai Masanari, our attention was drawn to his work specifically because of a poster. Murai, still active at 89, is a well-regarded and therefore expensive painter. It did not seem possible for us ever to be able to afford his work. We assumed at first glance that the poster we had discovered was based on one of his original oils; it turned out,
Plate 16 however, that it was based on a silkscreen print he had made. *Face,* the original numbered silkscreen, is a work resembling a *haniwa* face with the artist's typical use of abstract shapes set off among brilliantly contrasting colors.

The poster had been made to advertise the annual College Women's Association of Japan (CWAJ) Print Show, held annually since 1956. Each year this organization of volunteer women, working for the benefit of a scholarship fund, exhibits a large assortment of some two hundred prints by contemporary print artists, including brand-new printmakers who might not have the possibility of being seen elsewhere, along with many of the stalwarts of the print world. This "must see" event is held in Tokyo in the third week of October.

Another mandatory annual exhibition is the April show of the Nihon Hanga Kyokai (Japan Print Association) held at the Tokyo Metropolitan Museum in Ueno, an event that coincides with the cherry-blossom season. There are several hundred members of the association, which was established in 1919 by the founding fathers of the *sōsaku-hanga* movement. Today this exhibition is the primary showcase for providing an overall view of the contemporary print world, although we must add that not every printmaker chooses to belong to the association. However, both the JPA exhibition and the CWAJ show are important venues for learning about recent print works, and they have been important to us both in increasing our knowledge about prints and in expanding our collection. We have faithfully attended both exhibitions over the past thirty years.

Because of their appearance in the CWAJ catalogue we first became aware of and attracted to the works of Toneyama Kojin,
Plate 17 including *The Flutist,* and Yoshida Chizuko, including *Butterflies*
Plate 18 *A.* Toneyama has spent a considerable period of his artistic life in Mexico, to the point of being decorated by the Mexican government for his cultural achievements. One could not say whether or not the flute were Japanese; we picked the print because of its elegant composition and restrained color. We heard the music and

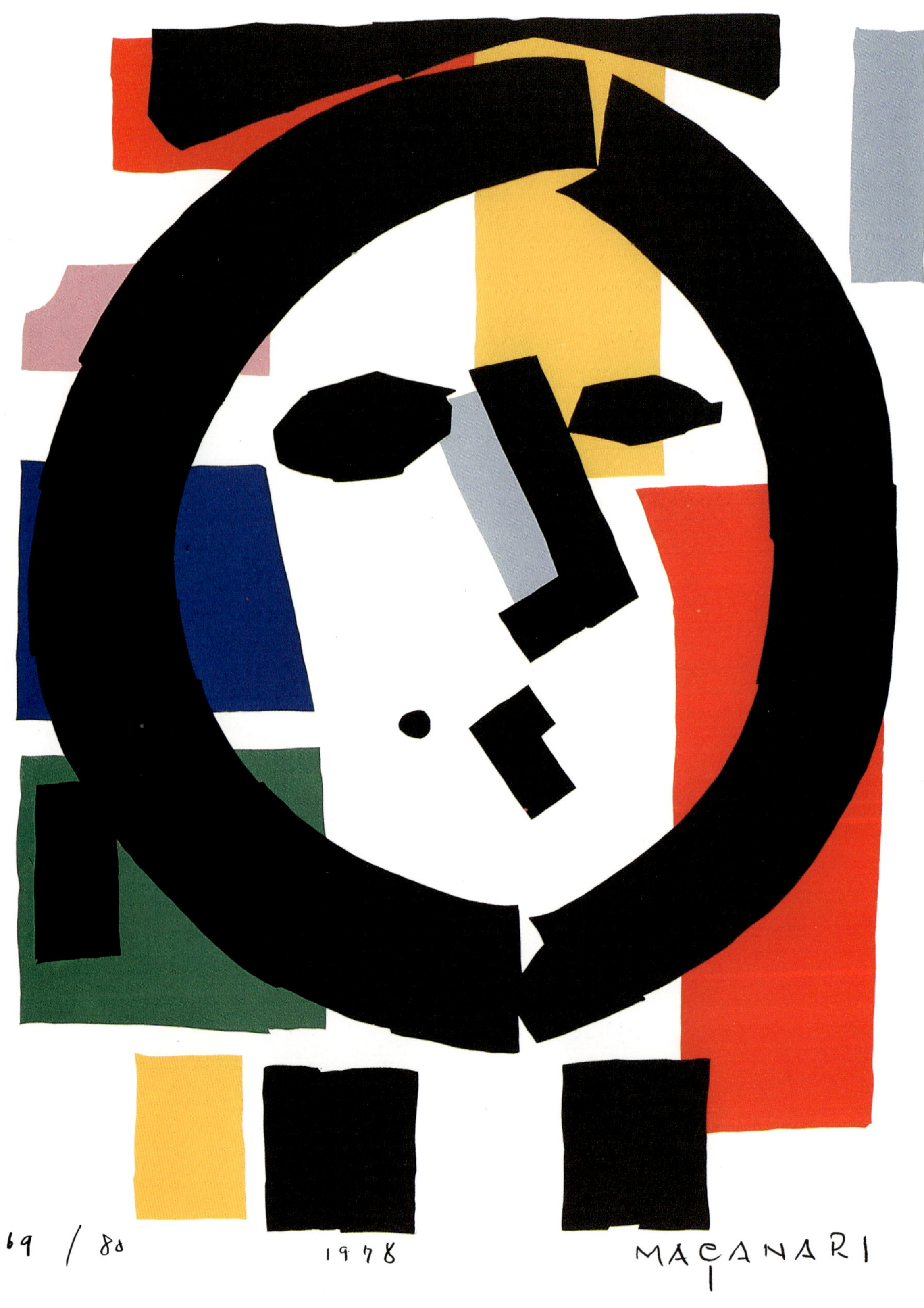

16. Murai Masanari (b. 1905). *Face,* 69/80, 1978, silkscreen, 76.5x56.5 cm. Signed Maçanari.

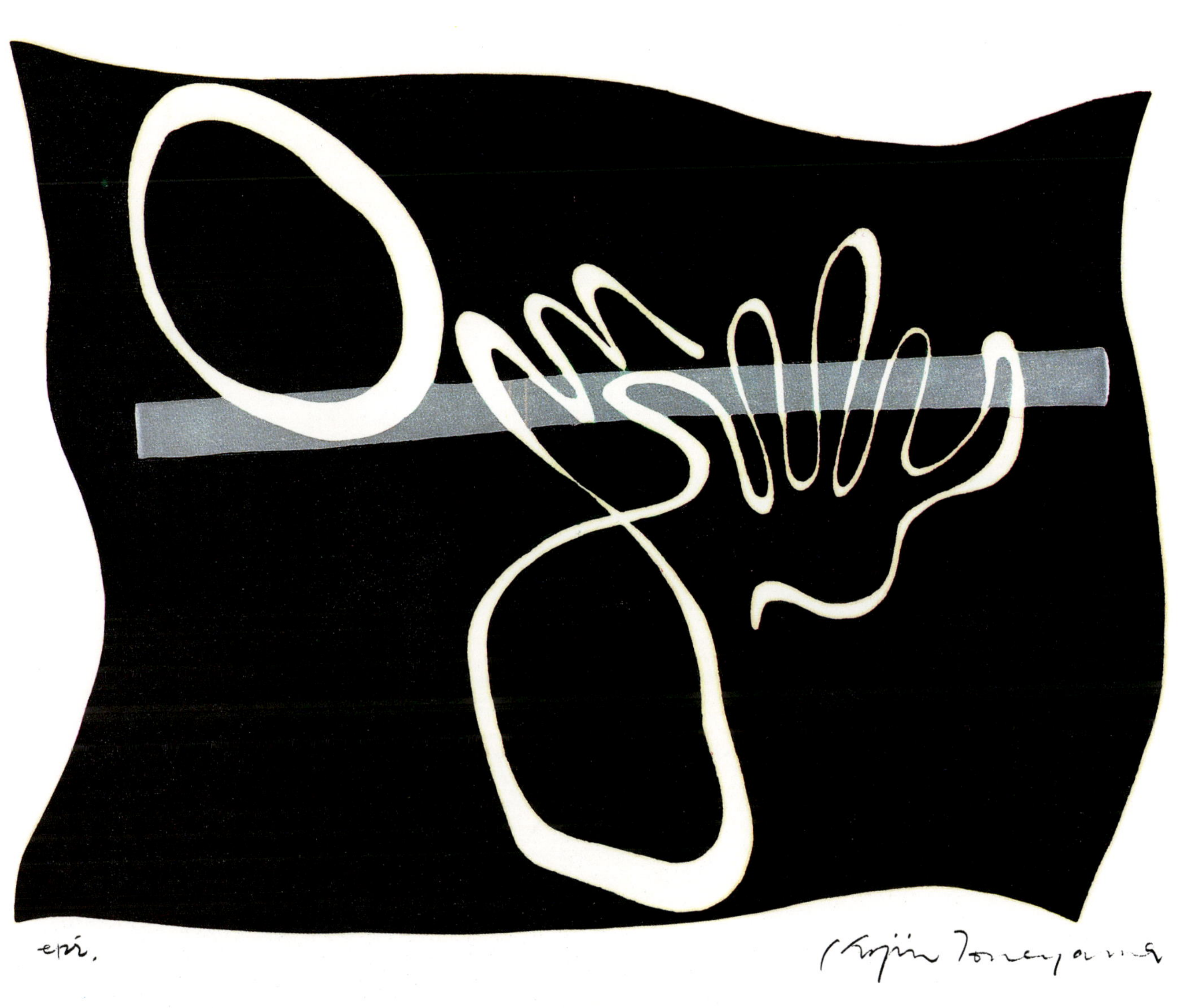

17. Toneyama Kojin (1921–94). *The Flutist,* 1970, E/A (edition known to be 10), undated, unlisted but known to be 1970, woodblock, 45x58.5 cm. Signed Kojin Toneyama.

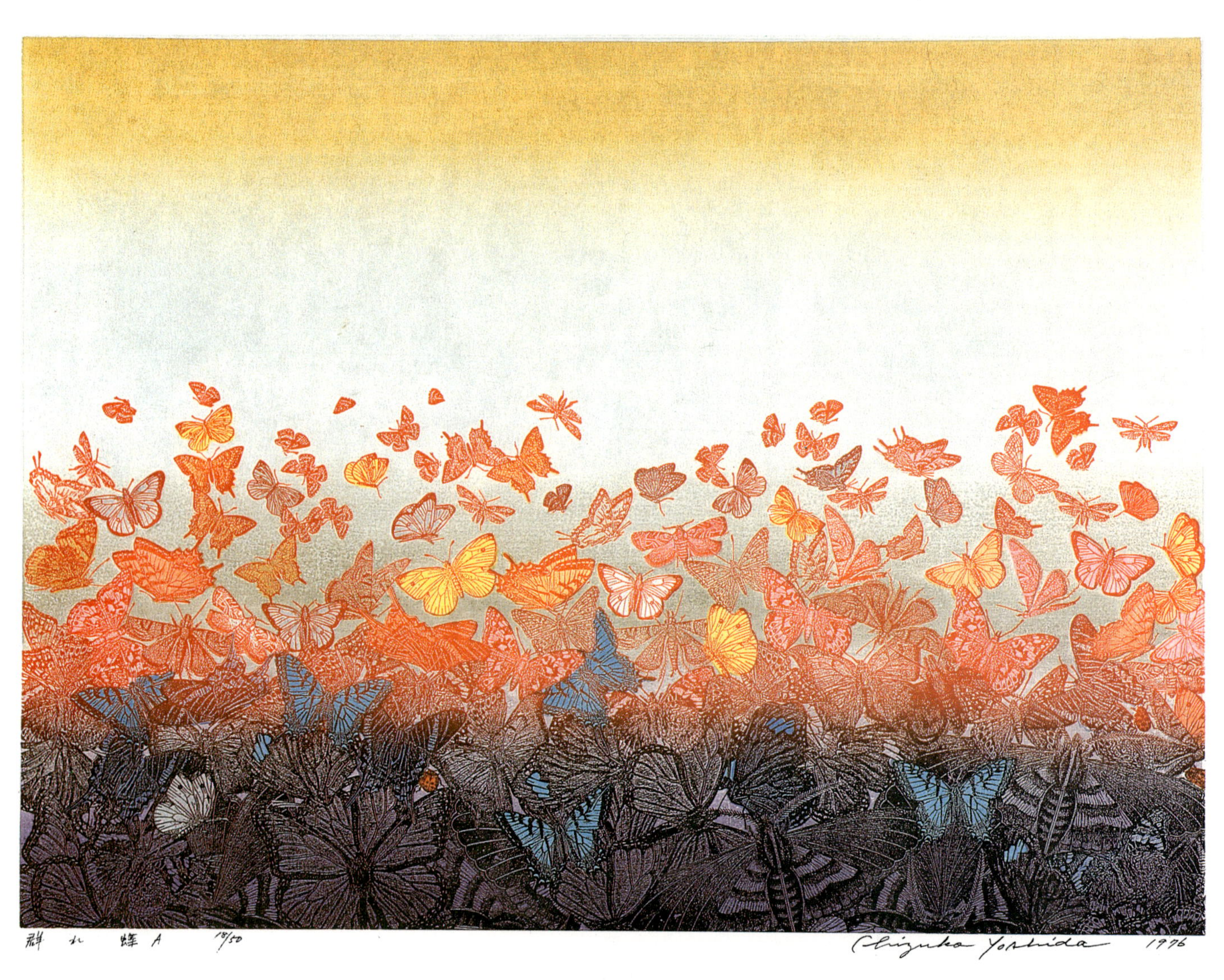

18. Yoshida Chizuko (b. 1924). Titled in Japanese *Mure Chō A* (Butterflies A), 18/50, 1976, woodblock, 42x55.7 cm. Signed Chizuko Yoshida.

did not question if it were Japanese or Mexican. By the same token, Yoshida Chizuko's butterflies flew no flag of national origin. They just fluttered about so appealingly on the cover of a CWAJ catalogue that when they landed, they alit right in our collection. Yoshida's work seems to draw on the old woodblock tradition, particularly in the shading at the top, reminiscent of *ukiyo-e*.

Chizuko is one member of the Yoshida family, all of whom have been so involved in the modern print world that they can virtually be called the Barrymores of twentieth-century prints. Chizuko's husband, Hodaka, her brother-in-law, Toshi, and their father, Hiroshi (the frontispiece artist) have all made major contri-
Plate 19 butions to the world of Japanese prints. Yoshida Toshi's *Light and*
Plate 20 *Shadow* and Yoshida Hodaka's *Omen* reflect their family woodblock heritage, and are typical of the artists' genius at free invention enclosed in a masterful unity of organization. All members of the Yoshida family have traveled extensively in America and Europe. They were especially enamored of Mexico in their early days, and one can detect some pre-Columbian forms in their works. These prints were steppingstones for us because they were pivotal in turning our attention to works that compelled our attention because of form, composition, and texture. Suddenly we realized that we had become very attracted to abstract prints.

Even the idea of this seemed quite foreign to us at the start. We had found it quite reassuring to look at a *haniwa* and grasp the fact that it was a figure of some sort. When we looked at a picture of a temple we did not necessarily have to know the inner workings of the religion or to which sect it belonged—knowing it was a religious edifice was sufficient. For abstract works, however, we had no frame of reference but simply had to develop our eye by looking, asking, feeling, and basically trusting our own aesthetic sensibilities. Increasingly we came to admire compositions for their balance, shapes, and colors. This sort of print offered a sort of spiritual refuge in a too-fast-moving world and provided immense emotional and intellectual pleasure. We also noticed that we were once again in the magic world of woodblocks, where the artists were able to achieve their incomparable effects with wood and simple tools, much as a potter could mold earth and clay into an admirable piece of pottery.

We were entranced next by the pre-eminent abstract artist
Plate 21 Yamaguchi Gen. He was very popular and his works were very hard to find, partly because he seldom finished printing his editions to completion. The excitement of creation was everything for him and he soon became bored by the tedium of printing the same thing. His stated edition number was usually fifty, but he never printed many. Yamaguchi's work was so admired by his peers that a prize for technical innovation has been created in his honor by the Japan Print Association.

Plate 22 Hagiwara Hideo caught our interest, again because of unusual

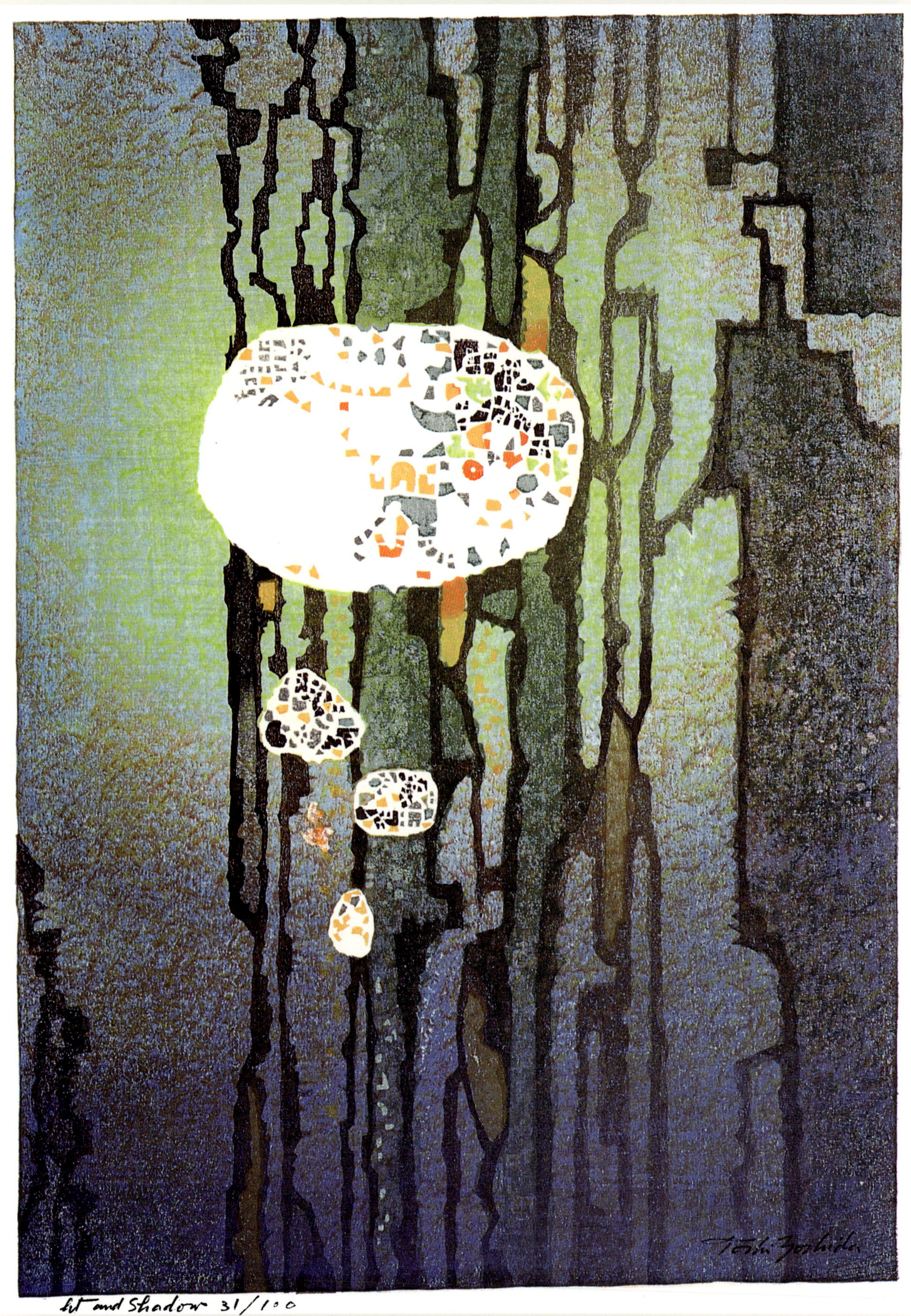

19. Yoshida Toshi (b. 1911). *Light and Shadow*, 31/100, undated, woodblock, 51.1x36 cm. Signed on the image Toshi Yoshida.

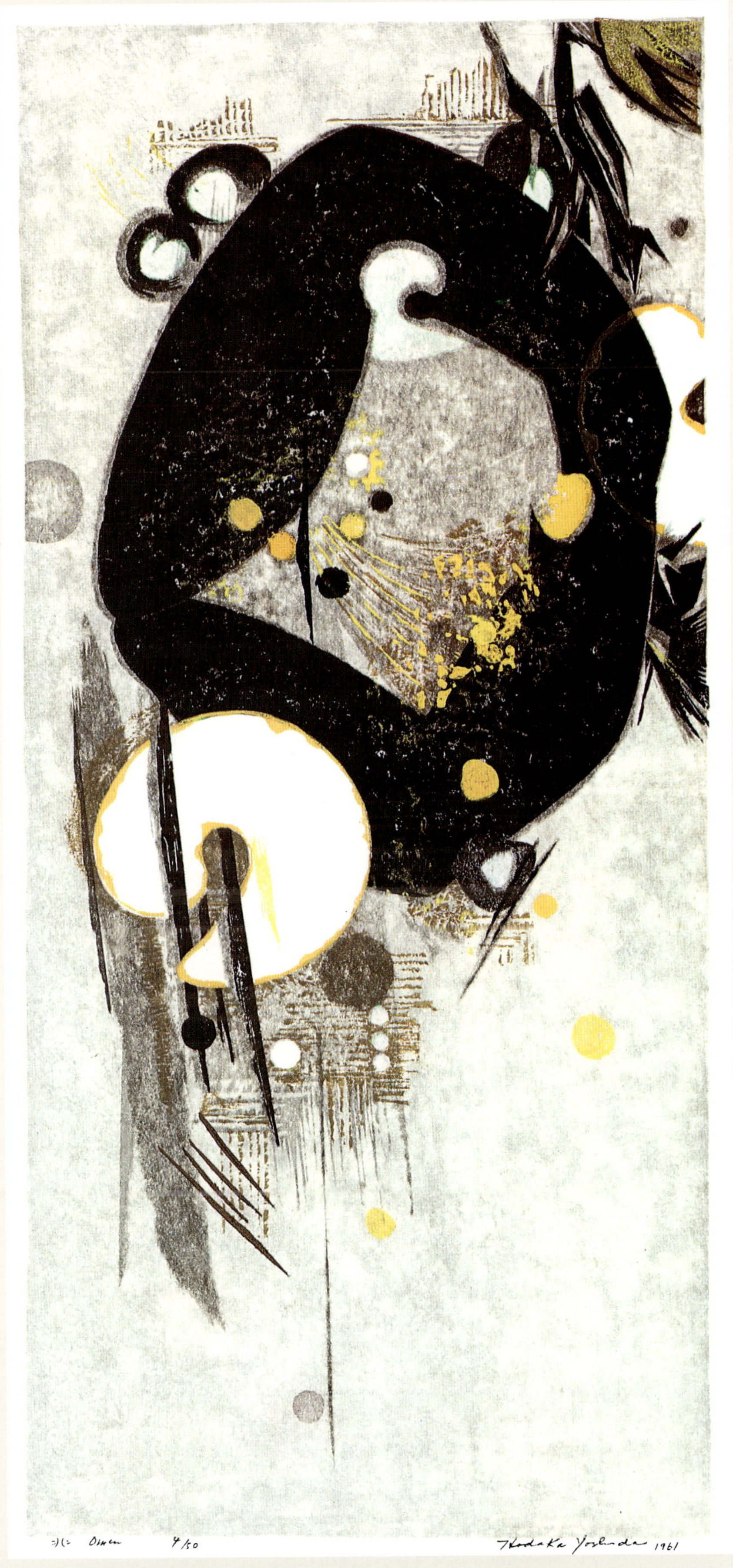

20. Yoshida Hodaka (b. 1926). Titled in Japanese *Kizashi*, titled in English *Omen*, 4/50, 1961, woodblock, 63x28.5cm. Signed Hodaka Yoshida.

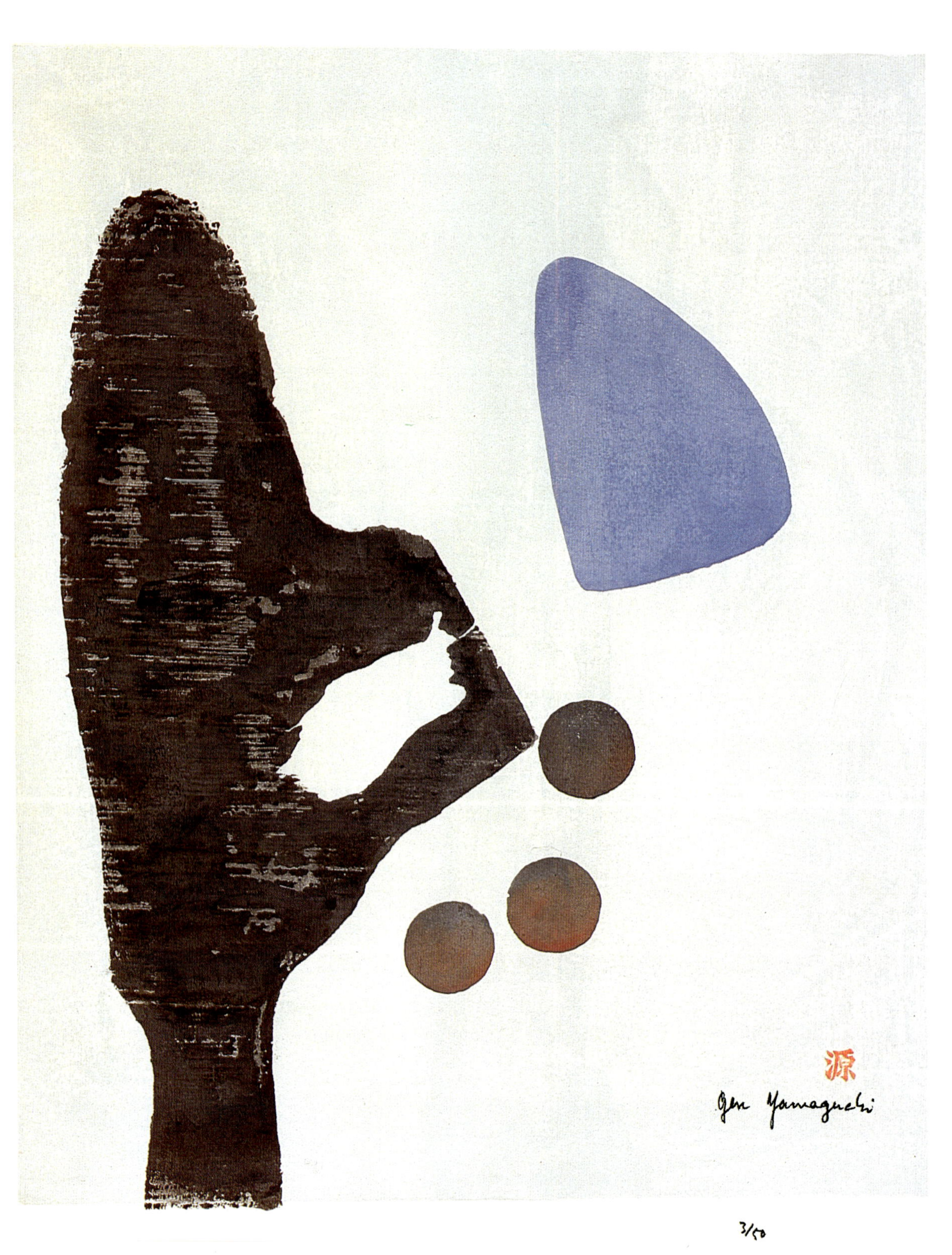

21. Yamaguchi Gen (1896–1976). Title unlisted, 3/50, undated, woodblock, 48.5x38.5 cm. Signed Gen Yamaguchi, sealed in kanji Gen.

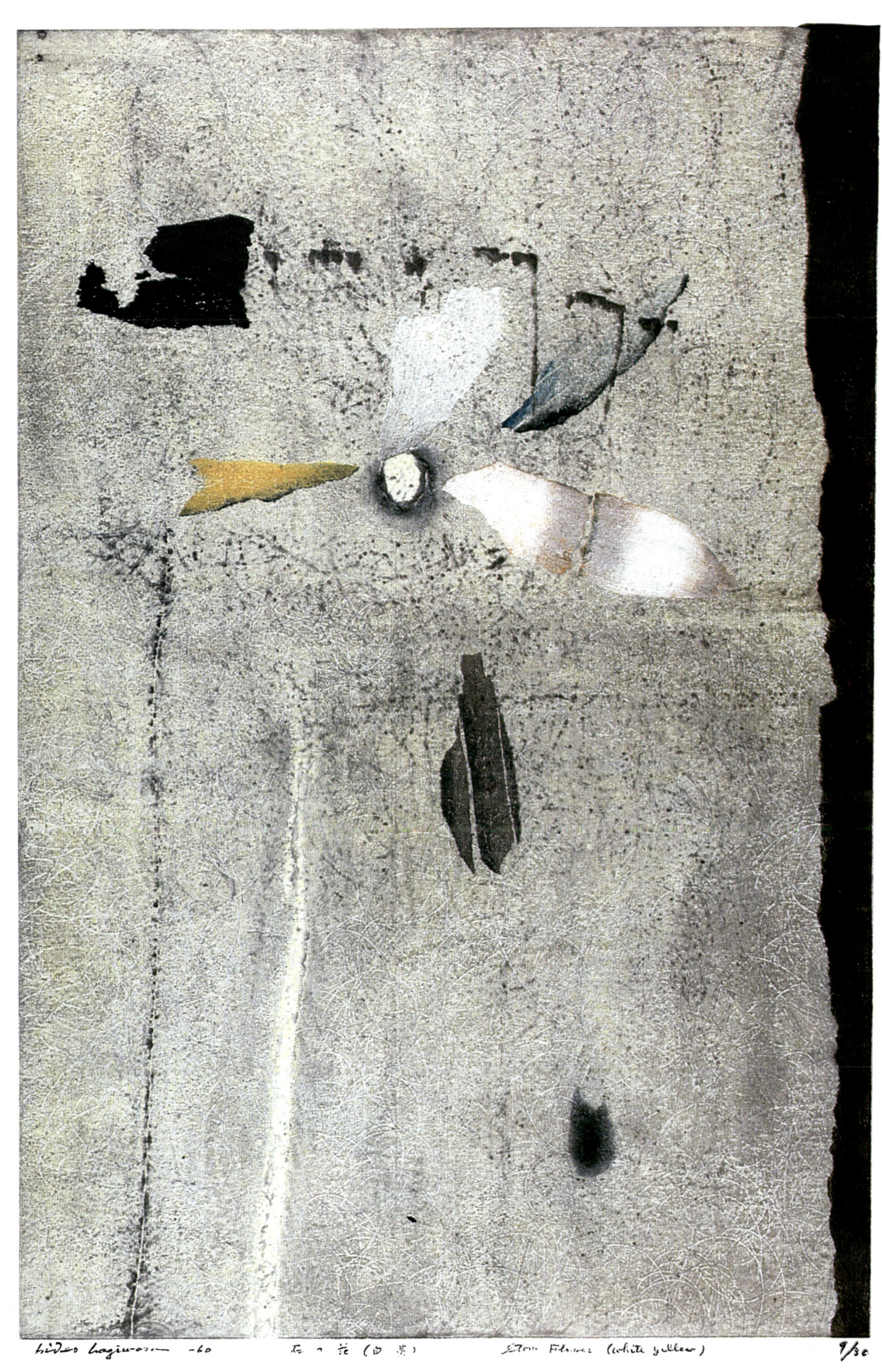

22. Hagiwara Hideo (b. 1913). Titled in Japanese *Ishi-no-hana (Haku-ō),* titled in English *Stone Flower (White Yellow),* 9/30, 1960, woodblock, 90.5x59.5 cm. Signed Hideo Hagiwara.

printing methods. We have never had a desire to make prints ourselves but can certainly appreciate the originality of someone like this artist who for years created an entire body of work by forcing the ink into the paper from the reverse. The result is an almost ethereal and subtle surface on which to work. Hagiwara too was famous for his never-ending search for new and original methods of printing.

Plate 23 *Plate 24* *Plate 25* These artists were rapidly joined by Shinagawa Takumi, Yoshida Masaji (no relation to the previously mentioned Yoshida family), and Uchima Ansei. We were fascinated by the exquisite coloring, the deceptively complex printing methods, and the intriguing asymmetrical balance of the compositions, which resulted in a vitality and harmonious tension reflecting the talent of the three printmakers.

Later we found that these artists were students of Onchi Koshiro (1891–1955), who is considered the spiritual leader of the *sōsaku-hanga* movement, and as such had as great an influence on a host of modern print artists as did Hiratsuka. Onchi was the master of the abstract, and his philosophy of searching out the new, of spatial organization, and of elegance of construction was absorbed by all of those who associated with him. At first it was not obvious to us, as newcomers to this genre, that the works of Shinagawa, Yoshida, and Uchima belonged to the Onchi school of thought, but years later when we viewed them all together it became clear that somehow they had a certain kinship. We have presented them here one after the other so that the impact of this type of work can be enjoyed as a whole.

The works of the next two artists seemed like dazzling, avant-garde, abstract compositions when we first saw them but, in fact, *Plate 26* they are based on realistic themes. Takahashi Rikio's *Tasteful, Kyoto Series No. 41* is just one of a series of numerous prints on Kyoto, the ancient capital, which has beguiled him during the entire course of his career. This print is his impression of a tranquil Kyoto garden, with each simple element arranged ideally to encourage our thoughtful meditation, and with his trademark of superimposing various blocks one upon the other to evoke unusual nuances of color.

Plate 27 Iwami Reika's *Silver Waterfall* is typical of her absorption with the theme of water, an interest so strong that she has often used pieces of wood with a grain resembling the flow of water. Iwami's work requires great physical strength, which would seem to be beyond the reach of this fragile, diminutive woman. She replies that she finds her force from within. "I like big, powerful things since I am very small," she says, "and that's what I try to create." Iwami is also a composer of haiku poetry. With its limited five-seven-five syllable form, haiku focuses on essentials, a strict discipline that Iwami uses as a guide for her prints. Her works are austere but powerful, with an integration of printing, embossing, and the

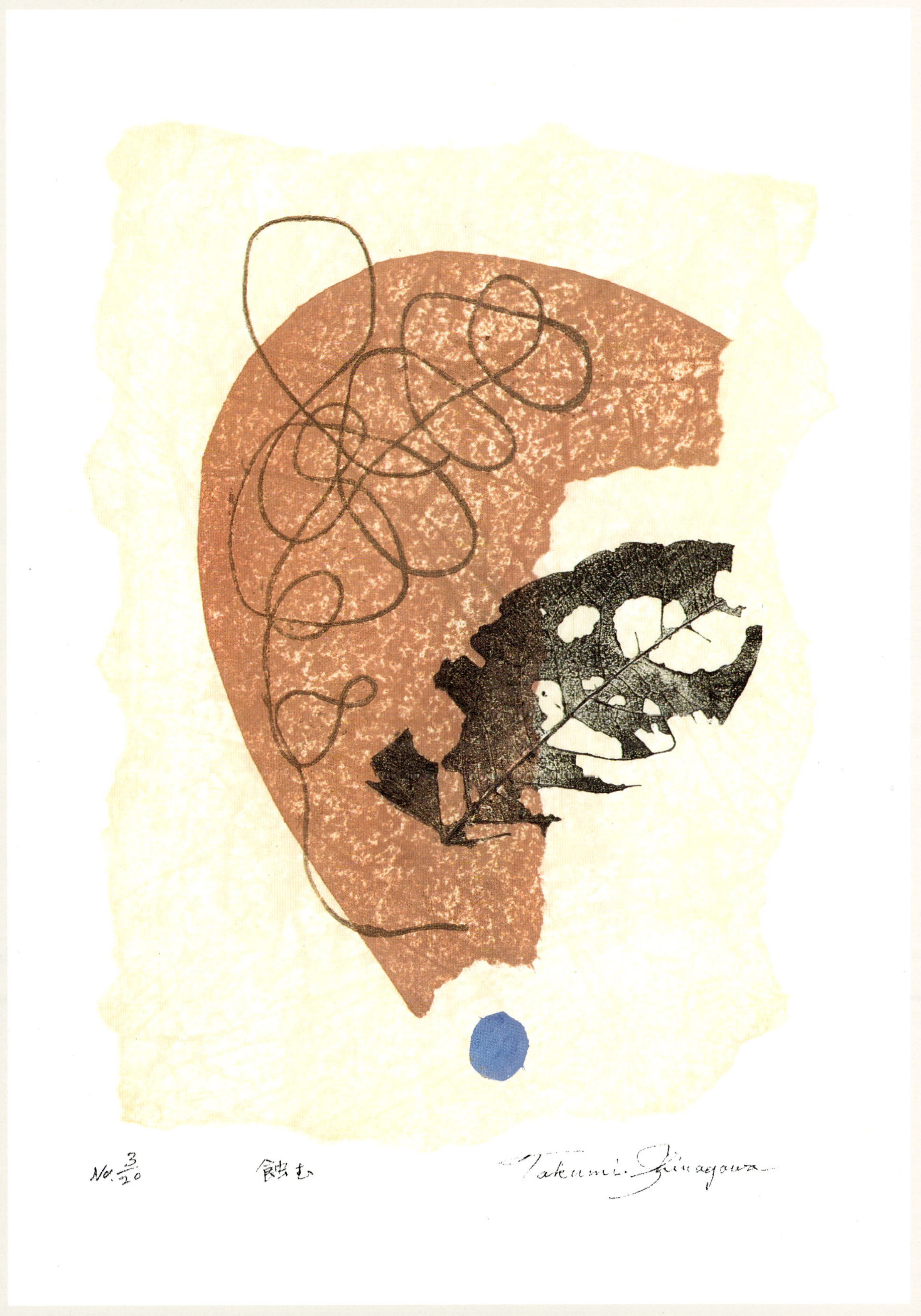

23. Shinagawa Takumi (b. 1908). Titled in Japanese *Mushibamu* (Eaten Away), 3/20, undated, woodblock/paper block, 50x31.7 cm. Signed Takumi Shinagawa.

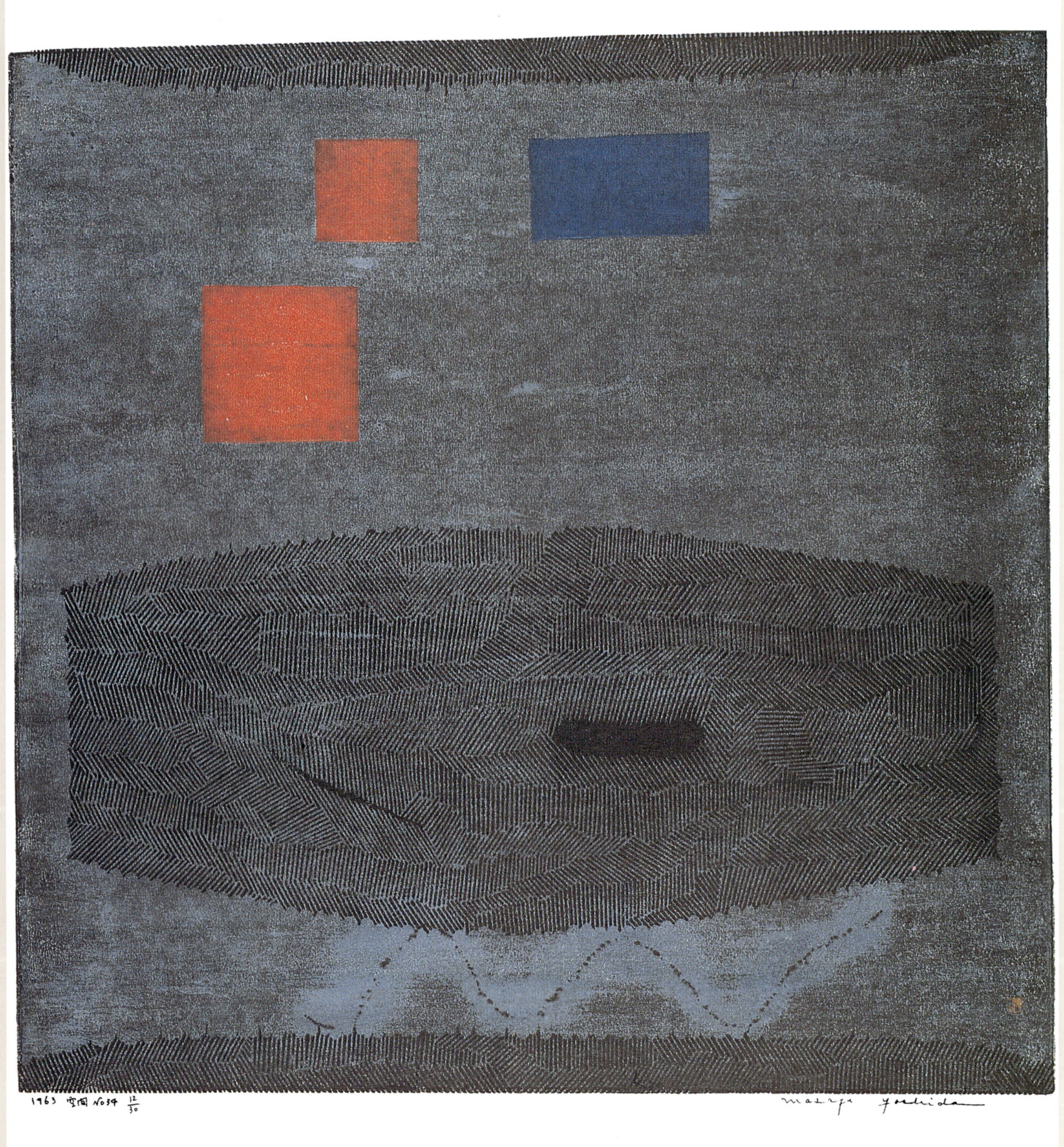

24. Yoshida Masaji (1917–71). Titled in Japanese *Kūkan 34* (Space No. 34), 12/30, 1963, woodblock, 61x61 cm. Signed Masaji Yoshida, sealed on the image in kanji Masaji.

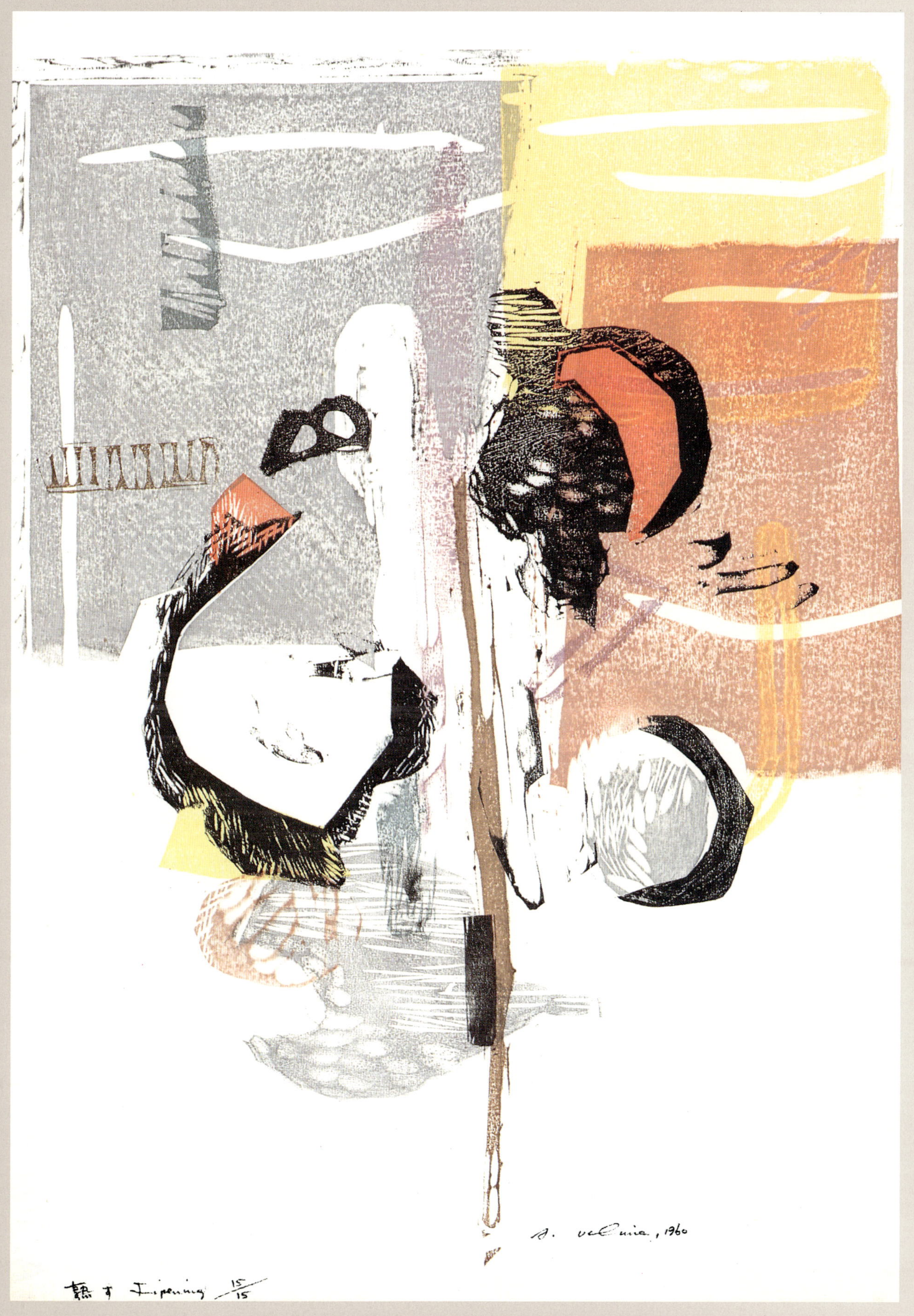

25. Uchima Ansei (b. 1921). Titled in Japanese *Jukusu,* titled in English *Ripening,* 15/15, 1960, woodblock, 60.8x40.5 cm. Signed A. Uchima.

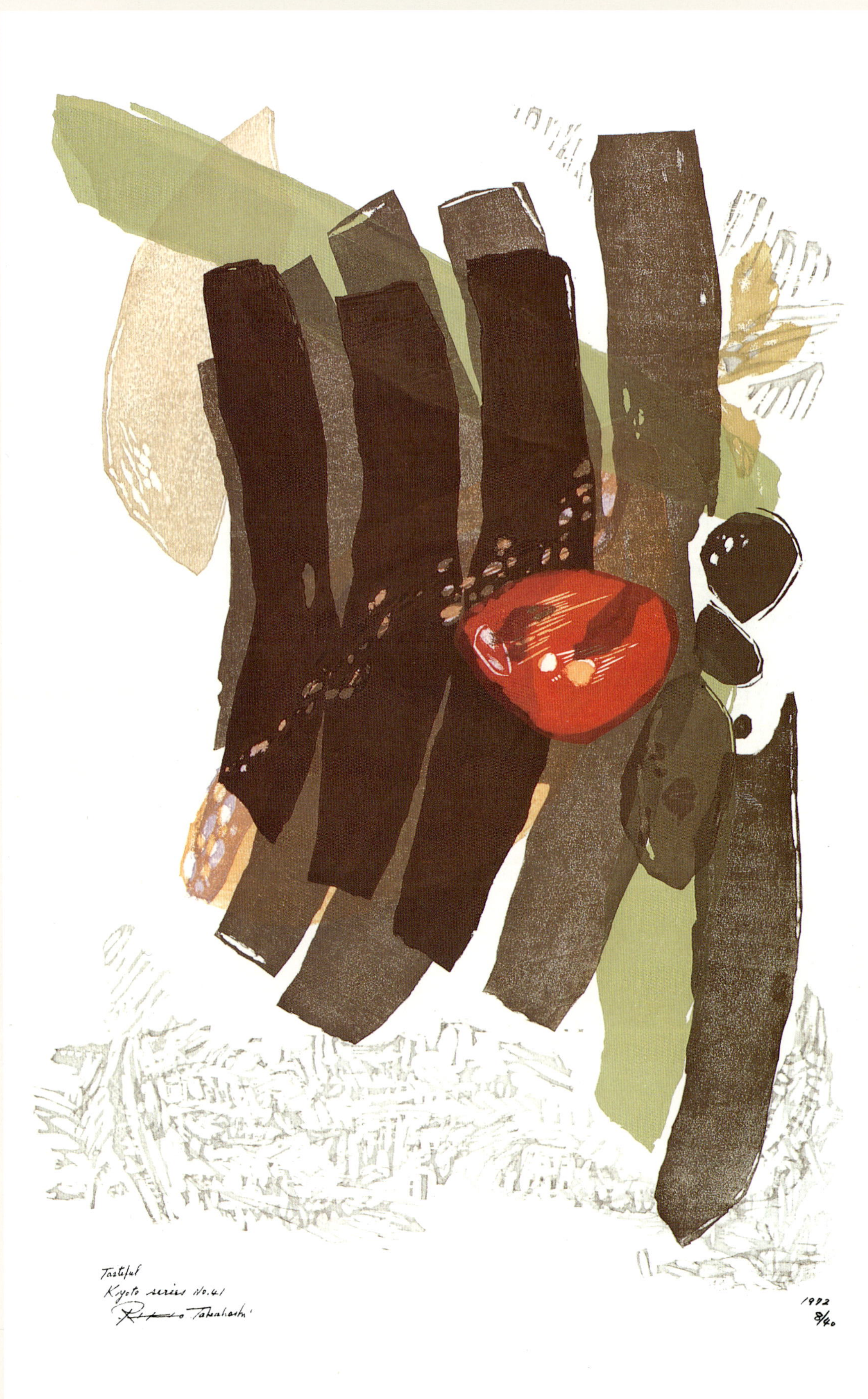

26. Takahashi Rikio (b. 1917). *Tasteful, Kyoto Series No. 41,* 8/40, 1972, woodblock, 94x60.3 cm. Signed Rikio Takahashi.

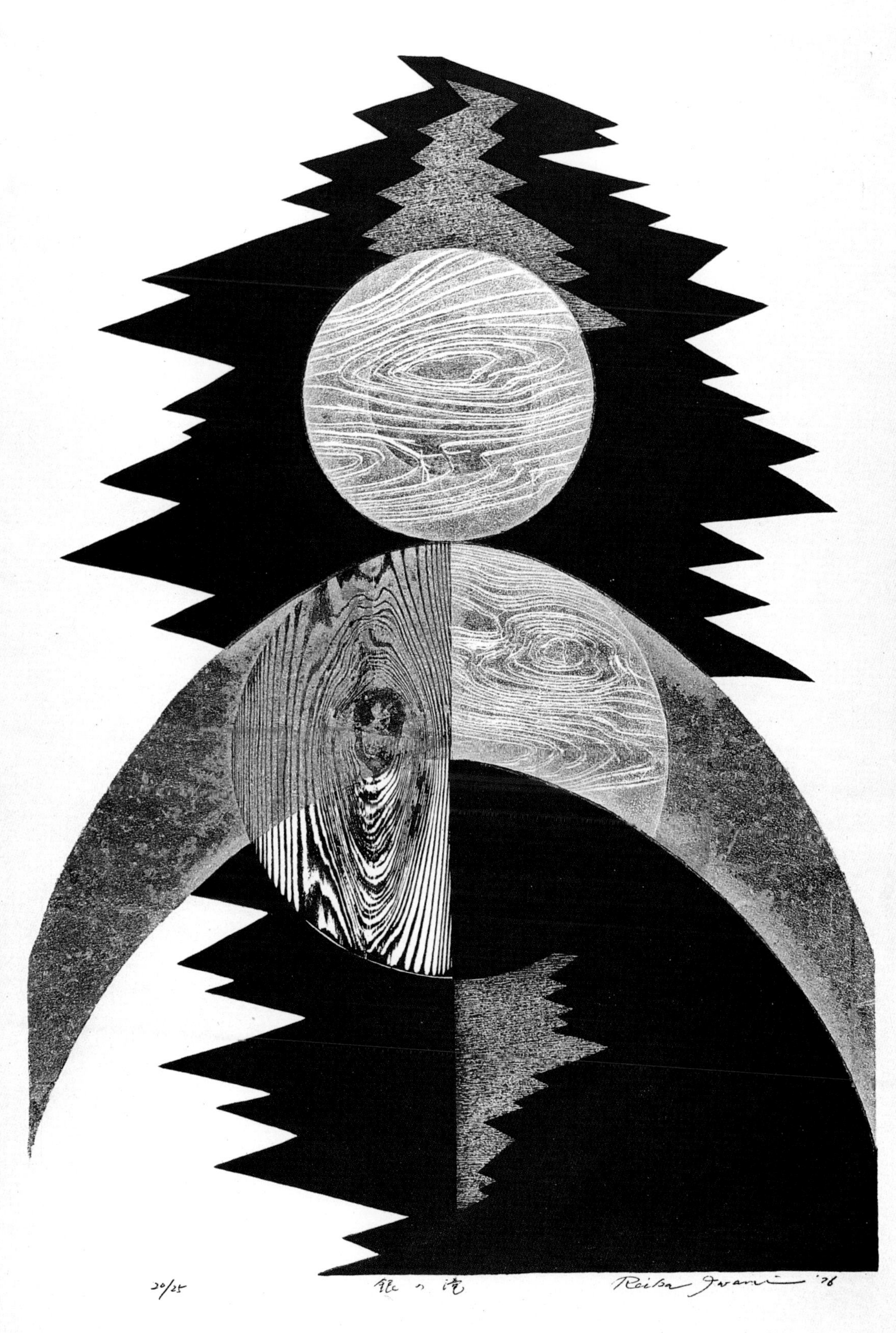

27. Iwami Reika (b. 1927). Titled in Japanese *Gin-no-taki* (Silver Waterfall), 20/25, 1976, woodblock with silver foil, 102x70.5 cm. Signed Reika Iwami. Published by the Tolman Collection, Tokyo.

occasional addition of gold or silver foil, adding up to art that is very satisfying in its structure and simplicity.

Our least favorite question asked by clients when they are faced with an abstract print is "What's this supposed to be?" As we have tried to indicate with the above examples, an abstract work is meant to satisfy not only the eye but the emotions, imagination, and spirit as well. These prints reflect the sense of order and balance, taste, and constant experimentation typical of the modern Japanese print artist.

To the novice collector it may seem frivolous to think about acquiring a piece of art simply for color, but by this stage in our lives we felt that our involvement with prints had turned out to be a serious one, and we began to analyze what we had gathered in order to fill in the gaps. We thus chose the following three artists simply because their use of color was exciting and dynamic, with nuances of color harmonies that were unfamiliar to our Western sensibilities.

Plate 28 Amano Kazumi's *Correlation—Pair A* attests to his mastery of both form and color integration as well as his ability to combine two techniques, woodblock and etching, effectively. Kusaka Kenji's *Plate 29* brilliantly pure lines in *Work 67.3* seem powerful enough to sweep us into space. For years Ay-O has been known as "the rainbow *Plate 30* man," and the reason is immediately obvious in his print *Wave C.* His bold juxtapositions of brilliant tones dazzle the eye and command attention. The usual silkscreen print artist employs one screen for each color, but Ay-O uses a separate screen for each band, sometimes as many as eighty screens, a method he perfected in the 1960s in the U.S., where he was caught up in the Pop Art movement and the era of "happenings." He was brought to international attention at a show at the renowned Louisiana Museum in Denmark. When we were to meet Ay-O, we were prepared to be overwhelmed by someone who had become a worldwide sensation and were afraid that he might be a serious and off-putting type. Instead we found him to be an atypical Japanese who laughed easily and found fun in everything, not a particularly Japanese concept. Even his name is fun. He made a survey of the five Japanese vowel sounds—*a, i, u, e, o*—and discovered that *a, i,* and *o* were more popular than the other two, so he chose them as his name. His real name is Iijima Takao.

It is not surprising for an artist to be able to achieve luminosity and depth of color in the silkscreen technique, but what surprised us *Plate 31* about Kurosaki Akira's *Forbidden Venture* was that, along with unparalleled use of shading and embossing, he could achieve this almost psychedelic effect with the traditional woodblock medium. He is one of a number of world-known Japanese artists like Shinoda Toko and Ikeda Masuo who were born in Manchuria, which leads us to reflect upon possible early outside influences on artistic creativity. When we first met Kurosaki in Kyoto he was just another

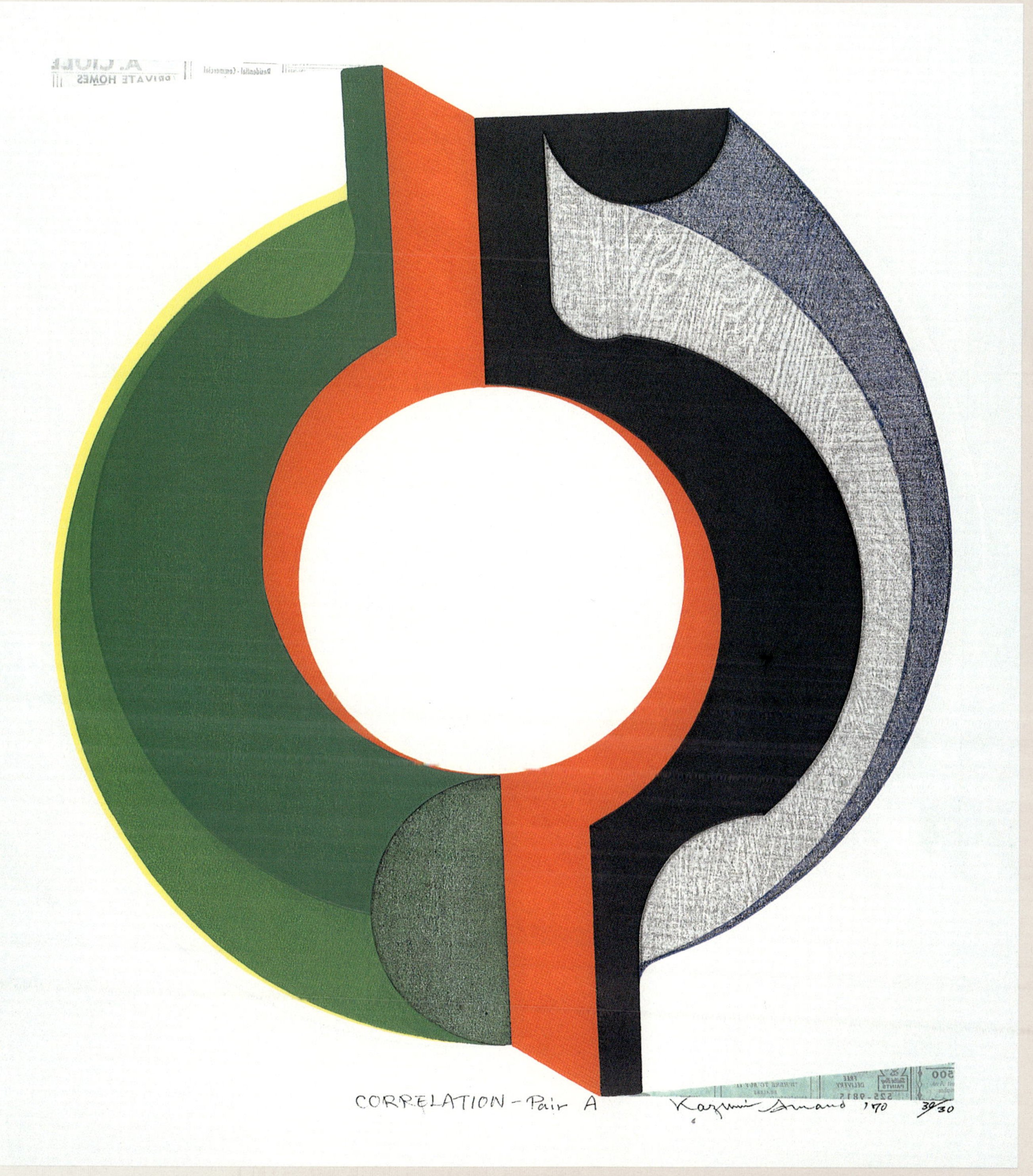

28. Amano Kazumi (b. 1927). *Correlation—Pair A,* 30/30, 1970, woodblock/etching, 55x50 cm. Signed Kazumi Amano.

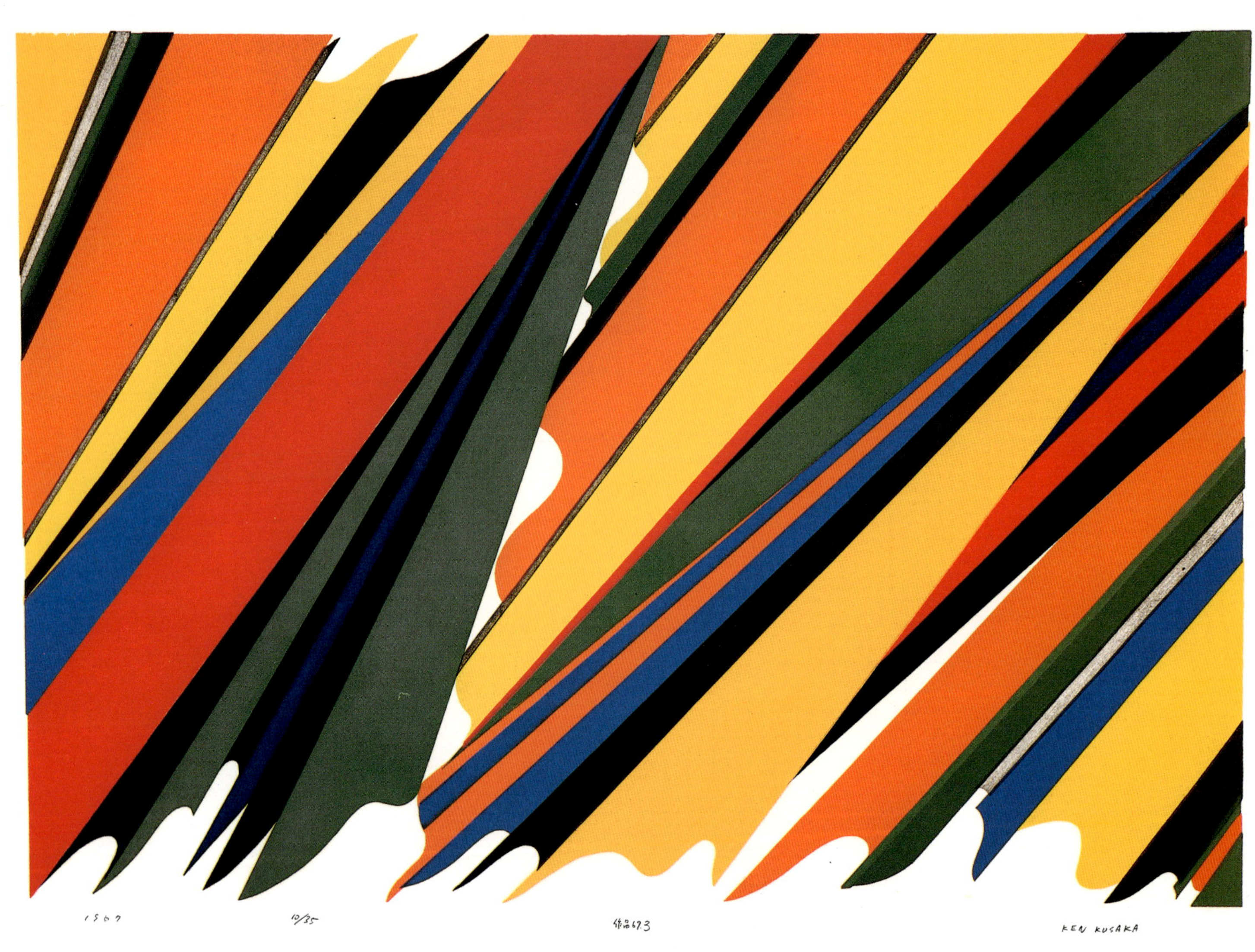

29. Kusaka Kenji (b. 1936). Titled in Japanese *Sakuhin 67.3* (Work 67.3), 10/35, 1967, woodblock, 55x77.4 cm. Signed Ken Kusaka.

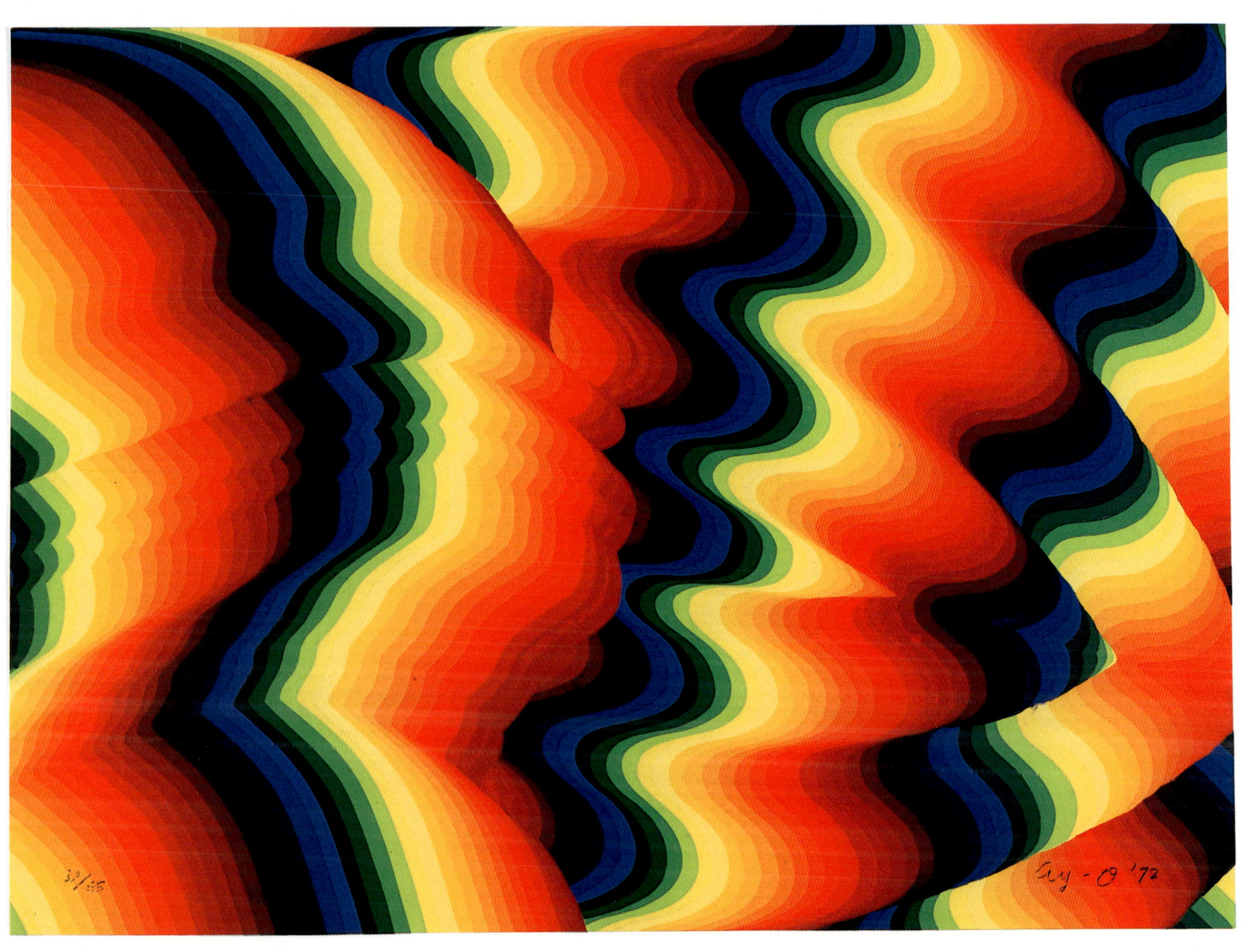

30. Ay-O (b. 1931). Title unlisted but known as *Wave C*, 39/65, 1972, silkscreen, 54.5x73.7 cm. Signed on the image AY-O.

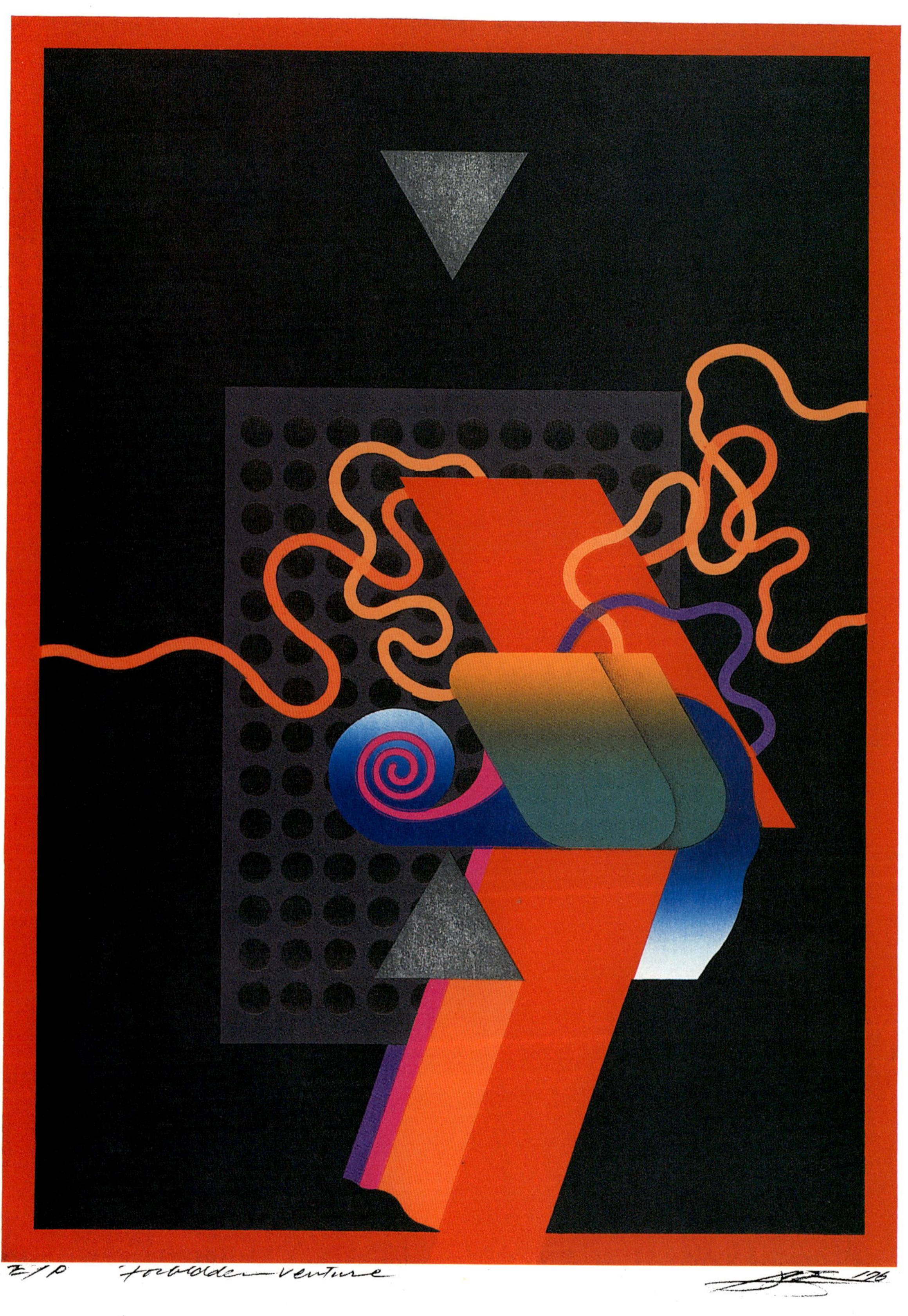

31. Kurosaki Akira (b. 1937). *Forbidden Venture,* E/A (edition known to be 75), 1976, woodblock, 57x41 cm. Signed A. Kurosaki. Published by the Tolman Collection, Tokyo.

hard-working artist creating his deeply mysterious worlds on paper, but he has gone on to win major prizes at international print competitions in Poland and in the former Yugoslavia. He spent one year in the U.S. studying English and participating in the art world there, and has now grown into a very famous artist and an excellent art teacher of a younger generation.

Continuing with the idea that there are no hidebound rules of collecting except for the criterion of what touches the heart of the collector, we further concentrated on color. Having experimented with the vivid and resplendent, we sought refuge in the soothing blues of Yuki Rei's kingdom of fantasy, *White Flames*, and Funasaka Yoshisuke's restful space. Funasaka has produced more than a thousand prints, and his series *My Space and My Dimension* is part of this grand continuum. The appeal of his work lies not only in its crafted simplicity but also in its formal purity. He manages to balance the shapes to carve out his own private space and to create tension with these elements. Since Japanese names are often confusing to foreigners, people are very grateful to have some device by which to remember who has done what. For a long time Funasaka incorporated the contours and color of lemons in his work, earning the nickname of "the lemon man" (just as Inagaki is "the cat man" and Hoshi is "the tree man," as well as the dozens of others who have been known for their subject matter rather than by their surnames).

Plate 32

Plate 33

At that time the goal of making the collection had not yet formed in our mind. We had been acquiring only those prints with a special appeal, shunning the small numbers of indecent or bizarre works that were never of any interest to us. We were acquainted with some collectors whom we felt had overspecialized. One of them had gathered sixty-five Hoshi tree prints and hung them all together, turning his house into a veritable forest. We wanted to be surrounded with only what made us happy and comfortable, works showing the wide range of talent and technique that abounded. With the sudden realization of the hold these prints had on us and the extent to which our collection had grown, we deliberately decided at this point to expand our horizons.

We had neglected a very important segment of Japan's culture, one dear to the hearts of the Japanese themselves and one that forms a seemingly impenetrable barrier to foreigners—the written language. Two artists at that time were noted for using written parts of the Japanese language as an art form, Shinoda Toko and Maki Haku.

From today's vantage point of being the leading dealers of Shinoda's lithographs, it is strange to recall that at first we felt her oeuvre might be a bit too intellectually sophisticated for us. She was already well established as a calligrapher and abstract painter who happened to produce the occasional lithograph. Most of our artists

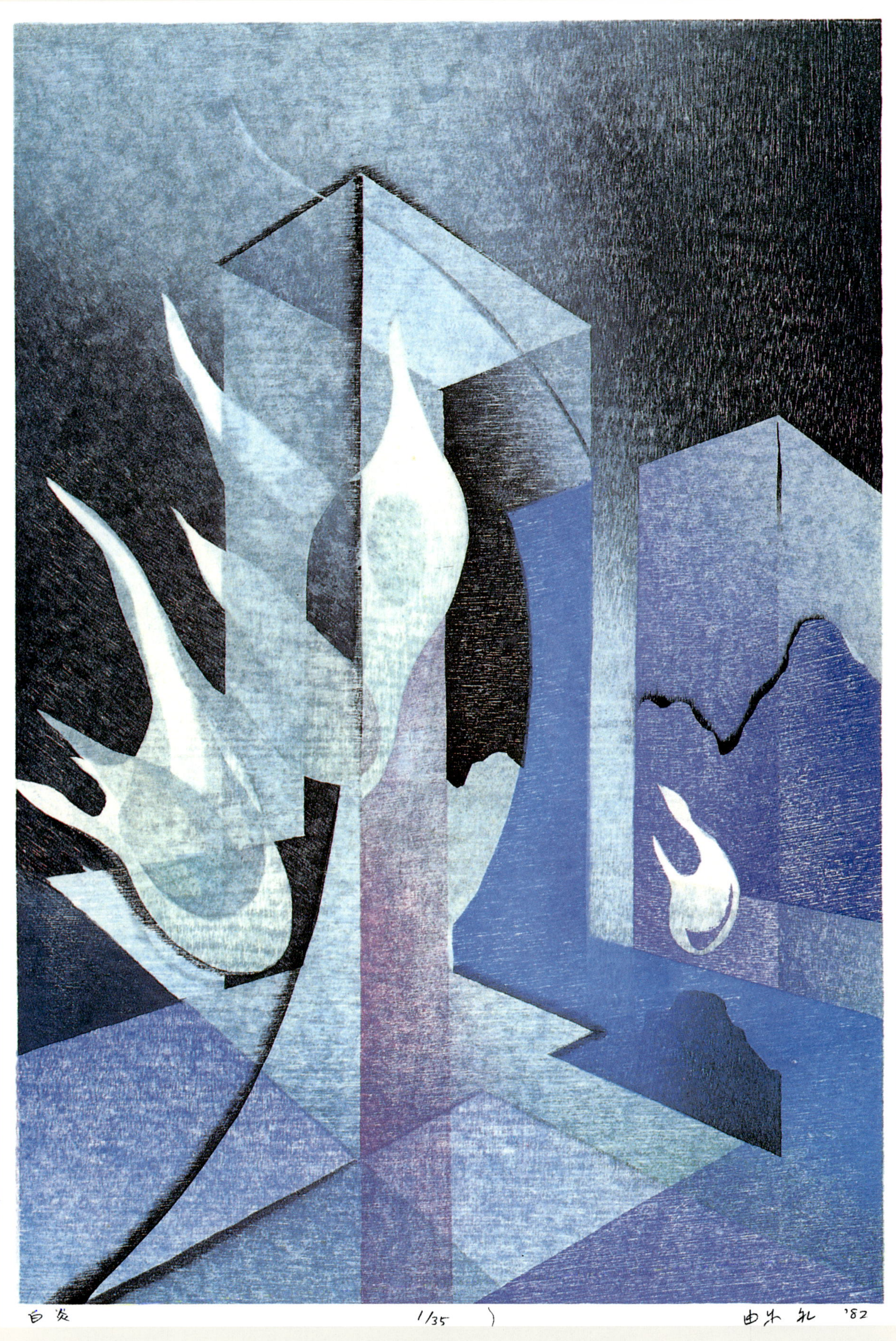

32. Yuki Rei (b. 1928). Titled in Japanese *Haku-en* (White Flames), 1/35, 1982, woodblock, 65x44 cm. Signed in kanji Yuki Rei.

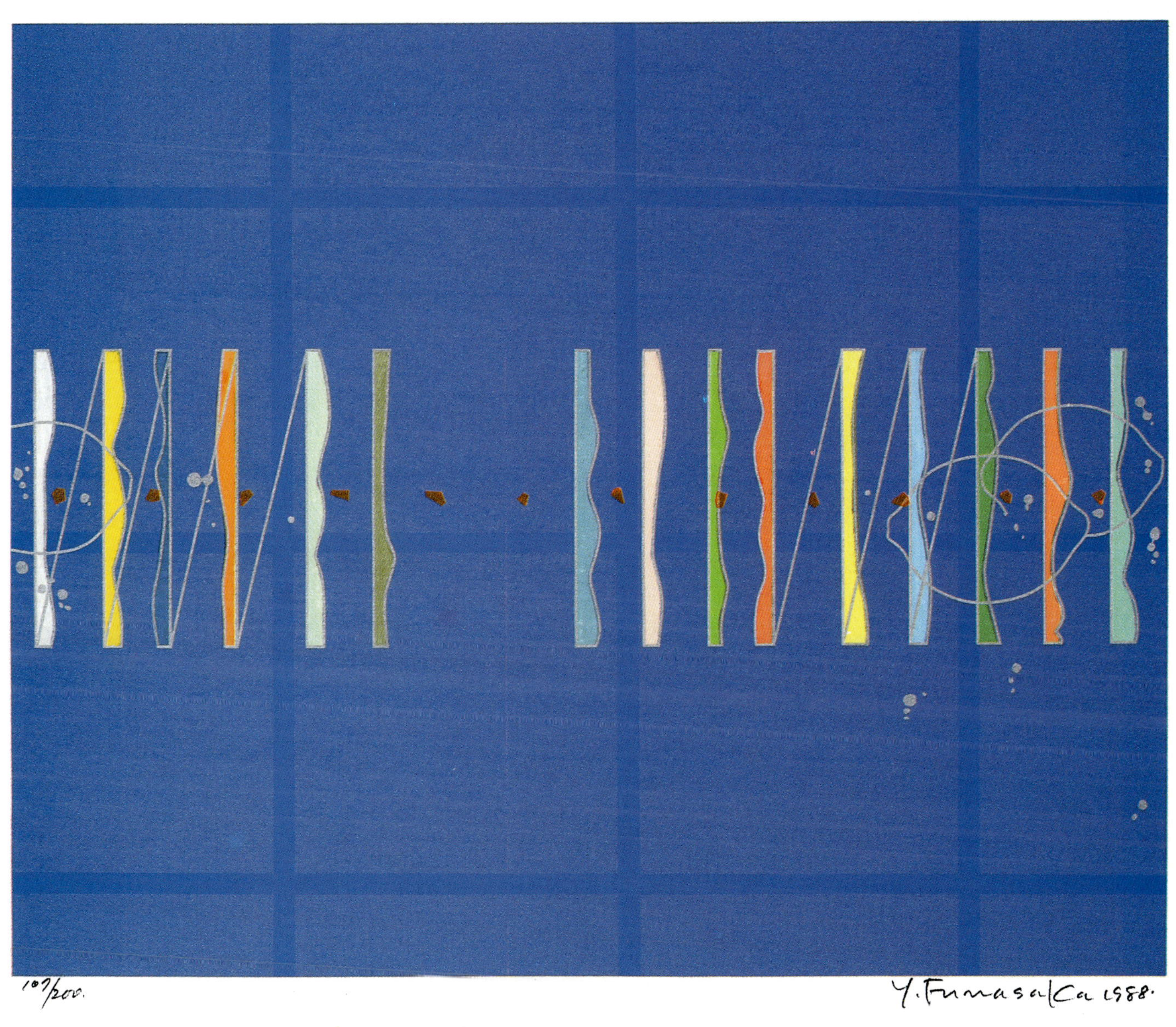

33. Funasaka Yoshisuke (b. 1939). Title unlisted but known as *M* (standing for 1,000, a production landmark for Funasaka), 107/200, 1988, woodblock/silkscreen, 35.5x43 cm. Signed Y. Funasaka.

were printmakers first, doing something else to earn their living, usually some form of teaching. We were reluctant to pursue the work of someone who was not fundamentally a printmaker. We learned that Shinoda had been introduced to this medium by the American artist Arthur Flory, who felt that her painting method would lend itself well to the lithographic technique. He printed the first few works for her and a new printmaking career was launched.

Lithography turned out to be the perfect method to satisfy Shinoda's stringent requirements and standards in presenting her

Plate 34

flowing and dynamic strokes. In *Iroha* she has drawn on a verse from a poem that includes forty-seven (of the forty-eight) sounds of the Japanese language. For many years she has used *hiragana* (a cursive syllabary representing sounds based on kanji) as subject matter in paintings and has found that it works equally well in prints. It was possible for her to create a vigorous composition based on ancient calligraphic strokes and then complete the work by adding her distinctive, inventive calligraphy, slightly altering it to make each print an original of sorts.

Plate 35

Maki Haku's works were another reason to delve into the written language. His prints, a combination of woodblock and cement work, were pulled in black and white, inviting us to concentrate on the subject matter. Whereas Shinoda was known for *hiragana* Maki preferred to employ kanji.

Students of Japan are frequently overwhelmed by its language. Learning to speak Japanese is a time-consuming, difficult, thankless, and never-ending task; learning to write Japanese, an amalgam of complicated, Chinese-borrowed characters ranging from those with a few simple strokes to others with more than twenty, is unbelievably harder. There are also the indigenous Japanese scripts, cursive *hiragana* and *katakana* (an angular script representing the same forty-eight sounds as *hiragana* but used chiefly to write words of foreign origin). Kanji and the two *kana* syllabaries are supplemented by borrowings in Romanization from other languages, borrowings whose meanings may differ from the meanings of the original foreign words. From this brief explanation it should be clear that gaining literacy in Japanese as an adult foreigner is quite a feat.

To the Japanese the written script is not such a monumental puzzle but an art form in itself. Shinoda once told us in a matter-of-fact way, "Of course, foreigners can appreciate my writing for its balance and form, but do not forget, we can read it too." Maki took advantage of the intrinsic design qualities of kanji for his abstract depictions. When I came across their work, I was very glad that I had paid attention during my study of prehistoric oracle-bone writings during my Chinese studies at Yale.

On the occasion of Shinoda's eightieth birthday in 1993 we authored our book *Toko Shinoda: A New Appreciation* to call

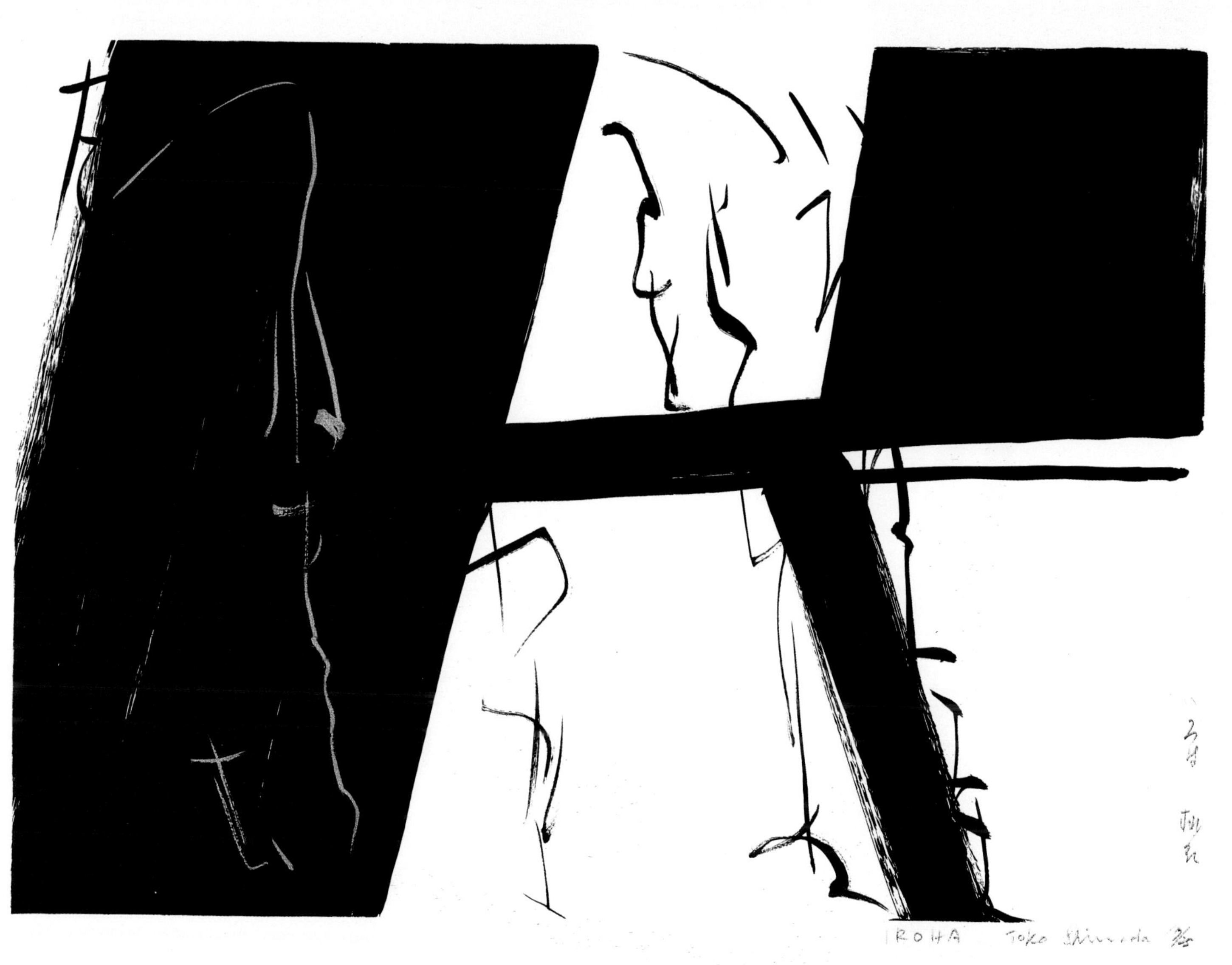

34. Shinoda Toko (b. 1913). Titled in Japanese *Iroha* (the first syllables of a famous poem), titled in English *Iroha,* 17/25, undated but known to be c. 1979, lithograph with hand-added silver color, 41.3x56 cm. Signed Toko Shinoda, signed in kanji Toko.

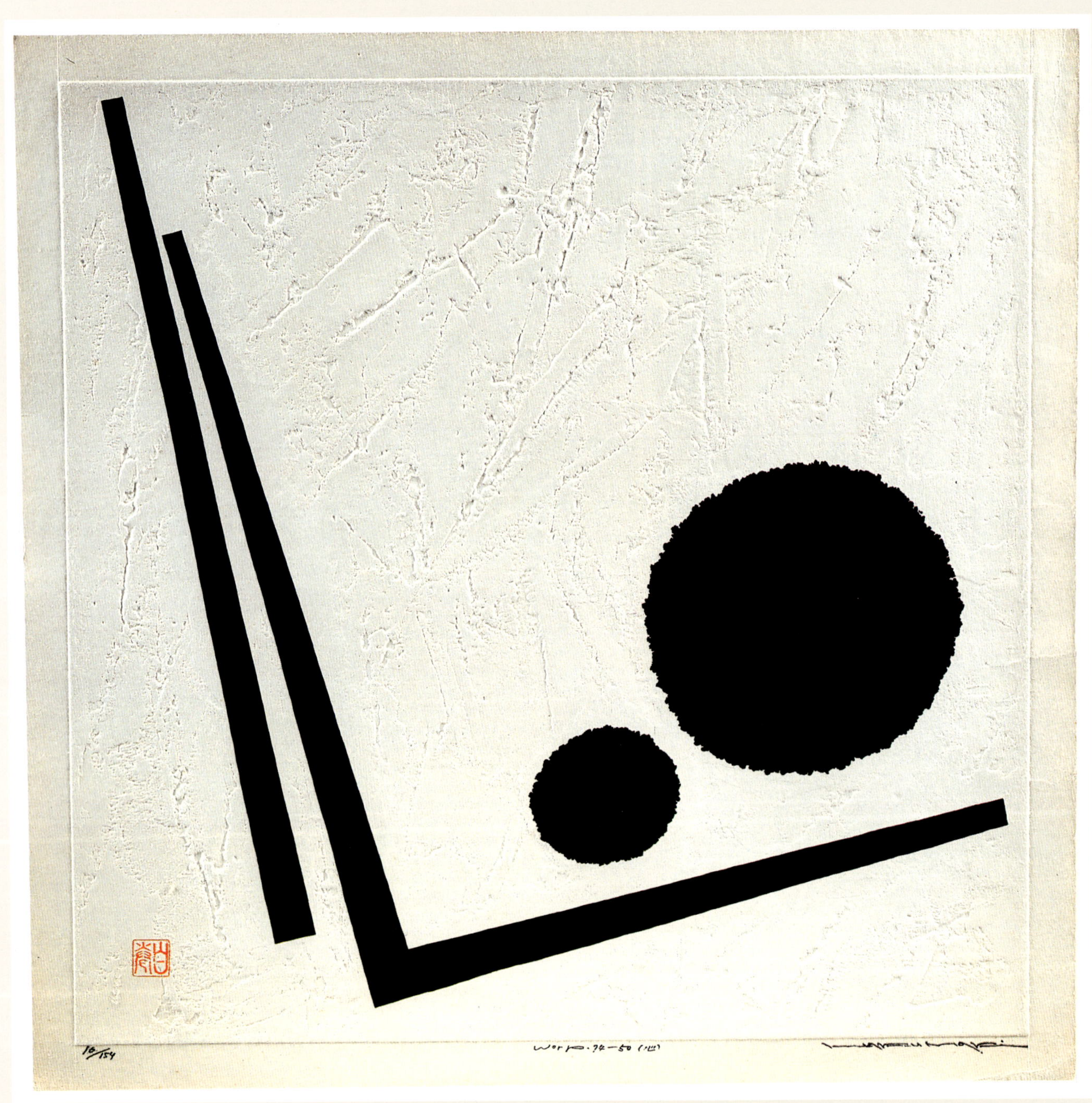

35. Maki Haku (b. 1924). Titled in Japanese *Kokoro* (Heart), titled in English *Work 74-50,* 16/154, 1974, woodblock/cement block, 49.7x49.8 cm. Signed Haku Maki, sealed in kanji Haku Maki.

attention to her role as a major participant in the print world. (That was the new of the new appreciation.) When we took into consideration her fame as a painter and calligrapher and balanced that with her lithographic accomplishments, we realized the extent of her genius. Searching for something to present to her on this special birthday, we discovered to our surprise that we had published nearly two hundred different editions of her lithographs and wrote our book about her.

As an additional surprise for Shinoda on this memorable birthday, we invited our older daughter, Allison, one of her favorite people, to come from New York especially for the publication party and to officiate with Nagao Eiji, our manager, as emcees at her black-tie birthday dinner.

We have mentioned that we were never interested in certain kinds of prints but did not intend to indicate a prudish attitude. In fact, the subject matter of Japanese prints is for the most part presentable to any viewer. Pornographic art has always been popular in certain quarters but we chose not to collect it. However, mildly erotic subject matter was part of the scene we next explored, and coincidentally all three of the following artists worked in lithography.

Plate 36 Ikeda Masuo, born in Manchuria, first achieved great fame in New York, where he lived and studied for many years. Ikeda, considered by many critics as the consummate print artist, has also been given kudos for his writing on a wide variety of subjects. Someone remarked that if he could not make a living as a graphic artist (which he certainly can), then he could easily support himself through his literary efforts. In addition, he has directed several movies, won awards for his ceramics, appears regularly on television, and is a lively and humorous fellow who seems to have a finger in every pie.

Plate 37 Yoshihara Hideo is a soft-spoken, easygoing teacher whose unconventional work belies the kind of man he appears to be. Our days in Kyoto brought about many meetings with this gentle man, and we were always left with a sense that his work was incongruous with his simple outward manner.

Plate 38 Tamura Fumio's work is something akin to old wine in new bottles. The idea of combining pieces of various shapes to create a new shape or of using divers parts of human figures to make a new figure had been done in woodblock much earlier, but not with Tamura's sense of color and style.

All three artists—Ikeda, Yoshihara, Tamura—enjoy portraying the female form in an enigmatic atmosphere. The eroticism of the prints is ambivalent and innocent because the creators are adroit in making us enter a dream world where artistic line, form, and color are paramount. We must be the dreamer too and share our personal fantasies with those of the artists, as we study their imagery. Ikeda

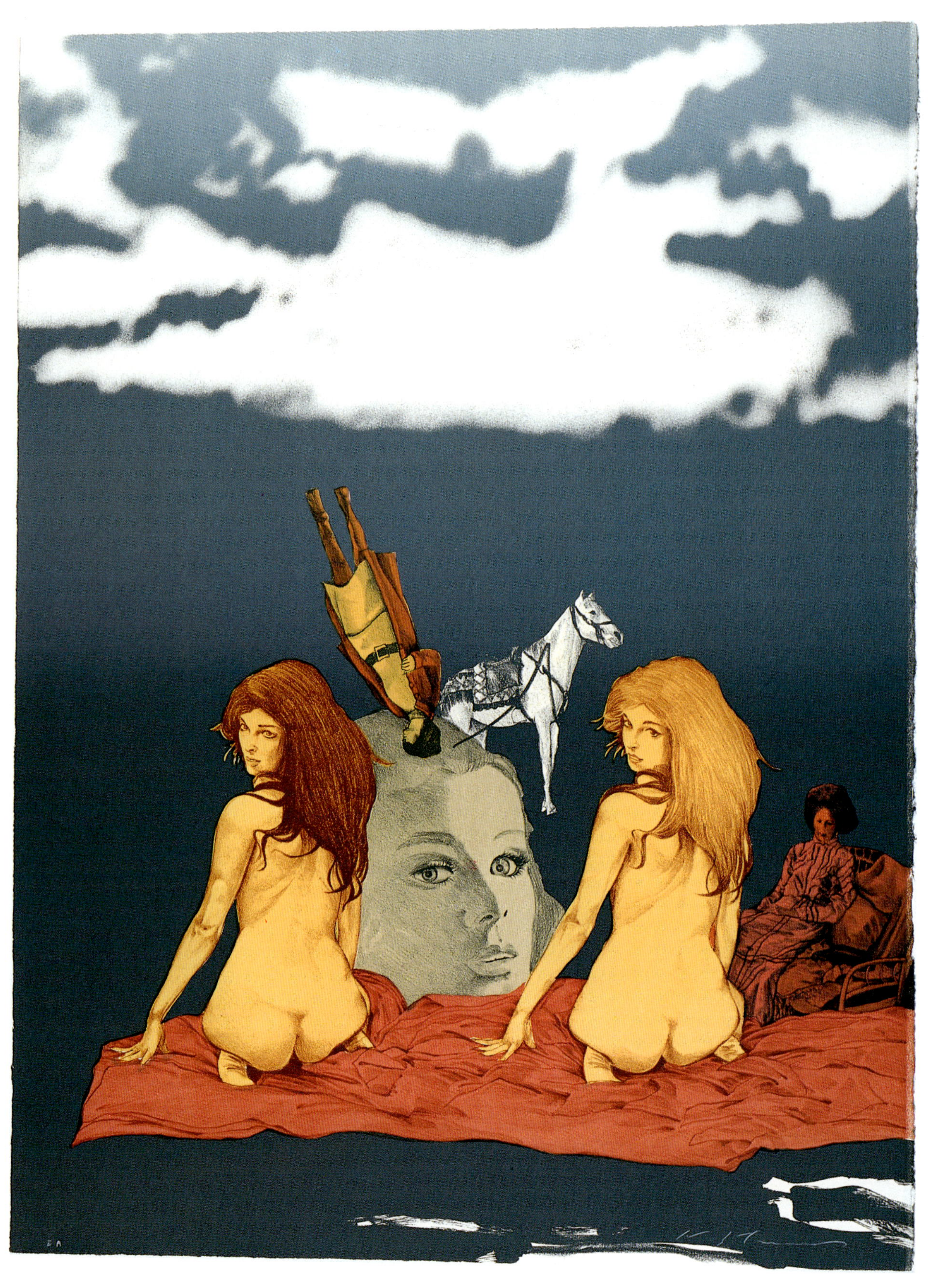

36. Ikeda Masuo (b. 1934). Title unlisted but known as *Waratte* (Laughing), E/A (edition known to be 100), 1970, lithograph, 76x56 cm. Signed on the image M. Ikeda.

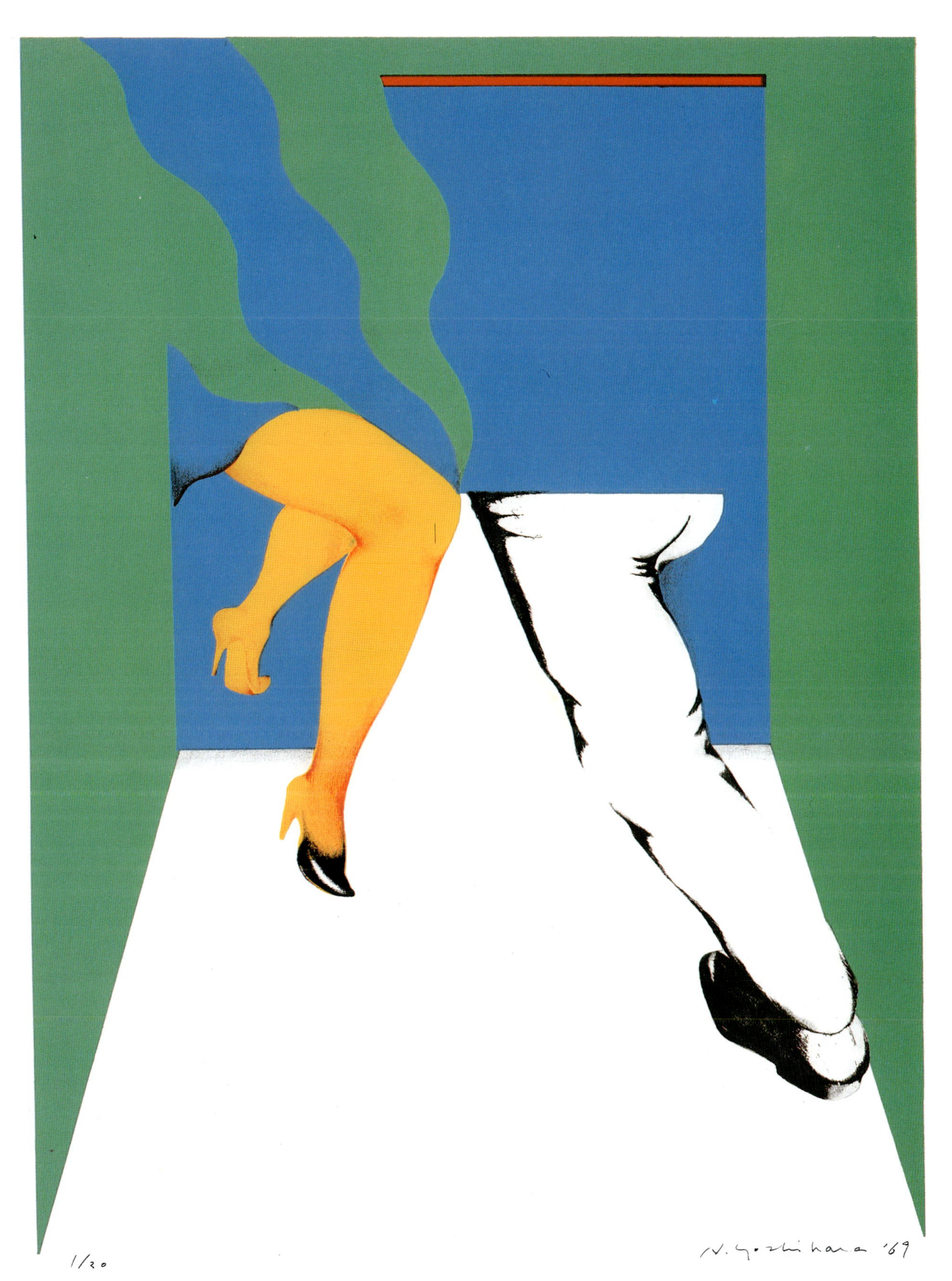

37. Yoshihara Hideo (b. 1931). Titled on the reverse *Ai* (Love), 1/30, 1969, lithograph, 54x40 cm. Signed H. Yoshihara, signed on the reverse in kanji Yoshihara Hideo.

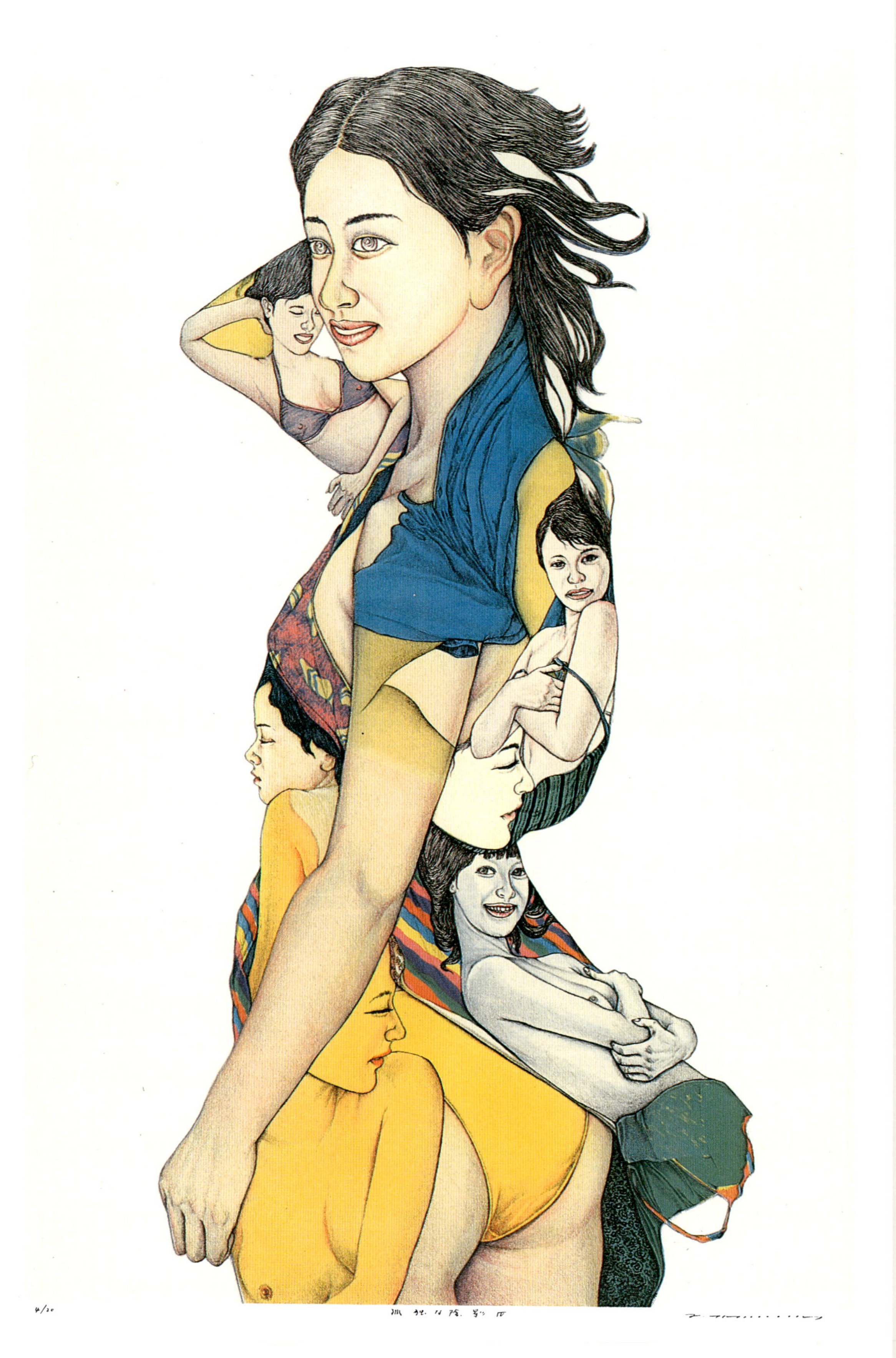

38. Tamura Fumio (b. 1941). Titled in Japanese *Kodokuna-in-ei IV* (Lonely Shadows IV), 4/20, 1983, lithograph, 60x39 cm. Signed F. Tamura.

used Western faces, Tamura a Japanese face, and Yoshihara no face at all, yet we appreciate their unique compositions and extraordinary imaginations.

Our path took us next to Sapporo, where diplomatic life provided the largest apartment in all Hokkaido, a car and driver, and a full social whirl, but unfortunately no proper Western school for our two small girls. Mary returned to Tokyo and the children were boarded at the Lycée Franco-Japonais de Tokyo. I was the vice-consul and director of the American Cultural Center, and one of the first things I did was sponsor a major exhibition of Saito Kiyoshi's work on Culture Day, November 3 and a holiday in Japan, at the Mitsukoshi Department Store. Up until thirty years before, Saito had lived for twenty years in Otaru, a neighboring city of Sapporo. The exhibition was attended by people whom Saito had not seen for decades, and it was a heartwarming reunion for those in Hokkaido who had a connection with prints. Of course, for me it was thrilling to meet so many artists and especially to be introduced to the art community by Saito himself.

Among the guests were Shibuya Eiichi (who had previously bought Saito's old press, which he still uses) and his then student Watarai Junsuke. When we started our business, they were among the first six artists we showed. During my time in Sapporo they became almost like relatives, exuding the warmth and hospitality for which Hokkaidoans are noted. The etchings they produce are an exact reflection of the sweet and gentle nature of the creators. I never look at their prints without thinking of how kind and generous they were to me in my solo days in Sapporo.

The work of Shibuya and Watarai appears to have a European flavor. One reason may be that they studied at a famous Paris studio, S. W. Hayter's Atelier 17, and also at the Paris Friedländer
Plate 39 studio, as did Minami Keiko. As Minami lived in Paris for several decades it is natural that her work would have a Western flavor. Her work is characterized by a lyrical charm; there is nothing extraneous in her composition, just the essentials presented in a naive and simple way. Minami now lives in San Francisco with her husband, Hamaguchi Yozo, the renowned mezzotint artist, whose prints command $30,000 prices.

Shibuya and Watarai also project a land of fantasy in their art, filled with animals, flowers, clowns, fairyland castles, musical instruments, circuses—in short, all that appeals to the child in us. Needless to say, our daughters adored their prints, as will anyone
Plate 40 who appreciates the land of make-believe. Shibuya's *Northern Town*
Plate 41 and Watarai's *Hanazono Convent Garden* were created at my request. I had been asked to write an article about Hakodate, and felt that rather than illustrate the piece with photographs it would be more interesting to use original prints. The works portray a Russian church and a Trappist convent, both in Hakodate. This

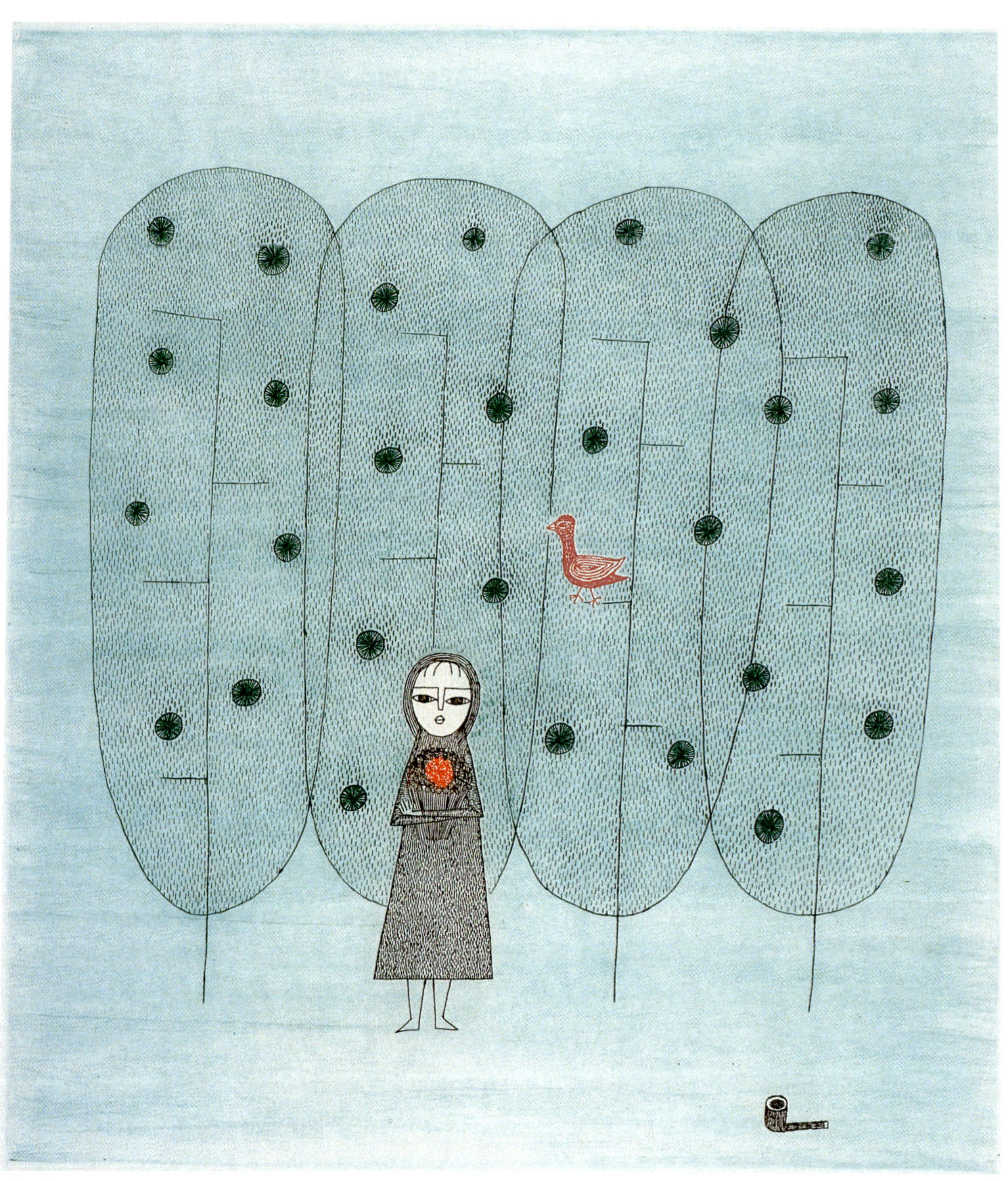

39. Minami Keiko (b. 1911). Title unknown, 27/50, undated, etching, 32.5x28.4 cm. Signed Keiko Minami.

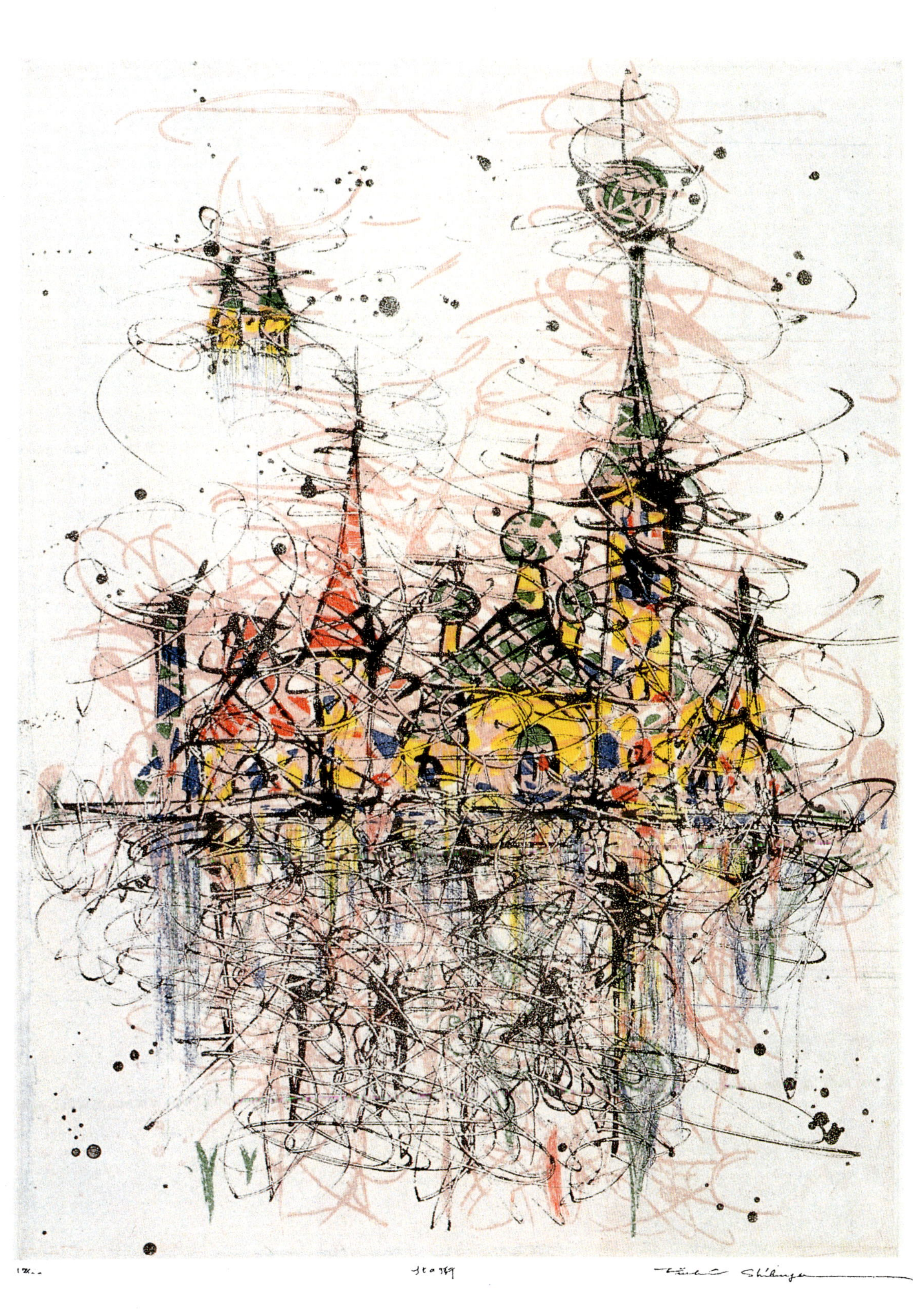

40. Shibuya Eiichi (b. 1928). Titled in Japanese *Kita-no-machi* (Northern Town), 17/100, 1975, etching, 36x26.7 cm. Signed Eiichi Shibuya. Published by the Tolman Collection, Tokyo.

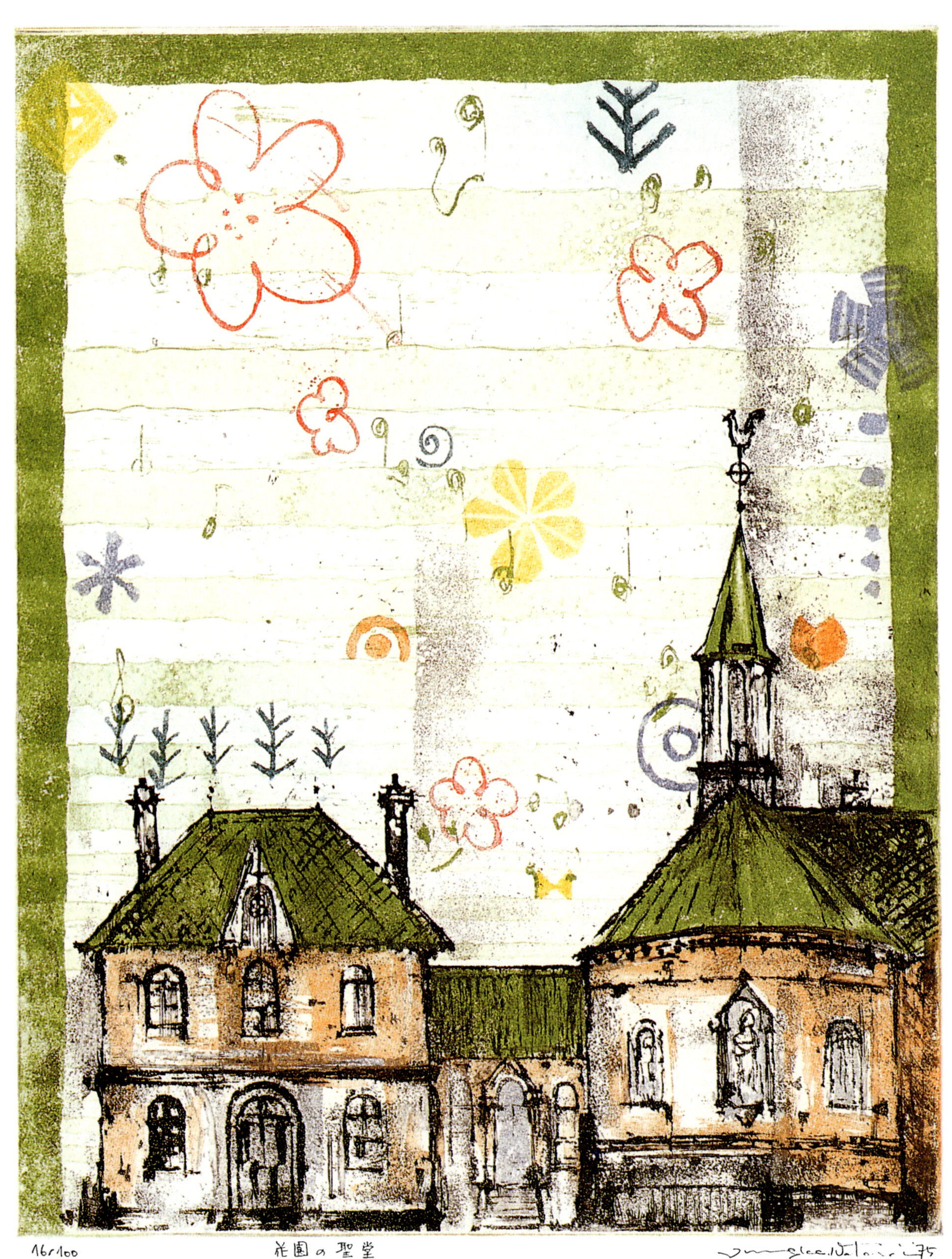

41. Watarai Junsuke (b. 1936). Titled in Japanese *Hanazono-no-seidō* (Hanazono Convent Garden), 16/100, 1975, etching, 36x27.8 cm. Signed Junsuke Watarai. Published by the Tolman Collection, Tokyo.

southernmost Hokkaido city was one of two places where foreigners were allowed entry to Japan by the 1854 Kanagawa Treaty. Americans, Germans, French, British, and Russians leapt into the breach, as a result of which there are many foreign-built structures in Hakodate. It is hard to believe that the sites depicted by Shibuya and Watarai are actual places in Japan because the delicate etching technique and the artists' learning experience abroad have both influenced the finished product.

After Hokkaido I was reunited with my family and promoted to director of the American Cultural Center in Kyoto and concurrently the consul attached to the Consulate General in Osaka and Kobe. With this assignment came a fifteen-room house, which easily could have passed as a branch of the National Museum of Modern Art, which it certainly rivaled in the number of prints exhibited. We festooned the place with our collection, and art lovers from everywhere were frequent visitors.

All eight of the American cultural centers in Japan were undergoing a metamorphosis, and in Kyoto this meant closing the old center and building a new one. In the interim between the closing of one and the opening of the other was a period of eight months when there was very little for me to do and, in addition, no place in which to do it anyway. Fortunately we still had the fifteen-room "art hotel," and the extra bedrooms were always filled with many of the artists you have read about in this book.

We used the time to think about our future and came to the conclusion that the amount of personal satisfaction we derived from our involvement with prints and artists far outweighed the benefits we might receive by working in an American cultural center without even the "culture." (The official name was to be changed to American Center. For years afterward, whenever we were asked what happened to the culture, we used to joke that we took it with us when we left.)

While we lived in Kyoto, the artist Clifton Karhu played a unique role in our lives, in much the same way Shibuya and Watarai had in Sapporo. Clif, a long-term Kyoto resident, was the best-known American there. By way of self-introduction to the expatriate community we invited all the Americans to a cocktail party. In those days "all" meant seventeen full-time residents. We did not own any Karhu prints, our rationale being that we were collecting prints by Japanese. We had invited him not because he was an artist but because he was an American. I still remember our first conversation, and, in fact, I just spoke to him on the phone and told him what I was going to write. He remembered the conversation too.

He asked why we did not have any of his prints in our collection. I felt that it was a startling question that deserved a bold answer, probably because I was on the defensive. So I said, "I don't really like your prints. They're too bright. I mean, have you ever actually seen an orange sky?" Karhu did not say anything. He just admired the rest of our collection. Several weeks later, reciprocating our hospitality, he invited me to dinner and then to go barhopping in the picturesque geisha quarter of Gion. We started out rather late, and after dinner had a drink here, a drink there, visiting one place after another, until it became really late. As we started on our way home Karhu silently pointed up at the sky and it was orange. I have been his biggest fan ever since. He frequently took me around in Kyoto, showing me how to look at things, how to edit with my eyes, and how to appreciate the beauty of Japan. Our continuing appreciation of that beauty is one of the factors that keeps us here.

It is of particular significance that when we left embassy life and began our business it was Karhu with whom we started and a Karhu work the very first print we ever sold. He is the artist who has created our logo, which represents us on the sign in front of our building, on our stationery, and on our business cards. Sometimes we chide him about the less-than-astute clients who cannot remember if it is the Karhu Gallery selling Tolman prints or the other way around. We feel grateful and fortunate even today that we two Americans have been able to succeed at our respective careers in Japan against the obvious odds.

When we wrote our first book, *People Who Make Japanese Prints—A Personal Glimpse,* it was taken for granted that a Karhu print would grace the cover of the English part and a Shinoda print that of the Japanese section. We even changed the title to accommodate our two important artists. After all, Karhu is not Japanese and Shinoda does not like to be thought of only as a printmaker—but they both make Japanese prints.

As natural as it was for Shibuya and Watarai to depict the foreign-style churches and monuments in Hokkaido, it was just as obvious for Karhu to be the recorder of the traditional Kyoto that may not always be here (though it has lasted for 1,200 years). Clif's print for the jacket of the book *Katsura Moonlight* pictures the Katsura Detached Palace, famous for moon-viewing and poetry-composing parties held by the imperial family since the seventeenth century. The print is a perfect example of why Karhu's work is as popular with Japanese as it is with foreigners; it depicts the soul of Japan as Japanese like to think of it and as Westerners like to imagine it.

Plate 42

In Japan's print history there have been several foreigners who have created prints better then many Japanese. The works of the Frenchman Paul Jacoulet are currently enjoying a resurgence of popularity; dealers are searching everywhere for prints by Elizabeth Keith; and at the moment there are American artists like Sarah Brayer, Daniel Kelly, and Joshua Rome, who specialize in prints. Of course, there is a host of other foreigners who paint in oils or

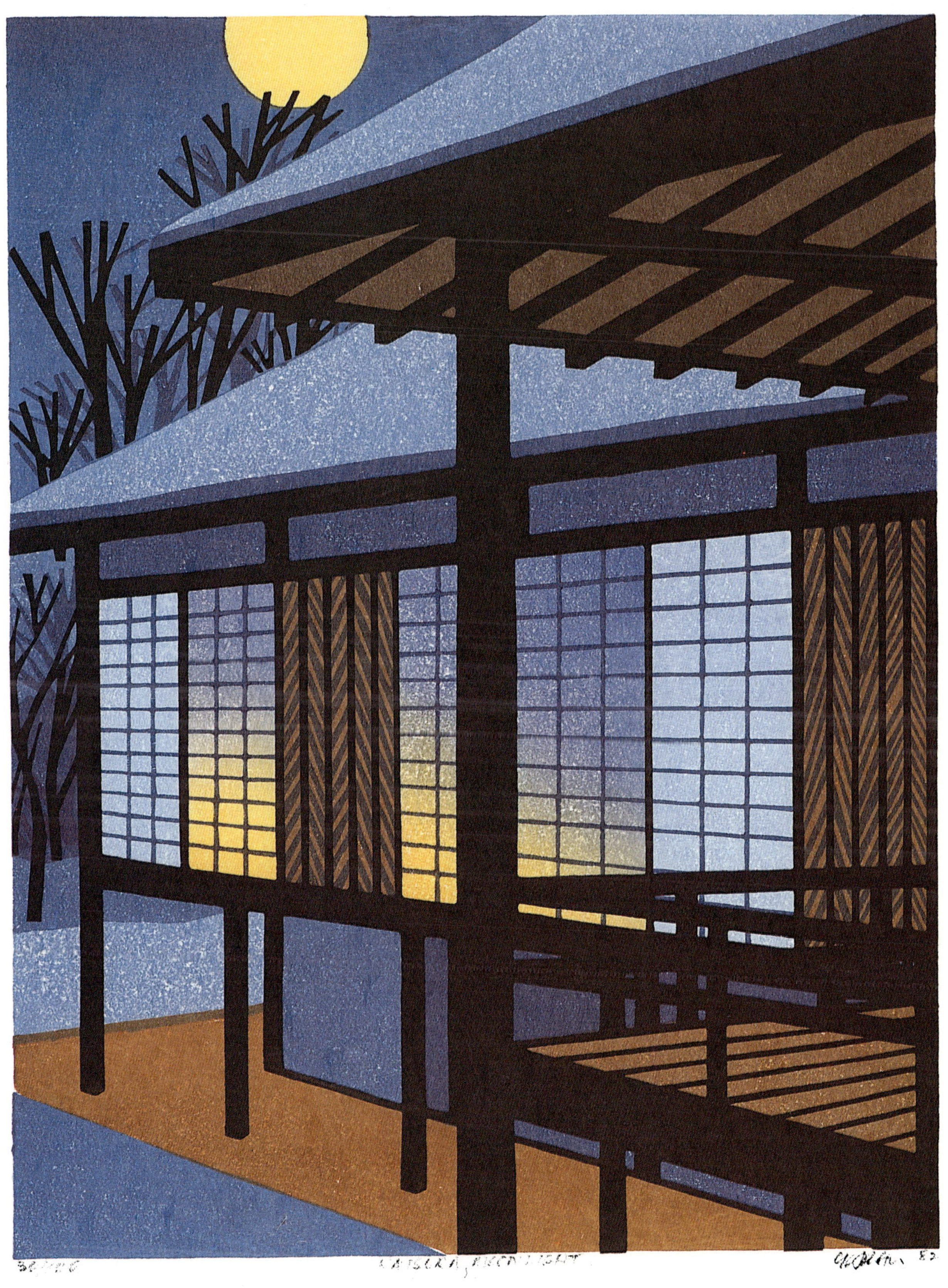

42. Karhu, Clifton (b. 1927). *Katsura Moonlight,* 30/100, 1982, woodblock, 40x30 cm. Signed C. Karhu. Published by the Tolman Collection, Tokyo.

watercolor or make pottery or paper, but one has to admit that Clif Karhu stands head and shoulders above them all. He has become a Kyoto institution, even being elected by his Japanese print-artist peers to head the Kyoto branch of the Japan Print Association. Karhu dresses only in kimono, and along with making prints can also carve netsuke and Japanese flutes and seals, create pottery, do ink paintings, and, in general, enjoys working and living the way many Japanese would like to.

By the time we met Karhu we were already becoming known as "famous collectors," and I had had the temerity to tell him that his colors were too bright! I am now reminded of the adage that one can only operate at the level of one's understanding. Receiving his kind instruction and looking through his eyes, we underwent a drastic change in our perception of line and color. As a result we find that we have almost four hundred of his works, many with colors that really do have to be seen to be believed.

At the beginning of this section we mentioned that occasionally we had been influenced in print buying by other people's recommendations of what should constitute a fine collection. And once again we heeded other voices but this time instead of cats and trees on the recommended list we were bullied into bicycles and umbrellas on the one hand and horses on the other.

Plate 43 In a recent statement Kuroda Shigeki said that he has never intentionally made sketches of real umbrellas and bicycles but used those images only to "express the change, flow, and expanse of time in a pictorial dimension." One can say that he has certainly met the challenge of depicting motion on paper. However, there is not a single person we know who owns his prints who does not think of them as bicycles and umbrellas. The subject has a universal appeal, but the reactions are different: Singaporeans think they are scenes of Paris; in Sydney art lovers know good and well that they must take place in Tokyo; and in Hong Kong people have it firsthand that they depict some exotic, unnamed locale. I am here to give testimony that the illustrated print is of Boston, and that the background commemorates my windshield being wiped clean with my own hand as I drove through rainy streets trying to locate the gallery in Harvard Square where Kuroda was having a show.

At that time, along with the relatively inexpensive prints by Kuroda that everyone could afford was the other side of the coin:
Plate 44 the "must have" prints by Nakayama Tadashi in the highest price range and therefore extremely desirable by those who had to have them <u>just</u> because they could not be bought by everyone, an attitude that represents another aspect of collecting. Nakayama is highly respected by other woodblock print artists who appreciate his innovative skill and exacting printing methods. He employs numerous blocks to create his richly decorative and painstakingly executed prints. Although he has used other subjects during his

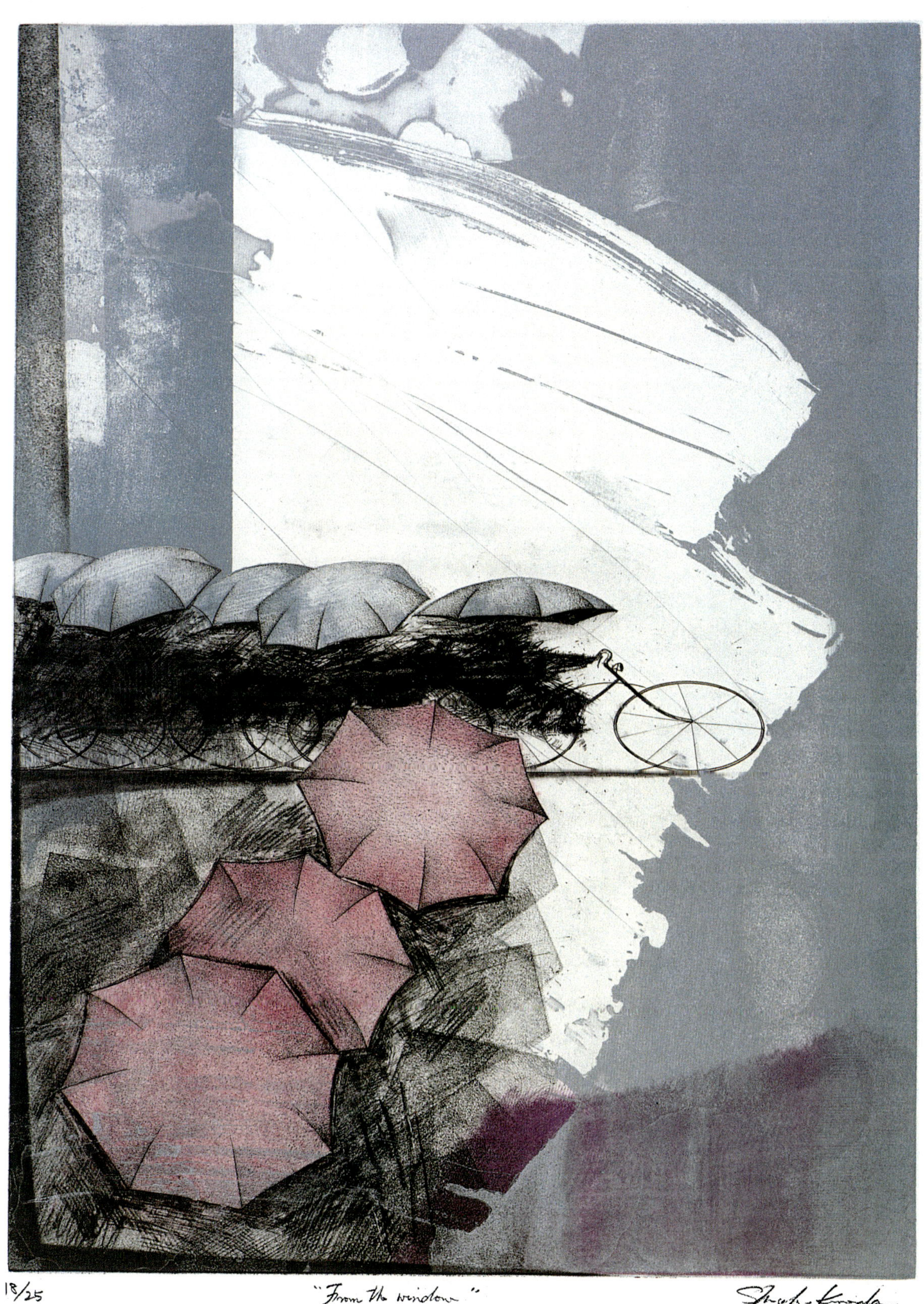

43. Kuroda Shigeki (b. 1953). *From the Window,* 18/25, 1981, etching/aquatint, 49.2x35.7 cm. Signed Shigeki Kuroda. Published by the Tolman Collection, Tokyo.

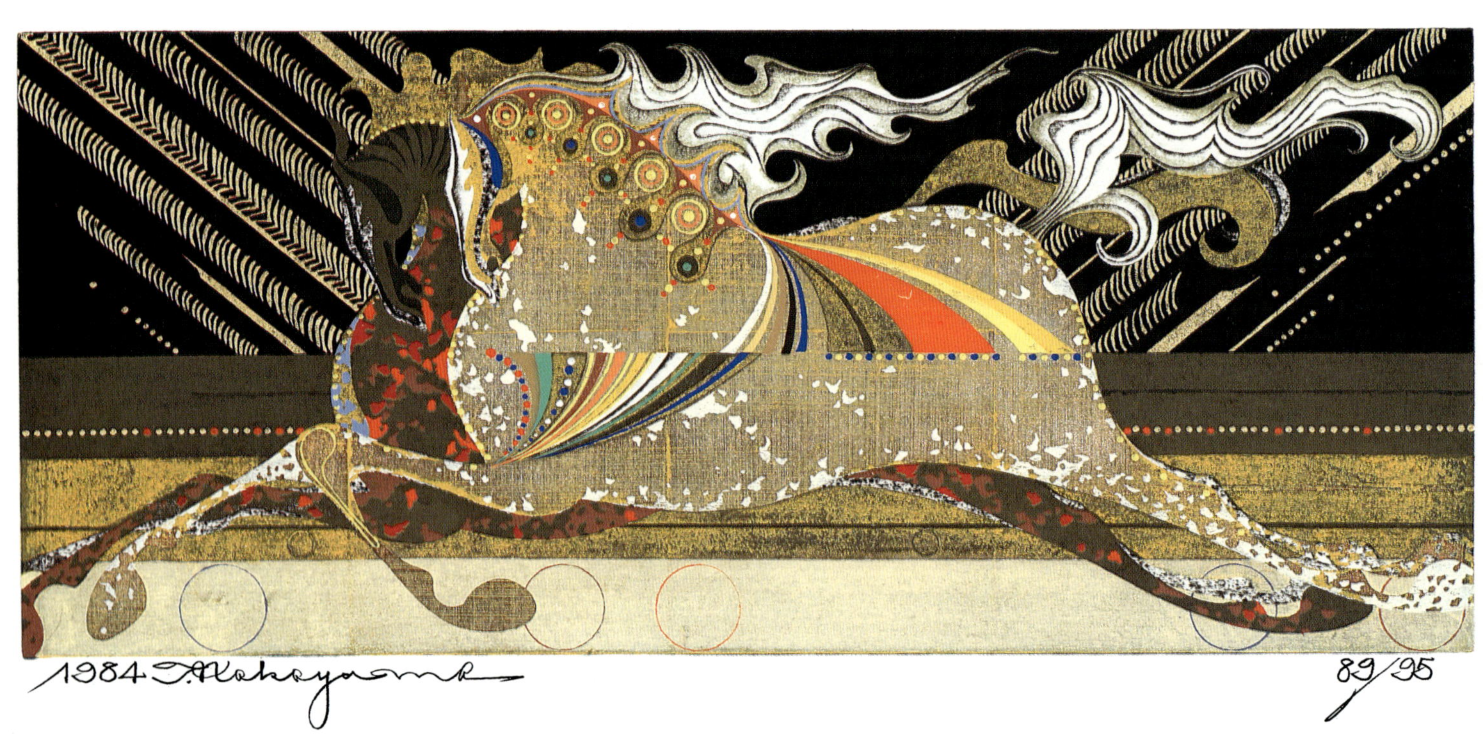

44. Nakayama Tadashi (b. 1927). Title unlisted but known as *Kyokuba Shissō* (Running Horses), 89/95, 1984, woodblock, 24.2x56.8 cm. Signed T. Nakayama, sealed on the reverse in kanji Nakayama.

THESE
THREE
WORDS

26/100 JIRO TAKAMATSU 1970

45. Takamatsu Jiro (b. 1936). Title unlisted but known as *These Three Words,* 26/100, 1970, offset, 73.8x54.5 cm. Signed Jiro Takamatsu.

long career, it was his large body of work depicting horses that brought him international renown. His works are also valued because he makes only a few prints a year.

Of course, we know that the expression "complete collection" cannot possibly be uttered in a country where equipment of every type is available and where the creators are blessed with the imaginations and skills to match the extraordinary range of printing methods. But still we felt that with the addition of the above two artists we would arguably have a rather sound basis from which to tell Japan's story of printmaking during this given period.

Not according to our friend Mary Baskett, former director of prints at the Cincinnati Art Museum, where the largest and broadest assemblage of modern Japanese prints in the U.S. is housed (due to the kindness of Caroline Porter, a longtime collector). Mrs. Baskett's gift to us of a Takamatsu Jiro work is an example of conceptual art and probably something we would not have chosen for ourselves. But it does prove the point that everything exists in the world of the Japanese print.

Plate 45

Our collecting continues to this day. I mentioned that when I went to Saito Kiyoshi's latest exhibition I bought another of his prints. Even though the first print we ever bought was a Saito, this latest purchase, one of his older prints, is certainly not our last.

We hope readers will understand that the above scenario is not the actual step-by-step description of how we formed our collection, but, in general, that is the way it happened. We simply wanted to offer some ideas on how we began, with no particular plan but simply buying a print here and there by chance; how our collection unfolded, not only in terms of the prints themselves but in our personal relationships with the artists who made them as well as in a deeper knowledge of the history and culture of Japan, so much of which is an inspiration for many of the works; and how the collection kept growing until it became one of the most important aspects of our lives, even to the point of our making a career as art dealers. Hundreds of adventures and thousands of prints later, we are still here to attest to our ever-present enjoyment in this field of art—and we are not finished yet.

Between Then and Now

The true collector is a treasure-trove of lore concerning the experience, the provenance, the how, where, why, and from whom each purchase was made, and the ease or difficulty of adding every precious piece he has to his holdings. This knowledge is part of the fun of pursuing, finding, and possessing. Every time the collector looks at a certain work the entire episode flashes through his mind, mostly with satisfaction, and the works spring to life in his heart.

The following story concerns three prints that came into our collection just as we were making the transition from being enthusiastic art collectors to being neophyte art dealers. A number of well-known people played a role in this drama, and our own delight certainly owes something to the fact that it occurred when we were just beginning our business.

The Osaka print artist Tanaka Ryohei, now 60 years old, is recognized as one of the most important contemporary etching masters of Japan. He is so well known that he signs his prints simply with his surname initial and given name—T. Ryohei.

His painstakingly etched prints are avidly sought after especially by foreign collectors. Charming scenes of thatched farmhouses, country lanes, bamboo groves, and idyllic villages capture a picturesque Japanese countryside that is fast disappearing and therefore all the more appreciated by those who wish that the traditional life of Japan would never cease to be. Ryohei depicts his scenery so invitingly that many viewers want to purchase the print and then go and find the actual place depicted. He lives in the western part of Honshu, Japan's main island, and he finds his pastoral subject matter in the surroundings there, much of it teetering on the brink of extinction in the wake of urban development.

If anyone were to look at Ryohei's work for social or political comment, he would not find it. Contemporary Japanese print artists, with few exceptions, avoid social or political comment in their works, and the audience does not look for it either. Perhaps this is a carry-over from the strict regulations of the Tokugawa period (1600–1868), when criticism of the government was discouraged and offenders were severely punished.

Plate 46

The political connotation was probably one of the reasons for my initial fascination with Ryohei's etching *Friarhood #2* (Takuhatsu), a print that we privately call "the Ron and Yasu print." The composition is of a long wall running beside a traditional Japanese building with a thatched roof. A monk is strolling away, up the incline alongside the wall, and it is beginning to rain. The maple leaves on the ground indicate that it is autumn. On the peeling wall someone—perhaps the monk, but we cannot be sure—has contributed a bit of grafitti: a sketch of an umbrella under which is written Ron in English on one side, and Yasu in Japanese on the other.

At the time of the release of this print, Ron obviously referred to America's President Ronald Reagan, and Yasu was a clear reference to then Prime Minister Nakasone Yasuhiro. The press had noted that they called each other by these nicknames during their many meetings.

The umbrella, in this particular context, could be a reference to the protection given by the U.S. to Japan in the form of the much-contested security treaty, occasionally referred to as "the U.S. umbrella." The simple drawing made one think about the important relationship between the two countries embodied in the friendship between these two world leaders. Although it could not be construed as a major political comment, the fact that it appeared in a print at all, and most particularly in a print by Ryohei, made it very interesting.

Friarhood #2, an etching/aquatint, was pulled in 1985 in an edition of 120 copies. It was an instant hit, not only because every one of Ryohei's prints is popular, but also because of its timely subject. Our gallery ordered and sold many copies and the print was soon sold out, but we saved one for ourselves and one to give as a present some day to the Ron of the print.

To backtrack a bit, when Nancy and Ronald Reagan visited Japan for the first time in 1970 as state visitors, he was then governor of California and I was the director of the American Cultural Center in Kyoto as well as vice-consul there. Part of my duties consisted of serving as liaison between the U.S. Embassy in Tokyo and the various important American visitors to Japan who inevitably found their way to the old capital. It was in this capacity that I became acquainted with the Reagans, and I was probably the only American they met on a daily basis during their eight-day visit.

In 1985, when I learned that then President and Mrs. Reagan were about to pay an official visit to Japan, I felt that this would be another chance to impress upon them the importance of the relationship between the two countries. I had hoped to avail myself of the good offices of my friend Ambassador Mike Mansfield to meet with the Reagans for a few minutes and present in person the print we had been saving for them. One reason for not having given the print previously was that I wanted to be sure it was completely sold out so that there would be no accusations of a commercial gallery trying to sell the print simply because the president had one.

Since Ambassador Mansfield was one of the chief proponents of amity between Japan and America, the above scenario of a meeting with the Reagans was not as impossible as it may sound. Unfortunately just when their visit took place, my own schedule took me to Singapore for an important exhibition of Japanese prints, and I was not able to meet with them.

However, my next visit to the U.S. on gallery business included a call on David Rockefeller, who has long been a well-known collector of modern Japanese prints and a friend and supporter of

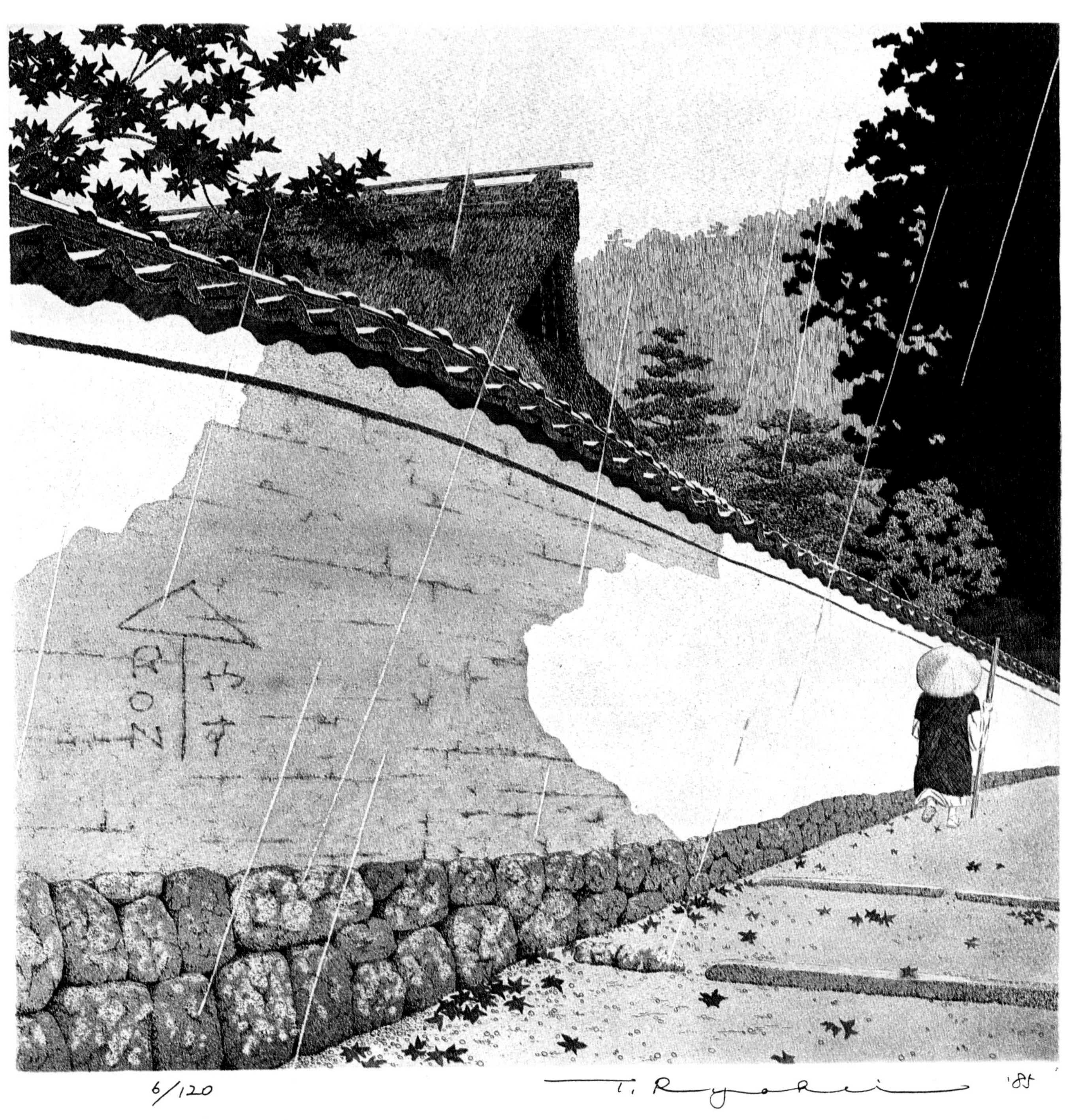

46. Tanaka Ryohei (b. 1933). Titled in Japanese *Takuhatsu #2* (Friarhood #2), 6/120, 1985, etching/aquatint, 30x30 cm. Signed T. Ryohei.

the Tolman Collection. On the day before our appointment, I read in the newspaper that President and Mrs. Reagan were to be the houseguests of the Rockefellers during their upcoming visit to New York to celebrate the rededication of the Statue of Liberty after its restoration work. I related the story of the Ryohei print to him and asked if he might find time to present it to the president for me.

Mr. Rockefeller, who is a kind and helpful person, quickly said, "Wonderful! The first day is taken up with various meetings and, of course, the last day with the Statue of Liberty ceremonies. But I've been thinking about what to do on the second day that might be fun. I'll borrow my brother Nelson's Japanese-style house, we'll have a small dinner there, and I'll make the presentation of the Japanese print the highlight of the evening."

In due course I returned to Tokyo and forwarded the framed print and a note for the president to Mr. Rockefeller. I attentively followed the news coverage of the presidential visit to New York and wondered how and if our print had fit into the proceedings. Soon I received a letter from Mr. Rockefeller saying that the dinner had been a huge success, the print had been greatly admired, and the Reagans had reminisced about their visit to Kyoto and had remembered my part in it.

One day about a week after receiving Mr. Rockefeller's letter, I was at home entertaining my friend Crocker Snow, president and editor-in-chief of *The WorldPaper,* based in Boston. We were interrupted during lunch by a messenger from the U.S. Embassy bearing a letter with the simple return address of The White House. I had heard that letters sent in the diplomatic pouch were always delivered by hand. I had never received a presidential missive and could think of no pending business with President Reagan, but I did have some inkling about the letter's contents.

After seeing the messenger off, I returned to find Crocker with a big question mark clearly written on his face. Eager to know what the letter said but at the same time wanting to tease Crocker, I nonchalantly said, "Oh, him again," and tossed the letter aside. The journalist in Crocker would have none of this. He urged me to open the letter right that minute (which, of course, I was secretly hoping to do). I found a charming note from the president, indicating that he liked the print and remembered our Kyoto times, and promising to keep in mind the importance of good relations between Japan and the U.S., as I had mentioned in my note.

Crocker felt that there was a lively human-interest story in the power of a Ryohei print to accentuate this point with the president of the United States. He interviewed me extensively for his newspaper, which is devoted to global news and is included as a special supplement in numerous magazines and newspapers throughout the world. If you think the above story sounds familiar, you may have read Crocker's article somewhere.

Considering the entire matter great fun, I was not prepared for the many copies of the article that I received from friends around the world who had spotted it in *The WorldPaper*. I made a file of them, along with the White House letter and the correspondence with Mr. Rockefeller. On my next visit to the Osaka area, I took copies of everything for Ryohei, who naturally was delighted with the exposure and the success of his work.

As a gesture of appreciation, he invited me to offer some creative suggestions for subject matter in a future print. Knowing that one of the very popular subjects for collectors is cats in any form, I hinted (though not as subtly as I would have you believe) that I would consider it an honor if he created an alluring cat in some special setting.

In what seemed no time at all, and just before I was preparing to leave for the U.S. on another print-selling trip, Ryohei brought forth the print *Summer Room,* which features a dozing cat on a wooden veranda in the situation cats seem to enjoy most—alone, napping, and luxuriating in the warmth of the day. The background of a vertical latticework window is flanked by *shōji* paper sliding doors. One of the special attributes of the print was that it had been printed in color, something quite unusual for Ryohei, who has generally executed his etchings in black and white.

Plate 47

On that trip, again meeting with Mr. Rockefeller, I teased him about being my presidential messenger, and to thank him, presented a copy of Ryohei's brand-new cat print for his collection. On viewing the work, he said he had a distinct feeling of *déjà vu*. He could not recall exactly but he knew that there was a work similar in subject and mood, and probably it was an older Japanese print, perhaps by one of the *ukiyo-e* masters of the last century.

The conversation then turned to other matters, in particular the catalogue of Mr. Rockefeller's collection of contemporary Japanese prints that we had agreed to write, a project that was now behind schedule. The cat print was forgotten for the moment.

The following day I continued my trip, planning to visit my friend and enthusiastic collector Leslie Stulberg at her summer home in Michigan. As luck and airline schedules would have it, I got there several hours before she had planned to arrive.

Not being one to sit around and stare into space, I wandered into the small town to browse around until my hostess was due. As collectors will, I stepped into the first gallery I came across, a small one featuring only posters. I began to leaf through stacks of them.

It was like Christmas, for what to my wondering eyes should appear but a poster reproduction of an *ukiyo-e* print by the famous artist Hiroshige, issued by the New York Metropolitan Museum of Art. There was no doubt in my mind that it was the very image Mr. Rockefeller had conjured up in his memory.

Plate 48

There was the cat again, this time from a back view, with the

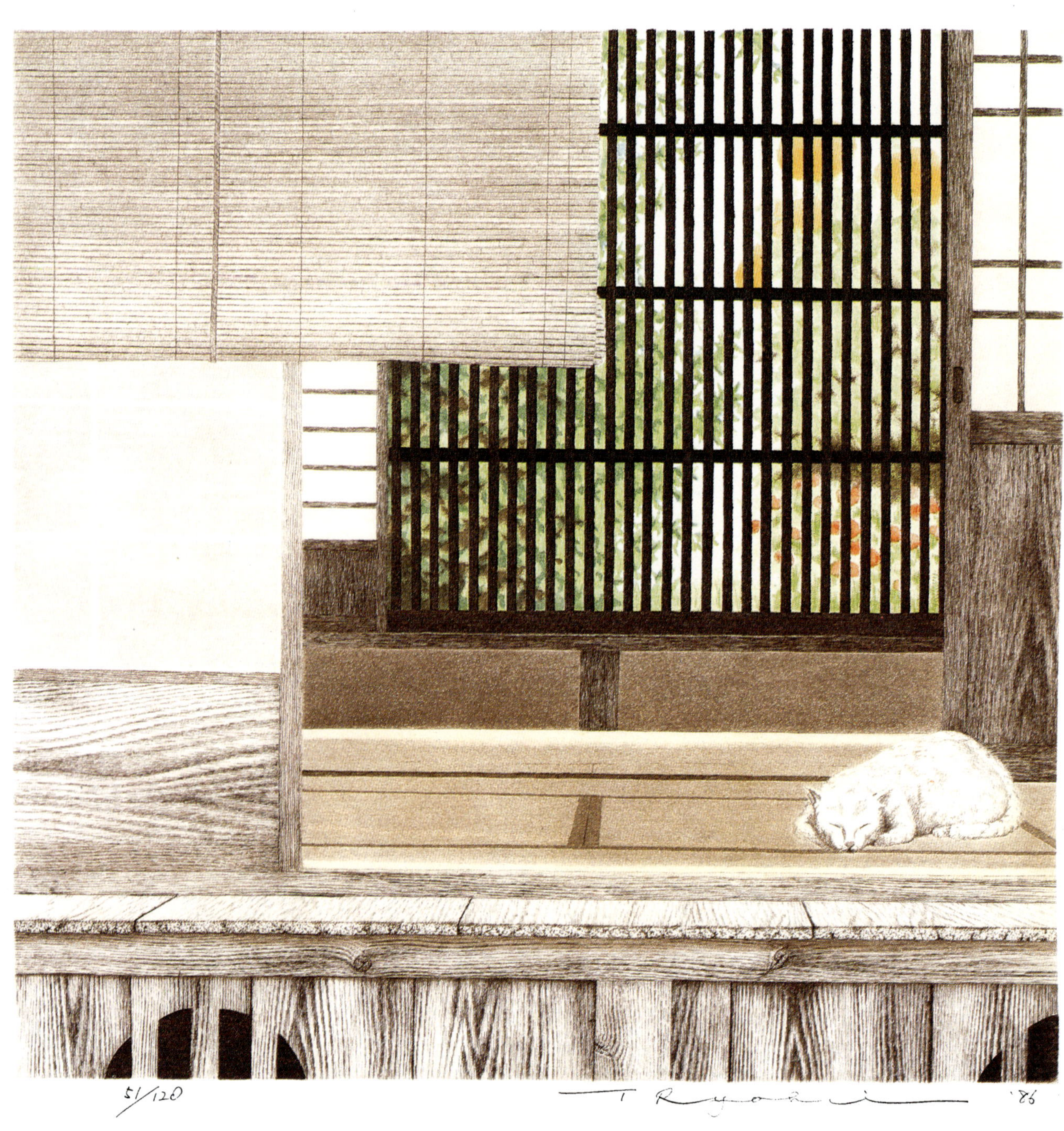

47. Tanaka Ryohei (b. 1933). Titled in Japanese *Natsu-no-heya* (Summer Room), 51/120, 1986, etching/aquatint. 29.5x29.5 cm. Signed T. Ryohei.

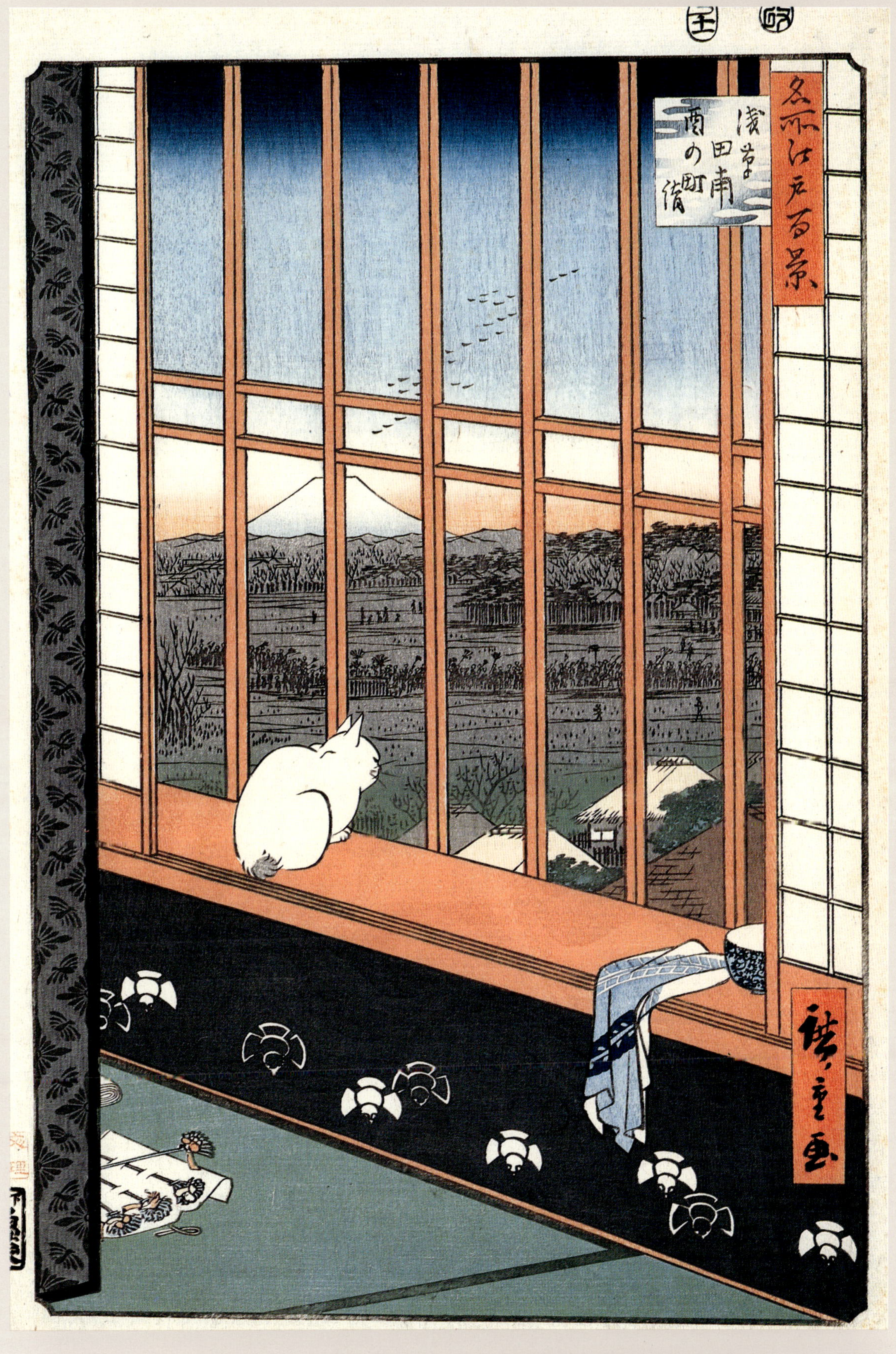

48. Hiroshige (Ando Hiroshige) (1797–1858). *Meisho Edo Hyakkei, Asakusa Tanbo, Tori-no-machi Mōde* (Asakusa Rice Paddies during the Tori-no-machi Festival), from the album *One Hundred Famous Views of Edo* (Tokyo), 1857, woodblock, 33.8x22.5 cm. Signed Hiroshige-*ga*.

cat looking musingly out of a window at the fields beyond, with Mount Fuji in the distance. Latticed windows flanked by *shōji* paper doors formed part of the composition. The original print is called *Asakusa Rice Paddies during the Tori-no-machi Festival,* from the album by Hiroshige entitled *One Hundred Famous Views of Edo.* Of course, I bought the poster, intending to delight my cat-loving, print-collecting friends with the story.

Next on this trip I traveled to Sanibel Island, Florida, home of Mrs. Caroline Porter. For decades Mrs. Porter has been the "angel" of the Cincinnati Art Museum, where her collection, probably the most extensive collection of modern Japanese prints in the United States, is housed. I do not know if she loves cats as much as prints, but they are certainly in close competition.

In any case, the Ryohei cat was an obvious addition to her collection and she enjoyed its story. Like all collectors, she has an inquisitive and acquisitive nature, with that underlying need to "complete the picture." Naturally she said, "I can't possibly buy the print unless I can buy the poster too." "Well, you can't," I replied, "because I'm going to give it to you." I was sure I could somehow get another poster, but I might as well admit right now that I have not seen another copy of it to this day although I have searched everywhere.

Having finished my business in the U.S., I returned to Tokyo, and soon after journeyed to Kyoto and Osaka to refresh myself, to visit artists, to keep up-to-date on the art scene in that part of Japan, and, of course, to select prints for our gallery. For me, these encounters with artists are among the most personally rewarding aspects of being an art dealer. I was looking forward with pleasure to having lunch with our good friend Clifton Karhu, still the foremost woodblock chronicler of Kyoto and the star of our annual year-end exhibition at Christmas time.

During lunch I related the saga of the two cat prints and the Hiroshige poster, and we had a stimulating discussion about how and where artists get their inspiration for subject matter, and the pluses and minuses of being an artist or an art dealer in general. We agreed that one of the pluses for both of us at that exact moment was that we did not have to report back to work in five minutes, a cheering thought as I accompanied Clif to visit an antique print shop in the area. I said I would go with him "just to have a look around," probably the most dangerous and untruthful words ever to escape the lips of the unabashedly tenacious and resolute collector.

As we entered the shop, which was full of old prints in various levels of desirability, our eyes fell immediately on Hiroshige's cat—the real one, not a poster, in beautiful condition, and definitely the work that Mr. Rockefeller had identified as the inspiration for Ryohei's etching. I had been searching so long for another copy of the poster, and here was the original in front of me. I was—for once—speechless. But by the time I recovered, Karhu had already purchased the print, begging my forgiveness and saying that my story had made the print irresistible to him.

As even the most fledgling of collectors can imagine, I found this a most unfriendly act and one that I must admit caused a certain amount of disharmony between us for a while. (Collectors, like a lot of other people, hate it when they cannot have what they want.) It certainly seemed to me that this cat was not to be mine. Now I had already lost two of them—the poster and the original Hiroshige print.

Over the next several years Karhu and I had many discussions and negotiations concerning this print. He remained my great friend, and I am sure he found all my whining and cajoling quite typical of what any collector must go through when he really wants something.

In the end, through the generosity (and persistence) of my wife and with the cooperation of Karhu, he allowed her to persuade him to let her buy the print as a birthday present for me. So the long-elusive feline finally came to rest in my collection, and I do not even particularly like cats.

Although each of our prints has its "story," not every one in our personal collection has such an involved and fascinating history as this. Nevertheless, every collector has his own saga to relate about what he encountered or felt when buying a certain piece, and he remembers vividly every tale that added to the piquancy of the purchase.

Obviously we cannot record such wordy descriptions and histories for every print featured in this book. However, each of the fifty prints in the following section, "Now," will be accompanied by a particular point that may help readers understand some of the salient features of Japanese prints, and in some measure bring the prints to life as well, making them more than just pretty pictures.

P.S. There has been an additional sighting of the Hiroshige cat. On a recent trip to Claude Monet's home at Giverny, outside Paris, my wife found another copy of it hanging on the wall among his famous collection of *ukiyo-e*. It is illustrated in color in the catalogue of his holdings, *La Collection d'Estampes Japonaises de Claude Monet,* page 167.

I'm still looking for the poster.

Now

The focus of this part of the book shifts from a detailed description of the assemblage of our collection to fifty points to keep in mind while you are forming your own. These points are not meant to be taken as strict advice but rather as guidelines when you are considering prints. We have based our comments on our twenty years' experience as dealers answering clients' questions and on the knowledge we ourselves acquired along the way as collectors, when we were asking many of the same questions.

Norman first came to Japan in 1955 and often says that if anyone had told him he would still be here almost four decades later, he would not have believed it. Japan was part of his military obligation, something that was viewed quite seriously in those days. Things were different in many respects then. For one thing, the exchange rate was 360 yen to the U.S. dollar, which meant that prints, though expensive on a meager military salary, were still within reach with careful planning. When his military service ended and Norman returned in 1964 on a student fellowship, bringing Mary and the children with him, the rate was the same but we now were a family of four. On a student budget, we looked at a lot of prints but could buy only a few. It was actually during our diplomatic days that we began to buy in earnest many of the works that we had been looking at and craving all those years. Each purchase was a major financial concern, but on reviewing those early years we fully believe that it was certainly worth all the deprivation we went through to come to possess what must be considered one of the finest collections of contemporary Japanese art anywhere. These are among the prints we will present in this section, some of which have become treasures not only for us but for print lovers around the world.

This passion for prints changed our lives and has occupied us for the past two decades. We find that this stage, NOW, is the most exciting time so far. Our gallery is, in fact, celebrating its twentieth anniversary this year. Even as we write this book, business travel has taken us to Honolulu, Hong Kong, Singapore, and Sri Lanka. Portions of the text and even the layout were discussed in Paris, where we attended our younger daughter Hilary's wedding and in Copenhagen, where we went next to establish a Danish connection for promoting Japanese prints. Our reception in Scandinavia has been especially warm. In 1990 we produced a major show at the Retretti Art Centre, a summer resort located four hours from Helsinki. The response was overwhelming. More than 200,000 people, approximately five percent of the population of Finland, attended the exhibition. In 1991, 1992, and 1993 we were able to produce other exhibitions at galleries in Helsinki and Hanko as a direct result of the Retretti show. In fact, we have just agreed to stage an exhibition of eighty prints at the Hämeenlinna Museum of Art in Finland in 1995.

Our pleasure at introducing these works around the world was heightened when we participated in Japan Week '94 at the invitation of Watanabe Taizo, the Japanese ambassador to Egypt. There we exhibited four dozen prints at the Cairo Opera House Gallery, the first showing of modern Japanese prints in the Arab world. The exhibition's warm reception encouraged us to continue our role of explaining this facet of Japan's culture internationally. All of our plans and hopes that we entertained when leaving our budding diplomatic career are finally coming to fruition.

This book has been written as part of several events that we planned to commemorate twenty years as art dealers, for ourselves and for our devoted clients. During its writing we organized a special anniversary exhibition of eighty artists' works, one hundred prints, at Ginza's Wako Department Store, Japan's most prestigious store and the venue for our very first—and their very first—exhibition of contemporary Japanese prints, truly a special celebration for both of us. That first exhibition in such an eminent place elevated Japanese prints to a higher position in the art world. We were happy after our years of challenging yet interesting work to be able to establish some sort of "tradition" and to have the pleasure of meeting the most important print artists working today at a level we have personally striven to establish for them.

Of course, we invited the artists whose work was being displayed, and we were delighted at the number who appeared. Among the many notables, Murai Masanari, lively and lucid at 89, came to see the show twice. Meeting this octogenarian made us stop and realize that Azechi Umetaro is 92, Shinagawa Takumi is 86, Saito Kiyoshi is 87, Minami Keiko is 83, Hagiwara Hideo and Shinoda Toko are 81. We are aware that Yamaguchi Gen died at 80, Sasajima Kihei at 87, Hashimoto Okiie at 94, and Mori Yoshitoshi, our oldest Japanese friend, also at 94. His passing caused us to accept the responsibility of recounting some personal anecdotes that would help keep these artists' personae alive. We have been very grateful for their company and friendship all through the years, and still rejoice at each encounter with their works. It has been our greatest pleasure to have served as a bridge to the West for these artists and their works, and to have brought them to the attention of many Japanese who might otherwise have neglected them. For us, the latter accomplishment is especially rewarding.

In these last twenty years, because of the wonderful prints that these artists have made for us to sell, we have been able to lead a life of interesting dimensions. We have become involved with people from all walks of life who have a curiosity about Japan and its material culture. In many cases the prints that we offer have filled a special place in their lives that will always remain a lovely memory of time spent in Japan, for some, years working here, for others, a print acquisition made on a vacation or business trip. We hope that in reading about the prints and the people who made them and the comments we have made, they will be able to add a new perspective to their collection.We also hope that readers will sympathize with our feelings of accomplishment in attempting this task and in carrying out many of our goals of intercultural communication, which we feel no one else would have considered and perhaps no one else could have done.

SEKINE Yoshio

COMMENT: *Japanese prints are produced as originals and are not copies of something else.*

Plate 49 For every rule there is at least one exception, and this print, *Soroban 305-S,* falls into that category. It is a photo-silkscreen made from an oil painting and is a typical example of the way Sekine Yoshio worked—and it is not typical of the work of other Japanese printmakers. A well-known oil painter and member of the renowned, now-defunct, avant-garde Gutai Group of Osaka, Sekine selected various of his paintings to be made into prints. This print holds a special place in our history as art dealers because it was the first print edition commissioned by the Tolman Collection.

One must not make the mistake of assuming that because this is a reproduction of a painting it falls into the category of mass-produced art. On the contrary, its production was closely monitored by the artist, and it is a limited-edition, signed, and numbered work. The photo-silkscreen process is a modern one and is used often for producing images on everyday articles. The difference is that those articles are not limited and signed. Photo-silkscreen prints in the fine-art world are handpulled. When the atelier doing the printing had made the first proof, we selected a copy and, for fun, trimmed it and put it into a frame exactly like that of the painting. When we hung them side by side and invited the artist to view them, to our delight he could not distinguish between them.

Sekine passed away in 1989, by which time he had created more than four hundred paintings of the *soroban* (abacus), some with small designs of beads, others on enormous canvases sporting just one large bead so skillfully done that it created a powerful optical illusion. Of course, he chose only a small portion of his painting output to be made into prints. Those who owned original paintings always felt honored that theirs had been picked to be executed in graphic form.

Why did Sekine choose the abacus to project his particular artistic vision? He unfailingly answered that he simply liked it—its oblong form, the interesting shape of its beads, and the infinite changes that could be accomplished by a movement of its parts. His imagination was challenged by the fact that the arrangement of the beads could be changed and a new order could be achieved with a single flick of the fingers. We admired the artist especially because he took one of the most common objects of daily use in Japan and elevated it to an art form. This ancient counting device, originally from China, is found everywhere today, right on the table beside the electronic calculator and computer. Even professional Japanese accountants are comfortable clicking away on it in preference to more modern methods.

Sekine once told us that as a young soldier he was stationed near Hiroshima at the exact moment of the atomic bomb explosion. From that instant and for many years after he felt that the reliable abacus served as a symbol of order and certainty, and it was this fascination that led him to use it so much that it eventually became his trademark.

At the end of the war he tried his hand at various jobs, from tearoom manager to surveyor's assistant, from billboard decorator to furniture mover. In 1949 he began working as a company employee in an industrial firm in Osaka but after retirement devoted himself completely to art on a full-time basis. He moved to Tokyo and spent every day for the next twenty years single-mindedly pursuing his theme, always succeeding in giving it freshness and new perspective. Sekine's subject may seem conventionally traditional but within it lies a sense of order and harmony that has universal appeal.

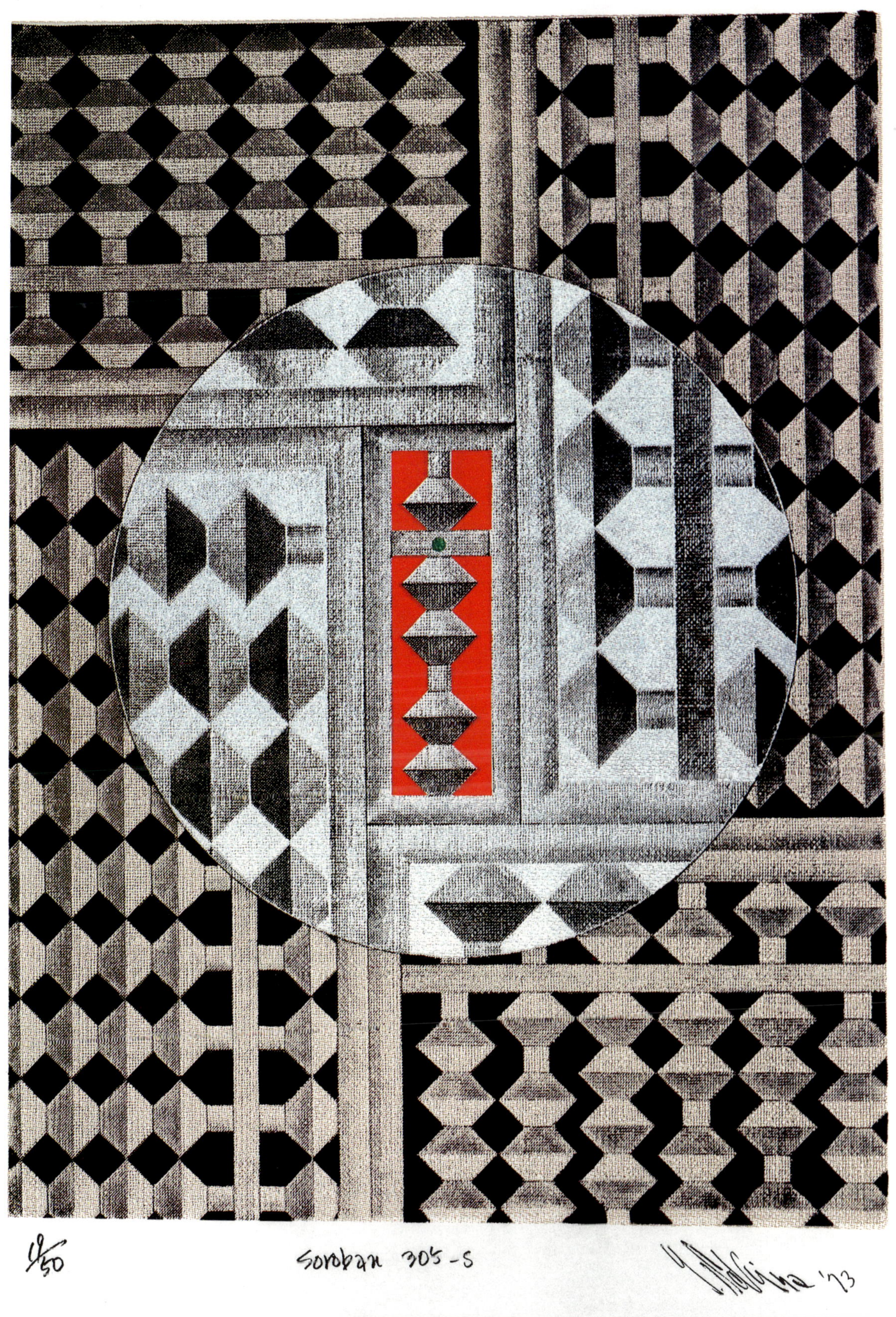

49. Sekine Yoshio (1922–89). *Soroban 305-S* (Abacus 305-S), 19/50, 1973, photo-silkscreen, 45.8x33.5 cm. Signed Y. Sekine. Published by the Tolman Collection, Tokyo.

MORI Yoshitoshi

COMMENT: *Artists are not always restricted to one medium.*

Since Mori Yoshitoshi's fame rests securely on his being the popularizer of the *kappazuri* (stencil) genre, it is hard to believe that he began this work at the grand age of 50 and continued with an amazing production until age 94. For the first half century of his life he worked as a designer of kimono patterns and studied with Serizawa Keisuke, the foremost supporter of the folk tradition in stencil art. Eventually, however, Mori wanted to achieve a more personal expression in his work, and spent the rest of his life portraying on paper his particular world—Kabuki figures, historical personages, markets, festivals, craftsmen, and fishmongers (which his father was). This was the world of *shita-machi,* the oldest and most traditional section of Tokyo, where Mori lived his entire life.

As a traditionalist Mori was not entirely comfortable when I first presented the idea of making a photo-lithograph of one of his gouache drawings. He had previously dabbled with the practice of having woodblock prints made by a professional *surishi* (printer) and even had some experience with silkscreens, but his heart belonged to the stencil and virtually his entire oeuvre was executed in that medium. Our gallery commissioned two lithographs and no others were ever made. Part of their value as collector's items comes from this rarity.

This print of the Tsukiji fish market was one made from a gouache drawing as a photo-lithograph. It was Mori's habit to go sketching with his cute little beret—how could he be an artist without it? Then from the gouache drawing, he would make a drawing in black and white and cut his stencil based on the drawing

Plate 50

in a free-flowing, spontaneous manner. Although I knew about this process it never occurred to me to wonder what happened to the original drawings. One day when I was visiting his studio, Mrs. Mori, his devoted wife who put up with his whims for sixty-five years, excused herself to make tea just as I happened to inquire about the contents of a drawer that had hitherto been off-limits. "She's gone," he said mischievously. "Let's have a look in here." In the drawer, rolled in helter-skelter fashion, were several hundred drawings, filed away as though they were mere reference works—or sketches. The artist may feel that way, but try to imagine how an art lover who comes upon such a treasure feels. This was a real "find" and I could immediately see the value of this discovery. The works were not simply sketches—they were masterpieces drawn with gusto by a genius who had spent his entire life surrounded by the very scenes he was depicting.

Mrs. Mori, returning with the tea and some *shita-machi* treats, was more worried about the mess than the discovery, since we had the works spread out on virtually every available surface. "What am I going to do with you two?" she asked. "Can't turn my back for a minute." But we hardly heard her. The impact of the artistic and monetary worth of the pieces was overwhelming. Mori was doubtful whether such paltry drawings (according to him) would be good enough to exhibit, and was positive that no matter what, no one would want to buy them. However, when we produced his very first exhibition at the most prestigious department store on the Ginza in 1975, Mori said, "I never dreamed that anything like my work would be shown at the same place where the empress buys her handbags." It was not only a smash success but served as a harbinger of many other Mori exhibitions at that same store throughout the years.

Mori was the most fun-loving, unpretentious, and direct artist we have ever met. His works—in which he manages to convey the charm of a certain gesture, the bustling activity of a fish market, or the glare of a warrior so that they seem to jump from the page—are imbued with these qualities as well. He also had a completely open mind, as witnessed by the fact that he was willing to try a new technique even at an age when most people are quite set in their ways. We are surrounded by his works and we think of him every day.

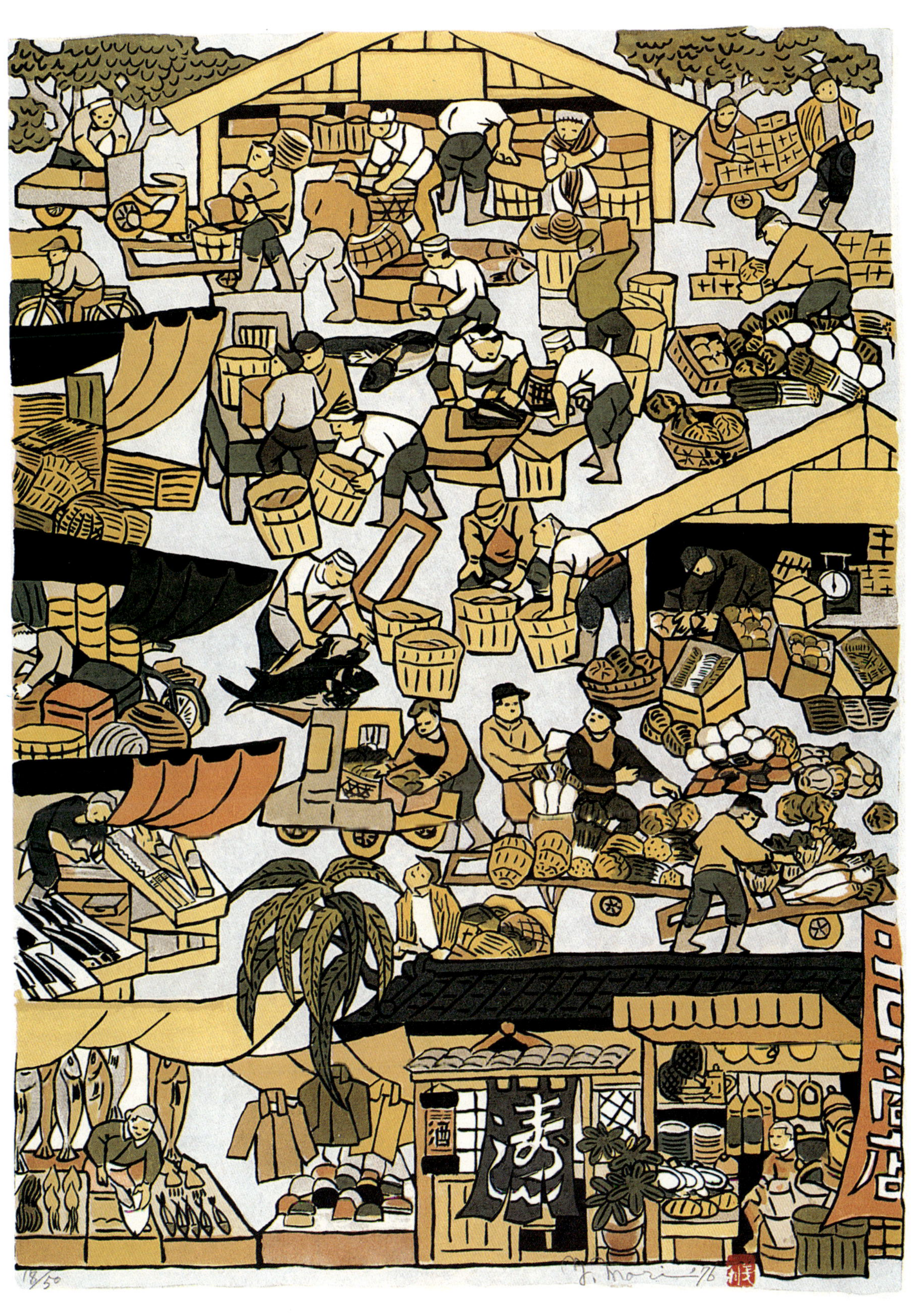

50. Mori Yoshitoshi (1898–1992). Title not shown but known as *Tsukiji Fish Market,* 18/50, 1976, photo-lithograph, 72.5x51 cm. Signed on the image Y. Mori '76, sealed on the image in kanji Yoshitoshi. Published by the Tolman Collection, Tokyo.

KINOSHITA Tomio

COMMENT: *Japanese print editions are not always printed out in the full edition originally intended by the artist.*

Plate 51 *Gray-Colored People,* a woodblock, was originally executed with the artist intending to pull an edition of fifty prints. However, the artist produced only the first three copies. We approached him and gained his reluctant approval to use his original carved blocks and to employ a professional printer to produce a slightly different limited edition of only twenty-five copies. We felt we were still preserving the integrity of the original edition by not making more than was stated at the outset.

Kinoshita Tomio is a seal carver by profession. These intricately carved "chops," used by Japanese as their official signature on important documents and as a personal identification at the bank, are maintained by all adults, and losing one's seal is cause for serious distress. When looking at Kinoshita's prints, one can immediately see that the boldly carved lines are cut by a master seal carver's sure hand, and that the carving is intrinsic to the drama presented by these very expressive humanoid forms.

For this particular artist the real pleasure in life is the physical act of carving. Subsequently he prints a few copies simply to enjoy the nuances of the result. Those few copies are all that is necessary for his artistic satisfaction. The task of printing the entire edition would definitely be tedium to an artist with Kinoshita's personality.

Kinoshita was pleased with our interest in his work and was satisfied with the finished print. This was vital because like all Japanese artists he would not be willing to sign his name to work that he felt was below his standards. We discussed possible future projects but he expressed only a halfhearted interest. He said he had no concern in his life to make art for commercial gain; he made art simply for pleasure and was happy making seals to earn his living.

Kinoshita is a good example of the fact that a lot of Japanese artists are not motivated like other people; he wants to make prints only when he feels in the mood to tackle a piece of wood and carve something creative of it. He does not want to be coerced into a commitment simply because some art lover is out there waiting.

To discuss this print's production and the possibility of other projects, I took the trouble to journey to the town of Yokkaichi near Nagoya, located in a rather inaccessible spot. There I always found Mr. and Mrs. Kinoshita leading a simple, unassuming life with their big fat cat, the focus of their life, snugly nestled and dozing lazily in a baby carriage in the entranceway.

Kinoshita told me quietly, "Sometimes when the weather is fine and the mood strikes me, I take down my tools [which he stores under the eaves of his old house] and I enjoy myself for the moment." It is hard to find fault with this sentiment except that there are a number of print lovers who admire his work and look forward with impatience to each new creation. But, of course, the artist's feelings are the most important factor in the creation of art. After all, how can one expect a work of art to be strong and vital if the artist's heart is not truly in it. We regretfully abandoned our hope for future collaboration in printing out old editions to their full extent lest we be accused of being the founders of the *foie gras* system of printmaking.

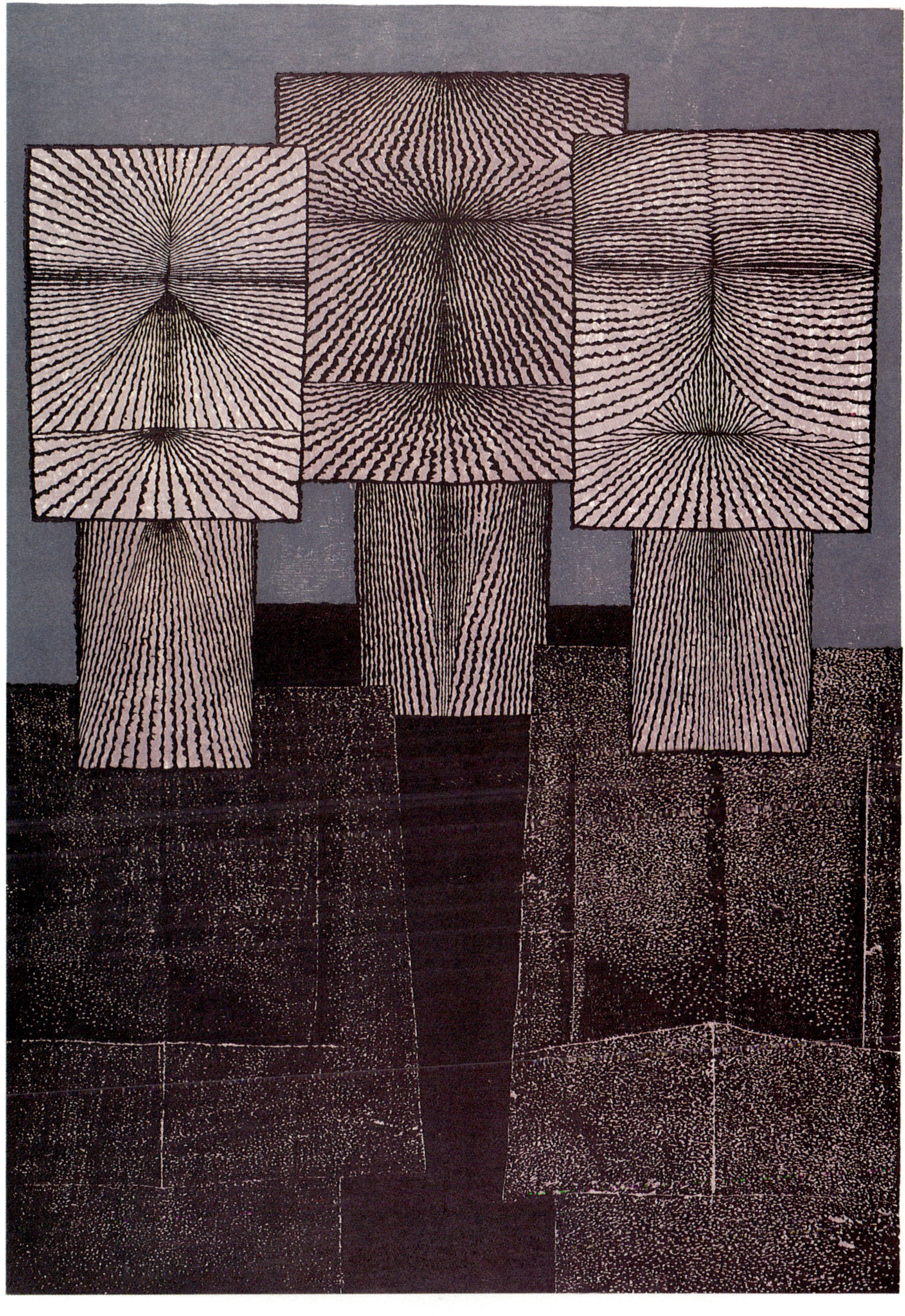

灰色の人々　　　Tomio Kinoshita　1980

51. Kinoshita Tomio (b. 1923). Titled in Japanese *Hai-iro-no-hito-bito* (Gray-Colored People), unnumbered but edition known to be 25, 1980, woodblock, 86x60 cm. Signed Tomio Kinoshita.

Clifton KARHU

COMMENT: *Commissioning an edition. One reason certain artists make certain prints.*

Plate 52

We commissioned the woodblock *House in Takaido* to commemorate the charming old house where our fledgling business had its start. A kind of structure that is vanishing quickly from the Japanese scene, the house, with its own classic tearoom, was spacious, grand, and ensconced in a huge and beautifully manicured Japanese garden. (Three Japanese gardeners are now living a life of carefree retirement because of what it took to maintain this beauty.) Surrounded by a high stone wall, it was a private preserve to which our clients could retreat, leave their shoes and daily cares behind them in the stately *genkan* (foyer), and enter not only the spiritual calm of a traditional Japanese house and garden but also the world of the Japanese print. Total immersion.

After years of contentment, when we learned that we had to leave our Takaido house because the landlord wished to raze the structure, uproot the garden, and redevelop the property, we very much wanted to preserve a visual record of that period of our life centered around the beautiful house. Commissioning a print seemed the ideal way to do this. Collectors who had enjoyed the cultural experience that the house offered were also eager to have a copy for their own memories.

An edition is commissioned for particular reasons and under particular circumstances. When we arranged a commission for the Caterpillar Corporation, which had various historic dates to commemorate, it was natural to ask Sekine Yoshio with his motif of the abacus since he enjoyed indicating numbers in abacus "spelling." When the Swedish packaging company Tetrapak wanted to have an artistic work that incorporated the various shapes of its products, the stylized colors and motifs of Wako Shuji were perfectly suitable. In these cases it was important to consider the artists' normal themes and insure that they were not overly compromised. Fitting the proper artist with the proper commission of a work can be an enjoyable endeavor. Gilbert and Sullivan felt the "punishment should fit the crime." Our job is more fun—"let the artist fit the commission."

When we wanted a memory of our house as a print, the artist who instantly came to mind was Clifton Karhu. His woodblocks are renowned for their depiction of traditional Japan—wooden houses, tile rooftops, decorative lanterns, and oil-paper umbrellas—evoking the essence of Japanese life and architecture, mostly of Kyoto, which also had special memories for us. He possesses a talent for creating a mood, with such images as a soft shaft of sunlight filtering into a courtyard, light rain falling in a quiet lane at dusk, or bright moonlight illuminating a mossy garden.

Karhu was the first artist with whom we set forth in our business and one who, with his wife, Lois, provided unstinting support to us during the trying times of getting our gallery off the ground. The accomplishments of Americans working successfully together in an almost exclusively Japanese milieu gave all of us a certain sense of comfort and mutual support.

Karhu, a frequent guest at our Takaido house, had enjoyed the house too. We knew that its architecture would appeal to him as an artist, and that he was attuned to our desire to want to capture not only a structure but an era. In short, we knew he was the perfect man for the job. He agreed to do it.

The print speaks for itself and underlines the adage that a picture is worth a thousand words. Commissioning this edition insured that our memories were captured in a lasting way. The most important thing was to have the right artist for the right portrayal. Karhu's skill and his empathy for what we wanted are evident in the print.

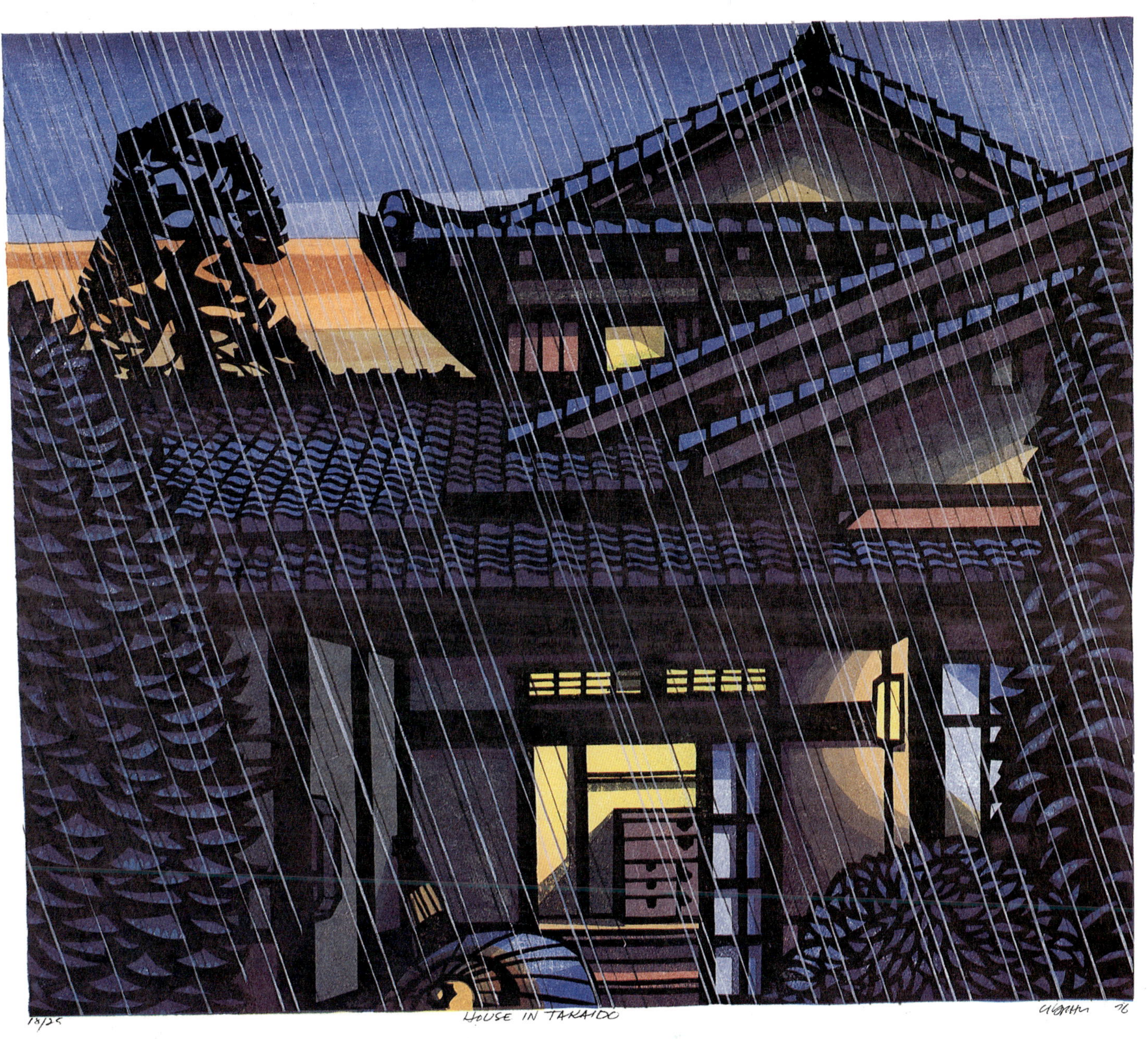

52. Karhu, Clifton (b. 1927). *House in Takaido,* 18/25, 1976, woodblock, 53.5x61 cm. Signed C. Karhu. Published by the Tolman Collection, Tokyo.

HARA Takeshi
(a k a HARA Ken)

COMMENT: *Collecting because of rarity.*

Plate 53

Tensor 76-1 was published by the Tolman Collection and was the only print created by Hara Takeshi in 1976. Japan's leading teacher of the lithographic technique, Hara was granted a generous one-year traveling fellowship by Japan's Cultural Affairs Agency that allowed him to visit the countries of his choice for study and observation and freed him from the need to create works to earn his living that year. Although his prints had long been prized internationally, this was his first trip abroad and he roamed for the entire year.

This print was part of a five-person portfolio (Hara, Iwami Reika, Yayanagi Go, Yoshida Katsuro, and Kurosaki Akira) that we published in an edition of seventy-five. We offered fifty sets as portfolios and twenty-five as individual works. Hara's print sold out on the first day because collectors and admirers were aware that it would be the only print he would make that year because of travel abroad.

Hara teaches lithography at Tokyo's Zokei University (University of Creative Arts) and is widely respected as an artist himself. As a teacher he has guided many artists, including Wako Shuji, whose own work reflects his mentor's fastidious attention to color and flawless technique.

One day, returning from a visit to Karhu in Kyoto, I was annoyed to find when the train stopped in Nagoya that the adjoining seat, luxuriously vacant until then, was about to be occupied. That is, until I realized that the occupant was to be none other than Hara, whom I had met but did not know well. As the train sped toward Tokyo, we chatted about this and that, and naturally our conversation turned to the art business. "You don't handle my work at your gallery," commented Hara. I replied that I had long admired his style but felt that our gallery was already featuring too many silkscreen print artists. "But," said the surprised Hara, "I've never made a silkscreen. All my works are lithographs." The conversation on the train was enlightening. Never ones to lose the momentum of spontaneity, we made the works of Hara our next major exhibition, and we have enjoyed a long, warm relationship with him ever since.

The particular effects that he realizes in his lithographs are more apt to be found in silkscreens. The delicate shadings, subtle blending of colors, and luminosity are difficult to achieve, but Hara has developed a special technique with a method of applying the ink with huge rollers to give his work an element of unbelievable smoothness, lushness, and control.

This artist's works are a study of the interrelationships of color, shape, and volume. The paths of projected light change in intensity and hue as they move across the paper, making the prints seem illuminated from within. Executed with supreme precision, these compositions reflect the personality of their maker: cool, quiet, dispassionate. His abstract work often brings to mind the rhythms of Oriental calligraphy. Hara is one example of an artist who would seem to be interested only in color or form but whose subject matter is, in fact, deeply rooted in his own culture.

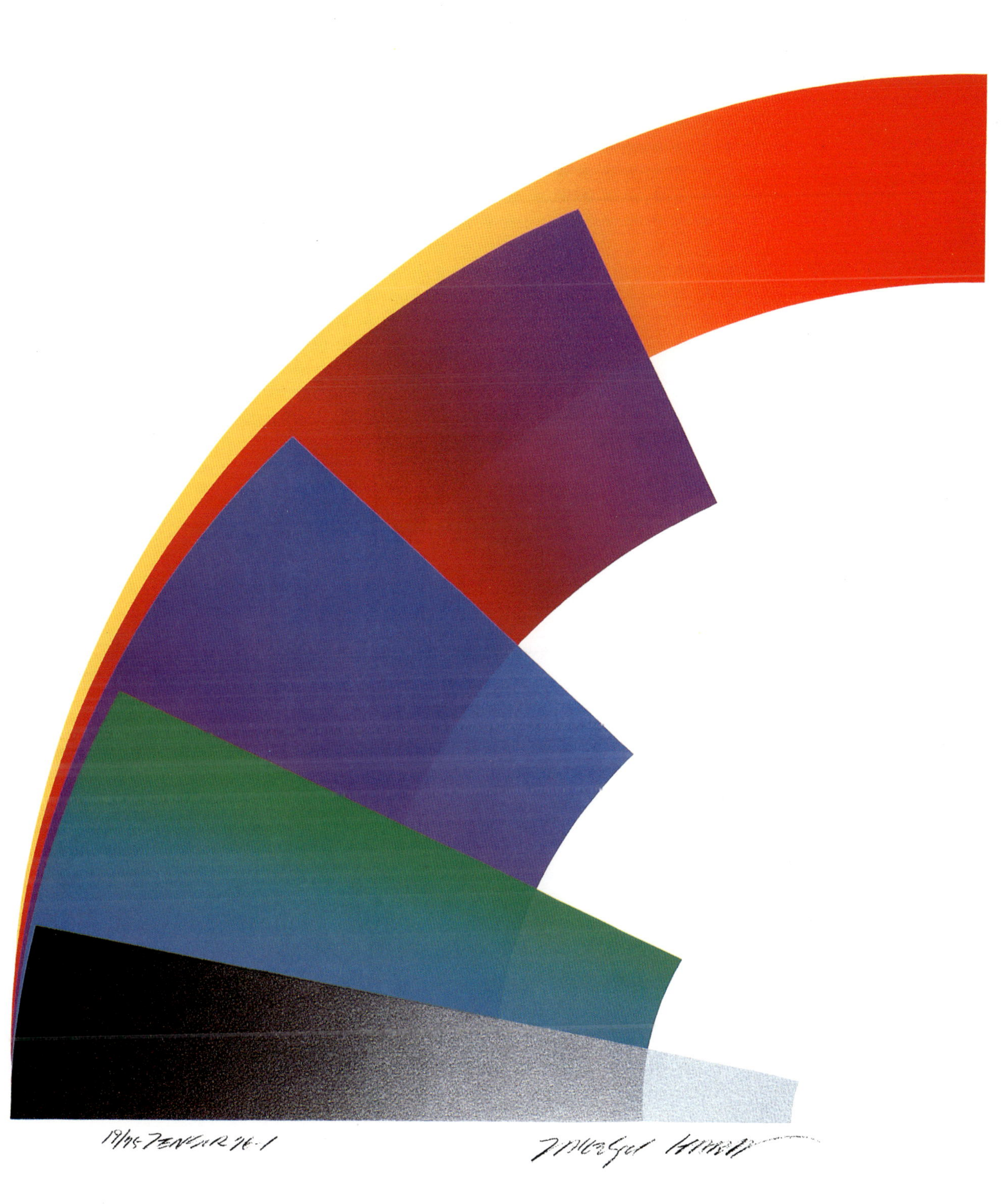

53. Hara Takeshi (b. 1942). *Tensor 76-1,* 19/75, 1976, lithograph, 66x50.5 cm. Signed Takeshi Hara. Published by the Tolman Collection, Tokyo.

SORA Mitsuaki

COMMENT: *There are prints available by artists who are more notable for their achievements in other media.*

A recent national census revealed that 70,000 Japanese list their occupation as "artist," but it did not provide a breakdown by medium. Further research by us indicated that many famous painters and sculptors also make prints. For print collectors, this is particularly good news. One may admire an outstanding artist's expensive oils, murals, or sculptures, which are often executed on a grand scale, but find that because of price or space limitations it is not possible to collect them. These limitations disappear when such artists also make prints.

The list of artists known first and foremost as painters who are also happy to make prints includes such luminaries as Onosato Toshinobu, Sugai Kumi, Yayanagi Go, Izumi Shigeru, Sekine Yoshio, and Shinoda Toko. It behooves the print collector who has a particular affinity for an artist working in another medium to make a few inquiries to learn whether or not that artist also makes prints. Often such artists find making prints another way of expressing their creative urge, and, of course, the price of a print will be much less than that of a large, original oil painting. It is a pleasant surprise to find that one can afford to buy what Fritz Eichenberg, founder of the Pratt Graphics Center, called "the most democratic form of art." Karhu phrased this sentiment more humorously when he said, "A print is something you should be able to buy without having to ask your spouse."

Plate 54

Sora Mitsuaki is a case in point. He is a renowned sculptor, and, in fact, the forms he uses in his prints strongly resemble his sculptural shapes. In his prints, however, he can enjoy the challenge of the flat plane and indulge his delight in color in the interlocking medley of his typical sculptural forms.

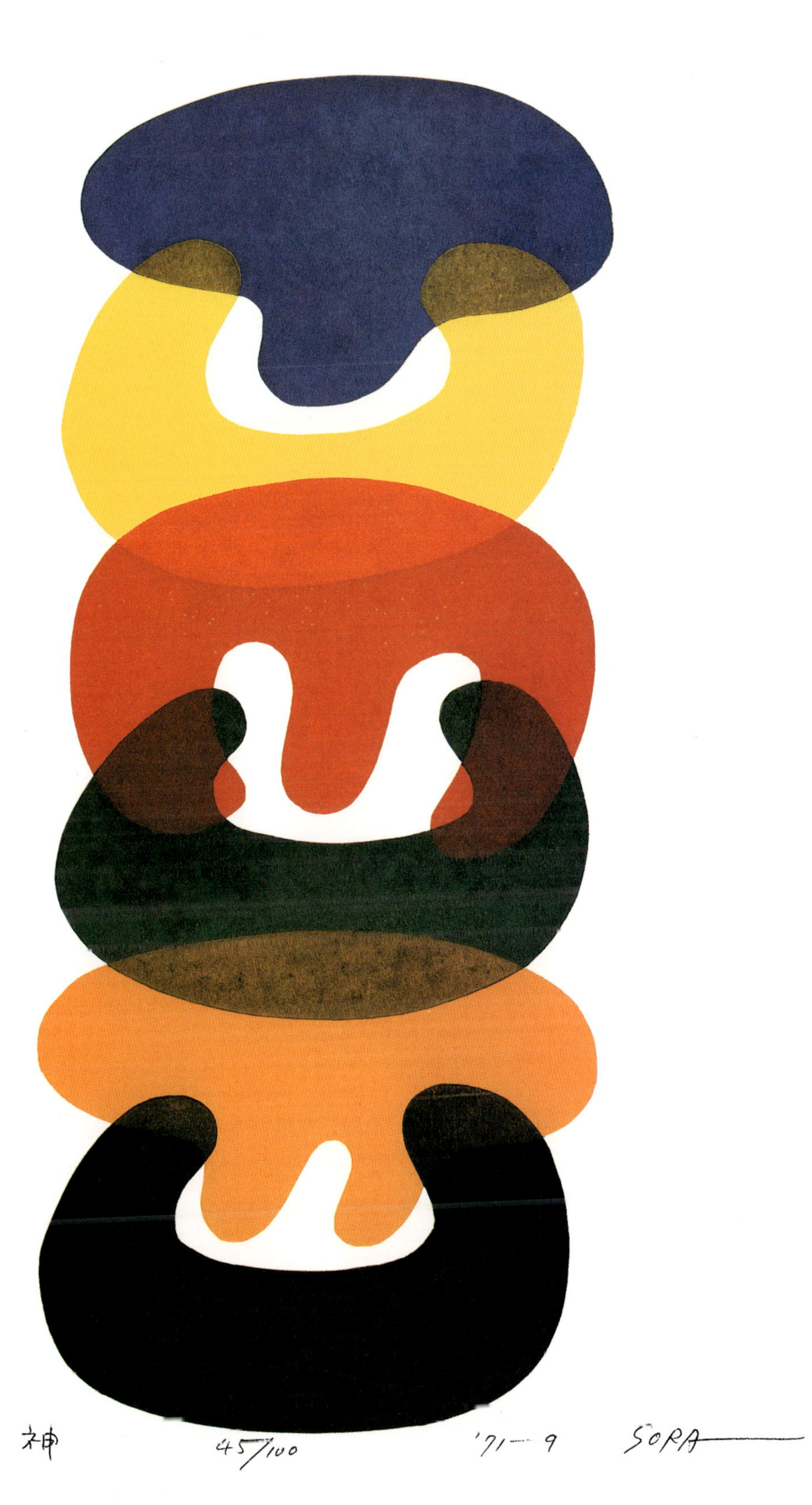

54. Sora Mitsuaki (b. 1933). Titled in Japanese *Megami* (Goddess), 45/100, 1971, woodblock, 62.5x46.8 cm. Signed Sora.

WATANABE Sadao

COMMENT: *What makes a print Japanese? Medium? Subject matter? What is "traditional"?*

We sometimes face a confused client who claims he is interested in a "traditional Japanese print" and then balks at an atmospheric old Kyoto scene in woodblock when he finds that the artist is an American of Finnish descent, Clifton Karhu. In the same way, others find it hard to accept an image of traditional subject matter executed in the latest laser technique. We explain that it is possible to employ a time-honored Japanese technique such as woodblock or stencil to create completely avant-garde subject matter. Similarly, an artist can depict a traditional subject using computer technology. In our gallery we try to decipher what people mean and strive to redefine a nebulous terminology.

Watanabe Sadao is one of the few Christian Japanese. He has utilized his religion for themes in all his works. His sources are both the Old Testament and the New Testament of the Bible so his prints appeal to both Jews and Christians. They are in collections all over the world, including even the Vatican.

Plate 55

In *Flight into Egypt* the subject is obviously not Japanese, but the stencil technique used has its roots in the old Japanese artistic tradition. This process was rejuvenated in modern times by Yanagi Soetsu (1889–1961), pioneer leader of the folk-art movement; Serizawa Keisuke (1895–1984), Living Cultural Treasure; and Mori Yoshitoshi (1898–1992), who adapted the art of textile dyeing to prints. Whereas Mori's subjects were invariably Japanese, Watanabe has availed himself of the extensive iconography found in the Bible. Other artists working today in this unique stencil technique include Kawada Kan, whose subjects are mostly famous Japanese places or country farmhouses, and Takahashi Hiromitsu, who has devoted his energies to depictions of the Kabuki world. Fortunately for the fans of *kappazuri* (stencil) prints, Hiromitsu is only 35 years old. We back him enthusiastically since the future of this endangered medium rests with him.

Watanabe's non-Japanese themes have caused some Western collectors to wonder why he should be part of their holdings of Japanese art. These would possibly be the same people who might be reluctant to buy a Kyoto woodblock print by Clifton Karhu. Yet there is no doubt that both artists are making traditional Japanese prints despite one's non-Japanese nationality and the other's non-Japanese subjects. Karhu, an American, is unsurpassed at extolling scenic Kyoto on handmade Japanese paper in the age-old Japanese woodblock tradition. Watanabe, though Japanese, is pursuing Western themes on beautifully wrinkled handmade Japanese paper in the folk-art tradition where black lines, rich color contrasts, and simple, naive forms are paramount.

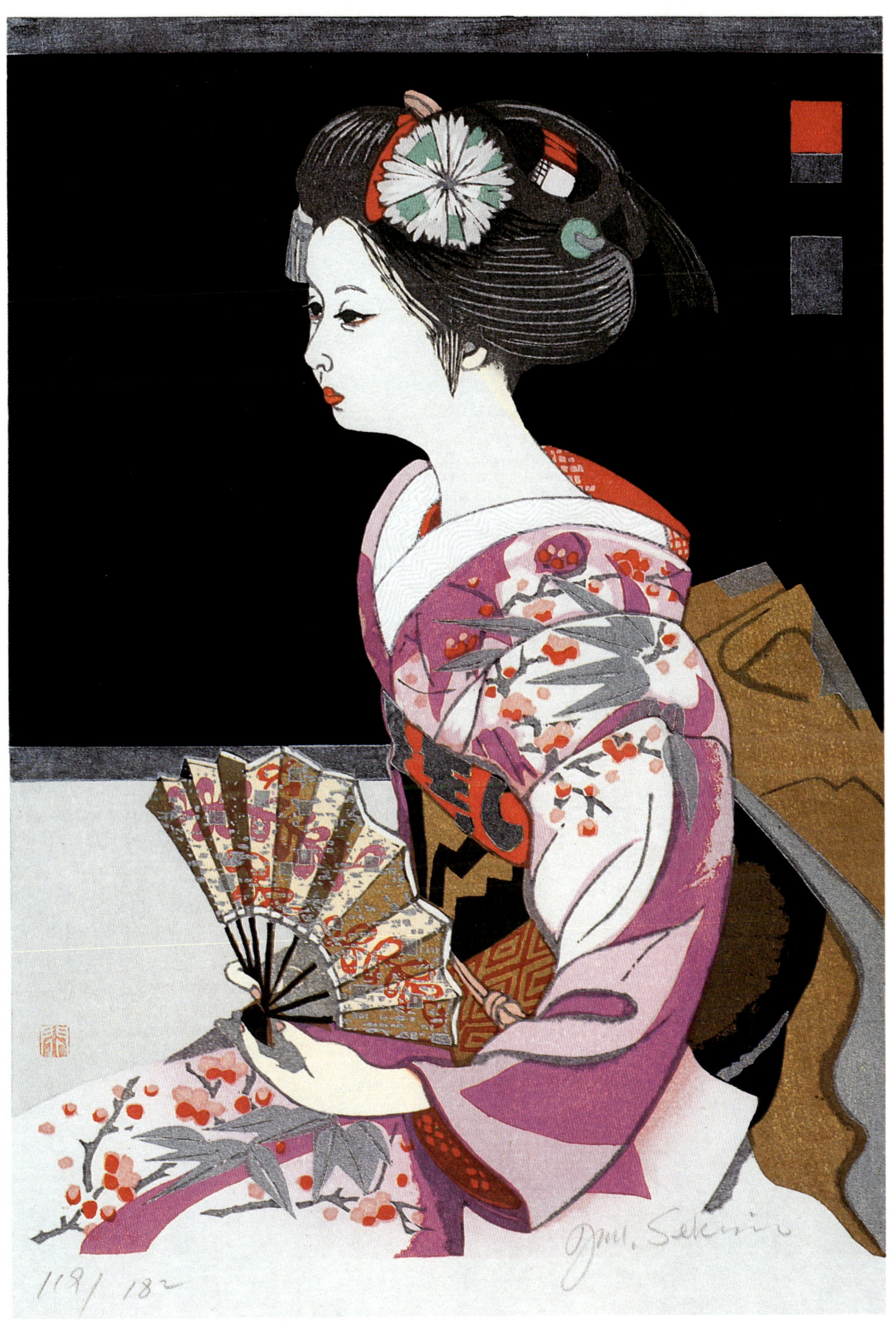

59. Sekino Jun'ichiro (1914–88). *Maiko,* 119/182 (actually an edition of 128 but the artist transposed two numbers), 1976, woodblock, 46.5x33 cm. Signed on the image Jun. Sekino, sealed on the image Jun.

MAKI Haku

COMMENT: *How important is the condition of the print?*

In the previous comment we listed several factors that affect print prices, including differences that would set a work apart and affect its value. In that comment we did not mention condition as a factor at all. This is not because condition is not important. It is because since we started collecting we have always searched for perfection and assumed the prints we actually purchased would be in perfect shape. Later on when we became dealers, we made it a rule never to allow clients to handle a print they might be considering for purchase. Our gallery staff members are like doctors, with a major hand-washing session before showing prints. We are determined to offer a print in pristine condition in return for a person's good money. We reasoned that the only way to insure this smooth and comforting exchange was to minimize careless handling by handling the prints ourselves.

After a first visit some would-be clients leave a bit unhappy from our testy admonitions of "Please don't touch the prints" and "We'll show them to you." To the more persistent touchers, our diplomatic gallery assistant, Taka, has been heard to say, "You are not encouraged to touch the prints." Stories of our severity are legion in Tokyo. The "lookers" seldom return, but somehow (as Mae West said) the good ones keep coming back. We have found that our strict policy has worked to our advantage since many clients have told us that they have looked at prints everywhere but always come to us when they are ready to buy something immaculate.

Plate 60

However, here we go again with an exception. This Maki Haku work is in miserable shape: the paper is stained and the edges are folded and bent. But the print was thirty years old when we first came across it, and there was no alternative. The image spoke to us and that was paramount, so we bought the print after much deliberation, not blaming it for what had happened over the decades. Just as we are encouraged to love the sinner and hate the sin, we decided to love the print and hate the stainer. Our advice is to seek prints in the finest condition, but if you love the image and feel the price is right, then buy the print for your emotional satisfaction. Obviously the cost should be less for something not in perfect condition.

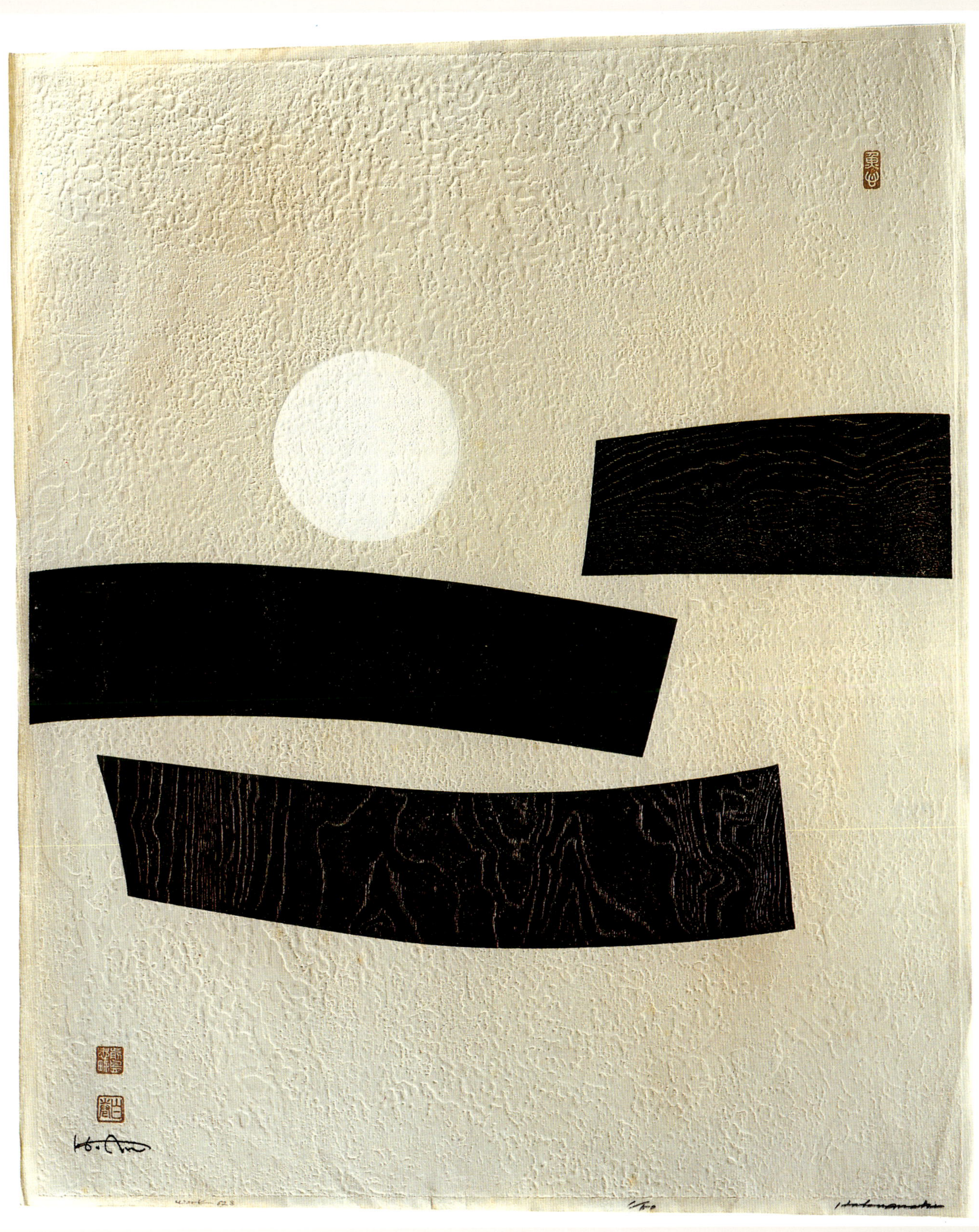

60. Maki Haku (b. 1924). *Work 62 3,* 1/50, 1962, woodblock/cement block, 63.5x52 cm. Signed on the lower left Haku Maki, sealed on the image Maejima Tadaaki, then Haku Maki; at the top right on the image another artist's seal.

IKEDA Masuo

COMMENT: *The unforeseen and totally unexpected in collecting—the role of the auction.*

The secondary market for contemporary Japanese prints, that is, the reappearance on the market of prints that are known to be sold out, is still in its infancy. But from time to time we hear of people who after a long residence in Japan decide to retire and return to their home country, move to a small condo, play golf or travel, and, in general, wish to divest themselves of "possessions" and lead a simpler life. After keeping their favorite works and bestowing some others on their children, they may put the rest up at auction. This is just beginning to happen.

Recently I had the pleasure of attending a Sotheby auction in New York featuring 350 modern Japanese prints. Since we were already the possessors of fifty of those on offer, I was particularly interested to see what prices they would command. The auction brought out the usual bidders, including many gallery representatives from Japan, and the enthusiastic bidding elicited respectable prices for all of the works, most of which had not appeared on the market for ten to twenty years.

I really intended only to look, but naturally was caught up in the excitement of the day and began bidding for a print that we had missed fifteen years earlier. On winning the bid and receiving the sought-after item, I learned that it was, in fact, the lead print in a "lot" containing two others, one of which was the Ikeda Masuo print illustrated here.

Plate 61

Ikeda is one of the most famous artists at work in Japan today. He is a major TV personality, prize-winning writer, etcher, lithographer, ceramicist, and bon vivant, so you can well imagine the pleasure of finding this print that he made during his sojourn in the U.S.—as a bonus! Since the print had not been made in Japan, it might never have come to my attention if I had not attended the auction. The lesson here is that collectors need to take advantage of every opportunity—and have a little fun at the same time.

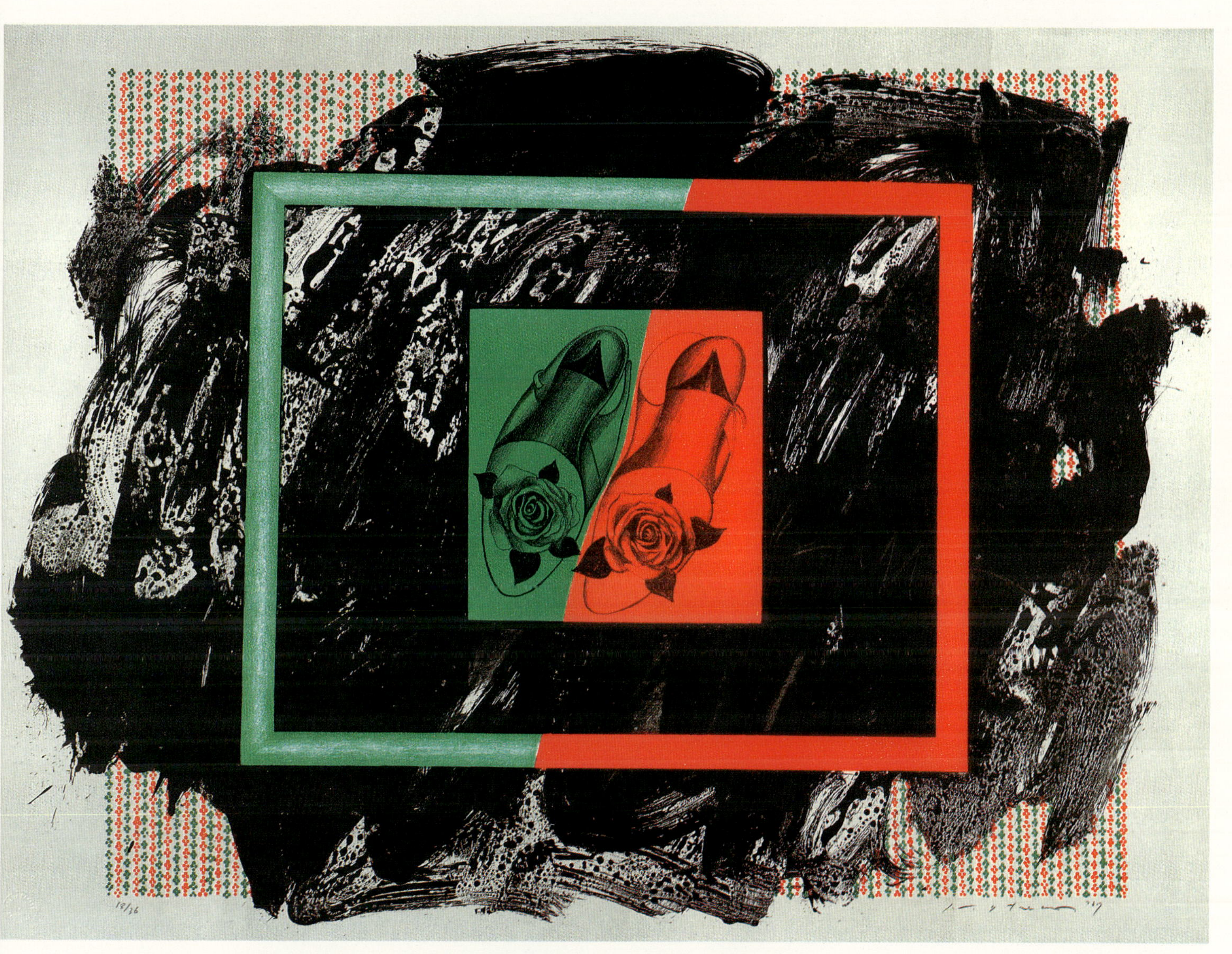

61. Ikeda Masuo (b. 1934). Titled on the reverse *Naked Shoes,* 18/36, 1967, lithograph, 56.3x76 cm. Signed M. Ikeda.

HASEGAWA Yuichi

COMMENT: *Japanese prints embody a wide range of unusual techniques, paper, and materials unknown elsewhere.*

Hasegawa Yuichi's woodblock technique is highly original and very complicated. Whereas most artists carve one block for each color, Hasegawa uses only one block in toto, for carving, printing, and effacing, until every color has been printed, requiring at least ten and as many as sixteen processes. Each stage is an entity in itself and cannot be retraced or repeated, certainly one of the reasons that this artist makes small editions of twenty.

Japanese woodblock prints are for the most part executed on *washi* (handmade Japanese paper). This paper is incomparable because it can be flattened, backed with other Japanese handmade paper to give it body, is easily restored if something happens to it, is long-lasting, and of great strength and resilience. Hasegawa has chosen to use a paper called *torinoko,* which possesses two distinctive properties: a pure white color and softness. Its white color is an important contrast to the brilliant hues of the artist's palette. However, since he prints and reprints from the same block, the wear and tear on the soft paper is of particular concern. To strengthen the entire sheet of paper, he uses a traditional technique that has been handed down through the ages by dyers of kimono fabric to strengthen their stencils: he paints a solution of *kakishibu* (persimmon tannin) on the back of the paper to give it a long-lasting body without affecting the color on the printed surface. Members of the artist's family were lacquer craftsmen, and the lustrous, shiny inks he sometimes uses are reminiscent of that art. Although his prints are abstract, everything about them is traditionally Japanese.

Hasegawa was recommended to us by his mentor, the great Saito Kiyoshi. Both artists live in Aizu Wakamatsu, which is aglow with persimmon trees in the autumn. Whenever we bite into a persimmon slice, we are reminded of both Saito and Hasegawa, Saito because the bright orange persimmon figures as frequent subject matter in his works, and Hasegawa because the very juice of this tangy fruit is an actual part of his print technique. In addition, every year during the season we are the lucky and grateful recipients of boxes of persimmons as gifts from our Aizu friends.

Plate 62

Hasegawa remarks about his work, "For a long time I have been influenced by the deep spirituality of Zen. The immense time and space of the Universe, arranged like a Buddhist mandala, has been my theme, along with the various forms of creation that can be observed in nature . . . I am striving to create works with a meaningful inner spirit."

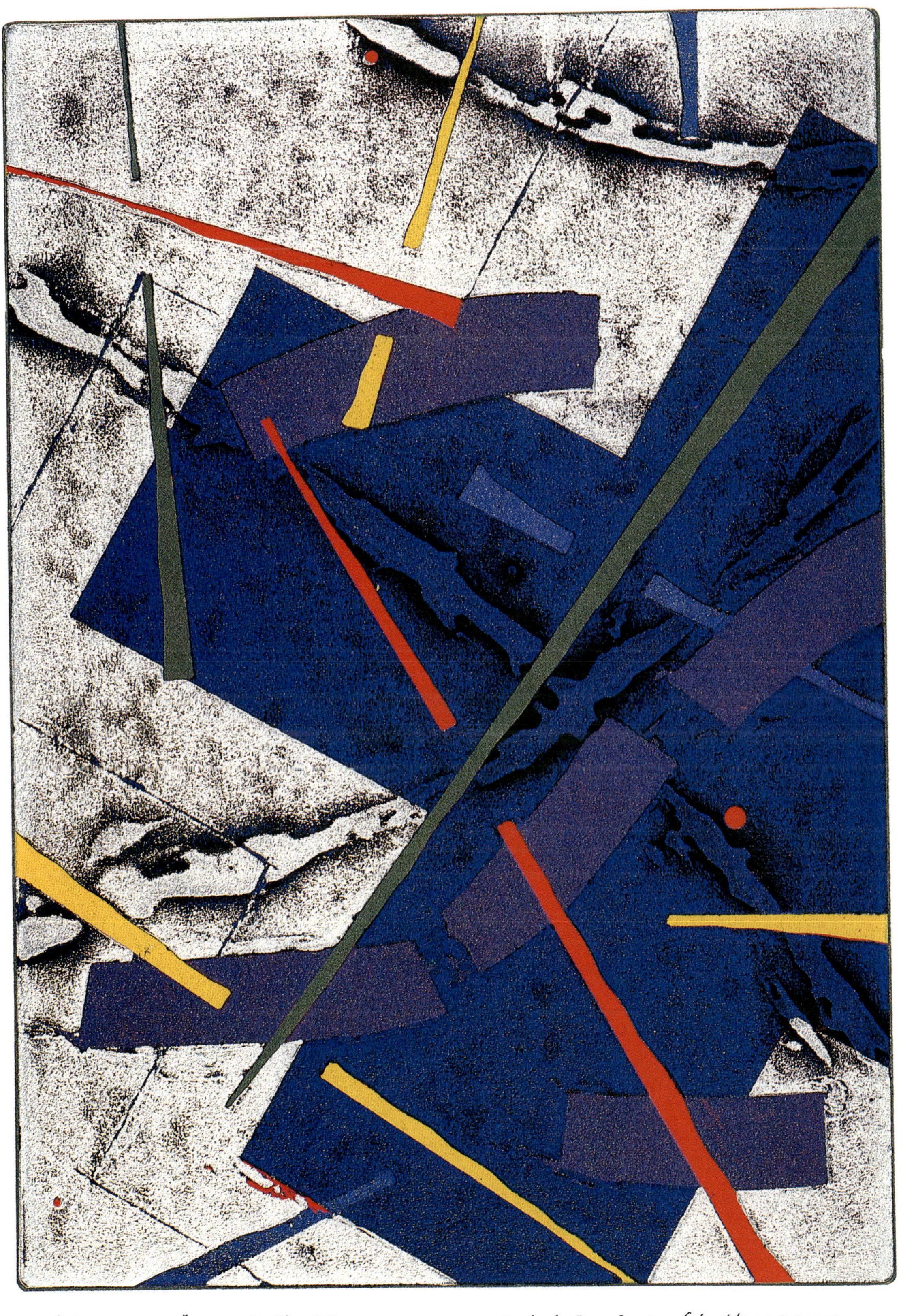

62. Hasegawa Yuichi (b. 1945). Titled in Japanese *Aoi-daichi (2)* (Earth in Blue [2]), 3/20, 1992, woodblock, 49x34.5 cm. Signed Yuichi Hasegawa. Published by the Tolman Collection, Tokyo.

SAWADA Tetsuro

COMMENT: *Perfection of technique and the use of* bokashi *(shading).*

The technique of *bokashi* has been used in Japanese prints since the early days of *ukiyo-e* and was an especially prominent feature of Hiroshige's landscapes. Modern Japanese artists avail themselves of their heritage, so it is no surprise to find this artistic technique cropping up even in the most avant-garde print works of today.

One may easily see that it is possible to use this delicate technique of an infinitesimal shading from a dark color into a paler one without any discernible point of change in one print, but if one lays out fifty prints of the same edition side by side and can discern no technical difference, one can then come to some appreciation of Japanese printing skill. The prints are not mechanically processed nor airbrushed; all are inked and printed by hand, their uniform excellence being the ultimate testimony to the talent of the printer. (Most silkscreen artists use professional printers.) An ordinary silkscreen may not present a great problem but one with the subtleties of shading inherent in Sawada Tetsuro's work needs a highly skilled printer who is responsible for bringing out the special attributes of his work: the interesting juxtaposition of matte and shiny inks, a clean, streamlined look, a stylistic precision, and the formidable process of *bokashi*.

Sawada, who is also a painter, has carried this method of *bokashi* shading from his paintings over into his prints and has been celebrated internationally for his technical achievements. For many years he did not title his prints; only when our gallery commissioned his editions did he begin the practice. He has made prints exclusively for us in much smaller editions than he normally produces.

Sawada is often referred to as "the skyscape artist" because he makes works
Plate 63 that remind people of the fantasy land they see from a plane. Layers of brilliant, complementary blue colors contrasted with muted tones of gradation suggest an escape from a mundane existence into the vast universe beyond. Sawada's scenes are stark, and yet from them emanates a hushed beauty that encourages contemplation and reverie.

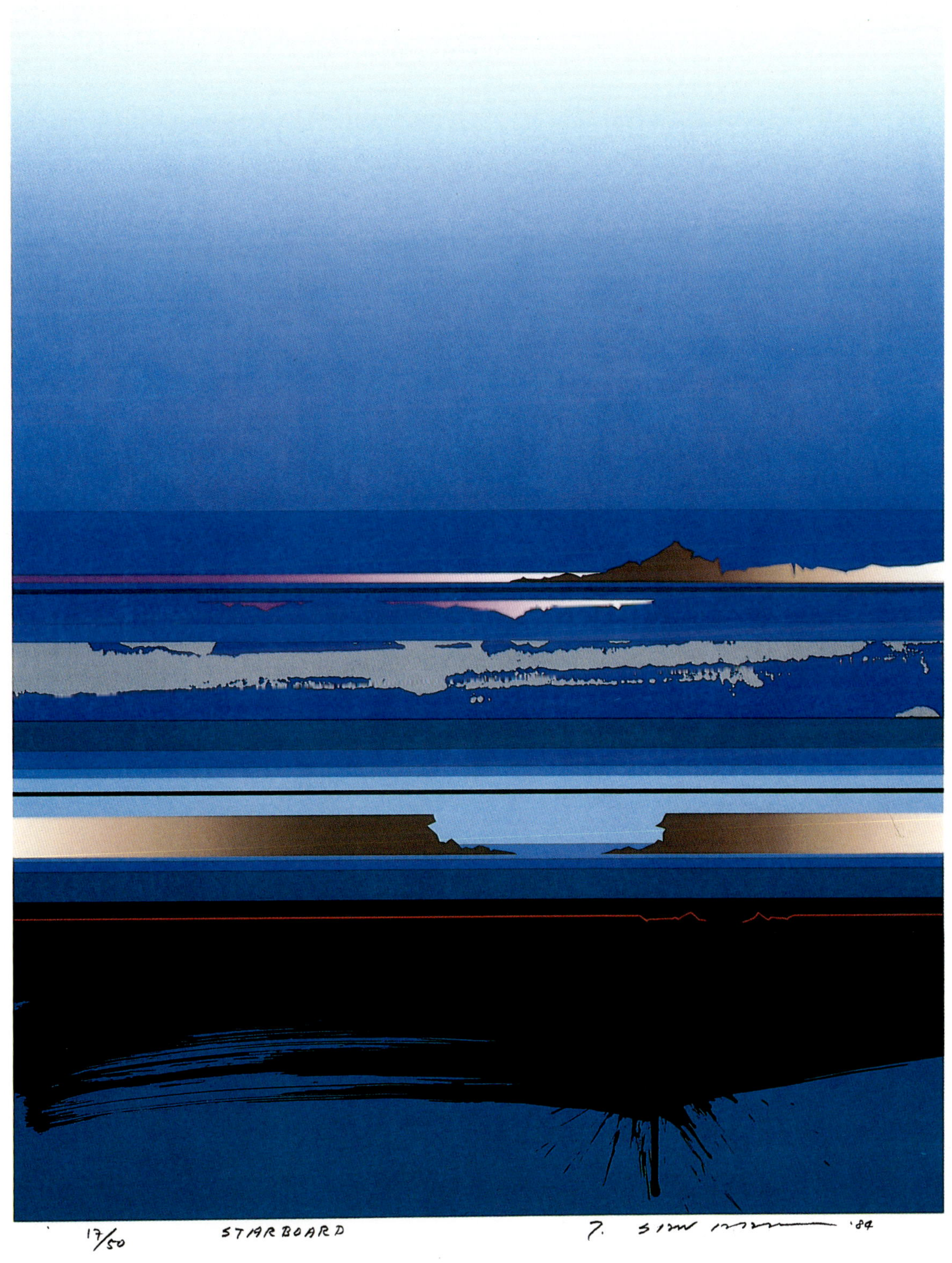

63. Sawada Tetsuro (b. 1935). *Starboard*, 17/50, 1984, silkscreen, 60x42.2 cm. Signed T. Sawada. Published by the Tolman Collection, Tokyo.

HAMANISHI Katsunori

COMMENT: *Superior technique.*

In addition to telling our own story in this book, we have continued to remind ourselves that the book is intended to be of help to collectors, pointing out reasons why they should enjoy collecting Japanese prints. This is not a book about technique but in the next few comments we wish to alert the reader to the subtleties and flawless perfection of techniques that make Japanese prints outstanding.

In this vein we felt that we had to start with Hamanishi Katsunori, who is one of the best in one of the most demanding of all printing methods, the mezzotint. Sometimes confusion arises because to the uninitiated Hamanishi Katsunori sounds like Hamaguchi Yozo, often referred to as the world's greatest living mezzotint artist, now 85 and living in semiretirement in San Francisco. (Aficionados of Japanese prints will recall Hamaguchi's velvety black prints with a few cherries as the focal point.) Hamanishi is only 45 years old but is the upcoming master in his field. He is what is called an "artist's artist" because when other printmakers look at his fastidious and detailed work they are left in awe.

His prints' appeal is obvious: Hamanishi has reached a new level of perfection (so taken for granted in virtually all Japanese printmakers) in a very difficult method. His subjects—twigs, branches, wires, ropes—are presented in a three-dimensional form on paper. They are not photographs; each image has been painstakingly burnished on the plate, raising the viewer's expectations to a higher level than usual, expectations that are fully met.

Plate 64

Hamanishi is not concerned with an all-encompassing view of the world, but more with a microcosmic look, like a close-up magician with his small captive audience. He loves shapes, their interlinkings, their details—all of which he slowly and deliberately reveals in his unparalleled, meticulous mezzotints. In recent years he has begun to add a bright touch of red or blue as a contrapuntal note to his detailed compositions, and these sudden bursts of color point up even more the dazzling brilliance of his creative imagery.

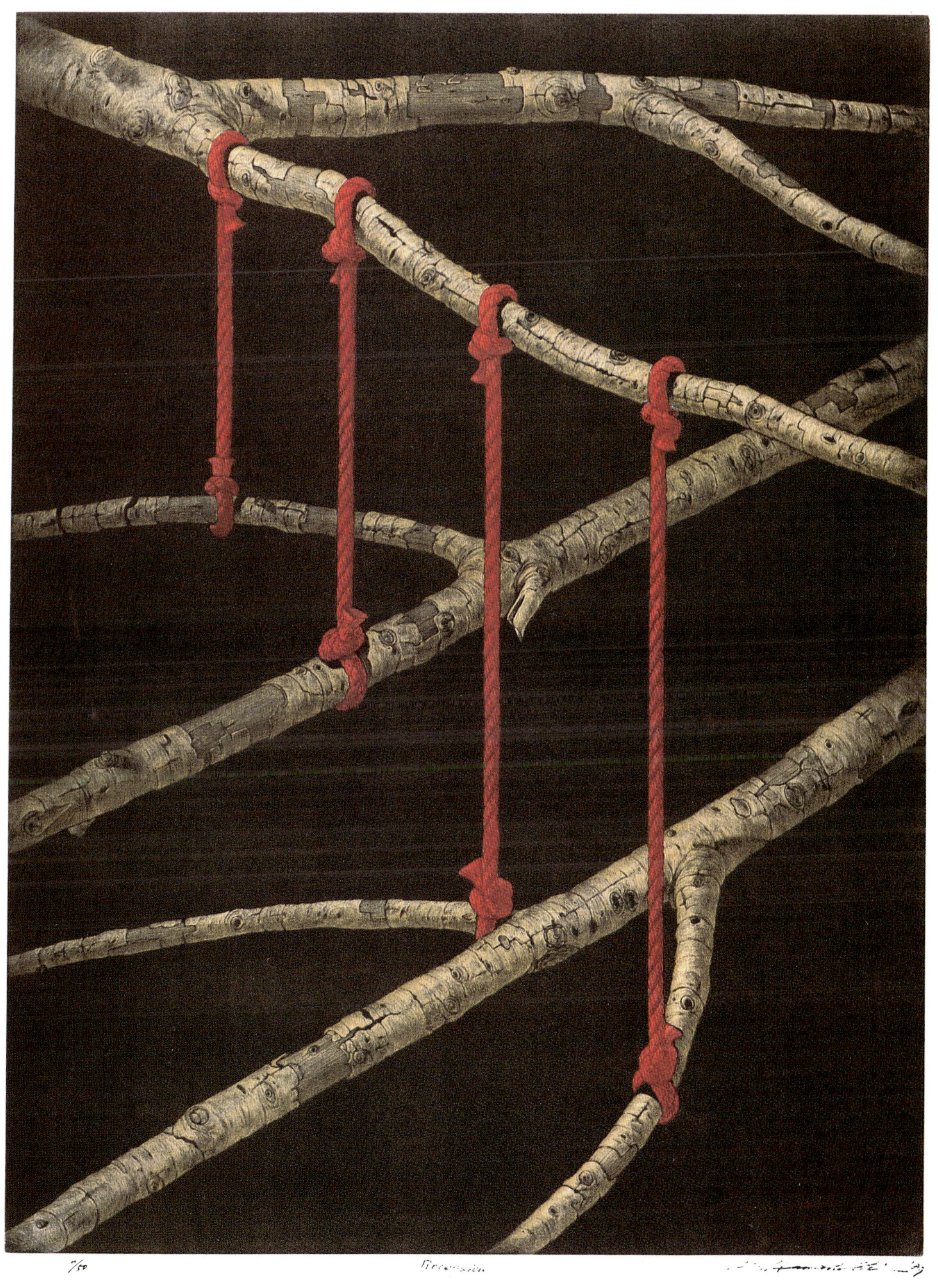

64. Hamanishi Katsunori (b. 1949). *Procession,* 8/50, 1989, mezzotint, 59.2x44 cm. Signed K. Hamanishi.

MIYASHITA Tokio

COMMENT: *Combining unrelated techniques on unusual paper.*

Miyashita Tokio's cheerful and outgoing personality may be the result of his having been born in Tokyo's *shita-machi* district, with its lively medley of tradesmen, peddlers, artisans, hawkers, and "just plain folks." Miyashita began studying woodblock printmaking with Hiratsuka Un'ichi while he was still in high school and continued in this technique for a few years. He then spent one year studying Western etching methods with Sekino Jun'ichiro and Komai Tetsuro. After learning the intricacies of both processes he decided to combine them, and therein lies the magic and inventiveness of his work.

Because of the demands of each technique, Miyashita must use a special paper that is absorbent enough to take the water-based ink of woodblocks, yet strong enough to bear the pressure of the intaglio process. One can always find the TM watermark in this paper, which he has made especially for him. His unique printing process, in which he actually solders small etched plates or actual wire onto the plate to be printed, needs an almost indestructible paper.

Plate 65

Fossil, with its intriguing insets, lush color, and seemingly casual disposition of elements, is a typical Miyashita work. The strong black line of the soldered wire is one of his trademarks, along with the deep, rich rendering of color that he achieves by printing the same area several times or by using the ink directly from the tube without dilution. In addition, this work is a full-bleed print, and the collector can enjoy the deckle edge of the beautiful handmade paper as well.

Although a serious and dedicated artist, Miyashita as a friend is a most relaxed and helpful person, who is always the first to lend a helping hand. One feels this aspect of his personality even on a first encounter, which is quite unlike meeting the stereotypical Japanese, who is supposed to be reserved and distant until he decides to accept you, a process that can take years. We have known this artist for nearly twenty-five years and recall especially his efforts on our behalf long ago when we wanted to have some bookcases made, a seemingly insurmountable task at the time. He came for lunch one day, heard our tale of woe, took the project in hand, and oversaw it until completion. We did not even ask him—he just did it. In fact, his role not only as a major artist, but also as an organizer and board member of the Japan Print Association has followed the same lines. When no one else is able or willing to carry out what needs to be done, Miyashita always does it, no matter what "it" is.

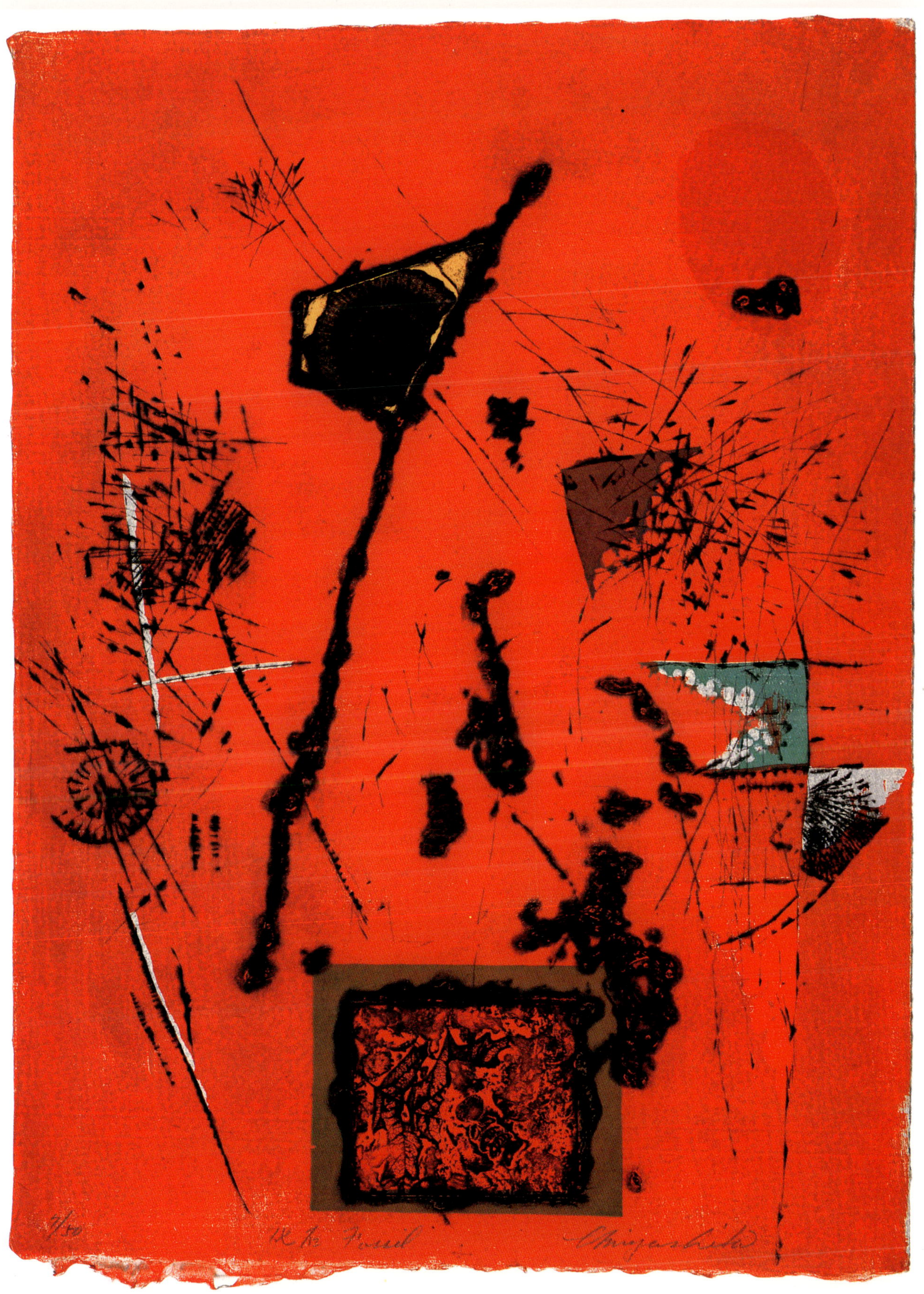

65. Miyashita Tokio (b. 1930). Titled in Japanese *Kaseki,* titled in English *Fossil,* 7/50, undated but known to be 1992, intaglio/woodblock, 65.5x47.5 cm. Signed T. Miyashita.

YOSHIDA Katsuro

COMMENT: *A man before his time: Yoshida Katsuro and his photo etchings.*

The idea of incorporating photographic processes in prints is widespread these days, but when Yoshida Katsuro made this photo-etching in 1976 it was still a novelty. The print was part of a five-person portfolio (including Hara Takeshi, Iwami Reika, Kurosaki Akira, Yayanagi Go, and Yoshida, in an edition of seventy-five, fifty to be sold as portfolios and twenty-five as individual copies). At the time Yoshida's work was the least popular print in the folio, probably because viewers were not used to the combination of techniques and needed time to absorb the idea. In the long run though, owners of the entire portfolio have repeatedly told us that Yoshida's print is one that has stood the test of time and the one they most cherish.

The artist has lived abroad, studying for a year in London on a grant from the Cultural Affairs Agency. Always traveling about with his camera and ever ready to capture scenes that intrigued him, Yoshida has shared his vignettes with us in his work. He is a funster, the personification of informality, possessor of a cheerful smile, an infectious laugh, and a perpetual wind-blown look. His sense of humor is often apparent in his work but sometimes the viewer needs a key to appreciate it.

Not lacking a sense of humor ourselves, we were quite amused to read in the British Museum publication *The Japanese Print Since 1900: Old Dreams and New Visions,* published in 1983, a short description of Yoshida's *Work 47(Expectations).* Among other things it states, "In this print the girl in the brutalized downtown area of a Japanese city has detached herself into a romantic, human vision." (Whatever that means.)

Plate 66

The facts are that this work was commissioned by us in 1976 (no credit given to us as publishers in the catalogue), and that it includes a photo of three young ladies about to enter the sacred precincts of the Egara Tenjin shrine in Kamakura. The deity of this shrine is renowned for listening to the prayers of those looking for the right person with whom to spend a happy married life. Nothing too brutal about that, we hope.

Yoshida has projected an enlargement of his photographic negative on a specially treated metal plate and has then proceeded to make an etching from it. His creativity is obvious, as he abstracts one of the girls from the group, presenting her standing alone in the forefront and gazing back at us in a questioning way.

Knowing the significance of the shrine, one can momentarily ignore the artist's technique and appreciate his whimsical presentation. He obviously was enchanted by the girl looking back to see if anyone had been watching her in her quest for matchmaking on a religious level. Or is she thinking, "I wish I weren't doing this."

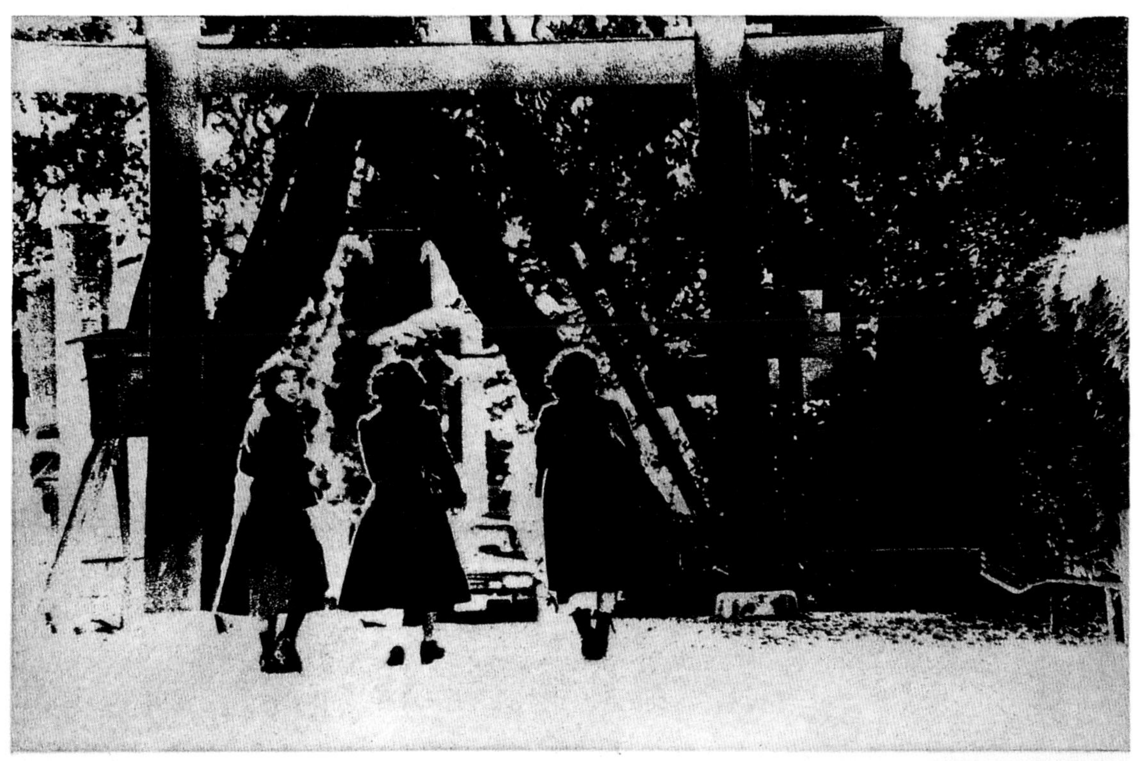

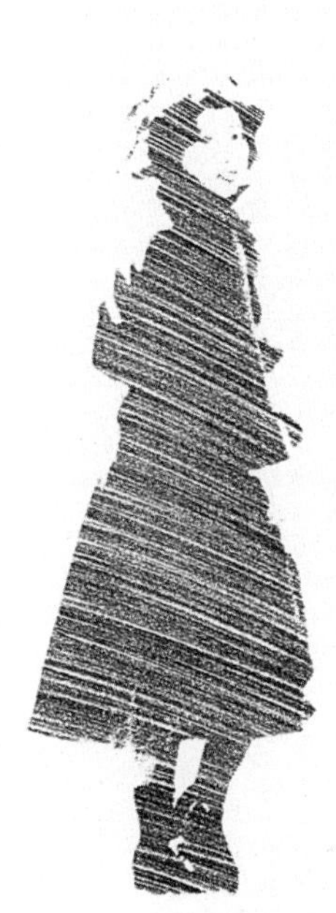

66. Yoshida Katsuro (b. 1943). *Work 47 (Expectations)*, 16/75, 1976, photo-etching, 56.5x40 cm. Signed Katsuro Yoshida. Published by the Tolman Collection, Tokyo.

IZUMI Shigeru

COMMENT: *Birds of a feather—great teacher, great students, great prints.*

At 72 years old, Izumi Shigeru has such a youthful appearance that everyone wants to push his own birth date back a little, and he has such an agile and fertile imagination that one simply bows low and stands back in awe. From the time we were introduced to his work we knew that our intellect was being challenged. We loved it—and went back for more. Izumi has always been in the vanguard.

When we first met him in 1970 Izumi was an inspiring teacher at Osaka University of Fine Art and leader of a talented group embracing the artists Funai Yutaka and Tsubota Masahiko, whose pages follow. Even today we are grateful to all three for stretching our minds and sensibilities toward appreciating concepts in art that we might never have known if we had not met them. They were also instrumental in making us aware that Osaka and Kyoto were hotbeds of artistic creativity, and that one did not always have to look to the capital to find great talent.

At the end of World War II, when there was little of anything available, especially artistic equipment, Izumi determinedly made his own printing press. In 1959, when he went on a study grant to the famous Pratt Graphics Center in New York, he was quickly elevated from the student ranks and made a teacher. After his U.S. stay he spent several years in France, where he enjoyed a bohemian life of freedom and artistic experimentation. In Japan he has had the benefit of great associates and teachers like Yoshihara Jiro, founder and benefactor of Osaka's famous, avant-garde Gutai Group, and also the help and counsel of such other notables as Ei-Q and Yoshihara Hideo.

Izumi's general lifestyle is one unfettered of any preconceived notions about anything. He hates edition numbers on prints, for example. He told us that is the business end of art and not his affair. He likes creating the work, and having someone else be in charge of bothersome details. His sense of adventure has even led him to produce some of his silkscreen prints on aluminum sheets, using different colors for each printing. The colors were selected according to his feeling that day. Of course, these glimmering metal sheets are show stoppers and probably influenced his next stage of work, in which he liked to print just a bit off-register to continue this effect. The result was a deliberate softening of what is normally a very hard edge of silkscreen printing.

We have long remembered the comment of one of our well-meaning but not well-informed clients who noted, "This guy is going to be really good as soon as he can master registering the colors in his prints," a comment indicating that one can operate only at one's level of understanding.

Plate 67

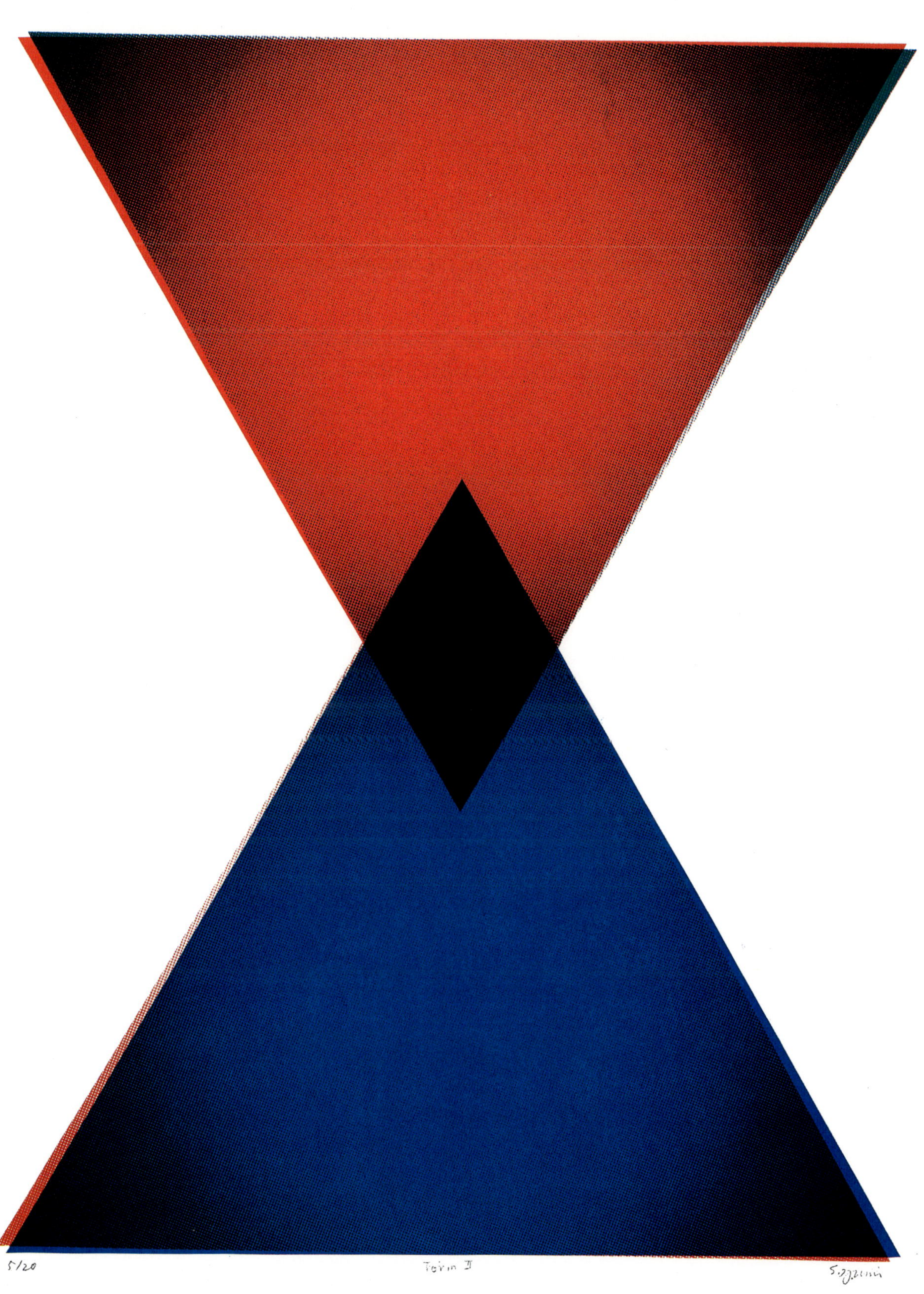

67. Izumi Shigeru (b. 1922). *Form II,* 5/20, undated, silkscreen, 72.5x54.5 cm. Signed S. Izumi.

FUNAI Yutaka

COMMENT: *Things are seldom what they seem.*

During our years in Kyoto, part of our cultural responsibility as diplomats was to immerse ourselves in the art scene of the western part of Japan. Since we were also interested on the personal level, it was easy to be a frequent visitor to the Osaka University of Fine Art. It was there that we were introduced to Funai Yutaka by his mentor in the printmaking department, Izumi Shigeru.

These were just about the days when Andy Warhol and his Campbell's soup cans were gaining notoriety in the international art world, and it is possible that Funai may have been the recipient of some unpleasant comparisons by the casual observer. Many people are of the opinion that Japanese are merely imitators and when they came across Funai and his "can" motif they probably felt confirmed in their suspicions.

However, we are here to attest that long before Andy ever dreamed of a can, Funai was using it as a theme in his work. Of course, each artist had a totally different concept in mind. Warhol was using the can as a Pop Art gimmick; Funai employed it more intellectually as an artistic concept to define shape and volume and to capture them on a flat plane.

Funai had first worked with simple lines, which eventually turned into boxes, then into stripes, and finally into angles dividing the can shape. We were interested to note that Izumi was concerned with presenting tubular shapes in his work at this same period, so it seemed likely that each artist was stimulated and influenced by the other. In *Major Scale* Funai chose the purest of colors—they almost make our eyes dance—to create a simple, uncluttered composition. We are riveted not only by the color but also by the rhythm of the lines, the precision of the printing, the placement of each segment of the composition, and the volume delineated and retrieved from the given space.

Plate 68

Before deciding to become an artist Funai had taken a degree in law. It is therefore not so surprising that his work reflects a logical orderliness and that after much research he likes to get down to the basics and work painstakingly from there.

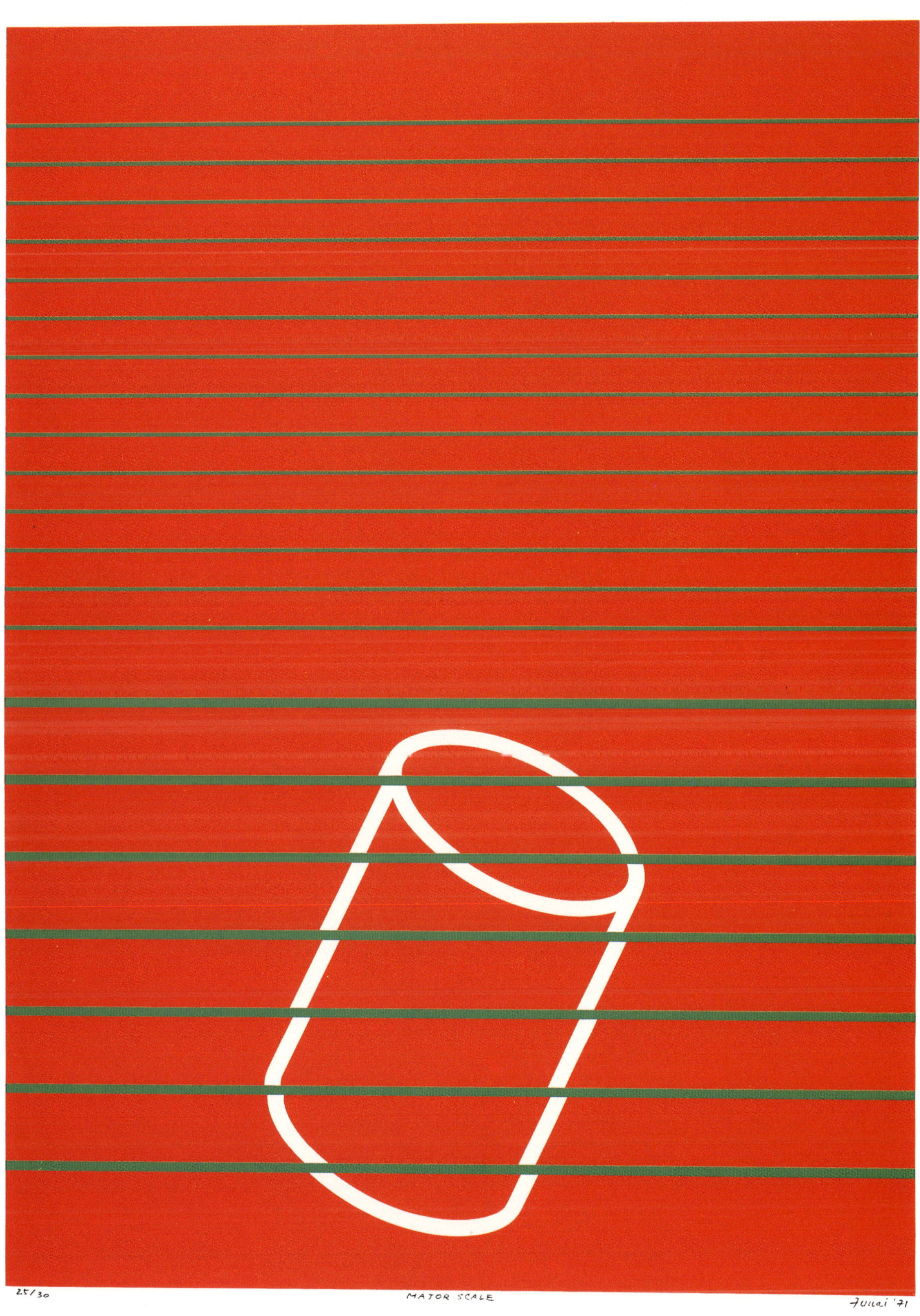

68. Funai Yutaka (b. 1932). *Major Scale,* 25/30, 1971, silkscreen, 65.3x47 cm. Signed Funai.

TSUBOTA Masahiko

COMMENT: *Being in the right place at the right time; influences on young artists.*

If one looks at the dynamism of Izumi Shigeru's talent and the perfection of Funai Yutaka's silkscreen technique and his determined pursuit of form, as described in the preceding pages, one will easily understand the premise that a marriage between their works would result in offspring looking something like Tsubota Masahiko's prints, with his own originality thrown in, of course.

Tsubota, as an excellent young student at Osaka University of Fine Art, was fortunate enough to study printmaking with Funai, who quickly recognized his talent and recommended him as a printer for Izumi. Tsubota was blessed by this coincidental crossing with two masters, and since he brought with him his own considerable abilities the results were preordained. We should note here that it is worthwhile for collectors to be acquainted with university art teachers, who can indicate the talents of their various students. This is a way to spot a winner before anyone else does, and to have the pleasure and fun of watching an artist grow (before his prices do). As collectors we became aware of Tsubota in this way and purchased virtually every print he made during the 1970s and early 1980s, delighting in each new image.

Each of his works grew simpler and yet more expressive over the years. One critic has said that he is a "subtractive artist," in that he tries to find the ultimate form by taking away all unnecessary elements. We are left with a meditative calm and also a realization of the density of space. In his work *Penetration-1* it is the clever addition of punched holes that adds to this effect.

Plate 69

When we first started our business we were asked to stage a major exhibition on very short notice. We accepted before carefully considering the details, such as the matting of the works. Having little money we thought we could economize by cutting the mats ourselves, but after several bitter and frustrating attempts, we found to our great dismay that cutting mats is an art in itself and we were doing a miserable job. A phone call made in obvious great distress brought our young artist friend Tsubota to Tokyo on the last night train from Osaka, mat cutter in hand. He worked through the night, producing only perfect mats with the same sense of carefulness that he would have given to pulling a print. We have never been able to look at a finely cut mat since without remembering our kind perfectionist with gratitude.

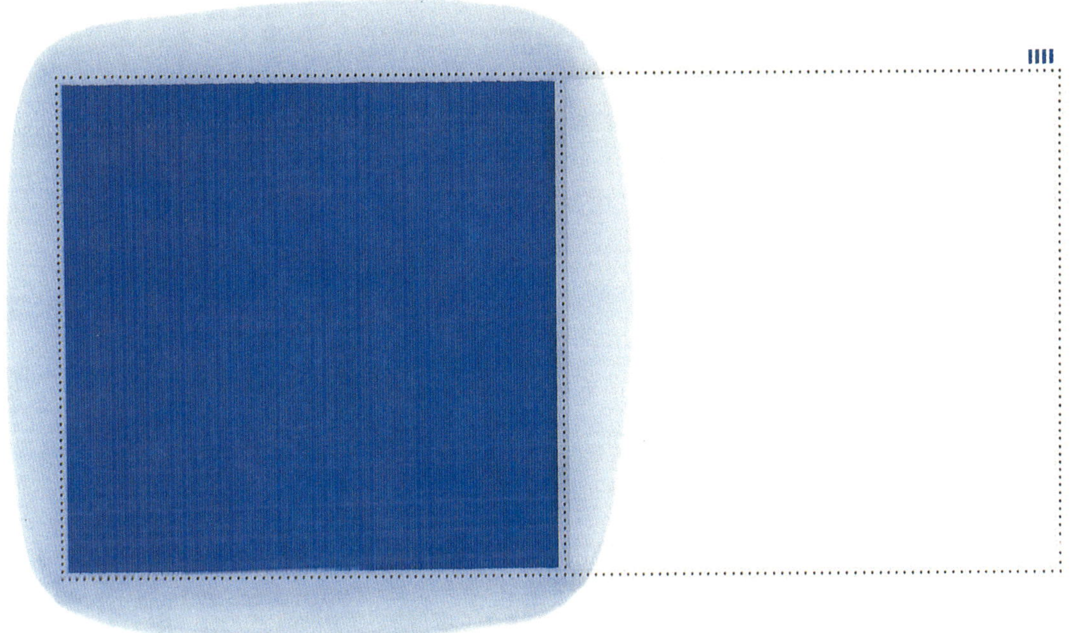

69. Tsubota Masahiko (b. 1947). Untitled but known as *Penetration-1,* 3/20, 1989, silkscreen and punch, 50.5x65.5 cm. Signed M. Tsubota.

TANAKA Ryohei

COMMENT: *Subject matter: the real and the spiritual Japan. One reason for large editions.*

Tanaka Ryohei (famous enough to sign his work simply Ryohei, his given name) has a knack of presenting a view of Japan that not only encompasses the realities of how one always wants it to remain but also the timeless serenity of each idyllic spot he chooses to portray. He insists that all of his etchings are of real places, and each invitingly beckons us to visit so that we can share the artist's pleasure. However, we fear that by the time we have located them, they might have been replaced by a housing development, a golf course, or, even worse, another McDonald's. That is an undeniable trend in today's fast-paced Japan.

The artist has been releasing his detailed etchings for more than thirty years, traveling in the countryside of western Japan where one can still find charming thatched farmhouses and peaceful country lanes. He works mostly in black and white, with an occasional appearance of a sepia or multicolored print. The appeal of his work is universal, probably because his own heartfelt pleasure and pride can be immediately sensed by the viewer.

Plate 70

Unlike Nakayama Tadashi, who has decided to make only a few prints each year and charge accordingly, Ryohei has opted to produce a large and varied annual selection in comparatively large editions (100 to 150, depending on size—the larger, the fewer), thereby keeping his prices low. This is certainly a boon for his collectors because it means his work is available virtually anytime to anyone who does not mind missing dinner out.

The most difficult aspect of the etching, aquatint, and drypoint techniques is the arduous task of making the detailed plate itself. Perhaps Ryohei feels that once this is accomplished the printing process is not so difficult, and that there is little point in making a small edition after the efforts that go into the plate. The metal plate is capable of withstanding the pressure, and an international audience is always clamoring for his work. Amassing Ryohei's engaging glimpses of the beauty of Japan suggests this variation on the slogan of a famous American potato-chip company—"Bet you can't have just one!" There are few collectors who have not repeatedly succumbed to a craving for yet another Ryohei treat, and not many who have had to do without their dinners, as they are so reasonably priced.

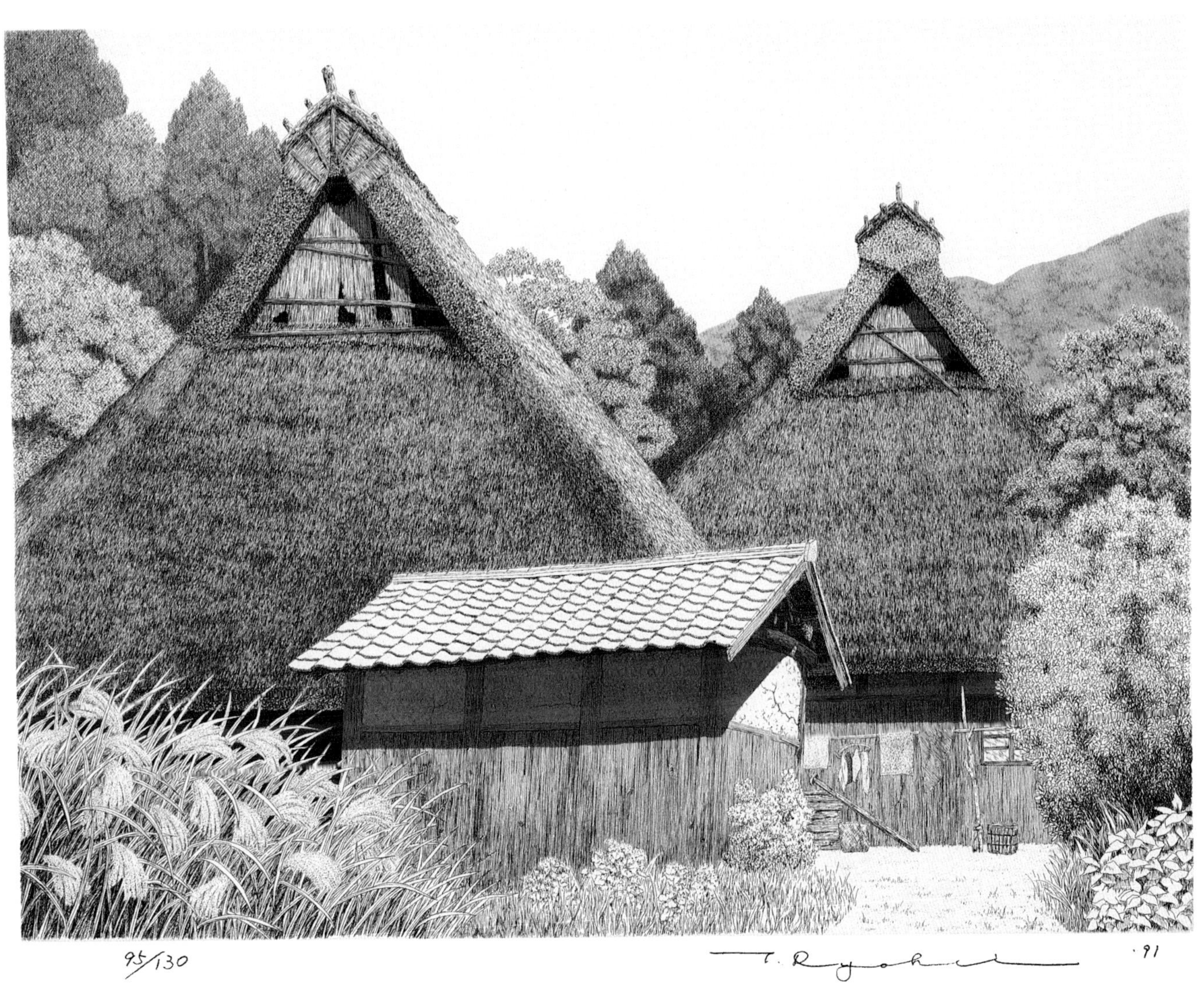

70. Tanaka Ryohei (b. 1933). Titled in Japanese *Arihara-no-aki* (Autumn in Arihara), 95/130, 1991, etching, 26.5x34.2 cm. Signed T. Ryohei.

SUGIURA Kazutoshi

COMMENT: *Age-old subjects and age-old techniques never lose their appeal.*

You can roam the world and be fairly certain of never meeting anyone who admits hating flowers. Sugiura Kazutoshi has been inspired by flowers for years, and he has an enthusiastic audience who appreciates every interpretation he makes of irises, peonies, roses, cosmos, camellias, chrysanthemums, or spider lilies. His beautiful silkscreens never need water, never droop, never lose their luster, and seem to exist simply to provide perpetual enjoyment. Although the artist depicts all of the flowers mentioned above, he is noted for his compositions of irises and has made more than one hundred different iris prints. *Plate 71*

Sugiura relies on traditional Japanese techniques to execute his works. He applies squares of gold leaf, in the same way old screens were made, onto handmade Japanese paper. His next step is to silkscreen his floral subjects onto the gold leaf. Next, blocking out the flowers, he uses a wash of pale shades of blue, purple, or green to cover the rest of the work, thereby toning down the glittering gold leaf and softening the effect. The result is visually relaxing, soothing even the most active A-type personality. The artist studied fine-art restoration at the Kyoto National Museum for four years, experience that has undoubtedly influenced his meticulously executed creations.

Sugiura, a full-time high school art teacher in Kyoto, makes his prints as the spirit moves him and his school schedule allows. His limited production insures that each eagerly anticipated work is a sellout, an example of the law of supply and demand at work. The prints are lovingly and skillfully made, and the traditional themes and method result in works highly prized by numerous collectors.

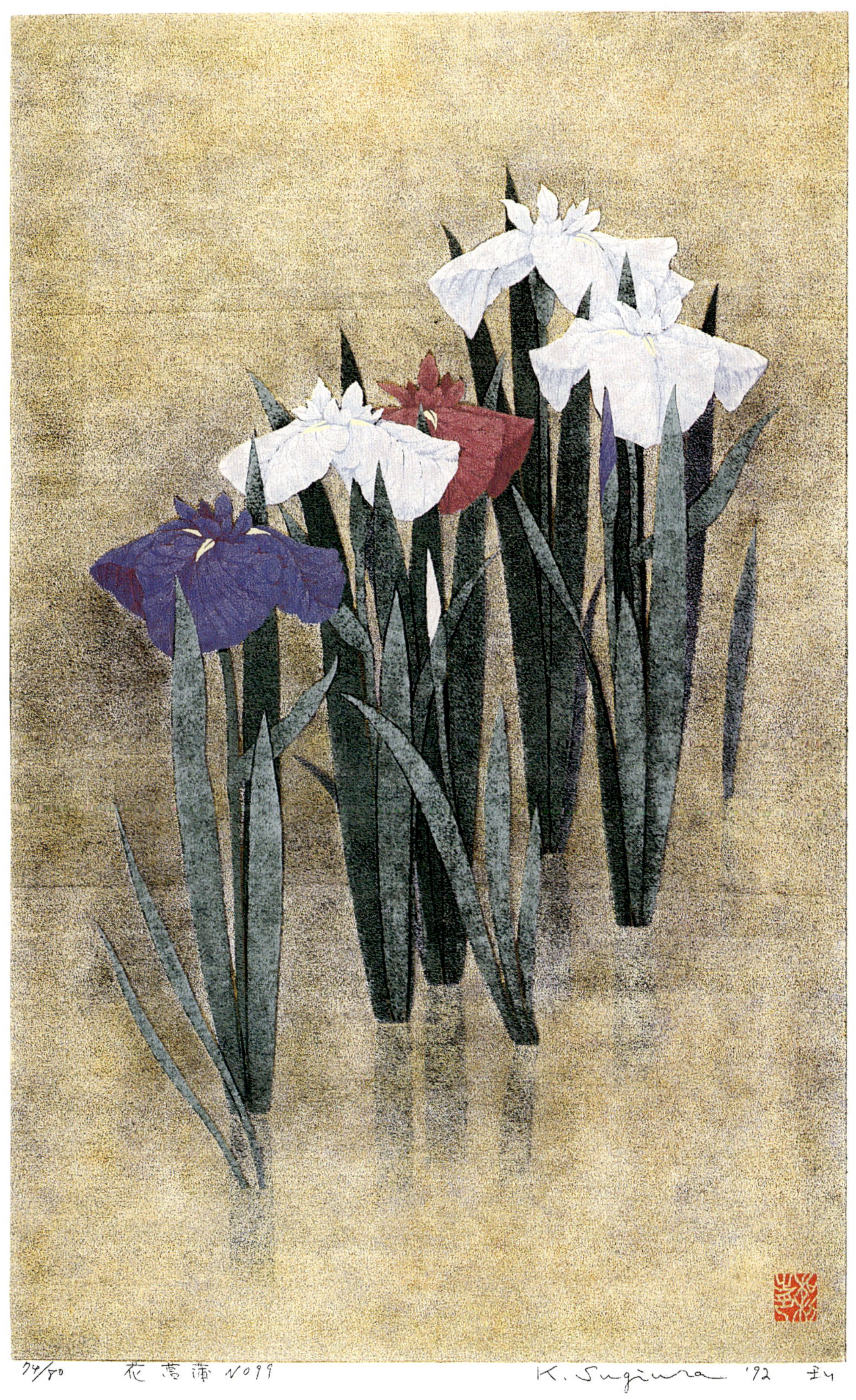

71. Sugiura Kazutoshi (b. 1938). Titled in Japanese *Hana-shōbu 99* (Iris No. 99), 74/80, 1992, silkscreen, 79x49.2 cm. Signed K. Sugiura, in kanji Kazu, sealed on the image in kanji Sugiura Kazutoshi.

HOSHI Joichi

COMMENT: *Becoming aware of irregularities in production and numbering.*

When we first began collecting Hoshi Joichi's woodblocks more than twenty years ago, he was being true to his name, which means star in Japanese. His fascination with the firmament resulted in prints of extraordinary vitality, explosive energy, and a reaching toward the boundless heavens that commanded the viewer's respect and reverence. His interest in the empyrean, with its connotations of pure and divine light, is exemplified in this 1970 print of a cathedral, *Morning Light*. This is the Hoshi we knew and loved.

Plate 72

Hoshi died in 1979 and today is best remembered as "the tree man." He was probably unaware of the poet Joyce Kilmer, who wrote, "Poems are made by fools like me, but only God can make a tree." However, Hoshi himself worked exclusively with the tree motif for many years, finding an appreciative audience that demanded more—and more—until finally the artist became leader of a "production team" with carvers, printers, and various assistants employed to turn out his work. This is an unusual practice for a woodblock print artist. We have found that most take great satisfaction in doing all of these processes themselves.

In any case, hordes of collectors were screaming for ever more trees, making it impossible for Hoshi to keep up with the demand. Now comes the worst part. Hoshi's normal edition was ninety-nine copies. First he made a gorgeous tree in red and gold. That sold out. But soon another edition of ninety-nine appeared, obviously printed from the same blocks, in blue and silver. That sold out. Hold on. Would you like it in green and bronze? Yet another edition with the same blocks. No one seemed to mind except us; as collectors and art dealers we were extremely disappointed to witness this practice. One of the factors in pricing prints is the size of the edition. What appeared in this case to be ninety-nine was, in fact, many more. In addition, the prints were astronomically priced (well, we did say that Hoshi was originally interested in the boundless heavens). But we must admit that we are in the minority who feel this way. Those who love Hoshi trees will pay whatever price is asked and either do not know or do not care about the particulars.

As if all that were not enough, after his death many of his works were released to the market, strangely inscribed "From the collection of the artist." We think this marks him as one of the largest collectors of his own work, and further, we wonder when these copies were actually produced and inscribed, and by whom. We enjoyed Hoshi most when he was reaching for the sky instead of plodding through the forest.

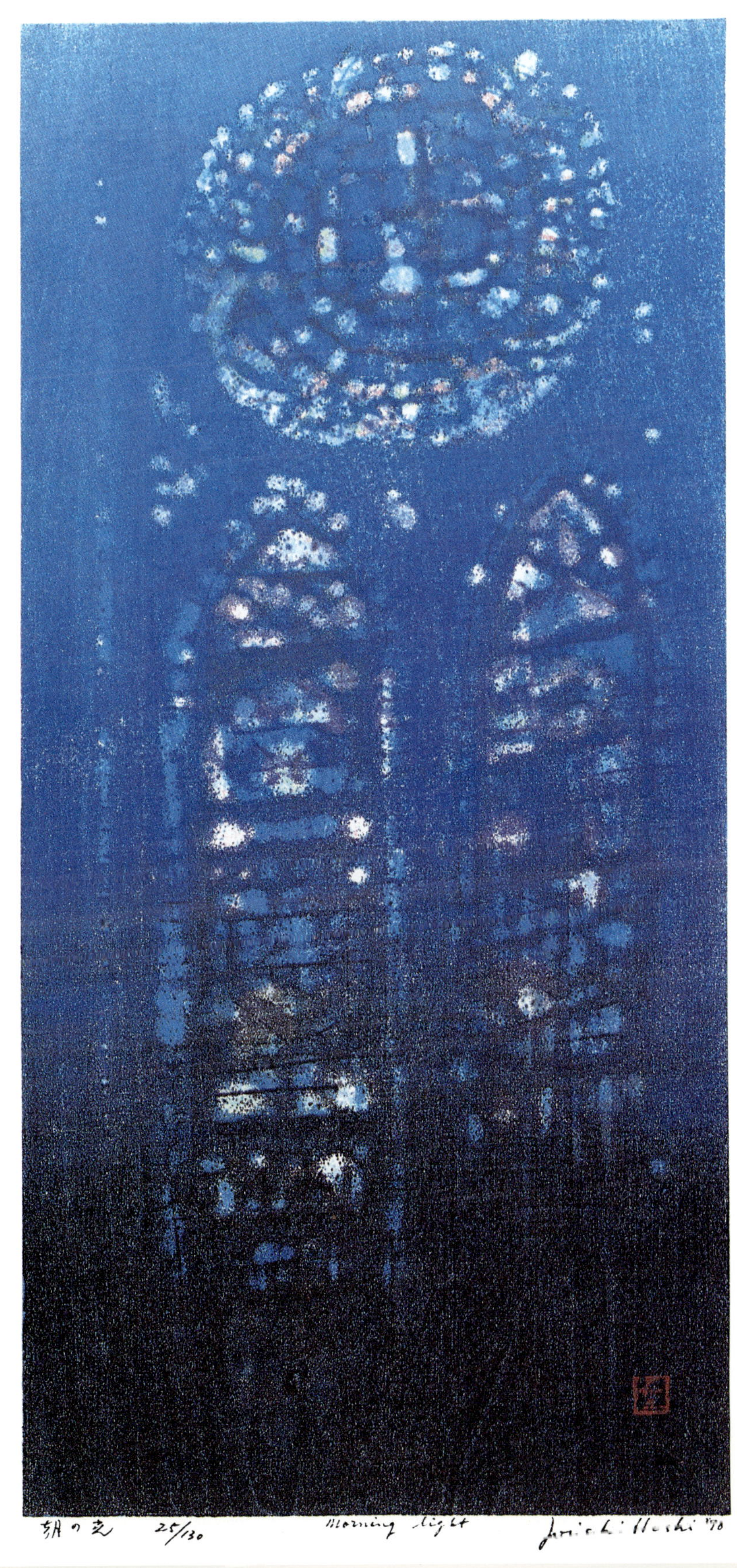

72. Hoshi Joichi (1913–79). Titled in Japanese *Asa-no-hikari,* titled in English *Morning Light,* 25/130, 1970, woodblock, 58x27.5 cm. Signed Joichi Hoshi, sealed with a logo of three trees and the earth on the image.

LIAO Shiou-ping

COMMENT: *Linking past and present.*

The ancient Chinese painting of five persimmons sublimely placed in space by the thirteenth-century artist Mu Ch'i immediately comes to mind when one contemplates Liao Shiou-ping's *Restful Time.* Liao too is Chinese, born in Taiwan and now an American citizen teaching at Seton Hall University in New Jersey. Before that, he studied and taught on three continents: at the renowned Atelier 17 in Paris, at the Pratt Graphics Center in New York, in his native Taiwan, and in Japan. He is included here as an "honorary" Japanese printmaker because of the substantial impact he has made on many young Japanese artists, even having been invited by the government to set up a printmaking workshop at Tsukuba University. Liao has exhibited widely here, and his themes and concepts of space link him to this part of the world. Although he is a master of Western printmaking techniques, often combining them in his works, his art is predicated on the Oriental philosophy of balance, of not ignoring either end of opposite poles, of utilizing both yin and yang to achieve symmetry and harmony.

Plate 73

During his stay in Japan from 1977 to 1979, Liao left his family behind in the U.S. He commented that when he returned to his lonely room at night, he took comfort in the simple things around him—a teapot and some cups, fruit, vegetables, a flower—that he unpretentiously began to incorporate as subjects in his prints. His work evokes a mood, sometimes one of nostalgia, always inviting reflection.

His prints often include a grid as the background, in unassuming tones of mauve, gray, or black. Though this can possibly be interpreted as a reference to the monotonous restrictions of our mechanized society, we think it also could be a subliminal influence from Liao's childhood. He has ten brothers, some of whom are architects and designers. In any case, this graphlike grid is the perfect spatial foil for the softly rounded shapes of the teapot and cups.

Whereas many artists strive for tension or dynamism, Liao deliberately intends the exact opposite. "In the rat race of life," he explains, "people get tired. I want them to sit down, look at my pictures, and relax." It is perhaps this quiet humanity in his work that is so appealing. Looking at this print one can easily imagine a few friends gathered for a quiet cup of tea.

As one of eleven sons he must have had to carve out his own space at an early date. Once, on a trip to Taiwan, we had reason to call him. When he gave me the number of his father's house he said, "When you phone, ask for Shiou-ping, not Mr. Liao. At that number <u>everybody</u> is Mr. Liao!"

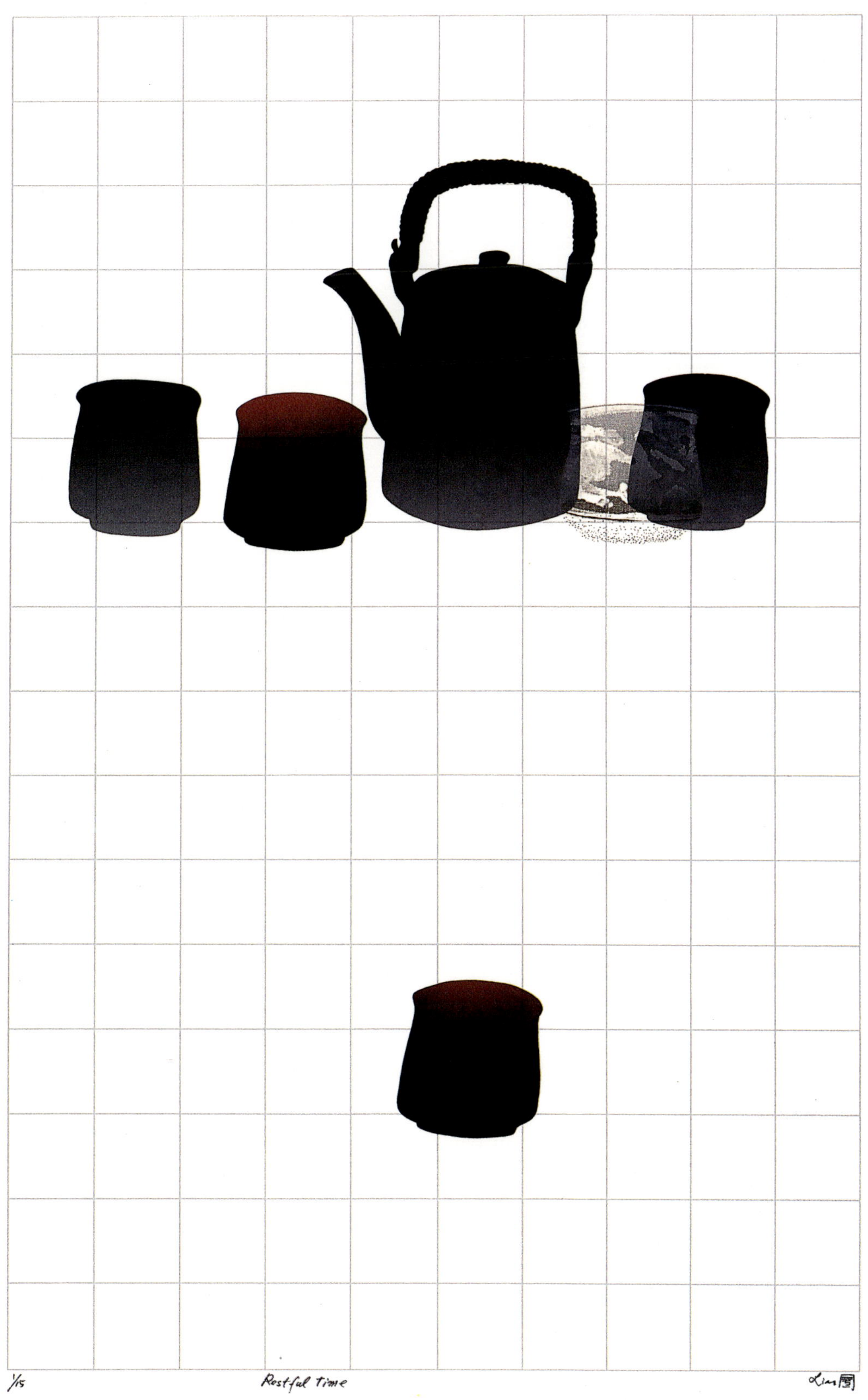

73. Liao Shiou-ping (b. 1936). *Restful Time,* 1/15, 1981, silkscreen/collagraph, 81x51 cm. Signed Liao, signed in kanji Liao.

ODA Mayumi

COMMENT: *Japanese prints are not normally a forum for social or political stands.*

Japanese print artists seldom air social or political comments through their work. Oda Mayumi is an exception, probably because although she was brought up in a traditional family in Japan, she has lived most of her adult life in the United States, where "causes" are the norm. Mayumi, as she always signs her work, has spent more than three decades in the United States, first on the east coast near Princeton, then after her divorce in a quiet spot just across San Francisco's Golden Gate Bridge near the Green Gulch Zen Center.

Mayumi is a devout Buddhist, a fact that is central to an understanding of her work. In addition, she has lived in the U.S. during the entire period of the feminist movement, and her theme over the years has been the celebration of Woman. Much of her work has been an interpretation of gods from the Buddhist pantheon, which she has transformed into seminude, voluptuous, earthy, life-enhancing goddesses full of color, beauty, *joie de vivre,* and power. Pixie-like Mayumi says she adores drawing plump, curvaceous women because she is so petite herself, and she wants to evoke the strength inherent in women. Her prints are characterized by their verve, simplicity, and bold color but most especially by their playful sense of fun. She has often been compared to Matisse because of her particular use of color and line.

"All women are goddesses," Mayumi says. "But each woman must discover this innate potential." She does not consider herself a feminist but simply wants to project the nurturing vitality of the female. Her lively nature and positive attitude are apparent in all her work. One of her exhibitions that we were happy to have attended was a show of Buddhist goddesses created as forty-foot-long banners at the Cathedral of St. John the Divine in New York City. If a particular Buddhist deity does not exist, Mayumi creates one. *Snow Goddess* is one of our favorite prints, a typical product of Mayumi's urge to be innovative, yet it still uses the age-old Japanese image of snow on pine branches and the traditional *seikaiha* pattern of waves in the sea as a setting for the imaginary goddess.

Plate 74

Up until now Mayumi has been a quiet activist, portraying women as creating and enjoying life. Recently, however, she has taken on a new interest, one of which she is an outspoken adherent—the banning of plutonium because of its threat to human life. Despite having lived in the U.S. for a long time, she has maintained strong ties with her mother country. Last year Japan began shipping plutonium from France for use in a nuclear reactor as an energy source, an action Mayumi strongly opposes. In our own effort to help her cause, we arranged for her to speak at the Foreign Correspondents' Club in Tokyo. The reaction to her plea was rewarding. One result was a ten-page story in the Japanese edition of *Newsweek,* excellent coverage and proof that one person with a belief can make a difference. Mayumi mentioned in her speech that the most recent Japanese nuclear reactor has been named Monju, the Japanese word for the Bodhisattva of Wisdom. She plaintively asked if we could imagine that.

Recently she has been making prints for the causes she is interested in, specifically the environment. She believes in a happy and simple life, grows all her own vegetables, and is close to Mother Earth in all of her endeavors. Although her work is likened to that of Matisse, her fabulous vegetable and flower garden makes one think instead of the luxuriance of Monet's garden at Giverny.

Both Allison and Hilary, our daughters, feel that their lives have been enriched by Mayumi. She has stayed with them in New York and Paris, they enjoy hanging her work, and admire her activities as a person. As dealers who have devoted a significant portion of life to prints and the people who make them, we are especially pleased when our admiration is carried on in the next generation.

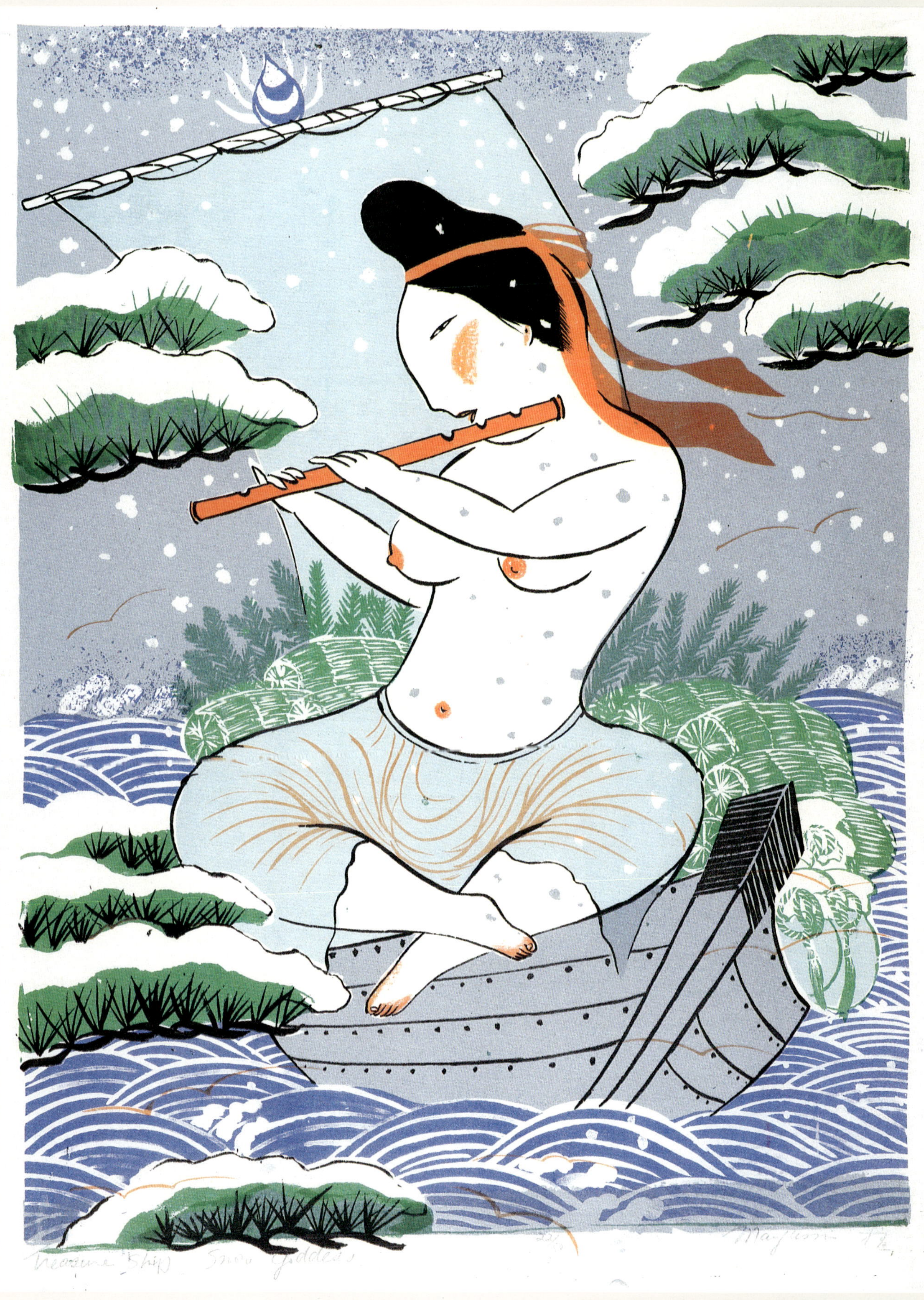

74. Oda Mayumi (b. 1941). *Snow Goddess,* from the *Treasure Ship* series, 22/50, 1976, silkscreen, 77.5x57 cm. Signed Mayumi, signed in kanji Mayumi.

MATSUBARA Naoko

COMMENT: *Living abroad can affect an artist's fame.*

Those who know the proverb "A prophet is a stranger in his own land" should not be surprised to hear that some Japanese artists have earned their initial fame abroad and only later gained it at home. This list includes such stars as Ay-O, Ikeda Masuo, and Shinoda Toko, all of whom became known in the United States before achieving even greater recognition and prominent positions in the art world here. And on the other side of the coin one can find Clifton Karhu, who is extremely well known in Japan and less so in the U.S., where he was born.

In this same vein, Matsubara Naoko's name and artistic reputation are more widespread abroad than in Japan. Brought up in the ancient capital of Kyoto amid the precincts of a Shinto shrine—her father was head priest of the Kenkun shrine and her mother of samurai lineage—Naoko left Japan after college, accepting a Fulbright assistantship at Carnegie-Mellon University. Later she traveled in Asia and Europe, studied at the Royal Academy in London for a year, taught printmaking at the Pratt Graphics Center under the wing of Fritz Eichenberg, and lived in Boston for several years. Her earliest teacher at the Kyoto Municipal College of Fine Arts was Frau Professor Lizzi Ueno, who encouraged her students to be independent, suggesting that instead of pasting their drawing on the block and carving in the usual manner, they should attack the block directly, hand and heart in tandem, a technique Naoko still uses today.

It is perhaps because of her early training, the influence of foreign teachers, and her extensive world travel that Naoko was moved to remark that she does not want to be known as a Japanese artist, just as an artist. She has even gone so far as to adopt Western methods of woodblock printing, using oil-based inks and a roller press, in contrast to the traditional Japanese style that features water-based inks and the interesting patterns created on the paper by the personal touch of the artist rubbing its reverse with his *baren*. However, to adapt a well-known adage—"You can take the girl out of Japan but you can't take Japan out of the girl"—she proceeded to create illustrations for a book called *Kyoto Woodcuts,* all of which she did completely from memory, she said proudly.

Naoko was imbued with the spirit of ancient Japan by her parents, and from them she has also received the sustaining legacy of an appreciation and reverence for nature and the will to persevere. No matter what subject Naoko chooses to portray—an Arctic sky, a Tibetan monastery, or a Korean dancer—all exude a dynamism and vitality peculiar to Shinto philosophy.

As befits the daughter of a Shinto family, Naoko is much concerned with nature and the spirit inherent in every tree, rock, or brook. In *Edge of Summer Lake* the location of the lake is not important. It is the artist's imagination and feeling that move us. Her work is not based on intellect and reason, as is much art in the West, but on a deep emotional response to what she sees, a response that is very Japanese.

Plate 75

For more than two decades Naoko has lived in Canada, where her husband teaches at the University of Toronto. The years of living abroad have provided an international perspective and reputation but have also reinforced certain aspects of the artist's inherited tradition.

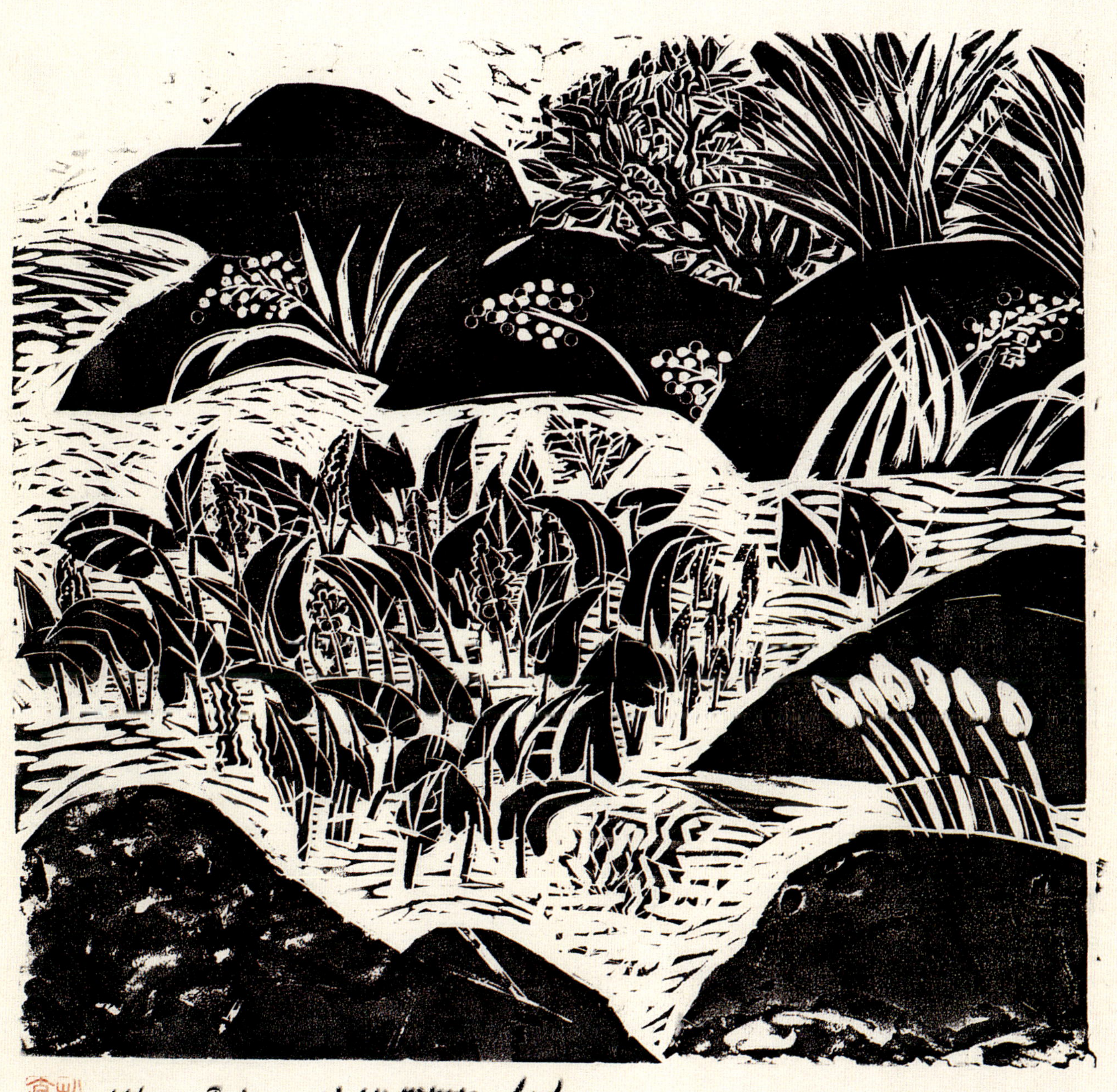

75. Matsubara Naoko (b. 1937). *Edge of Summer Lake,* 19/25, 1981, woodblock, 38x39.8 cm. Signed Matsubara, sealed in kanji Matsubara Naoko. Published by the Tolman Collection, Tokyo.

HIRATSUKA Un'ichi

COMMENT: *Do not give up the search for an "unavailable" print you want.*

Once the main body of a collection is formed, a collector may find that there are certain prints he needs to add. They may be prints he has seen reproduced only in a book or catalogue of long-past exhibitions, but there is something that makes an apparently unavailable work cause a great desire for possession in the heart of a true collector. In our gallery we are constantly besieged by people looking for prints that have long since been sold out. Even though we have the names and addresses of the purchasers, tracking them down and trying to convince them to resell is a difficult and generally fruitless task.

Even more laborious is locating a work from the early days of the *sōsaku-hanga* movement. *Rakan Temple in the Rain* was just such a print. I had seen it first in Oliver Statler's book *Modern Japanese Prints: An Art Reborn,* and then it kept popping up in various old exhibition catalogues. My quest was further complicated because I did not know how many copies had been printed, and in those days an edition of very few was the norm. Hiratsuka Un'ichi, one of the dedicated founders of the creative-print movement, was a devoted teacher and guiding light to many of the most admired artists in the history of woodblock prints. But more than that, he himself was a prolific artist, whose works number in the thousands. His compositions are well known, as they should be for an artist who has been active for eighty years. The trouble in tracking down his work, however, stemmed from the fact that he has lived and worked in Washington, D.C., for the past thirty years; in addition, the print I so desperately wanted was made in 1935, when artists were not particularly concerned with numbering their works. I also knew that at 99 Hiratsuka might not remember where the copies he printed had actually gone, so I almost gave up hope of ever seeing and perhaps owning this work.

Plate 76

In June 1990 I attended an auction of the collection of Roy Cole, whose holdings had been acquired with the help of Oliver Statler. When Statler was forming his own collection, around which he based his book, he had bought two copies of the prints in which he was interested, including *Rakan Temple.* In my successful bid for another print, I was lucky in finding a copy of this precious Hiratsuka work included in the "lot." The dedicated collector must persevere.

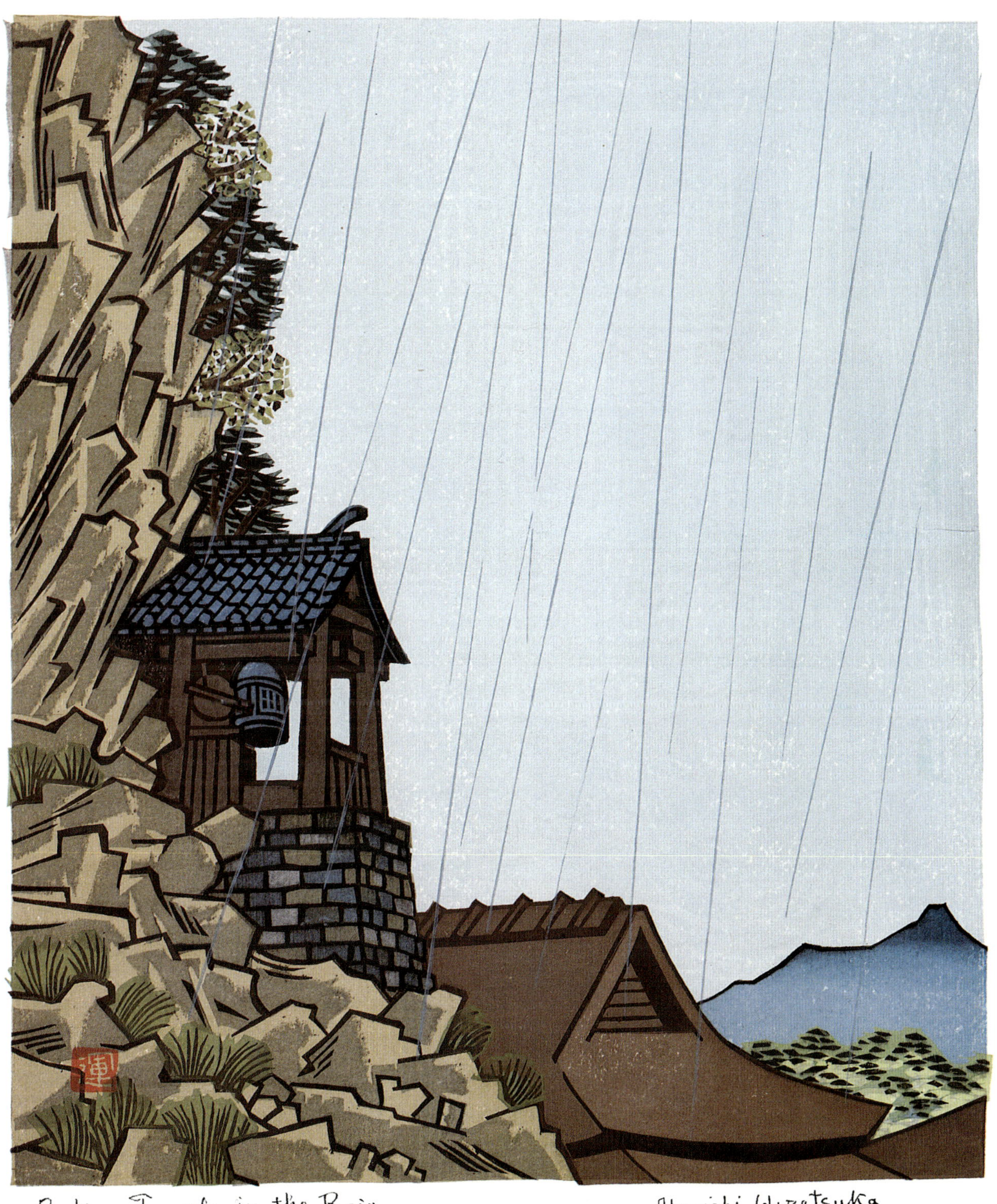

76. Hiratsuka Un'ichi (b. 1895). Titled along the right margin in Japanese *Ame-no-Rakanji* (Rakan Temple in the Rain), unnumbered, 1935, woodblock, 34.6x29.2 cm. Printed in kanji Hiratsuka Un'ichi, signed Un-ichi Hiratsuka, sealed on the lower left in kanji Un.

YAYANAGI Go

(*a k a* YAYANAGI Tsuyoshi)

COMMENT: *Unlocking the imagery.*

Looking at the brilliant colors and rich imagery in the prints of Yayanagi Go (or Tsuyoshi, as he sometimes calls himself), one might find it hard to believe that the artist comes from Japan, where restraint is allegedly a key word. Furthermore, the artist comes from cold Hokkaido, the northernmost island of Japan, considered the "boonies" by sophisticates from the capital. Yayanagi even studied pharmacology and graduated from agricultural college. So where do all these hot-colored, visually exciting prints come from?

Yayanagi has always loved art, but his travels in Central and South America and Africa from 1957 to 1959 obviously made a great impact. The intense tropical colors, the exotic flora and fauna, the voluptuous bodies—all made a lasting impression on the boy from the far north. Later he lived with his family in Paris for three years, studying at Atelier 17. There he achieved his excellence of technique and acquired the ability to put down on paper all those vivid concepts that were whirling around in his adventurous mind.

Once we hold the key to Yayanagi's past, we can understand what he is conveying in his work *The Island That Became a Bird*. There are his trademark black-and-white stripes relieving the intensities of color, his sensuous female forms, an unusual butterfly, the beautifully shaded blue sea, and—could it be?—yes, there are the shapes of Africa and South America, both clearly delineated and set off by two exotic birds. Very simple if you know the artist's work.

Plate 77

Japanese have a reputation for being conformists, but one look at a Yayanagi work makes one reconsider this idea. His international experiences have obviously added a great deal to his original open and warm Hokkaido personality and are the key to figuring out what this artist is hoping to communicate.

Yayanagi believes art should permeate life, and at the moment his colorful murals are in great demand with schools, corporations, and museums. In recent years he has designed fabric for clothing and furniture, and even in a crowd one can usually spot him, goateed and wearing his elegant tinted glasses and a Yayanagi shirt or cravat. His entire world is filled with color, excitement, and humor.

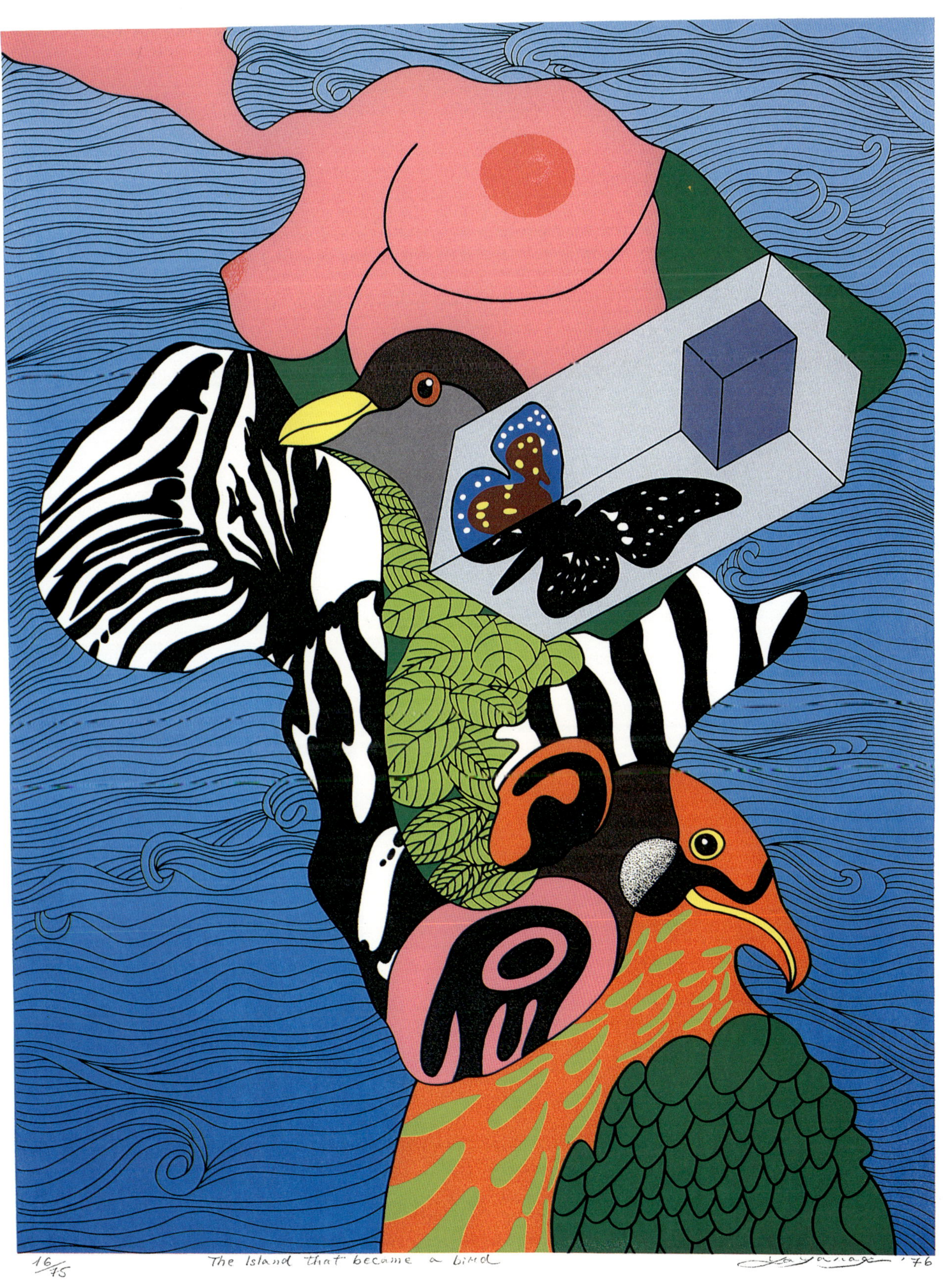

77. Yayanagi Go (b. 1933). *The Island That Became a Bird,* 16/75, 1976, silkscreen, 60x45 cm. Signed Yayanagi. Published by the Tolman Collection, Tokyo.

MIZUFUNE Rokushu

COMMENT: *Availability of prints: the collector should strike while the iron is hot.*

When we first started to collect, a vast mountain of desirable prints by a seemingly infinite number of talented printmakers seemed to be available. We knew that the artists we enjoyed were producing regularly and abundantly for each and every exhibition, so it was easy for us to fall into a state of "wait and see, we'll get it later."

Price was always a factor in those beginning days, but no matter how reasonable a work seemed to be, we had to make decisions. Because of the great availability we felt we had plenty of time. We could buy only a certain number of prints, and some artists would simply have to wait. That we still have virtually every print that we bought for our personal collection, even after twenty years as dealers, seems to attest to the amount of love and the determined selection that went into the collection's formation.

During those times, when so many works were available, it never occurred to us that there would come a time when we might go looking for a print and it would not be there. I suppose we were—then—as so many of our clients are—now—of the opinion that when we saw a print in an edition of thirty, the other twenty-nine copies were lurking somewhere waiting to be purchased. We found out the hard way that this is not always the case with Japanese prints.

Mizufune Rokushu was best known in Japan as a sculptor, but he was simultaneously a recognized and well-collected woodblock print artist. In his student days he had studied privately with the great Hiratsuka, and his involvement with prints was a long and distinguished one. He served on several organizing groups during the early days of the creative-print movement and, in fact, is known as the founder of the *Shin-hanga shūdan* (New Print Group).

Like many other artists Mizufune worked as a teacher to earn his living and eventually became a school principal. This man, so busy in so many fields, adopted a very relaxed attitude in pulling his prints, making only a few at a time in any one edition. It seemed that his ideas about numbering and dating prints were equally unstructured. Of course, we did not know all this then. His work was widely appreciated, we liked it all, but somehow it always seemed to fall into our "often a bridesmaid, never a bride" category.

We got to know Mizufune many years ago when he served as a judge of the College Women's Association of Japan Print Show with James Michener and Norman. We enjoyed his company and consequently became even more interested in his work. Just when we were thinking that we should buy one of his works, he passed away very suddenly. We had liked almost everything he produced, but apparently not enough to take a stand and make a purchase. Suddenly there was nothing—nothing to look at, nothing to choose from, nothing to buy at all. The few copies of works available after his death had been immediately snapped up, and we can still remember our disappointment. We later learned that he had printed only a few copies of many editions, but now, without Mizufune, they would never be printed to their full extent.

Plate 78

One day we came across this print, typical of his well-organized structure, brilliant colors, and inviting texture. Also, it was a fish, a motif he quite often used. The print was not our favorite Mizufune work but we grabbed it—because there were no others. It was outrageously priced, when one considered what his prints had usually commanded, but there it was, take it or leave it. We took it, and since then we have been more vigilant and less procrastinating in buying prints that we really liked on first sighting.

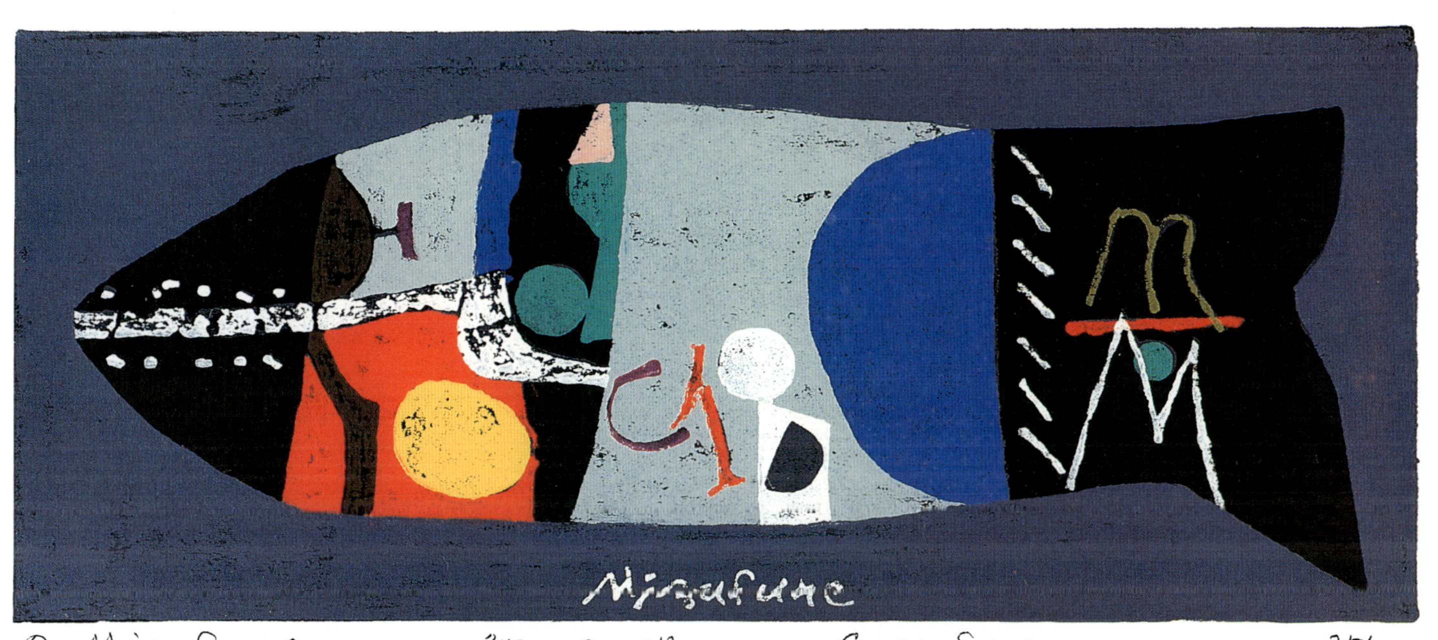

78. Mizufune Rokushu (1912–80). Titled in Japanese *Koi-no-uta* (Song of the Carp), 25/30, undated (probably 1975), woodblock, 13x31.2 cm. Signed R. Mizufune, signed on the image in white ink Mizufune.

SHINODA Toko

COMMENT: *Some prints are "must haves" that belong in every collection.*

A calligrapher, painter, and printmaker, Shinoda Toko is an artist whose work is found in famous public and private collections of Japanese art the world over. In Japan, her largest work, a twenty-eight-meter-long mural, is housed in the six-hundred-year-old Zojoji temple; her most famous painting graces a dining room in the new Imperial Palace. On a more accessible level, Tokyoites can enjoy her large painting on gold at the Tokyo American Club or her imposing two-panel screen in the dining room of the Foreign Correspondents' Club. Various hotels and corporations have her compositions as the center of their decor. All of these are original works and, as such, are much more expensive than prints, whose prices are lower because they are produced in multiple copies.

Shinoda's paintings are admired by everyone who appreciates her straightforward, powerful brush strokes. She is so well known and prized that her prints too have reached a great stage of desirability. Everyone wants a Shinoda, and those who cannot afford an original are delighted to know they can have one of her hand-pulled lithographs, made in very small editions.

Plate 79

Ascend is a typical example of the artist's signature work—simple, direct, and energetic. She usually adds by hand a touch of color to each print, here accents of red and silver, thereby making each buyer feel that he has a special Shinoda because no two of the hand-added strokes are exactly the same. Her work is collected widely, and because it is so universally esteemed one feels it must be part of any serious collection.

Knowing that worldwide attention up to now had been focused on Shinoda's impressive paintings, we were concerned that her accomplishments in the lithographic field might go unnoticed. For that reason we wrote *Toko Shinoda: A New Appreciation* as a tribute to the artist on the occasion of her eightieth birthday. Those wanting detailed information on Shinoda's life and her lithographic prints should consult that book.

Knowledgeable viewers often comment that Shinoda's work at first glance looks so simple that only a genius could do it. It certainly is true that she has devoted her life to perfecting her art, but not to the exclusion of everything else. Her interests are broad, and her vivacity and charm endear her to everyone, especially young people, who seem to feel no generation gap when speaking with her. When our daughter Allison would come to Tokyo from Yale on school vacations, dropping in for a chat with Shinoda was a must. Taka, our younger employee, is continually amazed at the range of subjects she is conversant with, and his five-year-old son, Kazuki, who enjoys visiting her too, has told us, "There's really no one like Toko-san, is there."

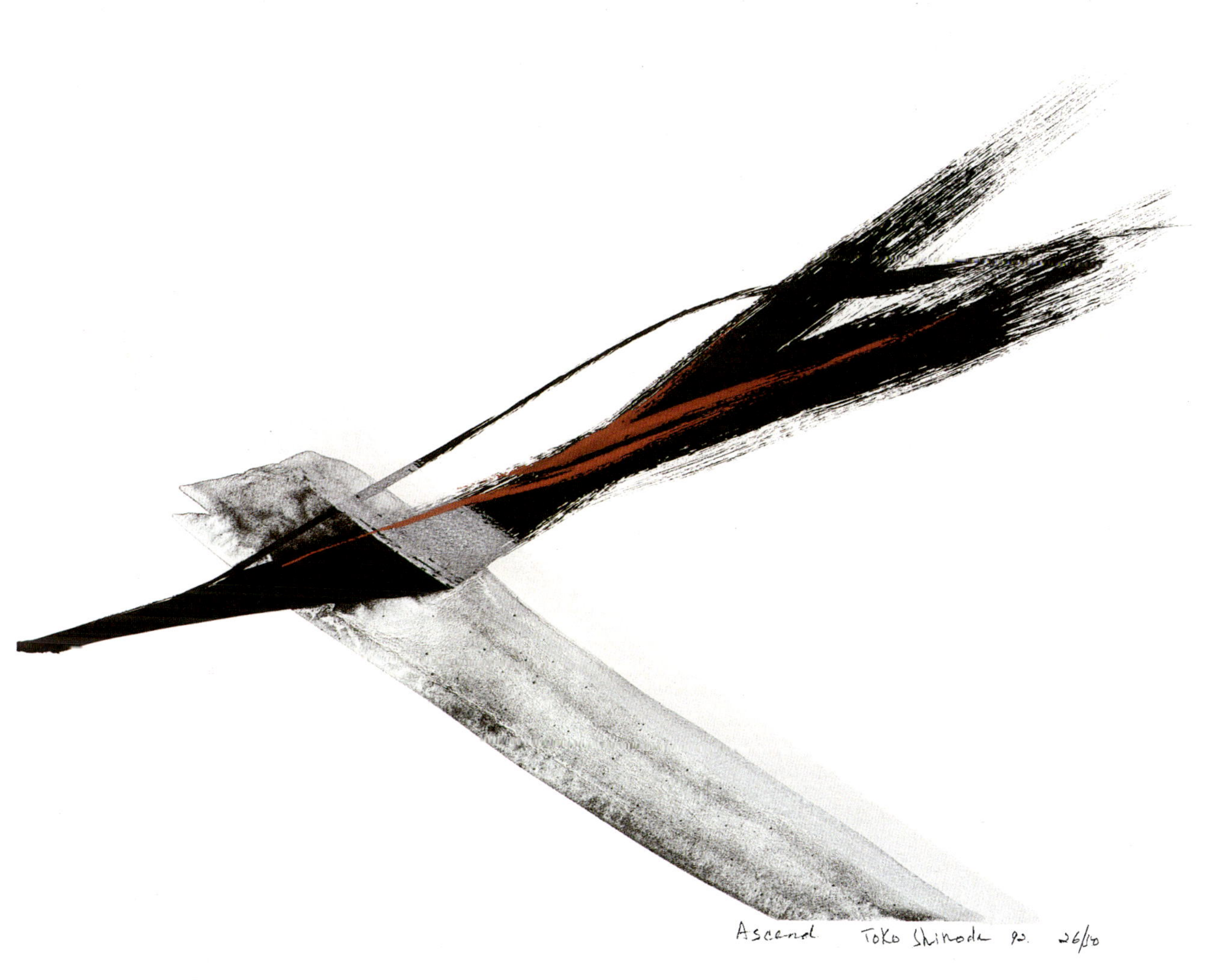

79. Shinoda Toko (b. 1913). *Ascend,* 26/50, 1992 (one of the few dated Shinoda prints), lithograph with hand-added color, 45.5x63.4 cm. Signed Toko Shinoda. Published by the Tolman Collection, Tokyo.

SUGAI Kumi

COMMENT: *Patience, though its own reward, can be costly.*

For years we have admired the work of Sugai Kumi. His delicate colors and lyrical shapes were appealing, and when he moved on to brighter and harder-edged works, we found them irresistible too. Unfortunately Sugai moved to Paris in 1952, so his prints did not surface in Japan very often. Occasionally we would see one in a catalogue and yearn all over again.

Each time we actually found a work we desired, it seemed beyond our financial reach. Sugai had gathered so much worldwide renown that he could command the prices of an internationally famous artist. Whatever he made sold out before we could bear to part with that much money.

Sugai was no longer in Tokyo but he seemed to be everywhere else, winning prizes at all the important biennials, at Ljubljana, Tokyo, Grenchen, São Paulo, Krakow. He seemed to be bobbing in and out of every catalogue or magazine we picked up, and we could not get him out of our minds. Rarity and unavailability undoubtedly spur interest in the print collector's possessive and never-still breast. Part of a collector's psyche seems to desire that which is not easily obtainable.

Last year we received an invitation to a showing of prints that had enjoyed special popularity in the 1950s. Included was Sugai's etching, title and date of publication unknown but clearly numbered 5/7. The print was rare enough all right, and more importantly, it was available. I bought it immediately at a horrendous price. But at least one more itch had been scratched.

Plate 80

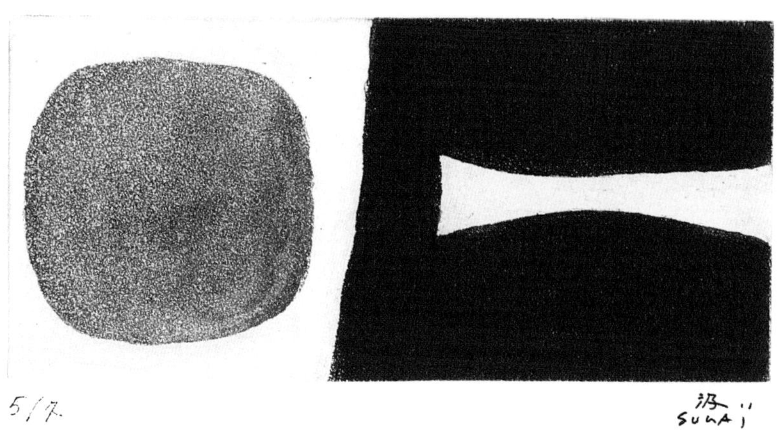

80. Sugai Kumi (b. 1919). Untitled, 5/7, undated, etching, 8.5x17.8 cm. Signed Sugai, signed in kanji Kumi.

NODA Tetsuya

COMMENT: *Collectors, to thine own self be true.*

Noda Tetsuya is a professor at the prestigious Tokyo University of Fine Arts, a respected teacher, and an artist of international repute who has shown his work in important exhibitions from Israel to Sapporo, where I first met him when I worked there during my diplomatic life. My official duties as director of the American Cultural Center called for me to be involved with the art scene, and in that capacity I attended an exhibition of the works of Yayanagi Go, Ay-O, and Noda that was sponsored by *Bijutsu Techō* (Art Notes), Japan's leading art magazine. As exhibitions of such sophisticated art were rare in remote Hokkaido, I was not surprised when Yayanagi later called on me, urging me to buy something at the show to help boost the sagging sales. It was at that exhibition that I was first introduced personally to Ay-O and Noda. I well remember having limited funds but eventually decided to buy one of Ay-O's colorful silkscreens. I was teased by Noda's then girl friend (now wife), who had accompanied the artists from Tokyo, for not buying one of Noda's works too but I had to admit to myself, if not to her, that my budget had already been stretched to its limits.

In later years, with less stringent financial restrictions, many times as I was just on the verge of deciding which Noda to add to our collection, I would invariably happen on the Nodas at some function in the very active social life of Tokyo. (Mrs. Noda is the daughter of a former Israeli ambassador to Japan). At these times I was always alert, knowing that I would be gently nudged by her, unfailingly being asked, "Have you bought some of my husband's work yet?" Although I could accept that she, as his greatest fan, wanted to see his prints placed in all the right collections, somehow she spoiled my motivation. It was my idea that I should decide what to include in our collection. Perhaps it was only a case of ego, but even now I find our own clients do not particularly enjoy being overadvised about which direction their collection should take. We always remind them that proper etiquette requires people to listen to advice, but common sense tells us that we do not always have to take it. Every collector must follow the dictates of his own heart.

Since it would be unthinkable to omit Noda's unique work in a book about the most talented Japanese printmakers of these times, *Diary April 1st, '88, Nashville* was acquired especially for this book, the only work to come into our collection for this express purpose. Noda's work is part of a continuum, a selected graphic diary of happenings in his life that he wishes to remember for his own reasons. The titles of the works are the dates on which the events happened. His technique, executing photography-based images in the silkscreen technique onto a woodblocked background, is his own.

Plate 81

Shortly after I purchased this print, chosen especially for its date to tease Mrs. Noda, we met the artist and his wife at a black-tie dinner at the U.S. embassy, a sayonara party for our cultural attaché. I found to my pleasure that I was seated between H.I.H. Princess Takamado and Mrs. Noda. Deciding to tell the story during dinner, I gained Mrs. Noda's amused permission to relate this incident of a stubborn collector who knows his own mind. I advise all collectors to know theirs too.

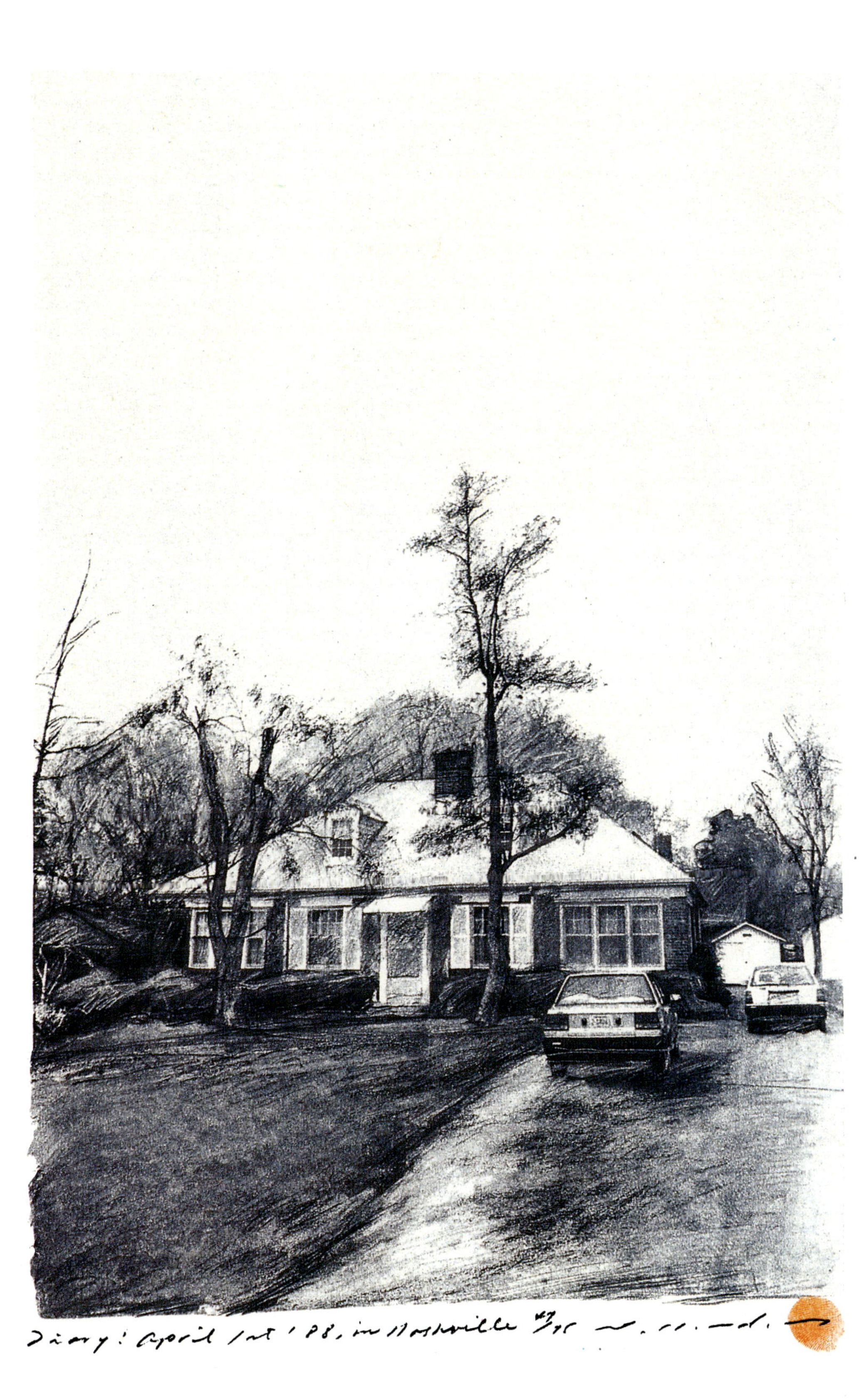

81. Noda Tetsuya (b. 1940). *Diary: April 1st '88, in Nashville,* 47/75, 1988, woodblock/silkscreen, 35x23 cm. Signed T. Noda, sealed with a fingerprint in red ink.

NISHIZAWA Shizuo

COMMENT: *Prints become known in various ways.*

When we first started collecting, we tried to gather information about the artists whose prints struck our fancy. As we could not afford to buy everything we wanted, we needed at least some visual reference of the subject matter that the artist usually created. We soon found that most published information included at least one picture of the artist's work. If the same image appeared in several places, we noticed that we became emotionally involved with that particular work more than with others by the same artist because we had seen it often and had come to know it. In addition, we may have subconsciously felt that this print must have been better than the others, or the artist, or whoever decided such things, would not have used it as a representative sample.

Now, as publishers of more than nine hundred print editions, when we release new prints for publication, we give much thought to which work to select as an advertisement for the show. We realize from our own experience that this is the print people will use as the ultimate example of that particular artist's work. The choice is difficult. Needless to say, we think all of the artist's works we have chosen are excellent, or we would not have selected them. But the fact remains that people tend to remember what they have seen in a newspaper or magazine, and so it is often the case that that particular work becomes more popular than others.

Plate 82

Nishizawa Shizuo's print appeared in full color on the cover of the catalogue of the 1983 College Women's Association of Japan Print Show. We had not paid attention to this artist before, but as dedicated collectors we quickly noted that the work was in an edition of only thirty and that it was a combination of silkscreen and aquatint, a difficult technique. Even though the print was priced much higher than most of the others in the show, in fact, the third most expensive of 217 offerings, we realized that it would become widely known because it had been featured on the catalogue cover.

There is an enormous audience for this annual charity exhibition so we knew we did not have time for reflection and bought Nishizawa's print on our first viewing. This did not mean that it was then among our favorite prints, although over the years we have come to admire its achievements greatly. Nishizawa has been depicting the puppets of the Bunraku theater for thirty-five years. Their lavish and colorful costumes and poignant expressions inspire him to reach for ranges and tones of color that would seem almost impossible to capture on paper. In any case, part of the appeal of this admirable work was that we knew it would become famous because of the wide dissemination of the catalogue. That is one of the ways collectors think.

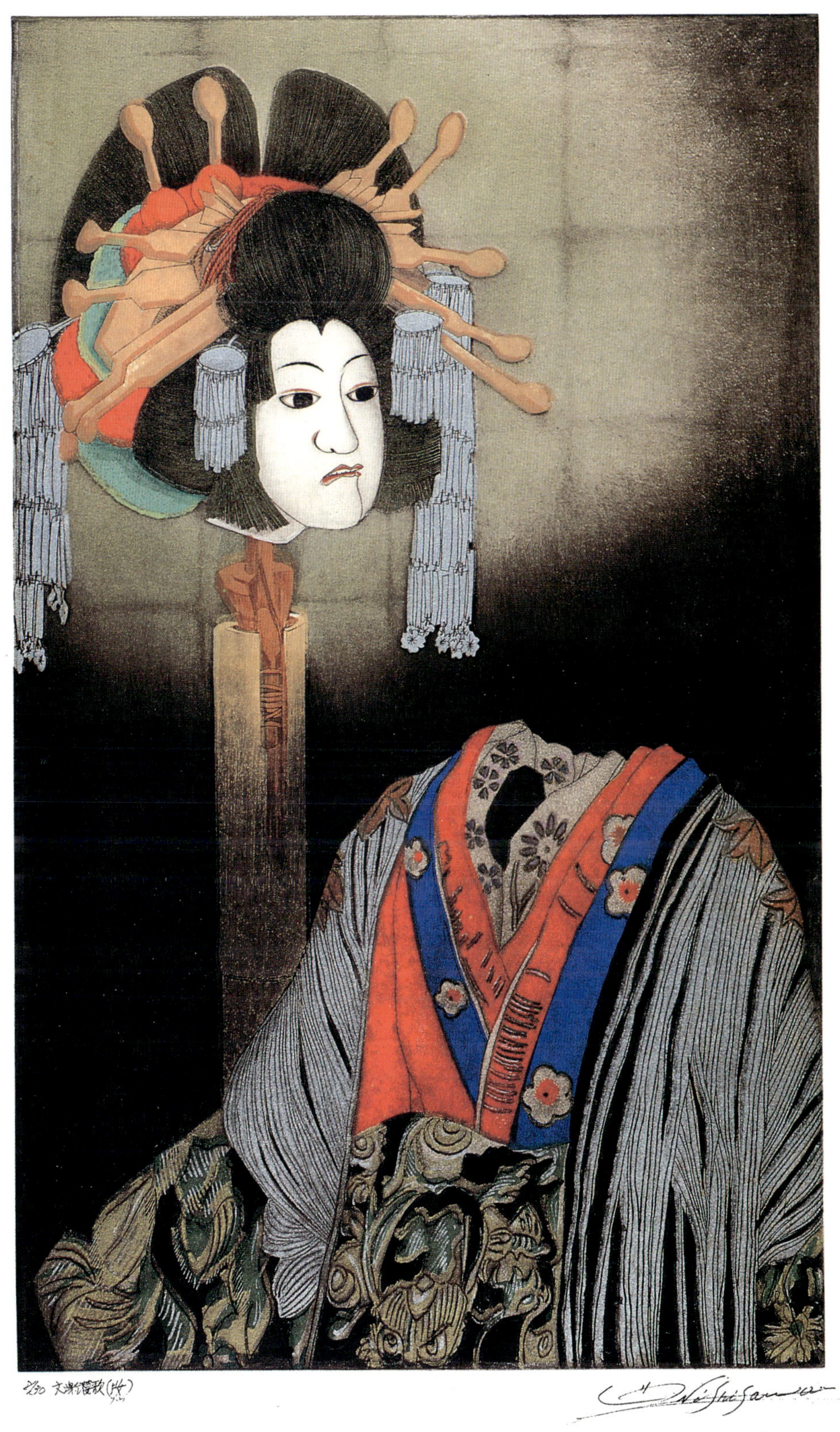

82. Nishizawa Shizuo (b. 1912). Titled in Japanese *Bunraku Sanka (Sou)* (under the kanji for *sou,* written in *katakana sou),* (Praising Bunraku [Pedestal]), 8/30, 1983, silkscreen/aquatint, 59.3x35.5 cm. Signed S. Nishizawa.

IMAMURA Yoshio

COMMENT: *Discovering new artists at the Japan Print Association show.*

One of the thrills of being an art dealer is being the first to recognize talent and to act on that conviction. One year when we attended the Nihon Hanga Kyokai (Japanese Print Association) annual show at the Tokyo Metropolitan Museum in Ueno, we had the pleasure not only of discovering a new artist whose work we felt would be an important addition to our gallery, but also the good luck in locating him and committing him to a one-man show. (The following year he was given a first prize at this same exhibition, and we came away with a certain feeling of self-satisfaction in knowing that we had spotted his genius first.) The above-mentioned exhibition occurs concurrently with the spectacular show of cherry blossoms in Ueno Park, awash with fluttering pink petals and revelers of every description and nationality. However, our determined gallery staff is always single-mindedly bent on being the first group through the exhibition when it opens at 9 A.M., and we save the blossoms for later.

In the early days of the print movement, especially the 1930s, the Nihon Hanga Kyokai provided an aegis for the strong-minded new makers of creative prints. The association is still thriving, but not all Japanese print artists belong to it. There are some very independent artists who, in fact, will not join any group or organization. Still, the Japan Print Association exhibition is <u>the</u> showcase for many important artists, and we find attending it an excellent way to keep abreast of certain happenings in the print world. Had it not been for our yearly pilgrimage to Ueno we probably would have missed Imamura Yoshio and his work. The artist lives in Iida City, Nagano Prefecture, which is hardly on our usual rounds. But because of seeing his work at this show we immediately contacted him and have been well pleased ever since.

Living in the country, Imamura is fond of nature and of taking walks in the woods. As a result, although one would probably categorize his work as abstract, he likes to incorporate actual details of his personal experiences into his prints. We might say that Imamura likes to "fossilize" time. If one searches hard enough, one will find images of insects, pebbles, stones, twigs, or fragments of other everyday objects worked into the composition. Imamura's prints are meticulously crafted, an amalgam of etching, woodblock, lithograph, and silkscreen. All are hand-pulled by the artist in our favorite mode of a limited edition of no more than twenty copies.

Plate 83

As we feel responsible for being among the first to recognize this artist's talent, we have been particularly proud of introducing his work into the collections of the Cincinnati Art Museum and the Gallery of New South Wales, Australia. Since we know Imamura is the father of four children who earns his living by running a design company in Iida, we were curious as to how he intended to fund his proposed three-month trip to France, where he told us he planned to study. Because of Japanese restraint in these matters we hesitated to probe.

I visited Paris during his stay to see about various matters concerning our gallery there and to see our daughter Hilary. Hilary was kind enough to prepare a sumptuous dinner for Imamura and me, at which he said he would like to propose a toast to express his gratitude to the Tolman Collection. He explained that he had made it a point to save the money we had paid him for print editions, and when he had accumulated enough he decided to take his study trip. Trying to retain memories of his Paris adventures, Imamura has fossilized fragments of his French experience in his work. The buff-colored background of his latest prints is often a blown-up, close-up image of a weather-beaten Paris wall that the artist captured with his camera.

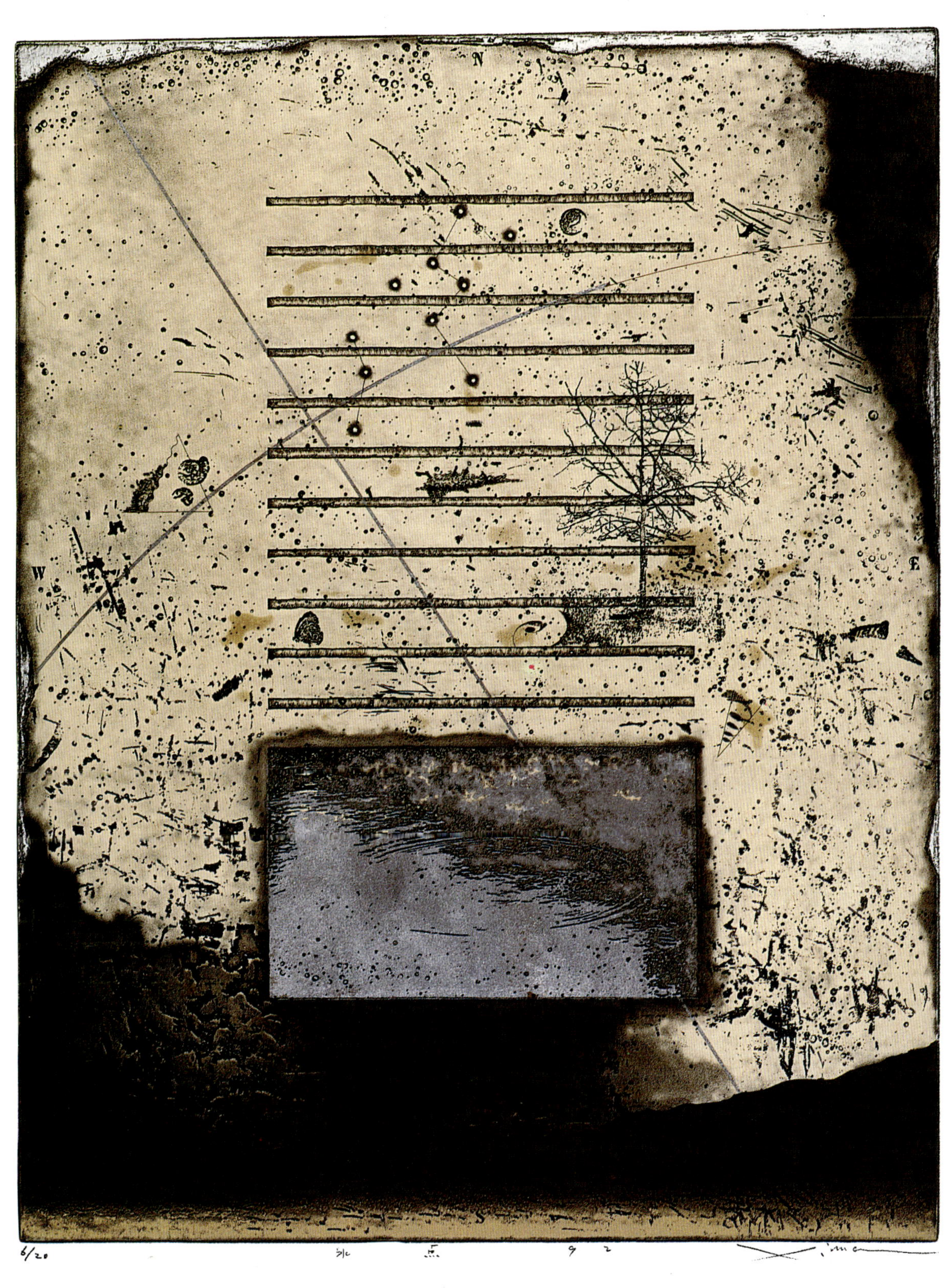

83. Imamura Yoshio (b. 1948). Titled in Japanese *Hyōten* (Icy Point), 6/20, 1992, etching, 60x45.5 cm. Signed Y. Imamura. Published by the Tolman Collection, Tokyo.

TOKUDA Akira

COMMENT: *Discovering new artists by chance in galleries.*

There is no better method of training the eye than looking at every opportunity. Visiting Kyoto with our Singapore dealer, Marjorie Chu, we were invited by an old friend who has a gallery there to see her current show. The featured artist was Tokuda Akira, and although he lives and works in Tokyo, we had to go all the way to Kyoto to become aware of him. We had a lovely vacation and a busman's holiday at the same time. As one never knows from where the latest talent will emerge, gallery-hopping is very much a part of maintaining one's knowledge of the current art scene. We find in our gallery that our most knowledgeable clients are those who drop in often just to see what is new. Often they are struck by an artist whom they had not noticed before, a discovery that can happen only when one is aware of what all there is and feels free to visit galleries when the mood strikes.

Tokuda has traveled internationally and was impressed by big cities like New York, Paris, Amsterdam, and Vienna, photographs of which often occur among his images. His intent is to convey the throbbing dynamism of big-city life and to create a textural surface in his prints that almost compels the visitor to reach out and touch the work (not in our gallery, please). Tokuda uses very thick paper and a metal plate for his deep embossing, and then hand-colors each print with pastel, which he must rub into the paper meticulously. The result has the *Plate 84* luster and smoothness of a silkscreen. The colors he chooses are bold, pristine, and vibrant, often shaded into paler tones of the same hue.

Tokuda has the dream of someday being a full-time artist, but at the moment he owns his own successful graphics-design company and makes prints only in his free time. His full workload and the labor intensiveness of his prints result in editions of generally fewer than ten. His teenage son helps him with the etching process of printing and insists on having his own embossed signature at the bottom of the print, which accounts for Tokuda's own signature in pencil and then the embossed circle at the lower right.

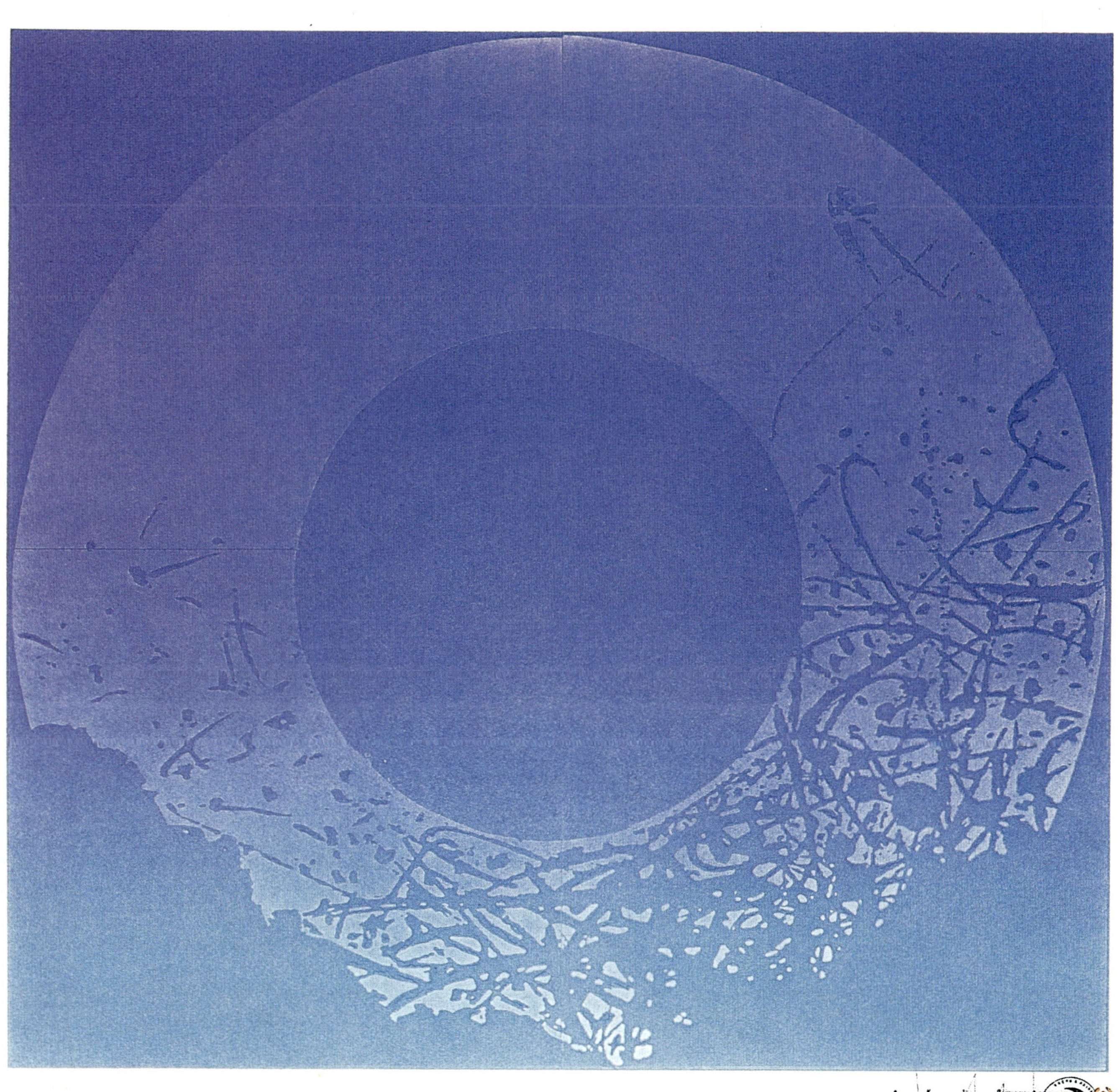

84. Tokuda Akira (b. 1946). *View 92-Pl BS,* 18/30, 1992, etching/hand-colored pastel, 47.5x50.5 cm. Stamped in black ink Akira, signed in pencil Tokuda, with a circular seal of K&A (Kaoru and Akira's Graphic Art Institute Japan) in black, and a red seal of A.T.

TANIGUCHI Shigeru

COMMENT: *The role of a gallery in backing an artist is a hard one if the artist does not wish to be backed.*

We started our gallery with only six artists: Clifton Karhu, Yayanagi Go, Funasaka Yoshisuke, Watarai Junsuke, Shibuya Eiichi, and Miyashita Tokio. Little by little as our eye, finances, and business sense improved we added one artist here and another there. We were always searching for those who had an originality we had not seen elsewhere, whether it be subject matter or technique.

One day Mary stopped by chance at a tiny gallery and came home carrying a roll of prints under her arm. We opened it up and found four prints that were so wonderful we decided on the spot to keep them for ourselves. Then we laughed when I asked, "What will we do about business?" "Don't worry," Mary laughed. "I only bought what the artist had with him. I've invited him for dinner tomorrow and he promised to bring everything he has made up until now."

The next night Taniguchi Shigeru came and we bought everything he had brought. He was a superior technician who could do virtually anything others could do and more, and he had an inventive, challenging imagination. He was always filled with new ideas, confidence, and humor. His subject matter went *Plate 85* through various phases, including Noh dancers, paper umbrellas, and sketches of some of Japan's national cultural treasures, all given fresh perspective through his technical virtuosity and personal interpretation. Taniguchi, however, did not particularly like to work with Japanese themes, and after trying a few he went on to the more international viewpoint that he preferred. Virtually self-taught, the artist has won countless prizes with his photo-silkscreens and lithographs in Japan and at far-flung international biennials from Miami to Ibiza in Spain, from Bradford, England to Ljubljana, in the former Yugoslavia.

As art dealers naturally we like to offer prints that sell, and sometimes we would broach the subject of working around a Japanese theme once again, since our clients had loved those prints so much. Taniguchi would have none of it. He was finished with that phase, was onto something new, and did not care if his work sold or not. He had a driving need to commit to paper what was inside him at that moment. He was working for his own artistic release, not to please others. If they liked what he made, that was a bonus.

We watched him progress with interest and often wondered whether he was just stubborn or a genius. We suspected the latter and continued to have faith in his talent. We knew that sometimes his limited finances prevented him from traveling and from artistic experimentation, so after long deliberation we decided to try to help. We proposed to buy at regular intervals one complete edition of whatever he chose to make, hoping this arrangement would provide a guaranteed income. Taniguchi politely refused, saying that he needed the pressure to produce art that people would truly understand and love from their hearts and not because they had contracted to buy it. Again we were forced to admire his position. The easy way is not necessarily the best for certain individuals.

To our dismay Taniguchi soon "graduated" to original oil painting, a course seldom taken by print artists. We tried one exhibition of his oils but our clients wanted more of his prints and he did not want to make them. We see him from time to time, but sadly the talk never turns to prints. Taniguchi is experimenting with being an oil painter at the moment, a course we must admire. All true artists must keep on seeking new directions or they would never command our interest.

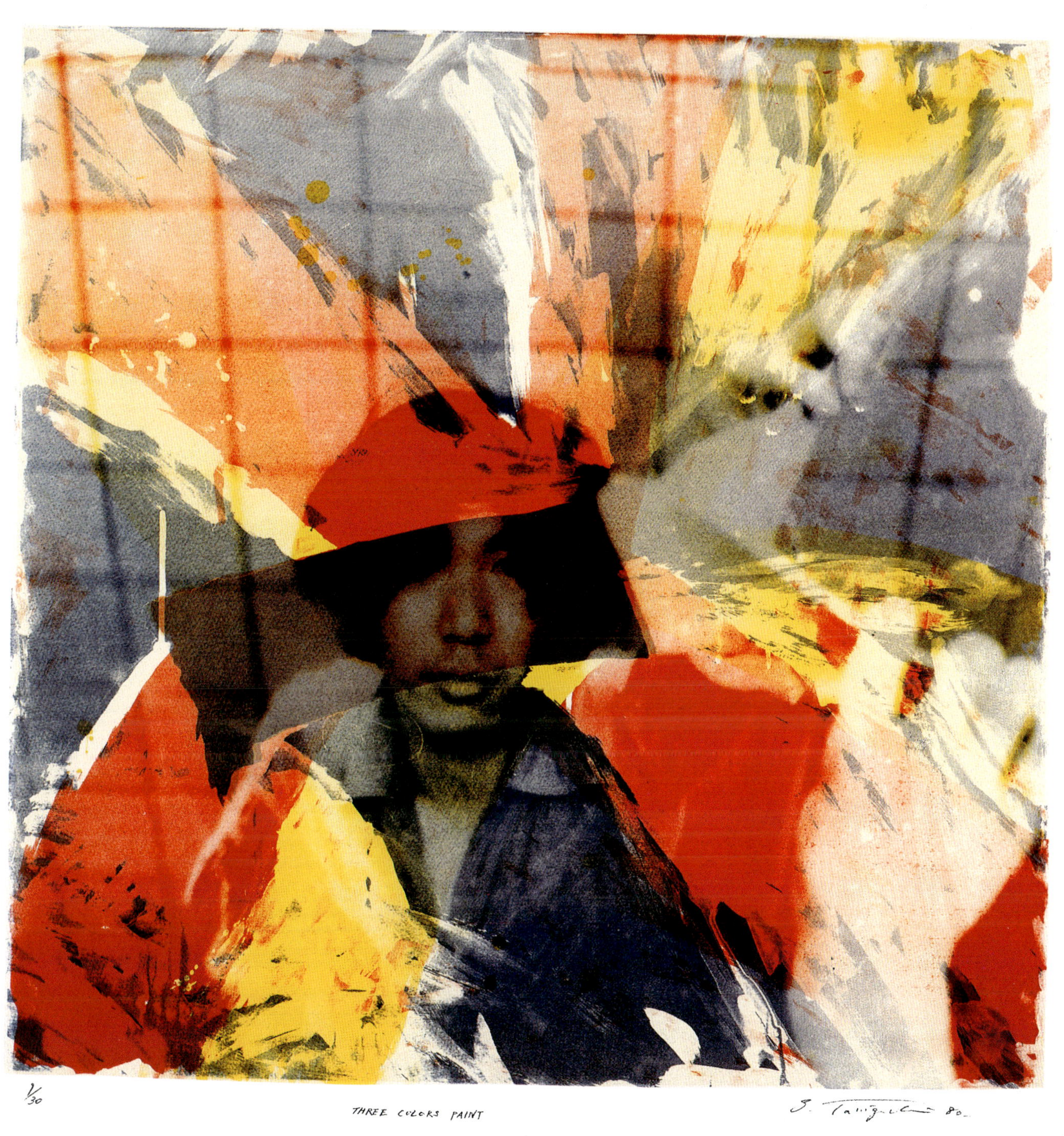

85. Taniguchi Shigeru (b. 1948). *Three Colors Paint*, 9/30, 1980, silkscreen, 65x64.5 cm. Signed S. Taniguchi. Published by the Tolman Collection, Tokyo.

KIMURA Kosuke

COMMENT: *The role of portfolios in introducing artists.*

In 1979 we decided to commission a special portfolio of prints, the idea being to show to what level Japanese graphic artists had risen by the end of the 1970s. We chose Shinoda Toko, Iwami Reika, Yayanagi Go, Ouchi Makoto, Kinoshita Tomio, and Kimura Kosuke, all well-established, world-famous artists. We wanted to include Taniguchi Shigeru too but hesitated because although his work was excellent he was not very well known. We consulted with Yayanagi, our friend, advisor, and also a great admirer of Taniguchi's work. Yayanagi indicated clearly that it was our responsibility to include Taniguchi. "If you don't put him in this portfolio, how can he ever be invited to participate in other fine things? You have to give him this chance." That night we discussed the project with Taniguchi, telling him of our misgivings and of our conversation with Yayanagi. He promised to make a print worthy of its company for the upcoming portfolio. Early the next morning we received a phone call from him telling us that he had just won a major prize in the Japan Art Festival exhibition. We were all elated—he, because he had received formal recognition, and we, because we had had the faith to ask him to be part of our project before we knew he had earned the prize.

Kimura was also part of this ambitious portfolio undertaking. He was a well-regarded artist with many biennial prizes to his credit, but we wanted him for other reasons as well. Firstly, his interesting juxtaposition of hard-edged, realistic images and softly blurred photomontages appealed to us. Secondly, he was an artist whose fame had its roots in the Kyoto–Osaka region and we wanted to bring him to further attention in Tokyo. Finally, we felt that his subjects were well suited to the times.

We did not specify any theme for the portfolio but just wanted each artist to work in his usual manner. The only requirement was that the finished works be uniform in size. Part of our hope was that the portfolio would be a sort of "instant collection," providing an overview of the current print world and of particular value to the true collector looking for something more substantial than a print to match a sofa. Our wish was that there would be enough collectors to buy the entire set, but because we were aware that not everyone could afford the whole set (or have adequate wall space, as prints in this portfolio were large ones), we made a certain number of the prints individually available.

Plate 86

Kimura's *Girl and Pagoda* was made in 1979 but it is still as technically and artistically fresh today as it was then. We were interested to learn that Kimura has recently carried his pagoda image one step further by designing a monument for the Ibaraki City Station plaza called *Rainbow Pagoda*.

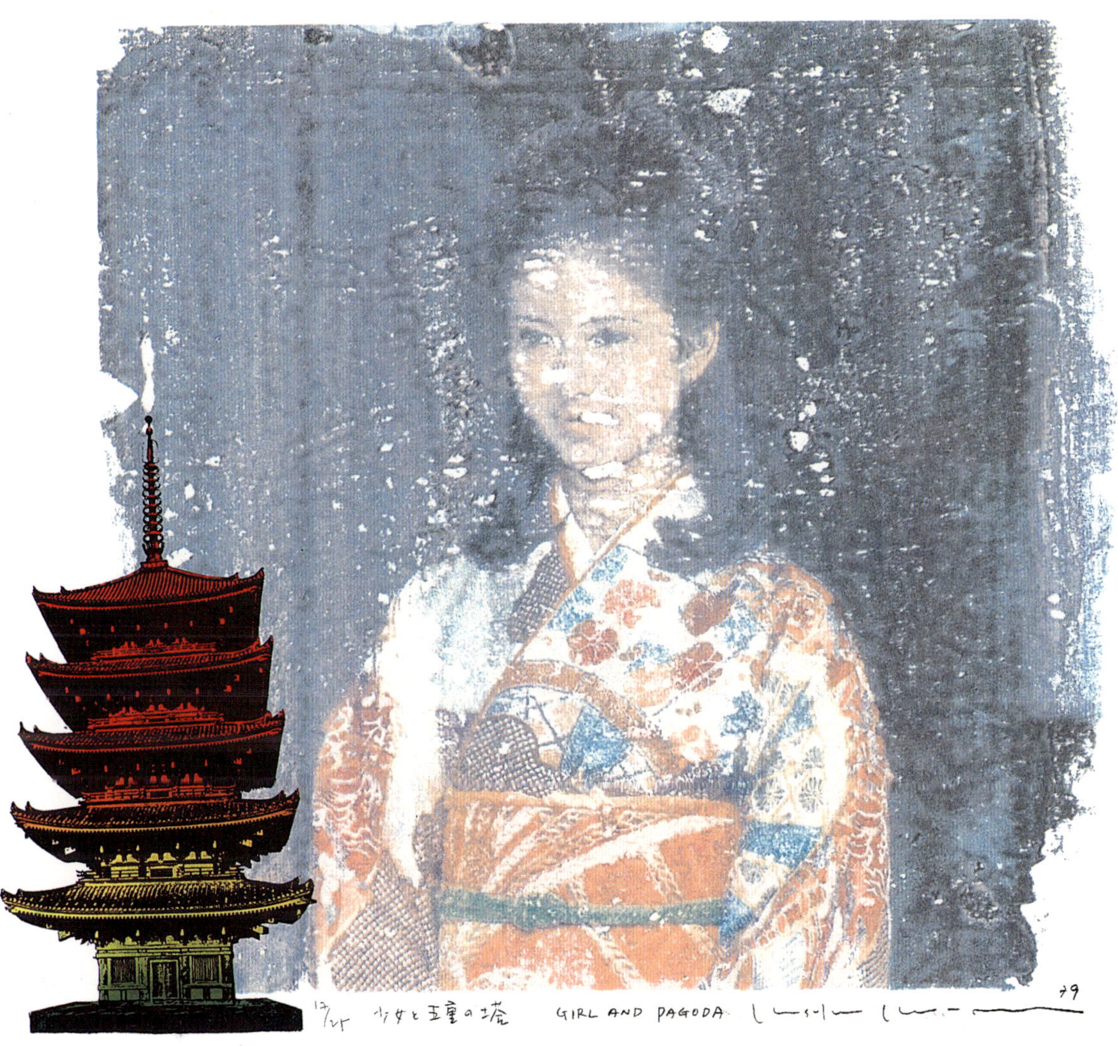

86. Kimura Kosuke (b. 1936). Titled in Japanese *Shōjo to Gojūnotō,* titled in English *Girl and Pagoda,* 17/25, 1979, photo-silkscreen, 62.8x90.5 cm. Signed Kosuke Kimura. Published by the Tolman Collection, Tokyo.

TAKAHASHI Ushio

COMMENT: *Technique makes all the difference.*

Plate 87 When we brought this print home we thought that perhaps we had succumbed to a bout of nostalgia. It reminded us of the depictions of "beauties" so prevalent during the *shin-hanga* era, of women combing their long hair or lazily and gracefully lounging in their kimonos after a bath. However, we both felt there was something different about this work. We liked the delicacy of the face and hands, and the deep, rich, impenetrable blackness of the hair. That's it, we decided. This black is not a woodblock black. Further investigation showed that the print was a mezzotint, and although subject matter may be culled from yore, it is no longer the same thing when it is portrayed in a technique other than the traditional woodblock. The black in this print is especially deep, mysterious, and unfathomable, adding to the overall enigma. Further investigation revealed that Takahashi Ushio uses real models in his work, that he has a daughter who continues to inspire his thoughts on femininity, and that his intent is to portray a type of graceful, sensuous, female beauty so achingly lovely that her scent almost rises from the paper.

Takahashi chose the mezzotint method because he felt it could provide the fine detail he required. Mezzotints are a hard taskmaster. Takahashi produces an average of five prints a year, mostly small ones. Employing a rocker, the tool used to prepare the mezzotint plate for inking, is an unbelievably tedious process. A machine has been invented to make the task easier, but Takahashi says that in the areas where he really needs subtlety of color and fine lines he must work by hand. His joy is to portray a kind of delicate, female beauty, perhaps an ideal that many people might consider passé, in one of the most modern of techniques. It is this anomaly that makes his work so interesting.

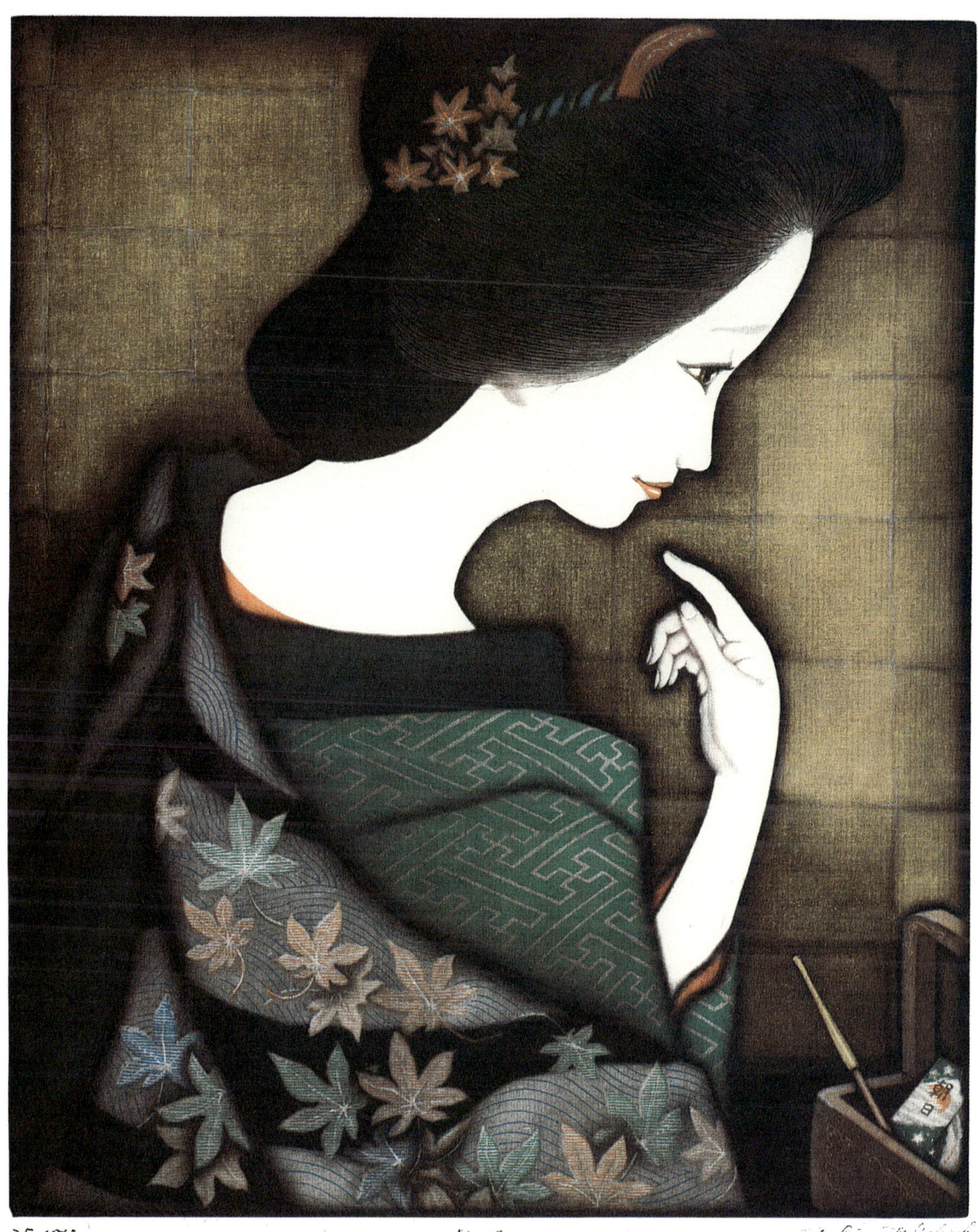

87. Takahashi Ushio (b. 1944). Signed in Japanese *O-Tama* (a girl's name), 35/75, 1983, mezzotint, 25.5x20.5 cm. Signed Ushio Takahashi, embossed seal Ushio Takahashi, under the signature an additional embossing in English stating that the work is an original print by Ushio Takahashi, with another personal seal of the wave pattern.

IKEGAMI Isao

COMMENT: *Perfect in composition, execution, and condition.*

We have already addressed the problem of condition of prints, a problem we faced as beginning collectors and are even more concerned with now as dealers. We operate our gallery on a very strict policy of "Do not touch, please," and we are aware that our reputation for offering prints in the best possible condition is part of what keeps our clients coming back.

The key words here are best possible condition. Modern Japanese prints are made in every possible medium, with endlessly varied techniques, each with its own peculiarities, on myriad types of paper, each with its own characteristics. All of these factors affect the finished print. For example, Sasajima Kihei's carving and printing method left the paper almost cut (sometimes actually cut), making the prints very fragile; Hasegawa Yuichi's repeated printing with the same block, even though he has strengthened his *torinoko* paper with persimmon tannin, occasionally makes the paper wavy; Hiromitsu's (Takahashi Hiromitsu's) complicated *kappazuri* stencils call for repeated washing of the paper, which often leaves it less than flat; when Shinoda Toko adds by hand elements to her lithographs, sometimes a tiny drop of color ends up on another part of the composition; Miyashita Tokio's printing technique calls for actually nailing the paper to the block, leaving two little permanent holes in the paper.

In Miyashita's case we tell clients, if you have a Miyashita print without the holes, then you do not have a real Miyashita. If you want a Shinoda lithograph with hand-added color, your print may include a dot of color in the margin where the artist did not intend it. Of course, you can press Hiromitsu's paper flat, but pressing takes life out of the paper and is not advised. Prints look the way they do because of all of the things that have happened to them; they were not simply extracted from some machine but have been involved in numerous personal, manual processes, all of which leave their mark.

Plate 88

However, talk about a print in "perfect" condition usually calls to mind the crisp, cool, clean silkscreens of Ikegami Isao. Ikegami is a fussy designer, and silkscreens are a fussy kind of print. They are made on glossy paper, usually with glossy ink, and one tiny scratch on the surface can ruin the effect. Ikegami has his prints pulled at the atelier of Okabe Tokuzo, probably the leading silkscreen printer in the land and teacher to many of the printers who now have their own ateliers. We were not surprised when Ikegami, who demands perfection, turned to Okabe, although he is one of the most expensive printers in Japan, to pull his work. If they were not perfectly executed, they would be failures.

Ikegami's black-and-white compositions with a touch of red have been part of the modern Japanese graphics look that our gallery has become known for. Ikegami says of his work: "I want to create a moment in life." Over the years he has gradually introduced a nuance of unexpected delicacy into his work. The hard-edged, black-white-red compositions now have an added celestial shade of blue-gray. They are always precisely executed, well-balanced prints, but the soft and subtle tones have introduced a new dimension and a new look.

For us, who look at art on a daily basis as our hobby, chief interest, and now as our business, it is refreshing to find original work with not only technical purity of color and composition but also with a philosophical foundation. Ikegami has a special regard for and certain fear of black—its mysterious depths, darkness, and beauty. He also says that for a long time he has been searching for the shapes he enjoys using. He wants to use inspiring forms that have a certain elegance and are unconsciously hidden in our minds. He says, "I want to create all the things that have existed in nothingness for only a brief moment: a form that doesn't take any shape; a color that doesn't show any hue; a sound that doesn't make any noise." How could we dare to present such works in less than perfect condition?

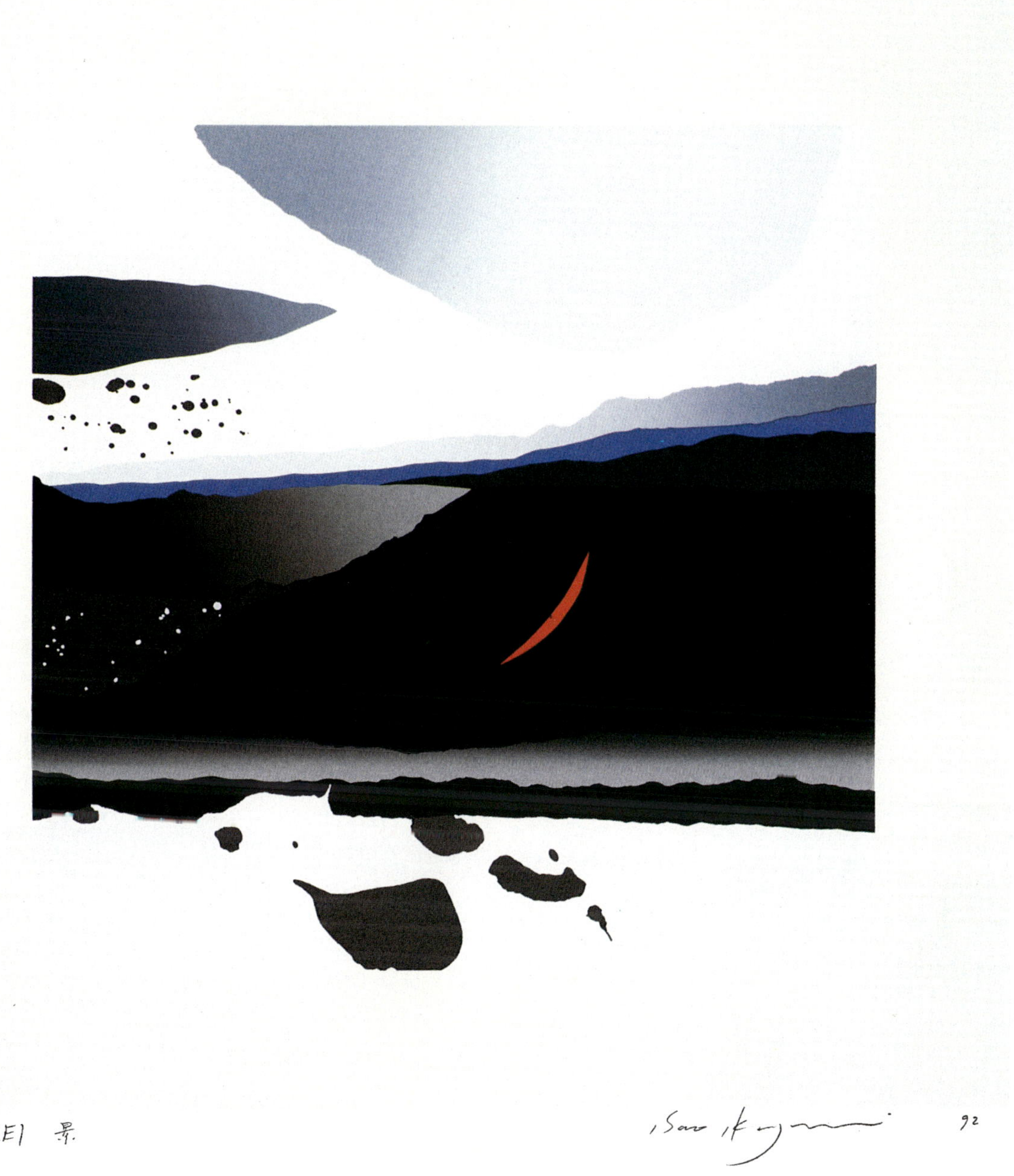

88. Ikegami Isao (b. 1938). Titled in Japanese *Kei* (Scenery), 22/55, 1992, silkscreen, 40x40 cm. Signed Isao Ikegami. Published by the Tolman Collection, Tokyo.

NAKAZAWA Shin'ichi

COMMENT: *Looking to the past and the future for subjects and titles.*

When we decided to write this book about our long involvement with Japanese prints and the people who make them, we were well aware of the paucity of information in English, a language in which much of the world gains its insights about Japan. We resolved to write in a clear and straightforward way, keeping in mind that many readers would not be native speakers. We intended this to be a book free of artistic jargon, a book one could read without having to consult a dictionary. Well, we tried, but you have Nakazawa Shin'ichi to thank for a possible trip to your dictionary to understand the meaning of chirality. We have had only one customer who knew the word, and he had a Ph.D. in physics.

Each artist has his own way of determining titles. Some titles really have nothing to do with the subject but are simply a way of identifying the work. With

Plate 89

Chirality, Nakazawa just liked the sound of the word. Artists have noticed that art lovers hate to be presented with a work known as *Opus 234* or *Work 94-1-1,* the mere indication that it was the artist's first work in January 1994. Since the word about the importance of titles is out, many artists play the game and try to come up with interesting titles, though a hard-core group refuses to go along with this practice. In our gallery, we feel the pressure for meaningful titles more than most, since our clientele consists of many non-Japanese and they like a frame of reference. Fortunately for them, most Japanese artists title their works in English because a large part of their audience speaks English.

Nakazawa's title is certainly as modern and avant-garde as his work. His technique too is rather unusual, a combination of etching and gold leaf. The background seems to consist of a secret written language, reminiscent of the Japanese *hiragana* syllabary. It is not. It is the artist's own made-up graffiti, which will probably drive future scholars crazy trying to figure out its "meaning," along with trying to decipher the mysteries of chirality.

Nakazawa's role model is the seventeenth-century Rimpa artist Sotatsu, who was renowned for his decorative screens with a poetic imagery, combining visual beauty with emotional intensity. It is always worth remembering that many young Japanese artists may appear to be ultramodern in their art (and their titles) but, in fact, serving as much of their inspiration is a rich cultural heritage on which they often feel free to draw.

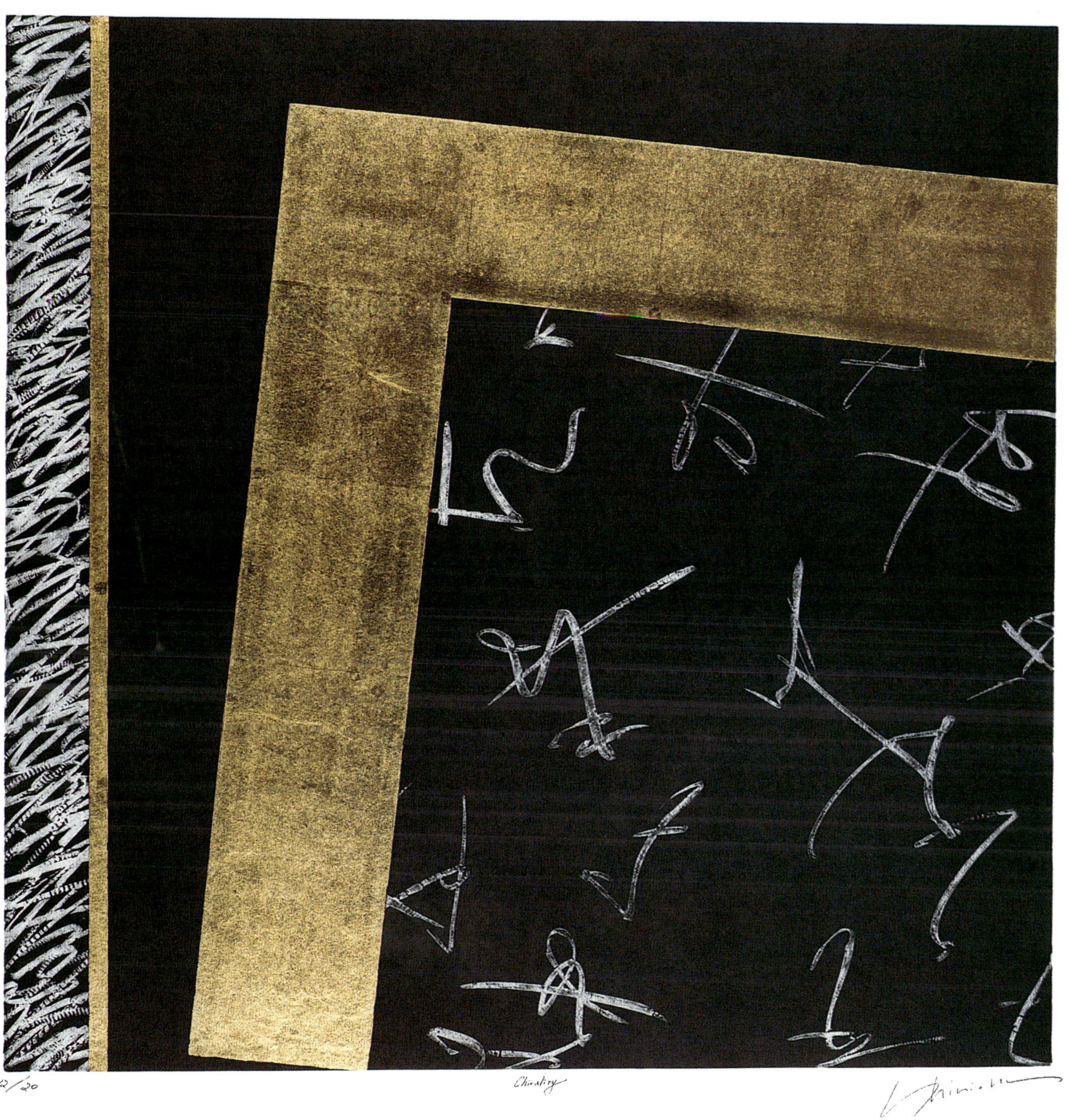

89. Nakazawa Shin'ichi (b. 1956). *Chirality,* 12/20, 1991, etching with hand-added gold leaf, 59x59 cm. Signed Shin'ichi, embossed in kanji Shin. Published by the Tolman Collection, Tokyo.

TSUBAMOTO Tatsuro

COMMENT: *Taking a chance on an unknown artist.*

We have noticed that people tend to buy prints by recognized names without reaching out for something new. This seems a perfectly normal thing to do for those who are set in their ways and insist that they know what they like. At the beginning of collecting this practice is understandable. It provides the novice collector with a certain feeling of reassurance and comfort to know that the path under his feet is not riddled with unforeseen mines. However, from another point of view, where would artists be if someone were not brave enough to take a chance on a new face? We feel our gallery's responsibility is to suggest to adventurous clients that they may wish to buy a work by a young, unknown artist. One advantage of such a purchase is that generally the editions are quite small because the artist too is feeling his way. Also, the prices are still reasonable because the artist has a reputation still in the making.

One must engage one's eye, taste, and sense of adventure to wade into uncharted waters even when only a small amount of money is involved. However, this type of purchase may bring a great deal of future pleasure, and, as Norman teases, you can always give it to your mother-in-law for Mother's Day. An individual considering a single print by an unknown artist is one thing, but for a gallery involved on a larger scale the risks can be quite scary. We felt that the work of Tsubamoto Tatsuro possessed all the elements that made a print exciting and desirable. In addition, one of our goals is to provide our clients with the chance to discover original and imaginative works.

There is so much on offer in the Tokyo art world that it is imperative for a gallery to be just as creative as an artist in order to capture the attention of the busy, art-oriented public. For that reason, we decided to stage an exciting show of three artists, thereby furnishing a three-fold reason for people to interrupt their hectic schedules to attend our exhibition. To great acclaim we showed the works of Tsubamoto Tatsuro, Imamura Yoshio, and Nakazawa Shin'ichi, artists using three different techniques and subjects, their common bond being excellence.

Plate 90 Tsubamoto's sophisticated lithographs seem to proceed from some dark dimension in infinity. The highlighted cylindrical or rounded shapes in the foreground appear to be floating in their own orbit. Because of their contrast with the endless depth of the background, the viewer feels their positive, glowing warmth all the more. The artist says he enjoys creating just such a "window" looking into space.

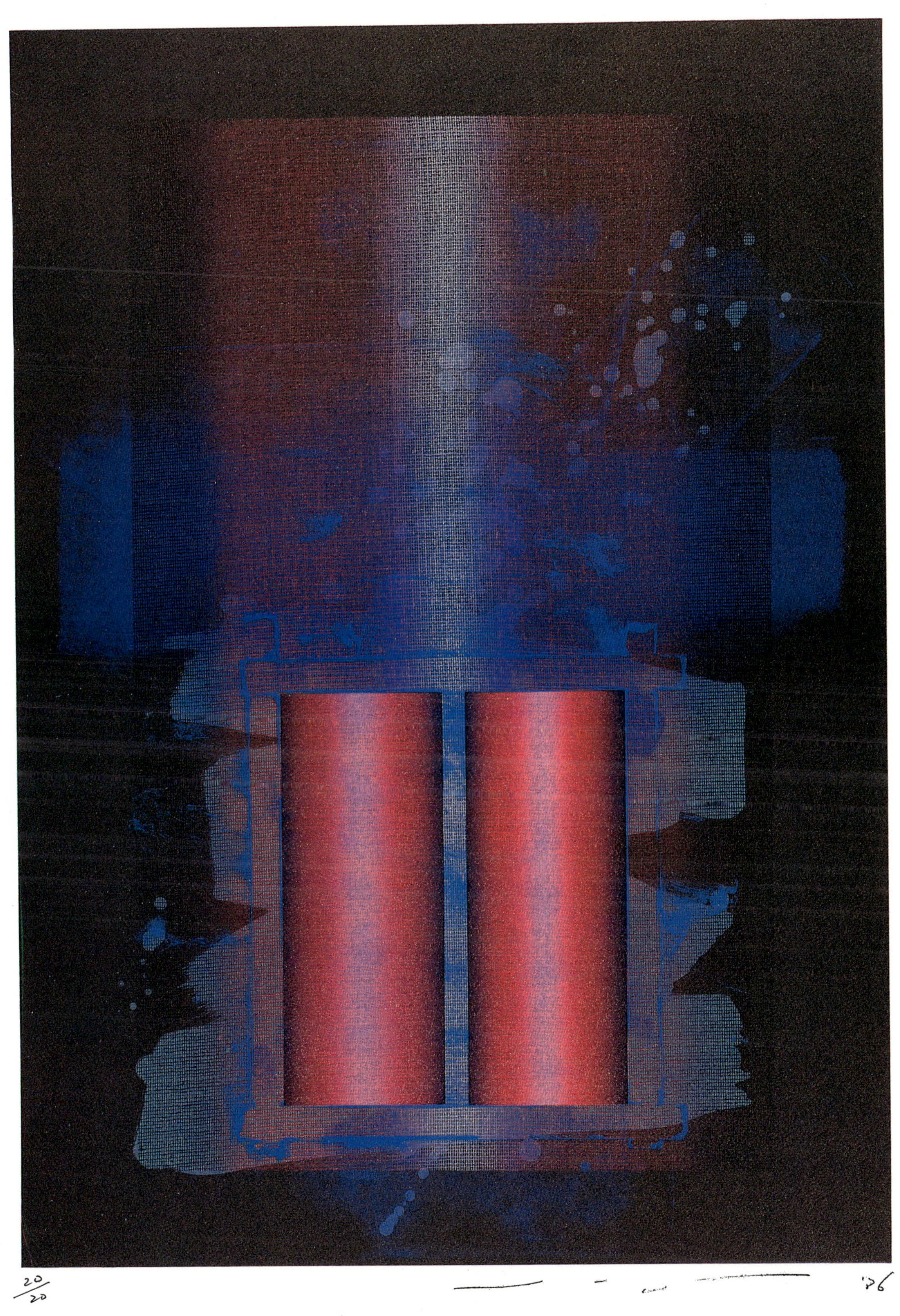

90. Tsubamoto Tatsuro (b. 1952). *In Black 86-17*, 20/20, 1986, lithograph, 54x38 cm. Signed T. Tsubamoto.

SASAJIMA Kihei

COMMENT: *Recognizing a bargain by knowing your art.*

Devoted collectors know that the chief ways they can continually sharpen their eye is by visiting galleries and museums, leafing through catalogues, buying relevant books, and, in general, being on the *qui vive,* until there comes a time when an artist's particular use of color or line is as familiar to them as their own name.

Plate 91

This print by Sasajima Kihei was found in one of the many Sunday flea markets held all over Tokyo and in other large Japanese cities. Our collection contains other finds: one turned up in Savannah, Georgia, and we have already related the story of our Saito unearthed in San Francisco. This Sasajima was stacked up with a strange assortment of badly framed works. The mat covered the signature and date, and only a portion of the print was peeking out from the heaped-up items, but there was no question about its maker. I know a Sasajima when I see one, and I fled with my discovery. The print is a joyful collector's item that came to me because I know this artist's work well.

Part of the delight in collecting is just this type of fortuitous experience—to stroll along, not really looking for anything in particular, and then suddenly to spot out of the corner of your eye a print you recognize from years gone by, in this case, a woodblock nearly fifty years old.

Galleries are not the only places to find prints. Keep your eyes open at flea markets too, but you have to be able to recognize a treasure when you see it!

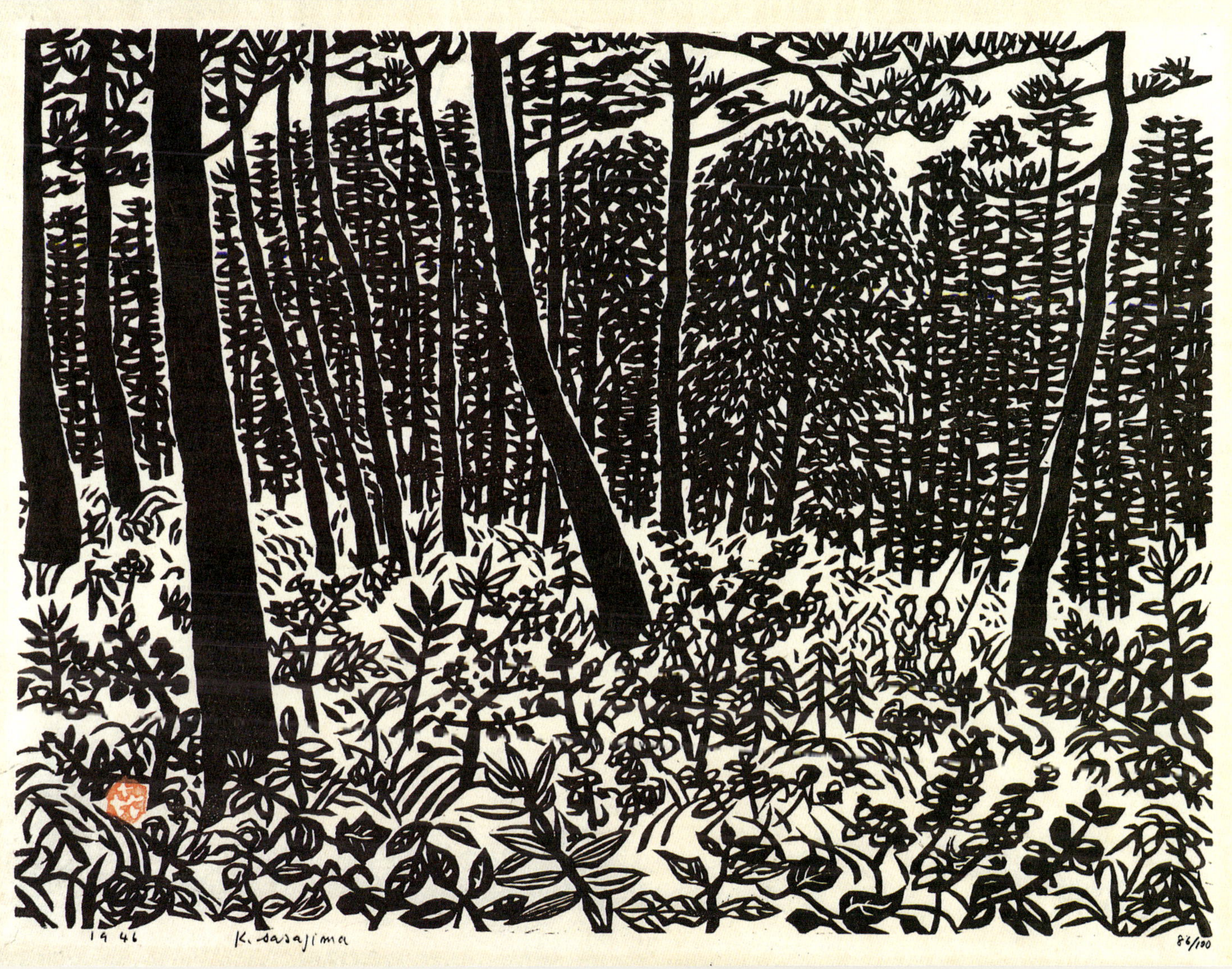

91. Sasajima Kihei (1906–93). Title unknown, 86/100, 1946, woodblock, 38.5x51.5 cm. Signed K. Sasajima, sealed on the image Sasa.

IWAMI Reika

COMMENT: *There are many surprises that make collecting fun.*

In the almost thirteen-hundred-year history of woodblock printing in Japan, Iwami Reika is the first woman to achieve the same status and worldwide recognition as male artists. And it took Iwami herself an unbelievably long time. Iwami was born in Tokyo and raised on the island of Kyushu, where she spent her first working years. Later she moved to Tokyo and began studying art on a part-time basis at Bunka Gakuin (Academy of Art). She devoted eleven years to learning dollmaking, and when this eventually proved insufficient to satisfy her creative spirit, she turned to printmaking. She has studied with three of the most important printmakers of Japan: Onchi Koshiro, Sekino Jun'ichiro, and Shinagawa Takumi.

Iwami's world is the world of "natural" Japan. *Sumi* ink, handmade paper, and real wood are blended to produce her austere yet powerful compositions. Embossing and overlaying silver or gold onto a velvety black background result in a finished work that is elegant in form and design, with a simplicity that is very satisfying to the beholder.

Iwami's subject is water and its flow, and her genius lies in the almost mystical ability to transmute the grain and texture of pieces of wood she has found into visual images of patterns of water. Contrary to popular opinion, she does not use driftwood in her work, simply old pieces of wood that she likes for their distinctive patterns resembling flowing streams or eddies. Sometimes she adds a touch of glittering mica (a stratagem of the *ukiyo-e* artists) to convey the feeling of water-washed sand in the sun.

The point that Japanese artists at an early stage in their careers identify their theme and then devote themselves to it could not have a better standard-bearer than Iwami. With only an occasional change in subject matter—a few short flings with butterflies, ducks, and, of course, Mount Fuji—Iwami has valiantly pushed ahead, regularly releasing prints that are black and white and occasionally include a touch of gold or silver leaf.

Plate 92

This is probably why *Circular Shadow No. 5* was such a surprise to us. We were almost ready to abandon our idea about Japanese artists refining a theme forever, until we remembered the key phrase "at an early stage in their careers." Obviously this print was made en route to that moment, and everything we have come to know Iwami by has happened since this early 1957 print.

Of course, surprises are not limited just to prints but also include the people who make them. We continue to be amazed by Iwami's perseverance in continually creating prints of great vigor and spiritual strength that belie her small and fragile person.

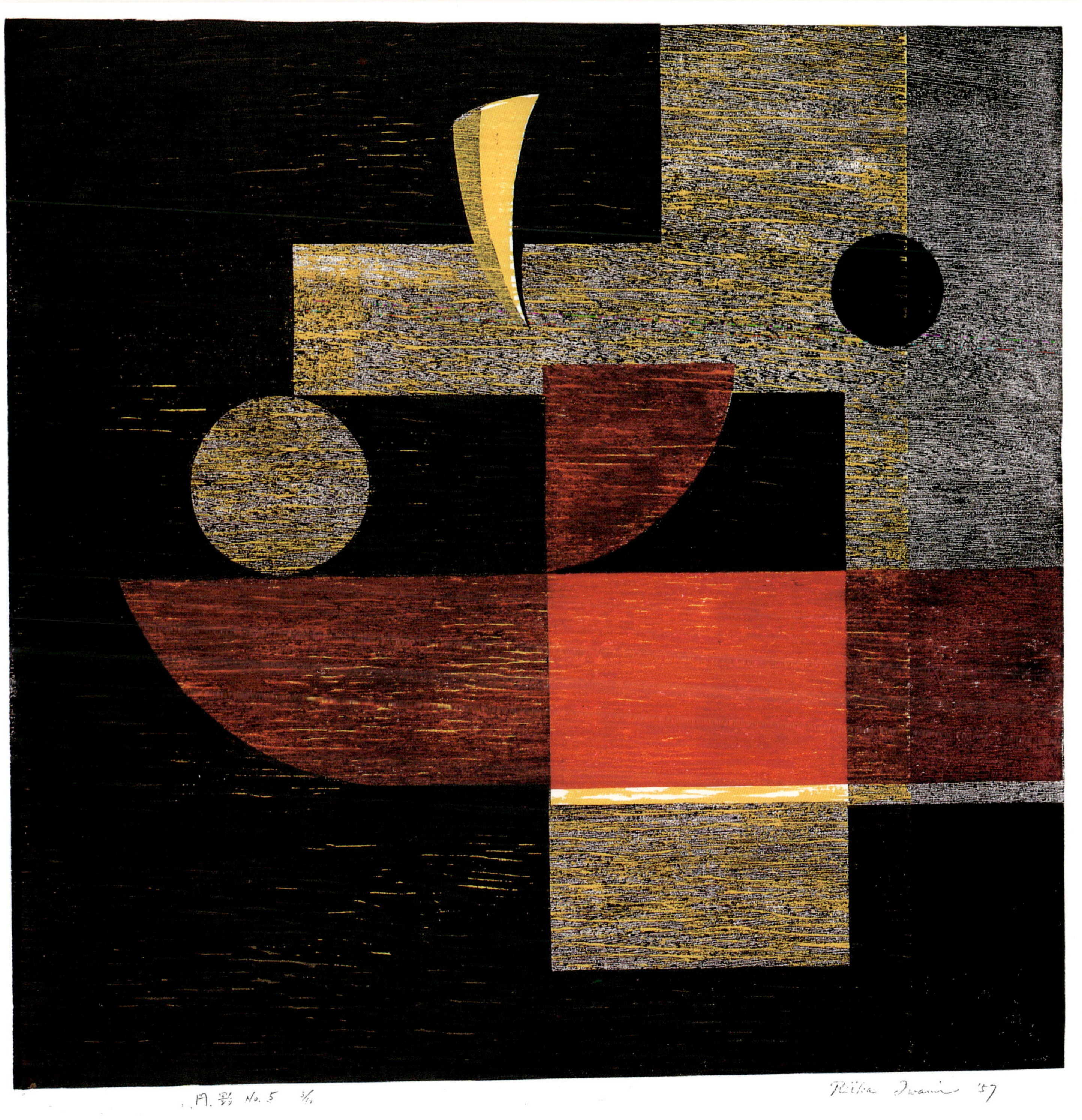

92. Iwami Reika (b. 1927). Titled in Japanese *Maru-ei No. 5* (Circular Shadow No. 5), 3/10, 1957, woodblock, 58.7x59 cm. Signed Reika Iwami.

ONOSATO Toshinobu

COMMENT: *Artists use professional printers for different reasons.*

It is probably safe to say that among Japanese print artists today it is the silkscreen printmakers who are most likely to use a professional printing atelier. This does not mean that they simply farm their designs out to the first available studio. The artist and printer work as a single entity, with the artist supervising every stage of the process to be certain that the printer is capturing every nuance he intended. A certain printer often works exclusively for a particular artist.

One cannot denigrate the role of the printer. In the case of silkscreens the work is extremely demanding. Especially in this medium, the execution has to be perfect or the print will not succeed as a work of art. Onosato Toshinobu, a famous painter, found it much easier to pay a professional printer to do his time-consuming silkscreening, an arrangement that freed him to create the designs and execute the oil paintings that were more rewarding to him.

Onosato's work translates very well into silkscreen printing. The bright coloring and the meticulous crafting of the complex patterns show up well in the glossy, clean result obtainable in screen printing. Onosato was preoccupied with

Plate 93

arranging circles and squares in a perfect and definite pattern. There seems to be no focal point, only the limitless sea of a carefully wrought design that almost brings us to the point of vertigo if we meditate on these mathematical mandalas too long. The intricacy of the work may help us understand why the artist would be willing, even anxious, to let someone else face the repetitive tedium of actually printing it.

Also, Onosato's paintings fetch handsome sums. I recently attended the auction of the estate of Mrs. J. D. Rockefeller III, where two of Onosato's small paintings each commanded a price in the neighborhood of $100,000. Paying the price of an expensive printer was not a problem for Onosato. He handed over his original painting to the best silkscreen printer in the business, Okabe Tokuzo, who did the rest.

This is perhaps one more reason to admire Ikegami Isao, whose quest for perfection we have touched upon earlier. Though younger and less well-off than Onosato, Ikegami has been astute enough to entrust his designs to Okabe, who can be relied on for matchless quality. Onosato wished to turn his designs over to a printer to have time to create new paintings; Ikegami wanted his work done by a perfectionist. Despite their different reasons, both artists were aware that paying the best professional printer to achieve their desired results was the appropriate path to follow.

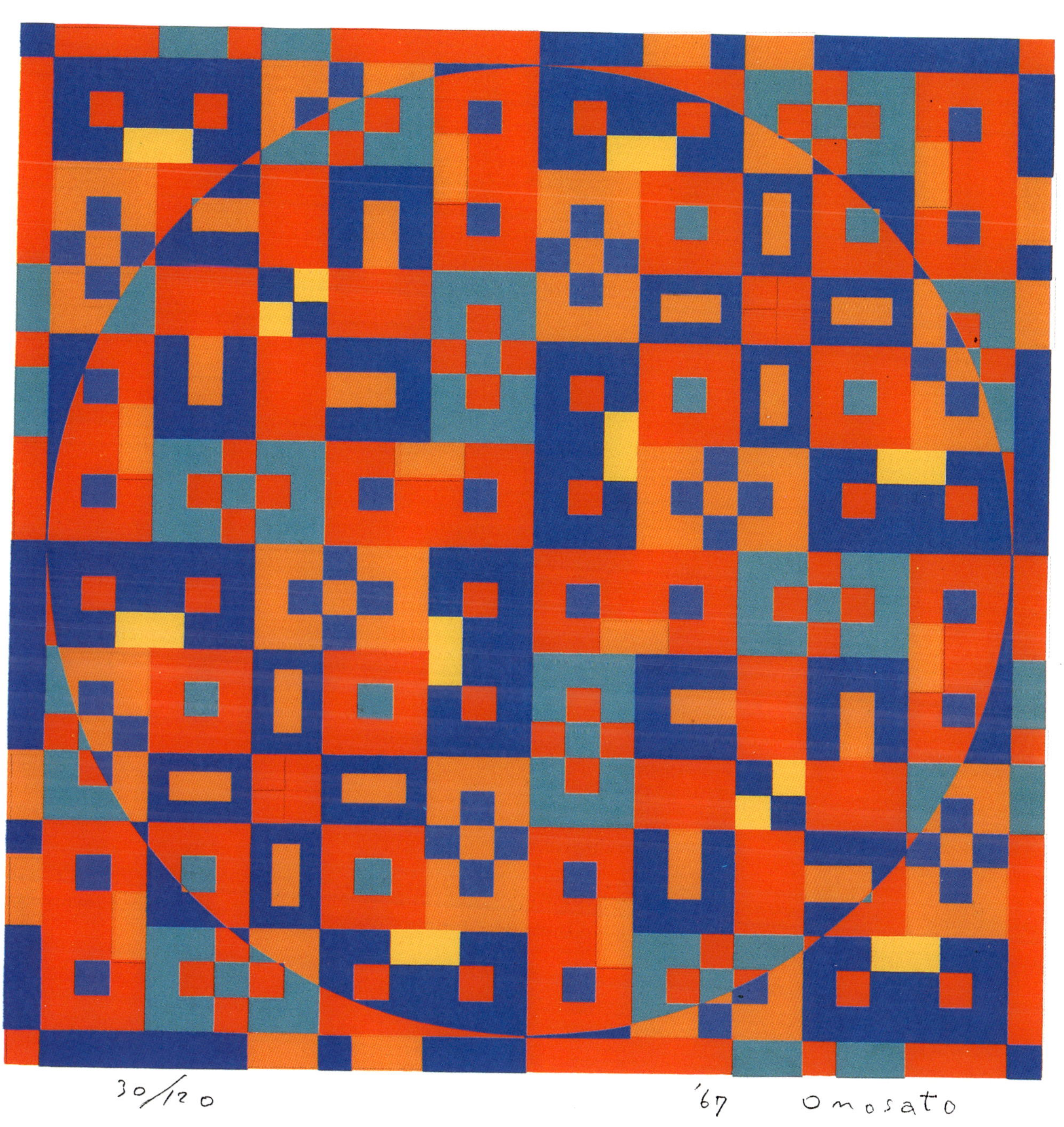

93. Onosato Toshinobu (1912–86). Titled on the reverse *67-G,* 30/120, 1967, silkscreen, 30x30 cm. Signed Onosato.

YUSE Yoshinori

COMMENT: *The enterprising gallery can play a role in getting young artists off the ground.*

Aspiring artists in Japan are caught in a vicious circle: established galleries are interested only in showing artists whose works are known and will sell; conversely, beginning artists cannot become known because no one will give them a show. Many Japanese artists find international biennials, where they often win prizes, excellent venues for making a name; others are fortunate enough to make contact with understanding, flexible, enterprising foreign galleries.

A peculiarly Japanese system of rental galleries also exists. These are set up specifically to rent space for exhibitions, usually a small room that a struggling artist rents for a week at a hefty fee. Sadly the artist's guest list is usually composed mainly of friends who are generally other artists, and the show does not attract buyers or critics who make a difference in an artist's career.

When we began our own business more than twenty years ago, we decided that one of our goals would be to introduce and support new artists who met our standards. When Yuse Yoshinori approached us in 1980, we gave him his first one-man show. We found his bold, clear colors and freshness intriguing, and his imagination lively. The artist hails from Akita Prefecture, where forests and lakes are abundant. He uses them in his fantasy landscapes, interchanging realism and abstraction in unusual perspectives and with luscious rhythms of color.

Plate 94

In 1970, before he began making prints, Yuse devised a philosophy of life about which he wrote a book, *Toward Absolute Nature Theory.* In the book he postulates that there is no termination to movement and flow but there is a "point" when the impact of a standstill may be felt; this is the "point" when Man feels at one with Nature, when he can affirm his own existence in this flow and movement. Yuse calls it the "running point." He further says, "While Nature continues to move and flow grandly and dynamically regardless of Man, Man steadily builds up his wisdom and power to control part of Nature for the sake of his well-being. Yet the flow and movement of human instinct is beyond Man's control. The moment when the flow and movement of Nature and those of Man cross, Man feels its 'running point' through his sensitivity. Art is the means I employ to communicate this feeling."

Getting a new artist started is the task of a gallery; keeping collectors interested by producing good work is the job of the artist; encouraging both gallery and artist is the pleasant responsibility of the collector.

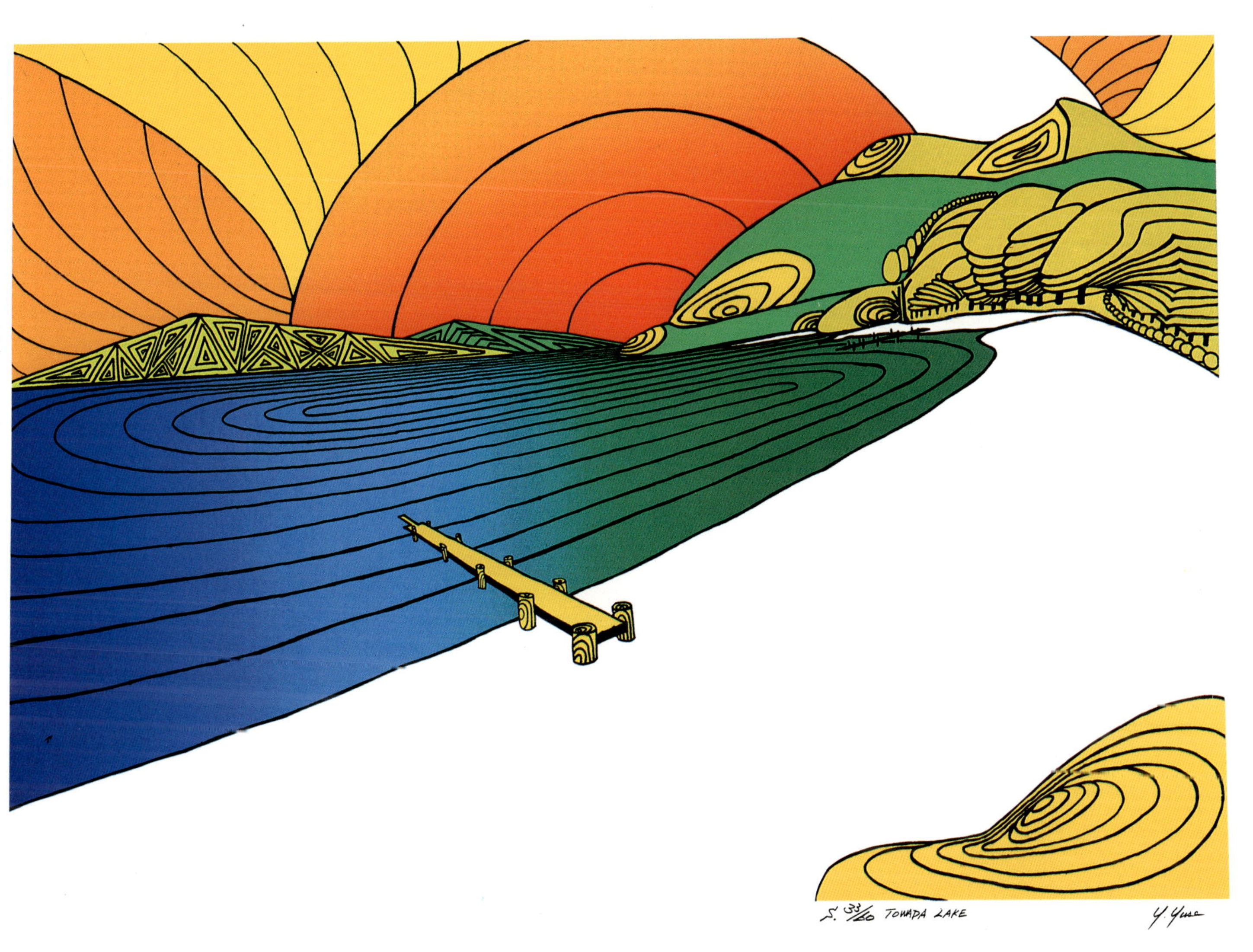

94. Yuse Yoshinori (b. 1947). *Towada Lake,* 33/60, 1979, silkscreen, 62.8x88.5 cm. Signed Y. Yuse.

MARUYAMA Hiroshi

COMMENT: *Once you have found them, never let them go.*

It can happen like this: a young, talented artist appears on the scene. At a large exhibition of prints, his is the work that is stellar, that is reviewed and praised by the critics, that takes the prize and is selected for purchase by a museum. One meets the artist, exchanges cards, and several months later an invitation to his one-man show arrives, a lure tempting enough to insure that one finds time in a busy schedule to attend the show. Among all the appealing works one finds favorites and buys them. And then . . . nothing more is heard from the artist. He has literally vanished from the scene. Unfortunately this scenario describes our initial experience with Maruyama Hiroshi.

Plate 95 We were intrigued with Maruyama's prints from the first time we saw them. The artist employed the traditional *bokashi* (shading) technique but in a complicated way, with abstract subject matter. He produced small editions. His colors were fresh and incandescent, and the forms reminiscent of the ribbon candy we used to enjoy in childhood.

At this point there were a number of young, fresh artists we were excited about, and we decided to stage a group exhibition of their works. Maruyama was the star of the show, and his works sold more than those of all the other artists combined. We then waited for some communication from him, but suddenly he was nowhere to be found. We learned later that he had received an irresistible offer to teach at Fukushima University, moved away from Tokyo, and consequently fell out of our circle.

To build a meaningful collection, one must keep abreast of an artist's latest accomplishments, commissions, prizes, etc. Of course, staying in touch is a mutual responsibility. Unfortunately artists who become academics are often caught up in a schedule that leaves little time for personal creativity and socializing. The result is that the collector loses interest, and the gallery owner finds another artist to replace the one he had tried to promote. What began as a promising relationship turns into a disappointing experience.

During the writing of this book I attended the opening party of this year's Japan Print Association exhibition in Ueno. The party occurred the night before I was scheduled to speak on Japanese prints in Fukushima, and I wondered if Maruyama might appear at my lecture. To my surprise, there he was in Ueno at the party. In our conversation he said that he had read in the newspaper about my forthcoming lecture, gave me his new business card, and promised to send an invitation to his next big Tokyo show. It seems that with Maruyama at least the cycle is beginning all over again.

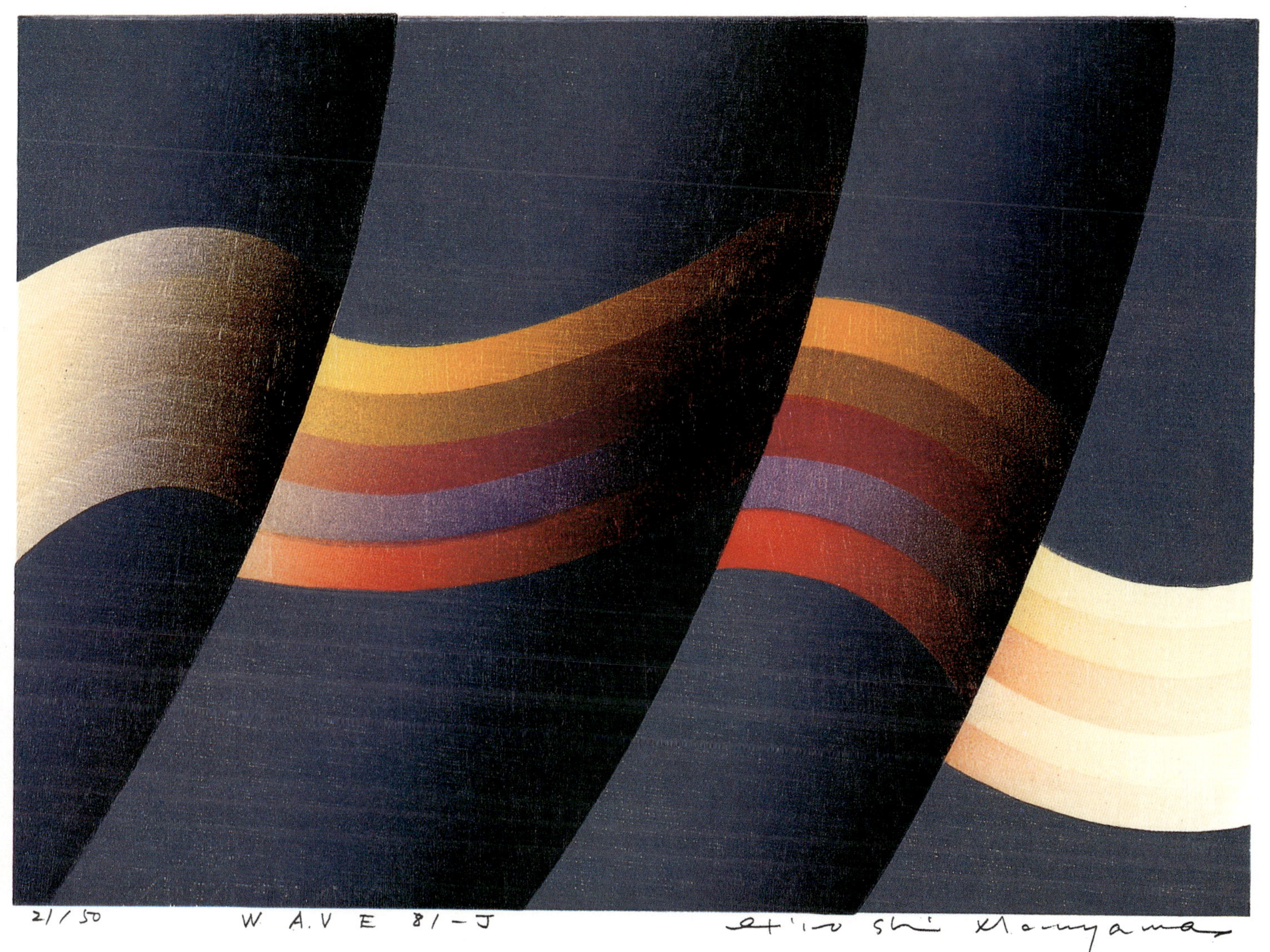

95. Maruyama Hiroshi (b. 1953). *Wave 81-J*, 21/50, 1981, woodblock, 30x42 cm. Signed Hiroshi Maruyama.

KAWADA Kan

COMMENT: *Choose your framer with care.*

Kawada Kan is one of a few Japanese artists active today in the world of stencil printmaking. He generally works in deep reds and blacks, with traditional subjects like old farmhouse interiors. We suppose we shall have to apologize to him at some point for linking his print with several negative comments that are not really his fault at all. In this essay we wanted to make a point, and unfortunately we shall have to use his beautiful print to do it.

Plate 96 We really wanted to have *Horyu Temple-Pagoda,* but in buying it we violated two of our basic rules: 1) Do not buy artist proofs, and 2) Be careful about prints that are already framed. We could see that the print was an artist proof when we bought it, as it was clearly marked as such. And the print clearly contradicted our policy of not buying prints in excellent condition. But for peculiar reasons that only the collector can fathom, we wanted the print, it was the only copy available, so we bought it. We loved the work per se, it was a *kappazuri* stencil work, it depicted a place in Nara that held memories for us, it was on the cover of a catalogue, etc., so we took the plunge.

We did not find out until later, when an earthquake knocked it off the wall, broke the glass, and split the frame, that the print had been pasted directly onto a piece of ordinary cardboard, endangering its condition and even survival as a work of art and, of course, seriously affecting its value.

As dealers who see many prints pass through our hands on both a retail and wholesale basis, we give the same strict advice to all: seek out a good framer who understands the framing of original prints (which is quite different from framing oils, posters, or cheap reproductions); insist that your framer use one-hundred-percent rag; do not hang your works in direct light or over heating or cooling apparatuses; if you insist on the modern "clip in" method, do not leave the print in that condition more than a month or two, as prints should not be in direct contact with the glass on a permanent basis.

It is beyond our comprehension why someone would invest a substantial amount of money in an original print and then feel that an inferior frame would suffice. In some do-it-yourself shops the frames are of a set size, and it is often necessary to trim a print to fit what is available. If one does not care about resale value or about aesthetics, that may be a quick solution. But that is exactly what it will turn out to be. Part of the buyer's complete interaction with his print should be the joy of selecting the proper mat and frame. It is also a creative enterprise because a poor mat and badly chosen frame will detract greatly from even the most beautiful print.

One small volume we can recommend that details all of this information is *A Guide to the Collecting and Care of Original Prints,* by Carl Zigrosser and Christa M. Gaehde, published by Crown Publishers, One Park Avenue, New York, N.Y., 10016. This informative essay, sponsored by the Print Council of America, is an indispensable source of information for the serious collector.

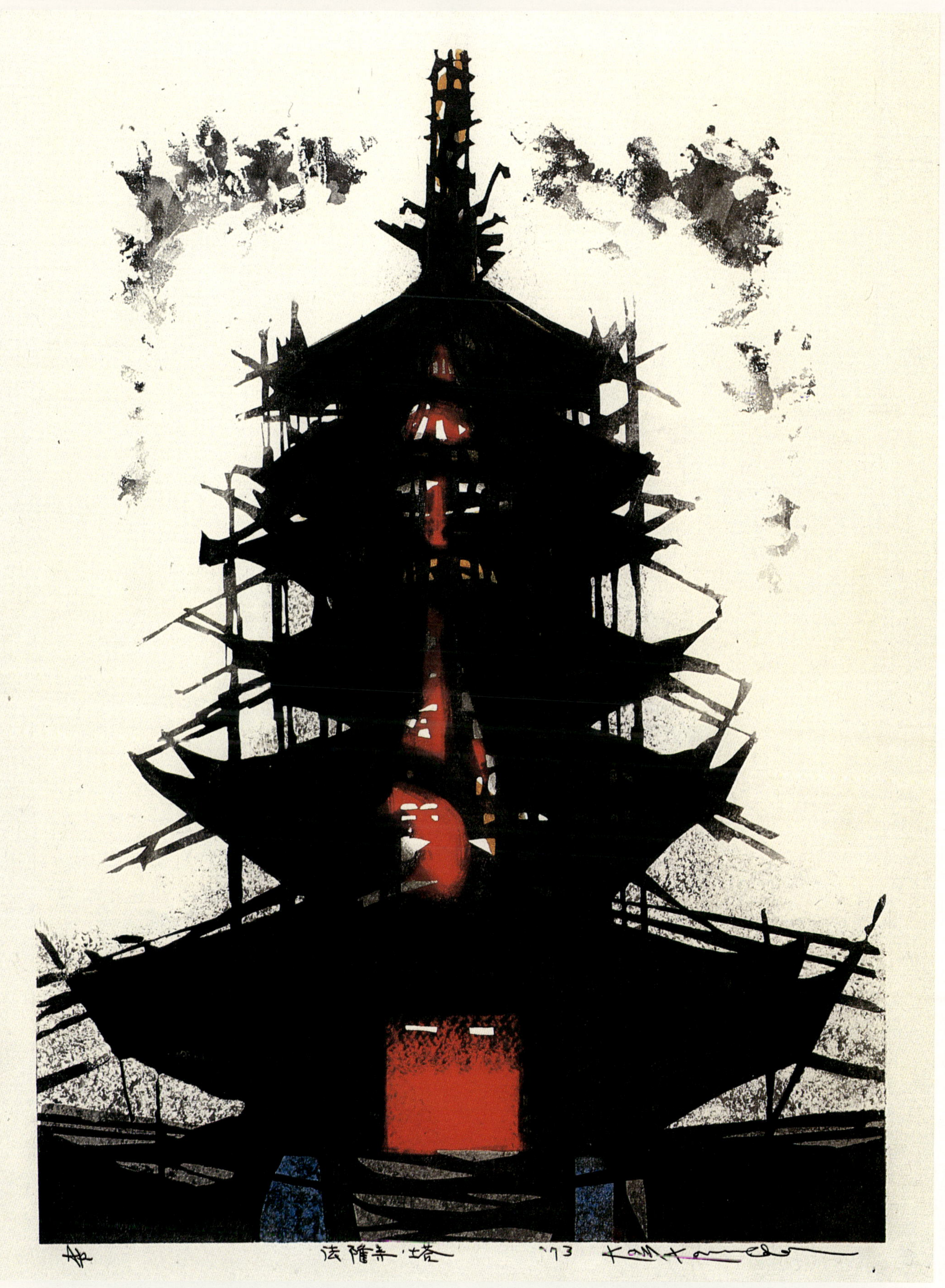

96. Kawada Kan (b. 1924). Titled in Japanese *Horyuji-tō* (Horyu Temple-Pagoda), A.P. (edition known to be 8), 1973, stencil, 58.5x41.5 cm. Signed Kan Kawada.

KAWACHI Seiko

COMMENT: *Let your imagination take part in the presentation of a print.*

An entire book could be written just about how to present one's collection: whether to use nonglare or regular glass; how wide the borders of the mats should be; should the print be floated; the choice of a silver, gold, or plain wood frame, etc. Framing is an important adjunct in complementing a print, but one should always keep in mind that a frame's main function is to protect and preserve the print. However, a tasteful frame is undoubtedly a noticeable contribution to the overall effect, and it is important to be in touch with a competent and caring framer who can advise one on all points of framing.

Sometimes for exhibitions we frame the same print in several different ways. Clients who love one example and hate another often refuse to believe that it is the same print, until we point out that it is the choice of frame that has made the difference. We have found that, in general, artists are the least likely to know what type of frame will enhance their work. Their egos tell them that no matter how the work is presented, it is so intrinsically wonderful that framing does not really matter. We try, as diplomatically as possible, to refrain from discussing the framing of a show with the artist. We try to mount an exhibition, frames and all, ready for everyone's enjoyment, and we devote a great amount of time to this aspect of our business as part of our contribution in presentation.

However, there are artists with flair and imagination in regard to framing. Fukazawa Shiro, for example, was once recognized in Mexico partly because of the elaborate frame on his work: he extended the actual composition to cover the wooden casing and made it part of the total work. His originality so impressed the judges that they awarded him a prize. *Plate 97* Kawachi Seiko's print *Sustain III* was recently offered for sale at a large department-store exhibition. It struck me instantly because it was an avant-garde woodblock full of taut lines and tensile vibration, yet it was mounted on a scroll in the most traditional way. The presentation was surprisingly effective.

In addition to being concerned with the proper display of his work, Kawachi Seiko reasoned that in Japan people have limited living space and might like to change their decor from time to time. If they saw art works in large, permanent frames, they might hesitate to buy them because of lack of both display space and storage space. However, a print mounted on a scroll could simply be rolled up and easily stored. Along with the convenience, the effect of a traditional mounting for an avant-garde work was original.

Among our clients we number more than a few who never frame the works in their collection. They store them in portfolios or in cabinets, taking them out occasionally for a little air and for enjoyment.

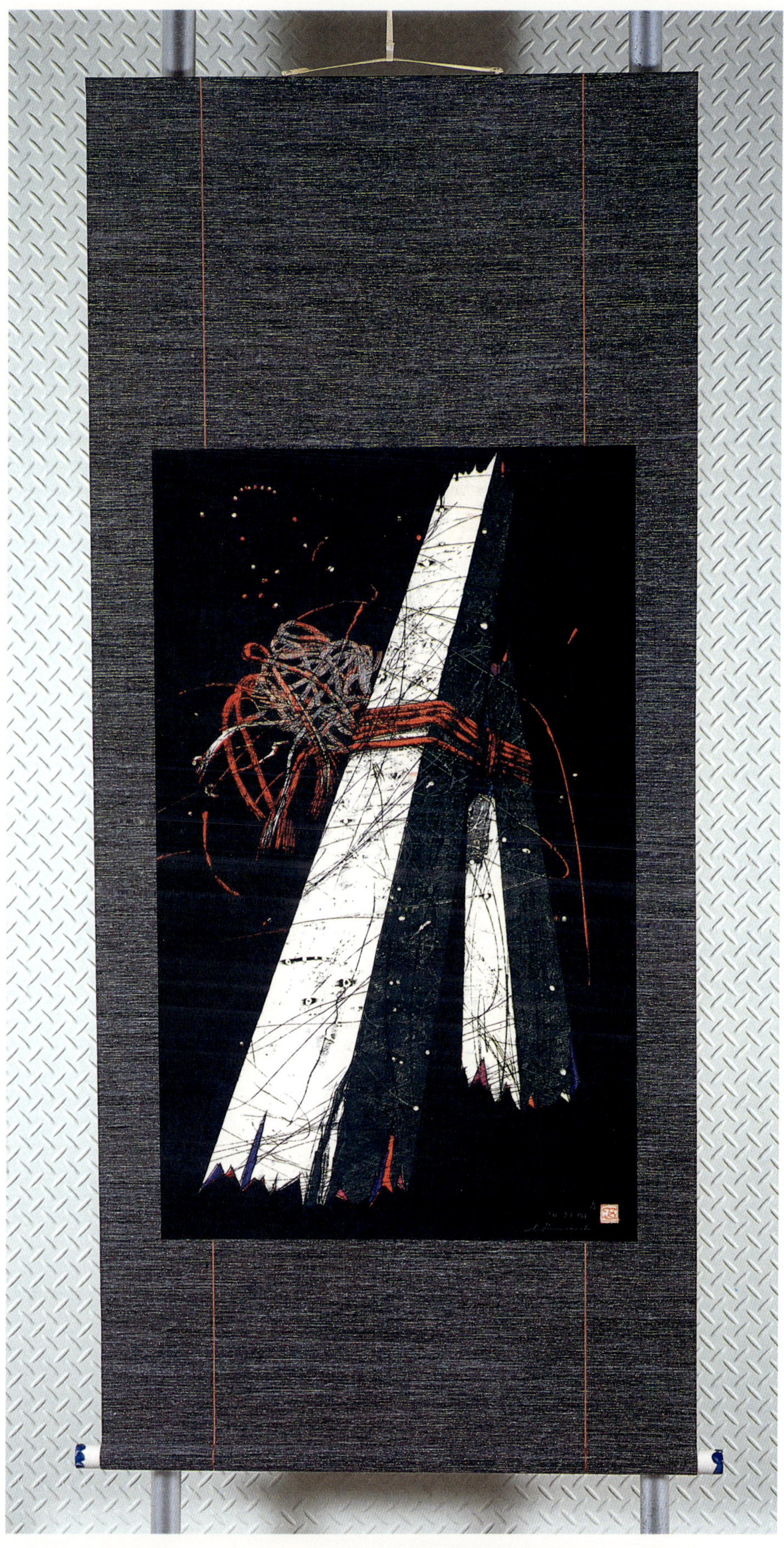

97. Kawachi Seiko (b. 1948). Titled in Japanese *Sasae (III)* (Sustain [III]), 1/5, 1993, woodblock, 90x54.5 cm. Signed on the image S. Kawachi, sealed in red on the image S K.

HIRATSUKA Yuji

COMMENT: *A new artist to fit our times.*

We have mentioned that this book is being written as part of our twentieth-anniversary celebration as art dealers. We felt for this special event that one big party, which we also held, would not be enough to commemorate our years of effort and fun in introducing Japanese prints. Knowing that our clients like us to do some of the work of finding new artists and works that lead them in new directions, we came up with the idea of adding a new artist to our stable on the occasion of this important anniversary.

When we started our search, criteria included the following: someone with a rising reputation but not someone too famous in Tokyo; someone whose work did not look like anyone else's but was easily recognized as that artist's personal style; someone whose subject matter was Japanese but whose work would possibly have wide international appeal. Hiratsuka Yuji met these requirements.

Hiratsuka has spent approximately the last decade in the U.S. studying and teaching. He has had more than forty one-man shows there, making him much better known in the U.S. than here, since he only occasionally contributes prints to important exhibitions in this country. His compositions have a slight suggestion of *ukiyo-e* prints, yet his interpretation and style are distinctively his own. His personal statement about his intentions in art expresses it best: "In my work I draw from the ancient and from the contemporary to express the mismatched combinations and hodgepodge that is Japanese daily life. The Zen aspect can also be seen in my portraits. In this case, I always leave the face blank or flat and profile very simple. I do not draw eyes or noses on my portraits. The human face is always changing; the face at work is different from the face enjoying love. Aging changes the face also. I want my prints to express this change. The portraits are left ambiguous so that the viewer can add his or her interpretation. This is the aspect of suggestion rather than expression. Also, I am interested in the humorous and colorful aspects of *ukiyo-e* art. In my portraits I want to incorporate an element of wit through exaggeration and distortion. For emphasis I fill in small areas with bright, whimsical colors. To express contemporary influences, I use the figure dressed in Western style."

Plate 98

Hiratsuka's work shown here, *be-ing,* is a portfolio of ten prints, each print depicting an aspect of being alive. All the prints are illustrated here, and you might enjoy fitting each print with a word from the following list: mending, predicting, contemplating, cracking, hoping, articulating, dreaming, praying, gesturing, engaging. The idea of publishing ten works by one artist in a single portfolio hand-pulled on handmade *kurodani* paper and presented in a handcrafted box appealed to us as an illustrious way to celebrate our twentieth anniversary.

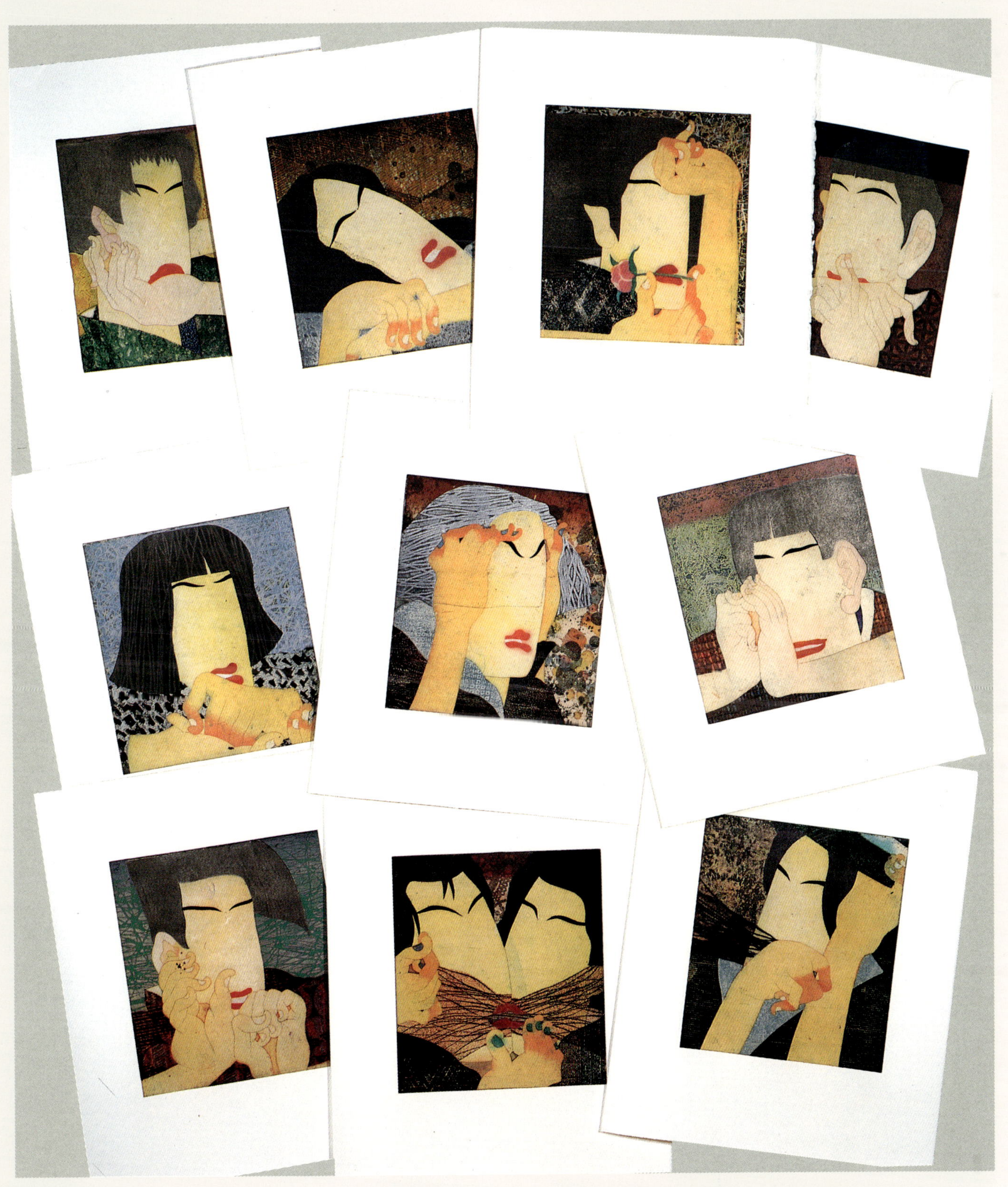

98. Hiratsuka Yuji (b. 1954). *be-ing* (a portfolio of ten prints), working copy photographed, to be produced in an edition of 50, 1994, etching/hand-coloring, 22.5x20 cm. Usually signed Hiratsuka. Published by the Tolman Collection, Tokyo.

WAKO Shuji

COMMENT: *An artist can work exclusively for one gallery.*

Earlier we discussed the many ways one could interpret the word traditional. It may seem strange but here we want to clarify the meaning of exclusive, which had seemed to us a straightforward concept. Not to everyone, it would appear.

We have noticed that now and then when we showed Wako Shuji's works to dealers and proudly announced that we were his exclusive representative, there were those who seemed not to believe us. This we would learn when Wako would phone in a panic, asking for someone from our gallery, usually Nagao Eiji, our devoted gallery manager, to come to his assistance. It generally turned out that some insistent dealer from abroad, apparently not understanding what the word exclusive means, had tracked down Wako's telephone number and demanded a meeting, for the purpose of making Wako an offer he could not refuse.

All of this usually took place a day or two after Eiji had patiently and courteously explained that we were responsible for and the source of all of Wako's lithographs. The dealer would then try to weasel out of his untenable position by saying, "Oh, when you said 'exclusive' I thought you meant just in Japan" or "Oh, when you said 'exclusive' I thought you meant only for the prints you handled." This is the place to set the record straight. When we say exclusive, that is exactly what we mean. It is only through the Tolman Collection of Tokyo that Wako's prints make their way to collectors and occasionally to other selected dealers.

Being very impressed with what we knew to be a unique talent and extremely high standards, almost ten years ago we engaged Wako in a special arrangement whereby we buy—exclusively—every print he makes. As with all contracts of any merit in Japan, ours is an oral one. Wako has been a loyal and consistently excellent artist, showing us only those prints that he feels live up to his high ideals. We never push him to make prints and, as a result, every one that he has released, a very limited turnout of only ninety-one different compositions in ten years, has sold out.

Wako describes his work as "expressing my inner sense of Japanese tradition seen through my modern eyes." In his compositions he often employs origami motifs like the folded crane, traditional tops and puzzles, and optical illusions. In addition, he uses lushly delineated fabric patterns set against a deep black background. These patterns evoke a sense of Oriental splendor.

If you have enjoyed the cover of our book, you have Wako to thank.

Plate 99 If you are enjoying the Wako print illustrated here, we have Wako to thank for making this print for our twentieth-year celebration.

And if you are really fascinated by Wako's work and wait about a year for him to make his hundredth work, you will have yourself to thank when you add *The Tolman Collection's One Hundred Views of Wako*, our next Tuttle book, to your collection.

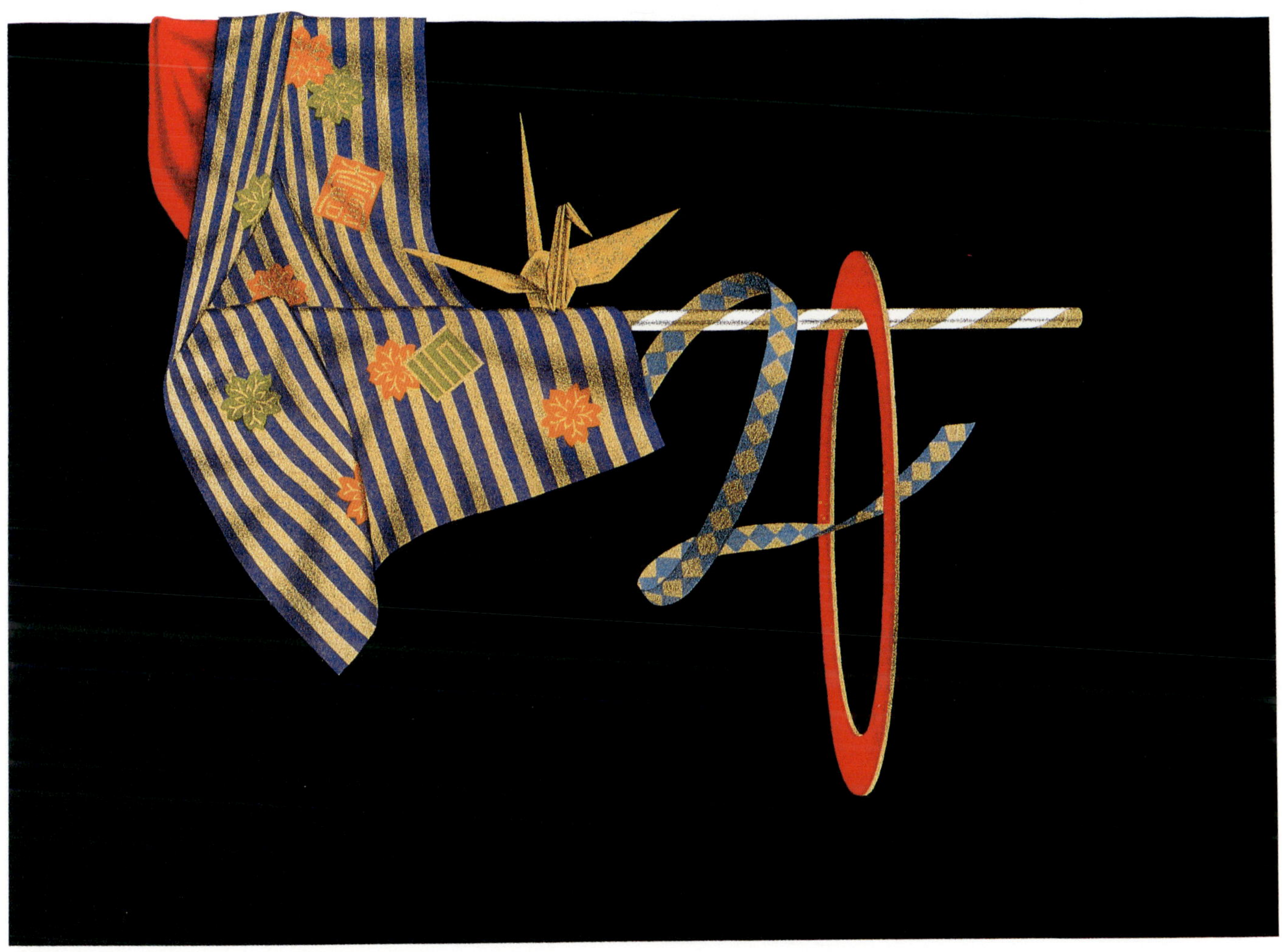

99. Wako Shuji (b. 1953). *Celebration*, 24/100, undated but known to be 1993, lithograph, 24.3x33 cm. Signed S. Wako. Published by the Tolman Collection, Tokyo.

The Artists

NOTES: The Japanese characters in this section are the kanji for the artists' names. Macrons, used to indicate long vowels in Romanized Japanese, are used for artists' names in this section only. The abbreviations CWAJ and JPA stand for College Women's Association of Japan and Japan Print Association respectively.

尼野和三
(plate 28)

AMANO Kazumi

1927, born in Takaoka, Toyama Prefecture; 1946, graduated from Takaoka Public College of Industrial Art; 1950, met Munakata and started making woodblock prints; 1957, 1st Tokyo International Print Biennial; 1962, 5th Contemporary Japanese Art Exhibition, Tokyo, Tokyo National Museum of Modern Art Prize; 1963, Tokyo International Print Biennial; 1964–68, Northwest International Print Exhibition, Seattle, prizes in 66, 67, 68; 1964, Lugano International Print Biennial, prize; 4th Tokyo International Print Biennial; 1965, Xylon International Wood Engraving Exhibition, Switzerland, second prize; 1966, 1st Krakow International Print Biennial; Tokyo International Print Biennial, honorable mention; 1967, Ljubljana International Print Biennial, prize; 1968, 2nd Krakow International Print Biennial, prize; 1968, taught four months at Augustana College and Marycrest College; 1969, Second Inter-Asia Print Exhibition, Manila, first prize; 1970, solo show, American Cultural Center, Tokyo; 1971, 73, Gallery of Graphic Arts, New York; has lived in New York since 1971.

COLLECTIONS: Tokyo National Museum of Modern Art; Cincinnati Art Museum; Zagreb Municipal Museum; Krakow National Museum.

靉 嘔
(plate 30)

AY-Ō

1931, born in Ibaragi Prefecture; 1954, graduated from Tokyo Art Teachers' University; 1955, first solo show, Takemiya Gallery, Tokyo; 1958, moved to New York; 1962, joined the Fluxus Group; 1964, first Rainbow Happening Performance, Carnegie Hall, New York; 1965, Environment Exhibition, Smoling Gallery, New York; 1966, Venice Biennial; traveled through Europe and India; solo show, Minami Gallery, Tokyo; 1967, Vancouver International Print Biennial, special prize; 1968–69, taught at University of Kentucky; 1970, Tokyo International Print Biennial, Tokyo National Museum of Modern Art Prize; 1971, São Paulo International Print Biennial, Bank of Brazil Prize; 1974, group show, Louisiana Museum, Denmark; 1976, exhibition of 36 works, Museum of Modern Art, New York; 1977, Rainbow Laundry event, World Trade Center, New York; 1979, Ay-O's World, Ikeda 20th Century Museum of Art, Itoh; 1982, 85, 90, solo show, Fuji Television Gallery, Tokyo; 1987, 300-Meter Rainbow Eiffel Tower event, Paris; 1990, solo show, Bunkamura Gallery, Tokyo; 1991, Whale Exhibition, Germany; 1992, Olympic Exhibition, Nantenshi Gallery, Tokyo; 1993, solo show, Emily Harvey Gallery, New York.

COLLECTIONS: New York Museum of Modern Art; Tokyo National Museum of Modern Art; Kyoto National Museum of Modern Art; Cincinnati Art Museum; Fukushima Prefectural Museum of Art; Machida City Museum of Graphic Art, Tokyo.

畦地梅太郎
(plate 14)

AZECHI Umetarō

1902, born in Uwajima, Ehime Prefecture; 1919, worked as a sailor; 1921, came to Tokyo and worked at various jobs, including one at the government printing bureau; accepted into the Japan Creative Print Association; studied woodblock printmaking with Hiratsuka Un'ichi; 1932, became a member of JPA; 1953, 57, São Paulo International Print Biennial; 1956, Lugano International Print Biennial; 1957, 60, 62, Tokyo International Print Biennial; 1974, 85, solo show, Ehime Prefectural Museum; 1979, solo show, Mikimoto Hall, Tokyo; 1987, 91, solo show, Machida City Museum of Graphic Art, Tokyo; 1988, solo show, Odakyu Department Store, Tokyo; 1990, solo show, Azechi Umetaro Memorial Museum, Ehime; honorary member of JPA since 1976.

COLLECTIONS: Azechi Umetaro Memorial Museum, Ehime; Machida City Museum of Graphic Art, Tokyo; Art Institute of Chicago; Boston Museum of Fine Arts; British Museum, London; Cincinnati Art Museum.

深沢史朗
(*plate 9*)

FUKAZAWA Shirō

(1907–78). Born in Tochigi Prefecture; 1930, graduated from Kawabata Academy of Art; followed a career as a portrait painter and began making prints in 1963; 1966, 69, Tokyo International Print Biennial; 1969, 71, Ljubljana International Print Biennial; 1970–76, Krakow International Print Biennial; 1972, 76, Frechen International Print Biennial, Germany; 1974, 76, Bradford International Print Biennial, England; 1978, International Drawing Show, Christchurch, New Zealand; 1975, first prize in the international competition for a coin design for the Montreal Olympic Games.

COLLECTIONS: Japan Culture Institute, Rome; Poznan National Museum, Poland; Warsaw National Museum; Krakow National Museum; Tampere Art Museum, Finland; Tochigi Prefectural Museum of Art; Cincinnati Art Museum; Japanese-Brazilian Cultural Society, Brazil; Mexico City Museum of Modern Art.

吹田文明
(*plate 13*)

FUKITA Fumiaki

1926, born in Tokushima Prefecture; 1947, graduated from Tokushima Teachers' College; 1948, sent to Tokyo University of Fine Arts as a research student by Tokushima Prefecture; 1957, 58, JPA show, Onchi Prize in 57 and JPA Prize in 58; Grenchen International Triennial, Switzerland, prize; 1960–68, Tokyo International Print Biennial; 1967, São Paulo International Print Biennial, Prize for Excellence; 1975, Miami Graphics Biennial, prize; 1987, Tokushima Cultural Prize; 1989, received *shijuhōshō* (Purple Ribbon) Medal from Japanese government; New Zealand International Print Show; 30-year participation in CWAJ show; member and director, JPA; member, Modern Art Association of Japan; presently professor, Tama University of Fine Arts, Tokyo.

COLLECTIONS: Tokyo National Museum of Modern Art; Kyoto National Museum of Modern Art; Prefectural Museums of Kanagawa, Tochigi, Tokushima, and Hiroshima; Tokyo Metropolitan Museum; New York Museum of Modern Art; Geneva Museum; Machida Museum of Graphic Art, Tokyo; Setagaya Art Museum, Tokyo.

船井　裕
(*plate 68*)

FUNAI Yutaka

1932, born in Kobe, Hyogo Prefecture; 1951–52, submitted work to Liberal Art Association exhibition, Tokyo Metropolitan Museum; 1954, participated in forming the Gutai Group but left in 1955; 1955, graduated from Osaka University of Fine Arts, majoring in law; participated in forming the Democrat Art Association; began printmaking; 1956, group show of lithographs, Hankyu Department Store, Osaka; 1956, Group Union Exhibition, Osaka Municipal Museum; Democrat Art Exhibition, Umeda Gallery, Osaka; 1956, 59, solo show, Hakuho Gallery, Osaka; 1958, Grenchen International Triennial, Switzerland; 1960, Asahi Young Artists Exhibition, Takashimaya Department Store, Osaka; 1962, 64, solo show, Kita Gallery, Osaka; 1965, 86, 87, group show, Shinanobashi Gallery, Osaka; 1966, 73, 75, 76, 78, solo show, Shinanobashi Gallery, Osaka; 1966, solo show, Gallery Azuchi, Osaka; Lithograph Best Three, Gallery CoCo, Kyoto; 1967, Tendencies in Modern Art group show, Kyoto National Museum; solo show, Akao Gallery, Osaka; 1968, 71, solo show, Gallery CoCo, Kyoto; 1970, solo show, Gallery Miyazaki, Osaka; 1971, 73, 75, Ljubljana International Print Biennial; 1972, Krakow International Print Biennial; Menton International Print Biennial, France; Bird's Eye View of Modern Art, Kyoto National Museum; 1973, Eikyu and Democrat Art, Umeda Museum of Modern Art, Osaka; 1974, 77, 78, solo show, Galleria Grafica, Tokyo; 1974, 79, solo show, Imabashi Gallery, Osaka; 1974, 76, Krakow International Print Biennial; 1975, Art Now, Hyogo Prefectural Museum; 1979, Yoshihara Jiro and After the Gutai, Hyogo Prefectural Museum; 1980, 81, 83, solo show, Ban Gallery, Osaka; 1980, Japanese Prints, Tochigi Prefectural Museum; 1981, Art Now 1970–80, Hyogo Prefectural Museum; 1983–84, Osaka Modern Art Fair; 1984, Modern Art

1950–70, Yao Seibu Hall, Osaka; since 1987 has not exhibited but continues to make new prints while working as professor at Osaka University of Fine Arts.

COLLECTIONS: Kyoto National Museum of Modern Art; Prefectural Museums of Wakayama and Miyazaki; Osaka Modern Art Center; New York Museum of Modern Art; Ljubljana Museum.

船坂芳助
(plate 33)

FUNASAKA Yoshisuke

1939, born in Gifu Prefecture; 1962, graduated from Tama University of Fine Arts, Tokyo, department of oil painting; 1960 to present, member of JPA; 1968, Geijutsu Seikatsu Gallery Competition, Tokyo, prize; 1970, 72, 74, 76, 79, Bradford International Print Biennial, England; 1970, Tokyo International Print Biennial, Tokyo Museum of Modern Art Prize; 1971–77, Ljubljana International Print Biennial; 1972, 74, 88, Krakow International Print Biennial; 1973, International Young Artists Competition, Tokyo, prize; 1974, began teaching printmaking at Asahi Culture Center; 1976–77, Japanese government fellowship to study in U.S. and England; 1977, solo show, London College of Printing and Jordan Gallery; 1976, 78, solo show, Yoseido Gallery, Tokyo; 1980, solo show, Soker-Kaseman, San Francisco, and Irene Drori Graphics, Los Angeles; 1991, Print and Paper Exhibition, Sweden; 1992, Contemporary Japanese Prints and Ceramics, U.S.; 1994, Japanese Prints: Then and Now, Wako Department Store, Tokyo, produced by Tolman Collection.

COLLECTIONS: Tokyo National Museum of Modern Art; Kyoto National Museum of Modern Art; Tochigi Prefectural Art Museum; Chase Manhattan Bank, Tokyo; Cincinnati Art Museum; Bibliothèque Nationale, Paris; Art Gallery of New South Wales, Australia; British Museum, London; Freer Art Museum, Washington, D.C.; Arthur M. Sackler Gallery, Smithsonian Institution, Washington, D.C.

萩原英雄
(plate 22)

HAGIWARA Hideo

1913, born in Kofu, Yamanashi Prefecture; spent childhood in Korea, returning to Japan in 1929; 1938, graduated from Tokyo Academy of Fine Arts; 1958, became full member of JPA; 1956 onward, annual solo show, Yoseido Gallery, Tokyo; 1960, 2nd Tokyo International Print Biennial, Kamakura Prize; 1962, 7th Lugano International Print Biennial, grand prize; 1963, 5th Ljubljana International Print Biennial, Science and Art Academy Prize; 1966, 5th Tokyo International Print Biennial, Minister of Education Prize; 1967, 7th Ljubljana International Print Biennial, Rijeka Museum Prize; 1979–90, chief director of JPA; 1984, honored by postal minister with silver cup for contribution to postal services; 1984, The World of Hagiwara Hideo, Yamanashi Prefectural Museum; 1988, awarded Small Cordon of the Order of the Rising Sun, 4th Class, by the emperor; 1989, awarded gold medal by Nobel Prize Committee for five works produced on themes from the novels of Kawabata Yasunari; 1992, Banska Bystrice International Woodblock Biennial, Czechoslovakia, prize.

COLLECTIONS: Tokyo National Museum of Modern Art; Prefectural Museums of Miyagi, Tochigi, Yamanashi, Wakayama, Oita, Toyama, Hiroshima, and Tokushima; Kamakura Museum of Modern Art; Honolulu Academy of Arts; Art Institute of Chicago; New York Public Library; Boston Museum of Fine Arts; Cincinnati Art Museum; Library of Congress, Washington, D.C.; Rockefeller Foundation, New York; Victoria and Albert Museum, London; Amsterdam Museum of Art; São Paulo Museum of Modern Art; Ljubljana, Rijeka, Scopjye, Krakow, Vienna, and Dresden Museums of Modern Art.

浜西勝則
(plate 64)

HAMANISHI Katsunori

1949, born in Hokkaido; 1973, graduated from Tokai University, Kanagawa Prefecture; 1986, visiting artist, Cleveland Institute of Art; 1987–88, studied at University of Pennsylvania on grant from Cultural Affairs Agency; 1988, visiting professor, University of Alberta; 1989, exchange artist between Japan and Canada. Partial list of prizes includes those of 1978, Ibiza International Print Biennial, Spain;

1979, Japan-France Contemporary Art Exhibition, Tokyo; 1982, Grenchen International Triennial, Switzerland; International Miniature Print Exhibition, Korea; 1983, Frechen International Print Biennial, Germany; Cabo Frio International Print Biennial, Brazil; 1984, International Mezzotint Competition, U.S.; 1987, Exhibition of Small Graphic Forms, Poland; 1989, Valparaiso International Exhibition, Chile. Partial list of shows includes those of 1984, l'Atelier 56, Tournai, Belgium; 1986, Gilbert Luber Gallery, Philadelphia; 1989, 91, Yoseido Reflections Gallery, Tokyo; 1989–91, Heian Gallery, Kyoto; 1994, Japan Week '94, Cairo, Egypt, produced by Tolman Collection.

COLLECTIONS: New York Metropolitan Museum of Art; New York Museum of Modern Art; Art Institute of Chicago; Library of Congress, Washington, D.C.; University of Alberta, Edmonton; Taipei Fine Arts Museum; Krakow National Museum; Osaka National Museum of Art; Achenbach Foundation for the Graphic Arts, San Francisco.

原 健
(plate 53)

HARA Takeshi (HARA Ken)

1942, born in Nagoya; 1967, B.A. in painting; 1969, M.A. in painting from Tokyo University of Fine Arts; presently full professor, Zokei University, Tokyo; 1969, Shell Art Exhibition, prize; 1972, 7th Japan Art Festival, Tokyo and Mexico; 1976, 12th Florence International Print Biennial; 1976, grant from the Cultural Affairs Agency for one year of study and travel abroad; 1982, Seibu Print Competition, Tokyo, first grand prize; 1985, Contemporary Japanese Prints, Tokyo Metropolitan Art Museum; 1990, group show, Retretti Art Centre, Finland; 1991, 5th Taiwan International Print Biennial; 1992, NICAF, Yokohama.

COLLECTIONS: Kyoto National Museum of Modern Art; Tokyo Metropolitan Museum; Cincinnati Art Museum.

長谷川雄一
(plate 62)

HASEGAWA Yūichi

1945, born in Aizu Wakamatsu, Fukushima Prefecture; 1970, influenced by Saito Kiyoshi, began making woodblocks; 1981, 35th Fukushima Art Festival, Grand Prix; 1983, 85, solo show, Takashimaya Department Store, Tokyo; 1987, 41st Fukushima Art Festival, Director of the Museum Prize; 1987, solo show, Elegance Gallery, Fukushima; 1988, solo show, Alphaflor Galerie, Freiburg, Germany; 1989, 90, 94, solo show, Tolman Collection; 1990, group show, Retretti Art Centre, Finland, produced by Tolman Collection; 1990–91, solo show, Galerie beim Roten Turm, Wurzburg, Germany; 1991, solo show, Tokyo American Club; 1992, solo show, Springmann Galerie, Freiburg, Germany; 1992, group show, Hankyu Department Store, Tokyo, produced by Tolman Collection; 1994, Japan Week '94, Cairo, Egypt, produced by Tolman Collection.

COLLECTIONS: Cincinnati Art Museum; Art Gallery of New South Wales, Australia; Hamburg Museum of Arts and Crafts; Singapore National Museum.

橋本興家
(plate 6)

HASHIMOTO Okiie

(1899–1993). Born in Tottori Prefecture; 1924, graduated from Tokyo University of Fine Arts; 1925–55, worked as high school teacher in Tokyo; 1937, began making woodblock prints, showing work in local and international shows; 1956, 58, 60, 63, solo show, Nihonbashi Mitsukoshi Department Store, Tokyo; 1957, 60, 62, Tokyo International Print Biennial; from 1962, exhibited work in England, Germany, Switzerland, France, Italy, Netherlands, U.S., Israel, Mexico, Australia, Austria, Sweden, and China; 1975, solo show, Yoseido Gallery, Tokyo; 1937–82, JPA show, serving as chairman 1973–78; 1971, awarded Medal of Honor by the Japanese government; 1980, awarded National Medal of Honor, 4th Class by the Japanese government.

COLLECTIONS: Tokyo Metropolitan Museum; Prefectural Museums of Hiroshima and Tottori; Berlin National Museum; Tikotin Museum of Japanese Art, Haifa, Israel; Cincinnati Art Museum.

平塚運一
(plates 5, 76)

HIRATSUKA Un'ichi

1895, born in Shimane Prefecture; 1913, left high school one day before graduation; worked for Matsue City office; heard a lecture by Ishi Hakutei and decided to become an artist; 1915, came to Tokyo to study art; 1917, returned to Shimane, got married, and worked as elementary school teacher; 1920, returned to Tokyo and became involved with the *sōsaku-hanga* movement; 1922, published the magazine *Journies and Literature* with Yamamoto Kanae; 1928, joined Japan Farmers' Art Promotion activities; gave lectures on printmaking; 1932, published *Study of Print Art;* 1934, published *How to Make the New Sōsaku Hanga;* 1935, was put in charge of the newly established printmaking department at Tokyo Art University (Tokyo University of Fine Arts); 1943, invited to Peking to teach printmaking; 1949, published *Printmaking Techniques;* 1955, published *How to Make Crayon Pastel Prints;* 1957, 73, solo show, Yoseido Gallery, Tokyo; Tokyo International Print Biennial; 1958, Lugano International Print Biennial; 1962, moved to Washington, D.C., where he lives with his daughter; 1962, solo show, North Carolina State University; 1962, 89, solo show, Smithsonian Institution, Washington, D.C.; 1971, Hiratsuka, Munakata, Matsubara: Three Generations, Cincinnati Art Museum; 1972, solo show sponsored by the Japanese ambassador to celebrate Hiratsuka's 77th birthday; 1973, solo show, Nihonbashi Mitsukoshi Department Store, Tokyo; Northwestern University; Art Institute of Chicago; 1977, received Medal of the 3rd Class from the Japanese government; 1979, solo show, Shimane Prefectural Museum; 1980, solo show for 20th anniversary of Isetan Department Store, Tokyo; 1983, solo show to celebrate his 88th birthday, Wako Department Store; 1984, solo show and demonstration, College of William and Mary; 1985, solo show, Japan-U.S. Cultural Center, Los Angeles; 1986, solo show and demonstration, World Trade Center, New Orleans; solo show, Ryu Gallery, Tokyo; 1987, solo show and demonstration, Smithsonian Institution, Washington, D.C.; 1989, solo show, Shimane Prefectural Museum; 1991, Hiratsuka Un'ichi Print Museum opened in Suzaka City, Nagano Prefecture.

COLLECTIONS: Tokyo National Museum of Modern Art; Kyoto National Museum of Modern Art; Smithsonian Institution, Washington, D.C.; Art Institute of Chicago; Boston Museum of Fine Arts; Honolulu Academy of Arts; Tokyo Metropolitan Museum; New York Metropolitan Museum; Rockefeller Foundation, New York; Library of Congress, Washington, D.C.; Cincinnati Art Museum; Prefectural Museums of Shimane, Saitama, and Shizuoka.

平塚雄二
(plate 98)

HIRATSUKA Yūji

1954, born in Osaka; 1978, graduated from Tokyo Art Teachers' University; 1987, M.A., New Mexico State University; 1990, M.F.A., Indiana University; 1992 to present, assistant professor of printmaking at Oregon State University; 1983, solo show, Clark Arts Center, Illinois; Central Museum Gallery group show, Tokyo; 1983, 84, 85, 93, solo show, Aunkan Gallery, Osaka; 1984, 87, 89–93, CWAJ show; 1985, group exhibitions in the U.S., Japan, Poland, Malaysia, Brazil, Korea, and Taiwan; 1986, Pratt Graphics Center show, New York, purchase award; 1987, World Print Membership Exhibition, California College of Arts and Crafts; 1988, São Paulo International Print Biennial, Superior Class Prize; 1988, solo show, Gallery Shirakawa, Kyoto; 1989–92, solo show, Greene Art Gallery, Guilford, Connecticut; 1989, 90, 92, 94, solo show, Chicago Center for the Print; 1987, 90, solo show, Gilbert Luber Gallery, Philadelphia; 1992, solo show, Oregon State University; 1993, solo show, Print Club, Philadelphia; Azuma Gallery, Seattle; 1994, solo show, Tolman Collection; Gresham City Hall, Oregon.

COLLECTIONS: Achenbach Foundation for the Graphic Arts, San Francisco; British Museum, London; Hallmark Cards, Inc., Kansas City, Missouri; Central Museum Gallery, Tokyo; International Graphic Arts Foundation, New Canaan, Connecticut; Print Club, Philadelphia.

星 襄一
(plates 12, 72)

HOSHI Jōichi

(1913–79). Born in Niigata; 1932, graduated from Tainan Normal School, Taiwan, and spent next 13 years there as a teacher; 1946, returned to Japan; 1949, JPA show, prize; 1952, became member of JPA; 1956, graduated from Musashino Art University, Tokyo; 1959, 61, 63, Tokyo International Print Biennial; 1970, traveling show of Japanese artists, University of Oregon, Eugene; numerous solo shows throughout Japan.

COLLECTIONS: Tokyo Museum of Modern Art; New York Museum of Modern Art; National Museum of Far Eastern Art, Berlin; Art Institute of Chicago; Haifa Museum, Israel; Rockefeller Foundation, New York; Helen and Felix Juda Collection, Los Angeles.

池田満寿夫
(plates 36, 61)

IKEDA Masuo

1934, born in Mukden, Manchuria; 1945, moved to Japan; 1951, Japan Students' Oil Painting Competition, Atelier Prize; 1954, graduated from Nagano High School; failed the entrance exam to Tokyo University of Fine Arts for the third time; 1955, established the group Existence with Ay-O and Manabe; 1956, began to create etchings with the encouragement of Eikyu; 1957, 60, 62, 64, Tokyo International Print Biennial, Minister of Education Prize in 60, Governor of Tokyo Prize in 62, Tokyo National Museum of Modern Art Prize in 64; 1961, first solo show of etchings, Shinobazu Gallery, Tokyo; 1963, São Paulo International Print Biennial; 1965, solo show Prints by Ikeda Masuo, New York Museum of Modern Art; 1966, visited U.S. on Ford Foundation grant; traveled abroad extensively but resided chiefly in the U.S. for the next 13 years; Venice International Print Biennial, grand prize; started making lithographs at Tamarind Workshop, Los Angeles; Krakow International Print Biennial, prize; 1967, Minister of Education Prize for Art Encouragement; 1969, Ljubljana International Print Biennial, Yugoslavian Art Academy Prize; 1970, 71, 73, 75, 76, solo show, Nantenshi Gallery, Tokyo; 1971, 74, 77, 80, 81, 82, 83, 85, 86, 88, 89, 90, 91, 93, solo show, Bancho Gallery, Tokyo; 1974, two-person show (with Ida Shoichi), Japan Society, New York; solo show, Central Museum Gallery, Tokyo; solo show, Staempfli Gallery, New York; 1976, three-person show (with Arakawa and Noda), Cincinnati Art Museum; 1977, Akutagawa Prize for his novel *For the Aegean Sea;* retrospective, Isetan Department Store gallery, Tokyo; 1978, two-person show (with Munakata), Los Angeles County Museum; 1979, returned to Japan; 1981, retrospective, Daimaru Department Store gallery, Tokyo; 1983, The Unknown World of Masuo Ikeda, Ikeda 20th Century Museum of Art, Itoh; 1984, first pottery exhibition, Nihonbashi Takashimaya Department Store gallery, Tokyo; 1986, designed tapestry for the National Diet Library, Tokyo; 1988–94, numerous solo shows throughout Japan.

COLLECTIONS: New York Museum of Modern Art; New York Metropolitan Museum; Tokyo National Museum of Modern Art; Kyoto National Museum of Modern Art; Tokyo Metropolitan Museum; Dresden National Museum; Cincinnati Art Museum; Los Angeles County Museum of Art; Brooklyn Museum; Hiroshima Municipal Museum of Contemporary Art; Prefectural Museums of Chiba and Hiroshima.

池上勇夫
(plate 88)

IKEGAMI Isao

1938, born in Tokyo; 1960, graduated from Musashino Art University, Tokyo; 1960–80, experimented with abstract painting while working as graphic designer; 1981, 15th Contemporary Modern Art Exhibition, Tokyo Metropolitan Museum; 1982, 87, group show, Tolman Collection; 1983, 85, 86, 88, solo show, Tolman Collection; 1985, solo show, Gallery Off, Nagoya; Tsutaya Gallery, Kyoto; Flower Collection, Osaka; 1986, solo show, Gallery Tamura, Hiroshima; 1990, group show, Retretti Art Centre, Finland; 1992, group show, Hankyu Department Store, Tokyo, produced by Tolman Collection; 1994, group show, Japan Week '94, Cairo, Egypt, produced by Tolman Collection.

COLLECTIONS: Cincinnati Art Museum; Rockefeller Foundation, New York; Tetrapak, Tokyo; Bayerische Landesbank, Tokyo; Oak Associates, Tokyo; Singapore National Museum; Hamburg Museum of Arts and Crafts; Bank of America, Hong Kong; Bank of America, Singapore.

今村由男
(plate 83)

IMAMURA Yoshio

1948, born in Nagano Prefecture; studied painting after high school; came to Tokyo at age 20 to work as a design assistant; self-employed as a designer since 1974; 1982 to present, JPA show; associate member of JPA; 1987, Most Promising Artist Grand Prix Print Contest, Japan, U.S., Israel, and Australia, purchase award; 1989, Miniature Print Biennial, New York, purchase award of John Szoke Gallery; 1989, Bharat Bhavan International Biennial, India, special prize; 1989, JPA show, associate member special prize; 1988, 89, group show, Tolman Collection; 1990, 92, solo show, Tolman Collection; 1990, 91, CWAJ show; 1989, Exposition France-Japon, *France Soir* second prize and *Figaro* third prize; 1990, Exposition France-Japon, *Figaro* first prize and *France Soir* first prize; 1991, *France Soir* first prize; 1992, solo show, Silk Gallery, Seoul, and Portfolio Gallery, New Zealand; 1993, solo show, Root Gallery, Tokyo, and Taller Galeria, Barcelona; 1992, group show, Hankyu Department Store, Tokyo, produced by Tolman Collection; 1994, Japan Week '94, Cairo, Egypt, produced by Tolman Collection.

COLLECTIONS: Cincinnati Art Museum; Tikotin Museum of Japanese Art, Haifa, Israel; Hamburg Museum of Arts and Crafts; Singapore Art Museum; Gallery of New South Wales, Australia.

稲垣知雄
(plate 11)

INAGAKI Tomoo

(1902–80). Born in Tokyo; 1923, studied printmaking with Onchi Koshiro; 1924, 6th Japan Creative Print Association exhibition; 1925, Los Angeles International Print Artists' show; 1932, became full member of JPA; 1948, Kokugakai Art Association show, award; 1960, Lugano International Print Biennial; 1966–80, honorary member of JPA and Kokugakai Art Association.

COLLECTIONS: New York Museum of Modern Art; Cincinnati Art Museum; Setagaya Art Museum, Tokyo; Machida City Museum of Graphic Art, Tokyo; Chiba Prefectural Museum; Yokohama Art Museum.

岩見禮花
(plates 27, 92)

IWAMI Reika

1927, born in Tokyo; 1955, graduated from Bunka Gakuin Liberal Arts College, Sunday art course; 1954–66, member of Kokugakai Art Association, Kokuga Prize in 59; 1954–94, member and annual participant in JPA show; 1956–65, Contemporary Women's Print Exhibition, Tokyo; 1957, 60, 62, 64, Tokyo International Print Biennial; 1957–94, CWAJ show; 1977, seven-person Japanese print show, Dusseldorf; 1977, 82, 87, solo show, Tolman Collection; 1983, solo show, Yoseido Gallery, Tokyo; 1984, Contemporary Japanese Prints, Warwick Arts Trust, London; 1986, Contemporary Japanese Prints, British Museum, London; 1989, Today's Yokohama, Sairin Gallery, Yokohama; 1992, 94, solo show, Tomy Gallery, Tokyo; 1993, 35th Anniversary Exhibition for Yokohama-San Diego Sister City Celebration; 1994, Japan Week '94, Cairo, Egypt, produced by Tolman Collection; Japanese Prints Then and Now, Wako Department Store Gallery, produced by Tolman Collection; three-person show (with Shinoda and Matsubara), Spirit Square Center for the Arts, Charlotte, North Carolina, produced by Tolman Collection.

COLLECTIONS: New York Museum of Modern Art, Study Collection; Cincinnati Art Museum; Library of Congress, Washington, D.C.; Rockefeller Foundation, New York; Yokohama Museum; Yokohama Municipal Gallery; University of Oregon; University of California; Yale University Art Gallery.

泉　茂
(plate 67)

IZUMI Shigeru

1922, born in Osaka; 1939, graduated from Osaka School of Arts and Crafts; 1948, Pan Artists Association exhibition, award; 1951, solo show, Hankyu Department Store, Osaka; with Eikyu and others formed the Democrat Art Association; 1951–57, Democrat Art Association exhibition, City Museum; Hankyu Department Store; Sogo Department Store; and Umeda Gallery, Osaka; Matsushima; Maruzen; Mimatsu; and Muramatsu Galleries, Tokyo; 1957, breakup of Democrat Art Association; 1953, 58, 64, solo show, Umeda Gallery, Osaka; started making etchings; 1955, Today's

Young Artists, Kanagawa Prefectural Museum; started making lithographs; 1957, Tokyo International Print Biennial, Young Artists Prize; 1957, 58, solo show, Hakuho Gallery, Osaka; 1958, three-person show, Yoseido Gallery, Tokyo; 1958, 64, solo show, Umeda Gallery, Osaka; 1958, solo show of watercolors, Minami Gallery, Tokyo; 1959, moved to New York; solo show, Pratt Graphics Center, New York; 1963, moved to Paris; 1958, 64, 68, 69, Modern Japanese Art Exhibition, Tokyo Metropolitan Museum; 1964, 65, 67, Salon d'Art Space, Museum of Modern Art, Paris; 1965, solo show, Paris and Germany; Japanese Artists Living in the U.S. and Europe show, Tokyo National Museum; 1968, 12 Japanese Artists exhibition, France; returned to Japan; 1970, became professor at Osaka University of Fine Arts; 1971, group show, Wakayama and Hyogo Prefectural Museums; 1973, 74, solo show, Shinanobashi Gallery, Osaka; 1973, Eikyu and Democrat Art exhibition, Umeda Museum of Modern Art, Osaka; 1976, four-person show (with Tsutaka, Hayakawa, and Motonaga), Shunko Gallery, Osaka; 1966, 76, 77, 81, Japan Art Festival, New York, Los Angeles, Tokyo, and Kyoto; 1979, three-person show (with Motonaga and Mio Kozo), Ban Gallery, Osaka; 1983, three-person show (with Tsutaka and Yoshihara Hideo), Wakayama Prefectural Museum; 1986, Eikyu and Izumi Shigeru, Central Annex Gallery, Tokyo; Eikyu and Surroundings, Prefectural Museums of Saitama, Miyazaki, and Wakayama; 1987, solo show, Keihan Department Store, Osaka; Eikyu and His Associates, Machida City Museum of Graphic Art, Tokyo; 1980, 81, 85, 86, 89, 92–94, solo show, Ban Gallery, Osaka; presently honorary professor at Osaka University of Fine Arts.

COLLECTIONS: New York Museum of Modern Art; Tokyo National Museum of Modern Art; Kyoto National Museum of Modern Art; Paris Museum of Modern Art; Carnegie Foundation, Pittsburgh; Rockefeller Foundation, New York; Tokyo Metropolitan Museum; Hyogo Prefectural Museum.

クリフトン カーフ
(plates 42, 52)

Clifton KARHU

1927, born a twin in Duluth, Minnesota; 1950–52, studied at Minneapolis School of Art; 1955 to present, has lived in Japan; 1961–63, Central Japan Pacific Art Society; 1961, Gifu City and Gifu Prefecture shows; 1963–68, Kyoto Print Society; 1964 to present, JPA show; 1966 to present, CWAJ show; 1966 to present, numerous solo shows throughout Japan, the U.S., Southeast Asia, and Europe; 1976, two-person show (with Doug Lawrie), Wako Department Store, Tokyo, produced by Tolman Collection; 1977 to present, annual Christmas exhibition, produced by Tolman Collection; 1977, elected Kyoto representative of JPA; 1986, solo retrospective, Tweed Museum, Duluth; 1988, solo retrospective, Takashimaya Exhibition Hall, Kyoto; 1990, solo retrospective, Retretti Art Centre, Finland; 1991, solo show, Hankyu Department Store, Tokyo; works commissioned by Matsushita Electric, National Panasonic, Hong Kong Shanghai Banking Corporation, IBM Japan, AIU Japan, Business Week, Boston-Kyoto Sister City Committee, Hong Kong Tourist Association, Cathay Pacific Airways, NHK Television of Kansai.

COLLECTIONS: Cincinnati Art Museum; East Asian Legal Studies Center, Harvard University; Kunst Museum, Salzburg; Minnesota Museum of Art, St. Paul, Minnesota; Museum of Fine Arts, Boston; National Museum of Australia, Canberra.

河内成幸
(plate 97)

KAWACHI Seikō

1948, born in Yamanashi Prefecture; 1973, graduated from Tama University of Fine Arts, Tokyo; 1973–84, taught at Tama University of Fine Arts; 1985–86, studied at Columbia University and traveled in Europe on grant from Cultural Affairs Agency; 1970, 38th JPA show, New Printmaker's Prize; 1976, Japan Print Association show, Grand Prix; 1978, 12th International Art Exhibition, Tokyo, Tokyo National Museum of Modern Art Prize; 1982, 6th Norway International Print Biennial, top prize; 1983, World Print Fair, California, special edition purchase prize; 1984, 1st Competition for Selected New Artists in Yamanashi, Yamanashi Prefectural Museum of Art Prize; 1986, gave print workshops at Columbia University, New York, and Atlantis Paper Laboratory, London; 1988, solo show, Tokyo Ginza Art Center Hall; Kyoto Art Center Hall; and Galleria Tega, Milan; 1991, Osaka International Print

Triennial, special prize; 1993, two-person show (with wife), Wako Gallery, Ginza, Tokyo.

COLLECTIONS: Tokyo National Museum of Modern Art; Tokyo Metropolitan Museum; Norway National Gallery, Oslo; Cleveland Museum of Art; Prefectural Art Museums of Hyogo, Yamanashi, Tochigi, Toyama, Niigata, Kanagawa, and Osaka; Library of Congress, Washington, D.C.; Gallery of New South Wales, Australia; British Museum, London; Yonago Public Art Museum; Machida City Museum of Graphic Art, Tokyo.

川田 幹
(plate 96)

KAWADA Kan

1927, born in Tokyo; studied under Serizawa Keisuke; graduated from Ochanomizu Bunka Gakuin Art Institute, Tokyo; 1953–59, Kokugakai show; 1960–67, Sankikai Art exhibition, Sankikai award in 61 and 67; 1973, 76, 87, solo show, Franell Gallery, Tokyo; 1982, 83, 84, Art Now exhibition, Chokoku-no-mori Outdoor Sculpture Garden, Hakone, grand prize in 82, Fuji TV Prize in 83, and Sankei Newspaper Prize in 84; 1985, Nitten Art Exhibition, grand prize; 1992, solo show, Bordeaux and Arcachon, France.

COLLECTIONS: Setagaya Art Museum, Tokyo; Cincinnati Art Museum.

木村光佑
(plate 86)

KIMURA Kōsuke

1936, born in Osaka; 1959, graduated from Kyoto Municipal University of Fine Arts; 1970, Bradford International Print Biennial, England, Richard Gainsborough Memorial Prize; 71, 83, Ljubljana International Print Biennial, grand prize in 71 and purchase prize in 83; 1972, Norway International Print Biennial, grand prize; 1977, 7th Contemporary Sculpture Exhibition, Japan, grand prize; 1978, 84, Krakow International Print Biennial, Award of Merit in 78, Gold Medal in 84; 1987, 1st Contemporary Print Exhibition of Shoto Museum, Tokyo, Grand Prix; 1988, poster commissioned to celebrate Osaka Centennial; 1992, monument *Rainbow Pagoda* for Ibaraki City; 1992, honored by the city of Osaka for cultural achievements; presently professor at Kyoto University of Art Crafts and Textiles.

COLLECTIONS: Kyoto National Museum of Modern Art; Tokyo National Museum of Modern Art; San Francisco Museum of Art; Krakow National Museum; Museum of Contemporary Art, Fredrikstad, Norway; New York Museum of Modern Art.

木下富雄
(plate 51)

KINOSHITA Tomio

1923, born in Yokkaichi, Mie Prefecture; 1958, JPA show, Best Prize; Modern Japanese Print Exhibition, St. James Church, New York, second prize; 1958, 59, Kokugakai show, Young Talent Prize in 58 and Kokuga Prize in 59; 1960, Northwest International Print Exhibition, Seattle, Seattle Museum Prize; 1961, two-person show (with Yamaguchi Gen), Seattle; 1962, Tokyo International Print Biennial; 1963, Excellent Contemporary Prints of the World, Philadelphia Museum; 1964, Show for International Prizewinners, Niigata Museum; 1971, Modern Japanese Print Art Exhibition, Belgium; 1982, Today's Artists in Mie, Mie Prefectural Museum; since 1982, has not submitted work for exhibitions or competitions, except at JPA show.

COLLECTIONS: New York Museum of Modern Art; Brooklyn Museum; Philadelphia Museum; Art Institute of Chicago; Houston Museum; Honolulu Academy of Arts; London National Gallery; University of Illinois, Urbana-Champaign; Oregon State University, Corvallis; Mie Prefectural Museum; Niigata Prefectural Museum of Modern Art.

北岡文雄
(plate 15)

KITAOKA Fumio

(Kitaoka submitted a fifteen-page autobiography, of which the following presents just a glimpse of his traveling, teaching, and working career.) 1918, born in Tokyo; 1939, began studying woodblock printmaking with Hiratsuka; 1941, graduated from Tokyo University of Art; 1943 to present, member of JPA; 1945, worked in Changchun, Manchuria, for Northeast Asia Cultural Promotion Society; 1946, evacuated to Andong, China, and began lifelong interest in Chinese woodblock art; 1955, studied in Italy, England, and at L'Ecole des Beaux Arts, Paris; 1956, moved to Sapporo and helped found the Sapporo Print Association; 1964–65, Fulbright Professor, Minneapolis School of Art; taught for one month at Pratt Graphics Center, New York; solo show, Minneapolis Institute of Art and Emerson Art Museum, Syracuse, New York; 1966, solo show, Boston Art School and Seattle Art Pavilion; 1971, visited Soviet Union at invitation of Soviet Painters' Union and Japan-Soviet Society; solo show, Soviet East Folk Museum, Moscow; 1980, invited by Beijing Central Art School for solo show and woodblock teaching; 1986, solo show, World Bank, Washington, D.C., and Nippon Club, New York; 1987, invited by Chinese government for solo show and to teach at Beijing Central Art School and Szechwan and Hangchou Art Schools; 1989, solo show, Gallery Yoshii, Paris; 1990, elected president of the Japan Artists' Association; 1992, received Silver Cup award from Ministry of Foreign Affairs for fostering international goodwill; 1993, solo show, Birmingham Art Museum, Alabama; World of Fumio Kitaoka solo show, Hokkaido Museum of Modern Art.

COLLECTIONS: Tokyo Museum of Modern Art; Boston Museum of Fine Arts; New York Museum of Modern Art; Warsaw National Museum; Tikotin Museum of Japanese Art, Haifa, Israel; Art Institute of Chicago; Cincinnati Art Museum; Rockefeller Collection, New York; Carnegie Museum, Pittsburgh; Soviet East Folk Museum, Moscow; Arthur M. Sackler Gallery, Smithsonian Institution, Washington, D.C.

黒田茂樹
(plate 43)

KURODA Shigeki

1953, born in Yokohama; 1977, B.A.; 1979, M.A., Tama University of Fine Arts, Tokyo; 1979, Bradford International Print Biennial, England; 1979, 81, Ljubljana International Print Biennial; 1979, 82, 85, 88, Grenchen International Triennial, Switzerland; 1979, 82, Miami Biennial, purchase prize; 1979, 81, 83, 89, 91, 94, solo show, Yoseido Gallery, Tokyo; 1981, Tolman Collection; 1982, 84, 85, 87, 91, 93, Gilbert Luber Gallery, Philadelphia; 1985, 86, 88, 91, 93, Azuma Gallery, Seattle; 1991, Verne Collection, Cleveland; 1993, Ren Brown Collection, Bodega Bay, California; 1979, 21 Contemporary Japanese Printmakers, Cleveland Museum of Art and Boston City Gallery; 1982, Yokohama-Shanghai Art Exchange Exhibition.

COLLECTIONS: Tochigi Prefectural Museum; Cleveland Museum of Art; Art Institute of Chicago; Art Gallery of the Citizens of Yokohama; Tama University of Fine Arts Museum; de Cordova Museum, Lincoln, Massachusetts; Yokohama Museum of Art; Shanghai City Museum; Odessa Museum of Art, Ukraine; Yokota U.S. Air Force Officers' Wives Club.

黒崎 彰
(plate 31)

KUROSAKI Akira

1937, born in Dairen, Manchuria; 1962, graduated from Kyoto Institute of Technology, design department; 1970, Tokyo International Print Biennial, Minister of Education Prize; 1972, 1st Florence International Print Biennial, Gold Prize; 1973–74, studied at Harvard University and Hochshule fur Bildende Kunst, Hamburg, on grant from Cultural Affairs Agency; 1975–76, visiting lecturer at Morley Art College, London; 1978, visiting professor at University of Washington, Seattle; 1979, Japan Art and Culture Association travel grant to China; 1980, visiting lecturer at University of Hawaii; 1981, 3rd Seoul International Biennial, grand prize; artist in residence at Bulgarian Arts Council, Sofia; 1982, artist in residence at Canberra School of Art, Australia; 1983, 2nd Biennial of Modern Bulgarian Graphic Art, first prize; 1st Exhibition of Yamaguchi Gen Grand Prize Show, Numazu, Japan, grand prize; 1983–84, visiting professor at Harvard; 1985, artist in residence at Cornell University; Japan Foundation travel grant to U.S.; visiting professor at University of Oregon; 1986, visiting lecturer at University of Michigan; 1987, Japan Foundation travel grant to the Netherlands; 1991, British Council travel grant; artist in residence at Glasgow School of Art, Scotland; 1992, Much Foundation research grant, Oslo

Much Museum and Japan Foundation; 1993, artist in residence at Pyramid Atlantic Workshop, Washington, D.C.

COLLECTIONS: Prefectural Museums of Tokushima, Toyama, Tochigi, and Wakayama; Bellas Artes National Museum, Santiago, Chile; Seoul Museum of Modern Art; Krakow National Museum; Warsaw National Museum; Rockefeller Foundation, New York; New York Museum of Modern Art; Cincinnati Art Museum; Los Angeles County Museum of Art; Louisiana State University, Baton Rouge; Hoganas Stadsbibliotek, Sweden.

日下賢司
(plate 29)

KUSAKA Kenji

1936, born in Okayama; 1955, 67, submitted work to the Mainichi International Art Exhibition, Tokyo; 1964, 66, Mainichi Modern Art Exhibition, Tokyo, Kanagawa Prefectural Museum Prize in 64; 1966, Tokyo International Print Biennial, Tokyo National Museum Prize; 1967, São Paulo International Print Biennial; 1967, 89, Ljubljana International Print Biennial; 1967, Premio International Print Biennial, Italy; Trends in Modern Art, Kyoto National Museum; 1968, Florence International Print Biennial; Tokyo International Print Biennial; 1969, Modern Print Exhibition, Kyoto City Museum; 1969, 75, 76, 83, 90, 93, Xylon International Print Triennial, Switzerland; 1971, Today's 100 Artists, Hyogo Prefectural Museum; 1981, 25 Years of the World's Modern Prints, Tokyo Metropolitan Museum; 1985, exhibition of modern Japanese prints traveling throughout the U.S.; 1987, mural commissioned by Matsuzaka Flex Hotel, Mie Prefecture; mural commissioned by Mito Yakult Company, Ibaragi Prefecture; 1992, Artists in Yokohama, Yokohama Municipal Gallery; 1993, International Print Biennial, Netherlands; presently teaches at Joshibi (Women's College of Fine Arts), Tokyo.

COLLECTIONS: British Museum, London; Library of Congress, Washington, D.C.; Tokyo National Museum of Modern Art; Tokyo Metropolitan Museum; Colorado State Museum of Modern Art, Denver; Kanagawa Prefectural Museum.

廖 修平
(plate 73)

LIAO Shiou-ping

1936, born in Taiwan; 1959, B.A., National Taiwan Normal University; 1964, M.A., Tokyo University of Education; 1965–68, studied at Ecole des Beaux Arts and Atelier 17, Paris; 1969–71, continuing studies at Pratt Graphics Center, New York; 1973–76, associate professor of art at National Taiwan Normal University; 1977–79, taught at College of Chinese Culture, Taiwan Academy of Arts, and Chinese University of Hong Kong; visiting professor of printmaking at Tsukuba University, Japan, and Daemen College, Amherst, New York; board director, Chinese Graphic Society, Taipei; member of Society of American Graphic Artists, New York, and Societé du Salon d'Automne, Paris; nearly 50 solo shows, including 1967, Maison des Beaux Arts, Paris; 1968, Crossley Gallery, Melbourne; Miami Museum of Modern Art; 1973, San Francisco Palace of the Legion of Honor; 1978, Shirota Gallery, Tokyo; 1979, Tolman Collection; 1982, National Art Gallery, Taipei; 1986, Newark Public Library; 1988, Yuna Gallery, Seoul; 1991, Striped House Museum, Tokyo; 1992, Museum of Modern Art, Liège, Belgium; Taiwan Museum of Art, Taichung; 1963, 69, 71, São Paulo International Print Biennial; 1971, Whitney Museum, New York; 1967–70, International Biennials of Buenos Aires, Paris, Bradford, and Tokyo; presently professor of art, Seton Hall University, New Jersey.

COLLECTIONS: New York Metropolitan Museum of Art; Tokyo Museum of Modern Art; Albertina Museum, Vienna; National Museum of History, Taipei; Victoria and Albert Museum, London; Museum of Modern Art, Haifa; Cincinnati Art Museum; Rockefeller Foundation, New York; Achenbach Foundation for the Graphic Arts, San Francisco; Bibliothèque Nationale, Paris; Museum Municipal d'Art Moderne, Paris.

馬渕 聖
(plate 7)

MABUCHI Tōru (MABUCHI Thōru)

1920–94. Born in Tokyo; 1941, graduated from Tokyo University of Art, department of industrial arts; 1951, 7th Nitten Exhibition, Tokyo; 1957, became member of Kofukai Art Association; 1960, founded Nipponkai Art Association; 1962, Tokyo

International Print Biennial; 1967, elected trustee of the Kofukai and Nitten Art Associations; 1971, commissioned by the Imperial Household Agency to make four prints for the Suzaki Detached Palace, Shimoda; 1973, founded Ashinokai Art Association, which held its first exhibition at Maruzen Gallery, Tokyo; 1974, group show, Nihonbashi Takashimaya Department Store, Tokyo; 1979, retired from teaching at Tokyo Women's College; 1980, began teaching at Hiroshima University; 1981, president of Nipponkai Art Association; 1982, became member of JPA; 1983, 47 prints purchased by Kure Municipal Museum, Hiroshima.

COLLECTIONS: Boston Museum of Fine Arts; Cincinnati Art Museum; New York Museum of Modern Art; Art Institute of Chicago.

巻 白
(plates 35, 60)

MAKI Haku (MAEJIMA Tadaaki)
1924, born in Ibaragi; 1945, graduated from Ibaragi Teachers' College; studied printmaking under Onchi and Hiratsuka; 1957–78, JPA show, prize in 57; 1957, 60, Tokyo International Print Biennial; 1959, began using cement and plaster of Paris in combination with woodblock technique; 1961–68, numerous overseas exhibitions; 1969, commissioned to make prints illustrating old Japanese poems for publication *Festive Wine;* 1970, 71, 74–82, 85–93, CWAJ show; 1974, solo show, Yoseido Gallery, Tokyo; 1991, solo show, San Francisco.

COLLECTIONS: New York Museum of Modern Art; Honolulu Academy of Arts; Art Institute of Chicago; Achenbach Foundation for the Graphic Arts, San Francisco; British Museum, London; Art Gallery of New South Wales, Australia; Tikotin Museum of Japanese Art, Haifa, Israel; Tochigi Prefectural Museum.

丸山浩司
(plate 95)

MARUYAMA Hiroshi
1953, born in Tochigi Prefecture; 1977, graduated from Tama University of Fine Arts, Tokyo; 1979, M.F.A., Tokyo National University of Fine Arts and Music; 1983 to present, assistant professor at Fukushima National University; 1976 to present, member of JPA; 1977, JPA show, prize; 1979, Ljubljana Graphic Arts Exhibition; Japanese Modern Graphic Art Exhibition, Cleveland; 1980, Tokyo International Print Biennial; 1982, Bilbao International Biennial, Spain; 1985–87, New York Art Expo; 1993, Taejon International Exhibition of Graphic Art, Korea.

COLLECTIONS: British Museum, London; Iwaki City Museum of Art, Japan; Machida City Museum of Graphic Art, Tokyo; Honolulu Academy of Arts; Tokyo National University of Fine Arts and Music.

松原直子
(plate 75)

MATSUBARA Naoko
1937, born in Tokushima Prefecture; 1960, B.F.A., Kyoto Municipal College of Fine Arts; 1962, M.F.A, Carnegie Institute, Pittsburgh; 1962–63, special student at department of graphic arts, Royal College of Arts, London; 1962, solo show, Carnegie Institute; 1963, Nihon Hanga-in Ten, Tokyo, Gold Medal; 1965, solo show, Galerie Viruly, Amsterdam; 1967, Penn State University Gallery; 1968, Pforzheim Museum, Germany; 1969, solo show, Haus Dornbusch, Frankfurt; Atelier Incontro, Vienna; Galerie in der Goldgasse, Salzburg; 1970, solo show, Wiggin Gallery, Boston Public Library; 1971, Three Generations (with Hiratsuka and Munakata), Cincinnati Art Museum; 1973, Japanese Artists in America, Kyoto National Museum of Modern Art and Tokyo National Museum of Modern Art; 1974, solo show, Hart House Art Gallery, University of Toronto; 1975, solo show, Gallery Graphics, Ottawa; 1976, two-person show, Mokuhan: the Woodcuts of Munakata and Matsubara, Art Gallery of Greater Victoria, British Columbia; 1979, 86, solo show, Tolman Collection; 1980, solo show, Barbara Fiedler Gallery, Washington, D.C.; 1981, solo show, Wako Department Store, Tokyo, produced by Tolman Collection; 1987, solo show, City Hall Gallery, Okinawa; solo show, Nihonbashi Takashimaya Department Store, Tokyo; 1994, Japanese Prints: Then and Now, Wako Department Store, Tokyo, produced by Tolman Collection; three-person show (with Shinoda and Iwami), Spirit Square, Charlotte, North Carolina.

COLLECTIONS: Albertina Museum, Vienna; Fogg Museum, Harvard University; Boston Museum of Fine Arts; Cincinnati Art Museum; Tokyo National Museum of Modern Art; Kyoto National Museum of Modern Art; Brooklyn Museum of Art; Detroit Art Institute; Art Gallery of Greater Victoria, British Columbia; Library of Congress, Washington, D.C.; Boston Public Library; New York Public Library; Yale University Art Gallery, New Haven.

南　桂子
(plate 39)

MINAMI Keiko

1911, born in Toyama; moved to Tokyo after World War II and wrote fairy tales; 1953, moved to France; 1954–56, studied etching/aquatint at Friedländer Atelier, Paris; 1957, print image used by New York Museum of Modern Art for Christmas card; 1958, image used by UNICEF for greeting card; 1962, produced illustrations for UNESCO books; 1966, work chosen for UNICEF calendar; 1969, featured in a movie for UNICEF; has participated in every Tokyo International Print Biennial since 1957; 1959 to present, numerous solo shows in New York, Tokyo, São Paulo, Los Angeles, Dusseldorf, Heidelberg, Chicago, London, Montreal, and Paris; 1982, moved to San Francisco; 1986, print commissioned by Nobel Prize Committee to commemorate Kawabata Yasunari's Nobel Prize for Literature; 1992, two-person show, Tokyo, Osaka, Nagoya; honorary member of JPA.

COLLECTIONS: New York Museum of Modern Art; Tokyo National Museum of Modern Art; National Gallery, Washington, D.C.; French Ministry of Education, Paris; Paris National Library; Fukushima Prefectural Museum.

宮下登喜雄
(plate 65)

MIYASHITA Tokio

1930, born in Tokyo; 1948, began making prints; studied under Hiratsuka, Sekino, and Komai; 1960, 62, 64, 66, 68, Tokyo International Print Biennial; 1965, Northwest International Print Exhibition, Seattle; Ljubljana International Print Biennial; 1967, São Paulo International Print Biennial; Vancouver International Print Biennial; Japan Art Festival, Mexico and U.S.; 1968, Lugano International Exhibition; 1969, Japan Art Festival, France and Italy; 1968, 70, Bradford International Print Biennial, England; 1973, India International Print Biennial; 1981, The World in Contemporary Prints: 1955–80, Tokyo; 1984, Xylon International Print Triennial, Switzerland; 1979, traveled in U.S. and Europe as a research worker for the Tokyo Metropolitan Museum; 1987, granted travel-study fellowship by Cultural Affairs Agency; member of JPA since 1955; presently full-time teacher at Tokyo University of Art and Education.

COLLECTIONS: Tokyo National Museum of Modern Art; Skopje Modern Art Museum, Macedonia (formerly Yugoslavia); Cincinnati Art Museum; Long Beach, California Modern Art Museum; Miami Modern Art Museum; New York Museum of Modern Art; Arthur M. Sackler Gallery, Smithsonian Institution, Washington, D.C.; Japan Culture Center, Rome; Japan Culture Center, Seoul; British Museum, London; Victoria and Albert Museum, London; Museum of History and Art, Hamburg; Bibliothèque Nationale, Paris.

水船六洲
(plate 78)

MIZUFUNE Rokushū

(1912–80). Born in Hiroshima; 1936, graduated from Tokyo University of Fine Arts, sculpture department; began to develop own woodblock approach under Hiratsuka; 1941, 47, 48, 50, Nitten Exhibition for Sculpture, grand prize awards; 1957, solo show, Matsuzakaya Department Store, Tokyo; 1960, solo show, Matsuya Department Store, Tokyo; 1960–61, taught woodblock printmaking, Marboro College and Putney School, Vermont; 1966, 75, solo show, Yoseido Gallery, Tokyo; 1970, Japan Academy of Arts award for sculpture; member of board of trustees of JPA; member of board of trustees of Nitten; 1960–77, principal, Kanto Gakuin Elementary School; decorated with 4th Class Order of Merit.

COLLECTIONS: Boston Museum of Fine Arts; Tokyo National Museum of Modern Art; Yokohama Museum; Hiroshima Museum; Kure Museum, Hiroshima.

森　義利
(plates 8, 50)

MORI Yoshitoshi

(1898–1992). Born in Tokyo; 1923, graduated from Kawabata School of Fine Arts; studied stencil fabric dyeing with Yanagi Soetsu and Serizawa Keisuke; after age of 50 began making stencil prints on paper; 1949–62, annual participant in Kokugakai Art Association show; 1960–65, solo show, Nihonbashi Gallery, Tokyo; 1966, traveling show in U.S. sponsored by Japan Society, New York; 1971, 73, 76, Isetan Department Store, Tokyo; 1972, 79, 83, Yoseido Gallery, Tokyo; 1975, first show at Wako Department Store, Tokyo, Enduring Images of Old Japan, produced by Tolman Collection; 1977, two-person show (with daughter Eiko), Wako Department Store, Tokyo; 1978, 82, 85, 87, 90, 92, solo show, Wako Department Store, Tokyo ; 1979, Honolulu Academy of Arts; 1980, 85, Matsuzakaya Department Store, Tokyo; 1980, 81, 83, Kabutoya Gallery, Tokyo; 1983, Kato Gallery, Tokyo; 1985, National Museum of Ethnology, Leiden, the Netherlands; 1957–90, international group shows, including ones in Barcelona (prize), Brussels, Cologne, Paris, the U.S., El Salvador, Mexico, Brazil, and Australia; 1976, awarded Silver Medal with Blue Ribbon by Prime Minister Miki Takeo; 1984, honorary Ph.D., University of Maryland; 1990, honored by head of Chuo Ward, Tokyo, for long-time merit to the ward; 1991, named Distinguished Citizen of Tokyo.

COLLECTIONS: Tokyo National Museum of Modern Art; Kanagawa Prefectural Museum of Modern Art, Kamakura; New York Museum of Modern Art; Barcelona Museum of Arts; San Diego Museum; Detroit Institute of Arts; Art Institute of Chicago; Boston Museum of Fine Arts; Machida City Museum of Graphic Arts, Tokyo; Japan Folk Art Museum, Tokyo; official residence of the prime minister of Japan.

村井正誠
(plate 16)

MURAI Masanari

1905, born in Ogaki, Gifu Prefecture; 1928, graduated from Bunka Gakuin, school of liberal arts, Tokyo; 1927, work accepted at the Nikaten Art Association show; 1928, moved to France; exhibited in the Independent Exhibition; 1932, returned to Japan; 1934, instrumental in organizing the New Age Exhibition with Hasegawa Saburo and Yamaguchi Kaoru; 1950, established the Association of Modern Art; 1951, exhibited oil painting in São Paulo International Biennial; 1952, International Art Exhibition, Carnegie Institute, Pittsburgh; 1953, participated in the organization of the Japan Abstract Art Club; 1955, began making silkscreen prints; 1962, 5th Contemporary Japanese Art Exhibition, Tokyo, grand prize; 1963, São Paulo International Print Biennial, prize; 1973, retrospective, Museum of Modern Art, Kanagawa Prefecture; 1979, retrospective, Museum of Modern Art, Wakayama; 1987, solo show, Galerie Tokoro, Tokyo; 1992, Contemporary Japanese Art Exhibition, Paris; 1993, solo show, Setagaya Art Museum, Tokyo.

COLLECTIONS: British Museum, London; Tokyo Metropolitan Museum; Kanagawa Prefectural Museum.

中山　正
(plates 44, 57)

NAKAYAMA Tadashi

1927, born in Niigata; 1947, left Tama Art College; 1950, began making woodblock prints; 1957–78, 10 solo shows, Tokyo; 3 solo show, Italy; 2 solo shows, U.S.; 1962–63, lived mainly in Milan; 1964–65, lived in London and Bath; taught at Bath Academy of Arts; 1989, solo show of personally selected works, Wako Gallery, Tokyo; 1993, solo show, Wako Gallery, Tokyo; has participated in several overseas shows, including Krakow International Print Biennial and Northwest International Print Exhibition, Seattle; annual participant in CWAJ show.

COLLECTIONS: Cincinnati Art Museum; Achenbach Foundation for the Graphic Arts, San Francisco; Fogg Art Museum, Harvard University; Honolulu Academy of Arts; Minnesota Museum of Art; National Gallery of Victoria, Australia; Philadelphia Museum of Art; Western Australian Art Museum, Perth; Library of Congress, Washington, D.C.

中澤慎一
(plate 89)

NAKAZAWA Shin'ichi

1956, born in Tokyo; 1975, began to teach himself to make etchings; 1979, graduated from Rikkyo University, Tokyo; 1978, 79, JPA show; 1983, 85, International Miniature Print Exhibition, Pratt Graphics Center, New York; 1984, International Mezzotint Exhibition, Philadelphia; 1984, 85, Promising Young Artists Exhibition, Isetan Department Store, Tokyo; 1985, Prizewinning Print Artists Exhibition, Central Museum Gallery, Tokyo; 1984, solo show, Art Space Koa, Tokyo; 1985, group show, Nishi Ginza Gallery, Tokyo; 1986, International Grafik Triennial, Frechen, Germany; 1986, 88, Pratt/Silvermine International Print Exhibition, New York; 1986–91, 1993–94, CWAJ show, Tokyo; 1988, 89, group show, Tolman Collection; 1990, solo show, Tolman Collection; 1990, group show, Retretti, Finland, produced by Tolman Collection; 1992, Six Japanese Artists on the International Stage, Hankyu Department Store, Tokyo, produced by Tolman Collection; 1994, Japan Week '94, Cairo, Egypt, produced by Tolman Collection.

COLLECTIONS: Cincinnati Art Museum; Rockefeller Foundation, New York; Gallery of New South Wales, Australia; Bayerische Landesbank, Tokyo.

西澤静男
(plate 82)

NISHIZAWA Shizuo

1912, born in Kobe; graduated from Osaka School of Art; 1963–94, JPA show; 1968, Pistoia International Print Biennial; 1969, became member of JPA; 1971, solo show, Modern Sculpture Centers of Tokyo, Okayama, and Hiroshima; 1984, Taiwan International Print Biennial; invited to participate in exhibition of modern Japanese prints, Spain; 1986, invited to participate in Modern Japanese Artists exhibition, Canada; commissioned by Nobel Prize Committee to make a portfolio of five prints to commemorate Kawabata Yasunari's Nobel Prize for Literature; 1990, prize in an international exhibition of Japanese prints, Australia; 1991, participated in a traveling show of Japanese prints, Rome and Athens; 1992, International Print Exhibition, Brazil; has been an annual exhibitor at the CWAJ show since 1975.

COLLECTIONS: Petit Palais Museum, Geneva; British Museum, London; Pistoia Municipal Museum; Hamamatsu Municipal Museum; Osaka Modern Art Center

野田哲也
(plate 81)

NODA Tetsuya

1940, born in Kumamoto; 1963, B.A.; 1965, M.A., Tokyo National University of Fine Arts and Music; 1968–76, Tokyo International Print Biennial, International Grand Prize in 68; 1969–87, Ljubljana International Print Biennial, grand prize in 77, Belgrade Museum Prize in 81, Grand Prize of Honor in 87; 1970, 72, 74, 80, Krakow International Print Biennial, second prize and Warsaw National Museum Prize in 70, Lodz Museum Prize in 70, 74, 80; 1984, Norway International Print Biennial, gold medal; submitted works to several biennials during the next two decades, including ones in England, Seoul, São Paulo, Venice, Frechen (Germany), Canada, and Valparaiso; exhibitions include Four Artists: Ay-O, Ikeda Masuo, Noda Tetsuya, Yoshihara Hideo, Nantenshi Gallery, Tokyo; 1974, Japanese print exhibition, Louisiana Museum, Denmark; 1976, Arakawa Shusaku, Noda Tetsuya, Ikeda Masuo, Cincinnati Art Museum; 1977, 81, solo show, Shirota Gallery, Tokyo; 1978, 83, 87, solo show, Fuji TV Gallery, Tokyo; 1980, solo show, Ikeda 20th Century Museum of Art, Itoh; 1981, solo show, Fukuoka City Museum; 1990, Last Century to Present Day, Still-Life Exhibition, Shizuoka.

COLLECTIONS: Tokyo National Museum of Modern Art; Kyoto National Museum of Modern Art; Prefectural Museums of Kanagawa, Tochigi, Oita, Kumamoto, and Miyagi; New York Museum of Modern Art; Warsaw National Museum; Brooklyn Museum; Cincinnati Art Museum; Los Angeles County Museum of Art; Oslo National Museum; Tikotin Museum of Japanese Art, Haifa, Israel; Achenbach Foundation for the Graphic Arts, San Francisco; Hirshhorn Museum, Washington, D. C.; Arts Council of Great Britain, London; Fort Worth Art Museum; Ateneum Art Museum, Finland.

小田まゆみ
(*plate 74*)

ODA Mayumi

1941, born in Tokyo; 1966, graduated from Tokyo University of Fine Arts; 1966–68, studied at Pratt Graphics Center, New York; 1971, 75, National Exhibition of Prints, Library of Congress, Washington, D.C.; 1972, Bradford International Print Biennial, England; 1973, Ljubljana International Print Biennial; 1975, 78, 83, solo show, Gallery Mukai, Tokyo; 1976, 78, solo show, Gallerie Humanité, Nagoya; 1979, 88, 89, solo show, Mary Baskett Gallery, Cincinnati; 1981, 83, 88, 91, solo show, Tolman Collection; 1981, solo show, CoCo Gallery, Kyoto; 1982, Tucson Museum of Art; Queen Emma Gallery, Honolulu; 1985, artist in residence and solo show, East-West Center, Honolulu; 1985, group show, Galerie Scheidegger, Zurich; 1986, Ginka Gallery, Tokyo; Mills College, Oakland, California; 1987, Honolulu Academy of Arts; Cathedral of St. John the Divine, New York; 1989, Verne Collection, Cleveland; 1992, Foreign Correspondents' Club, Tokyo.

COLLECTIONS: New York Museum of Modern Art; Boston Museum of Fine Arts; Cincinnati Art Museum; Tochigi Prefectural Museum of Art; Princeton University Graphics Collection, Princeton, New Jersey; Library of Congress, Washington, D.C.; Cleveland Museum; Yale University Art Gallery, New Haven.

オノサト トシノブ
(*plate 93*)

ONOSATO Toshinobu

(1912–86). Born in Nagano Prefecture; 1931, entered Tsuda Yoga Juku school to study oil painting; 1935, work accepted for the first time by Nikaten; organized Black Painting Exhibition with Nohara and Yamamoto; 1937, participated in the establishment of the Free Artists' Association; 1941, drafted into the army; held in Siberia as POW; 1954, Abstract and Illusion exhibition, Tokyo National Museum of Modern Art; 1958, began printmaking; 1963, Japan International Art Exhibition, prize; 1964, Guggenheim International Exhibition, New York; Venice International Biennial; 1974, Japan: Tradition and the Present, Museum of Modern Art, Dusseldorf; posthumous retrospective, Nerima Art Museum, Japan.

COLLECTIONS: Tokyo National Museum of Modern Art; Rome Museum of Modern Art; Guggenheim Museum, New York; Hara Museum of Contemporary Art, Tokyo; Louisiana Museum, Denmark; New York Museum of Modern Art.

大内マコト
(*plate 10*)

ŌUCHI Makoto

(1926–89). Born in Kawasaki, Kanagawa Prefecture; 1945, graduated from Kanagawa Prefectural Industrial High School; 1958, solo show, Japan Club, New York; 1962, 64, 66, Shell Award Exhibition, honorable mention; 1964, 71, 78, solo show, Yoseido Gallery, Tokyo; 1965–89, CWAJ show; 1976, First Western Pacific Print Biennial, Australia; traveled to Sydney and Melbourne; 1978, 79, 81, 82, solo show, Tolman Collection; 1979–86, Ibiza International Print Biennial, Spain; member of JPA since 1968.

COLLECTIONS: National Library, Tokyo; Bridgestone Museum of Art, Tokyo; University of Sydney, Australia; Cincinnati Art Museum; Rockefeller Foundation, New York; Fogg Museum, Harvard University; Art Institute of Chicago.

斉藤　清
(*plates 2, 58*)

SAITŌ Kiyoshi

1907, born in Fukushima; 1924, designed signs for shop fronts; 1927, set up own studio for designing shop signs; 1929, began studying oil painting; 1931, moved to Tokyo and worked part time while studying; 1936, JPA show; 1939–40, oil paintings accepted at Nikakai exhibitions; 1942, first solo print show, Kyukyodo Gallery, Tokyo; 1944–62, full member of JPA; 1944, hired by *Asahi* newspaper; 1946 to present, Kokugakai show; became full member of Kokugakai Art Association in 1949; 1948, Salon du Printemps, Mejiro, Tokyo, first prize; 1951–70, annual solo show, Mitsukoshi Department Store, Nihonbashi, Tokyo; 1951, São Paulo International Print Biennial, first prize (with Komai Tetsuro) in Japanese section; 1954, left *Asahi* to become full-time artist; 1955, Saito and His Associates, Seattle Art Museum; 1956, invited to U.S. and Mexico by Asia Foundation; 1956, Munakata and Saito, Chuokoron-sha Gallery, Tokyo; 1957, solo show, Corcoran Gallery of Art, Washington, D.C.; 1959, traveled in France; 1964, solo show, Honolulu Academy of Arts; 1967, cover portrait of Sato Eisaku for *Time;* 1969, solo show, Greater Victoria Museum, Canada, and San Diego Museum; 1970, moved to Kamakura; 1976, retrospective, Fukushima Cultural Center and Odakyu Department Store, Tokyo; 1977, cover portrait of Fukuda Takeo for *Time;* visited Prague for show at Czechoslovakia National Museum; 1978, moved to Kamakura; 1981, awarded 4th Class Order Medal by Japanese government; 1983, 245 works exhibited at Kanagawa Prefectural Museum of Art, traveling to Mie Museum of Modern Art and Odakyu Department Store, Tokyo; 1984 to present, solo show, Hakudotei Gallery, Tokyo; 1987, moved to Fukushima; 1988, Otaru Municipal Museum, Hokkaido; *Winter in Aizu* series, Portland, Oregon Museum of Art; 1992, Kawaguchiko Town Museum; Fukushima Prefectural Museum of Art; Odakyu Department Store, Tokyo; 1993, exhibition of entire works, Tochigi Cultural Center and Odakyu Department Store, Tokyo; 1994, solo show, Odakyu Department Store, Tokyo.

COLLECTIONS: Cincinnati Art Museum; Greater Victoria Museum, Canada; Philadelphia Museum of Art; Achenbach Foundation for the Graphic Arts, San Francisco; Denver Art Museum; New York Public Library; Art Institute of Chicago; Gallery of New South Wales, Australia; Tikotin Museum of Japanese Art, Haifa, Israel; Fukushima Prefectural Museum of Art; Kanagawa Prefectural Museum of Art.

笹島喜平
(plates 4, 91)

SASAJIMA Kihei

(1906–93). Born in Mashiko, Tochigi Prefecture; 1927, graduated from Tokyo Aoyama Teachers' School and taught until 1945; 1928, went to Mashiko and studied with Hamada Shoji; 1935, studied with Hiratsuka Un'ichi; 1936, studied with Munakata Shiko; 1945, began working exclusively as a woodblock print artist; 1954–71, 12 solo shows, Takashimaya Department Store, Tokyo; 1960, Modern Japanese Print Exhibition, Art Institute of Chicago; 1962, 66, Tokyo International Print Biennial; 1964, Modern Japanese Print Exhibition, Dublin; 1965, solo show, Mashiko; 1967, São Paulo International Print Biennial; Modern Japanese Print Exhibition, Tokyo National Museum of Modern Art; 1968, solo show, Ashikaga Municipal Hall Gallery, Gunma Prefecture; 1970, solo show, Keio Department Store Print Salon, Tokyo; 1978, solo show, Mito Cultural Center, Ibaragi Prefecture; 1989, solo show, Machida City Museum of Graphic Arts, Tokyo; 1992, solo show, Nara Prefectural Museum.

COLLECTIONS: Hamamatsu Municipal Museum, Japan; Oxford University, England; Berlin Oriental Art Museum; Tokyo National Museum of Modern Art; Boston Museum of Fine Arts; Tochigi Prefectural Museum.

沢田哲郎
(plate 63)

SAWADA Tetsurō

1935, born in Hokkaido; 1958, graduated from Musashino Art University, majoring in Western painting; 1960, began doing abstract oil painting; around 1973, began making lithographs and then silkscreens; 1966–67, traveled in North and South America; 1969, studied in France and Spain; 1980, Norway International Print Biennial, prize; 1971, 75, 76, 81, solo show, Franell Gallery, Tokyo; 1981, Tolman Collection; 1984–88, Kato Gallery, Tokyo; 1986, 88, 94, Gallery Vivant, Tokyo; 1986, 88, 90, 92, American Art Gallery, Seattle; 1988–91, Tower Gallery, Sacramento; 1986–93, Just Looking Gallery, California; 1991–93, Butter Gallery, Oregon.

COLLECTIONS: Cleveland Museum; British Museum, London; Cincinnati Art Museum; Honolulu Academy of Arts; Queensland Art Museum, Australia.

関根美夫
(plate 49)

SEKINE Yoshio

(1922–88). Born in Wakayama Prefecture; 1948–49, studied with Yoshihara Jiro; 1949–54, All West Japanese Art exhibition; 1951, 55, Nika Group Exhibition, Tokyo and Osaka; 1952, Seven Osaka Artists, *Mainichi* Newspaper Prize; 1958, International Art of a New Era traveling show, Osaka, Nagasaki, Hiroshima, Tokyo, and Kyoto; 1965, 66, solo show, Tokyo Gallery, Tokyo; 1966, solo show, Staempfli

Gallery, New York; 1966, First Japan Art Festival, New York, Pittsburgh, Chicago, and San Francisco; 1970, Contemporary Japanese Art group show, Staempfli Gallery, New York; Fourth Japan Art Festival show traveling throughout Europe; Human Documents 1970 group show, Tokyo Gallery, Tokyo; 1973, solo show, Galleria Grafica, Tokyo; 1975, 83, solo show, Tolman Collection; 1975, group show, Central Museum Gallery, Tokyo; Contemporary Japanese Art group show, Tokyo National Museum of Modern Art; Today's Art group show, Yokohama Municipal Gallery; 1977, Graphic Images of Japan group show, Wako Department Store Gallery; 1981–82, The 1960s—A Decade of Change in Japanese Art, Kyoto National Museum of Modern Art.

COLLECTIONS: Tokyo National Museum of Modern Art; New York Museum of Modern Art; Chase Manhattan Bank, New York; Chase Manhattan Bank, Tokyo; Cincinnati Art Museum; Nagoya Museum of Contemporary Art; Munich Modern Art Museum; Tochigi Prefectural Museum of Art; Caterpillar Co., Peoria, Illinois.

関野準一郎
(plates 3, 59)

SEKINO Jun'ichirō

(1914–88). Born in Aomori; 1932, studied etching under Kon Junzo; 1936, elected member of JPA; 1939, came to Tokyo and studied under Onchi Koshiro; 1940, Kokugakai show, prize; 1946, elected member of Kokugakai Art Association; 1958, traveled to U.S. and Europe for a year on invitation of the Japan Society; 1960, Northwest International Print Exhibition, Seattle, prize; taught at Kanazawa Art College; 1961, Ljubljana International Print Biennial, prize; 1963, went to the U.S. for a year on a grant from the Ford Foundation; taught at University of Washington and University of Oregon; 1965, taught at Kobe University; 1971, honored for cultural achievement by Aomori prefectural government; 1972, honored for cultural achievement by Aomori City; 1975, Minister of Education's Art Encouragement Prize; solo show, Museum of Art, University of Oregon; 1976, solo show, Oregon State University; 1981, awarded the Purple Ribbon Medal by the Japanese government; 1982, solo show, Central Museum Gallery, Tokyo; 1987, awarded the 4th Class Medal by the Japanese government.

COLLECTIONS: New York Museum of Modern Art; Cincinnati Art Museum; Tokyo National Museum of Modern Art; Machida City Museum of Graphic Art, Tokyo; Prefectural Museums of Wakayama and Fukushima.

渋谷栄一
(plate 40)

SHIBUYA Eiichi

1928, born in Hokkaido; 1951, graduated from Hokkaido Gakugei (Art Teachers') University; 1958 to present, JPA show, award in 59; 1969, elected member; 1965, Shunyokai show, award; 1972, elected member; 1965–66, studied etching at Friedländer Atelier, Paris, and drawing at Academy Grand Chaumiere, Paris; 1971–72, studied etching at Hayter's Atelier 17, Paris; 1977, 88, 91, visited Europe to continue studies of wood engraving and art in general; numerous solo shows, including those in Paris, Tokyo, Kyoto, Kitakyushu, Kofu, Shizuoka, Sendai, Sapporo, and Asahikawa; group exhibitions include 1986, 90, Print Adventure Exhibition, Hokkaido; Japan-U.S. Print Show (with Watarai Junsuke), U.S.; Young Etchers Exhibition, France; 1990, group show, Retretti Art Centre, Finland, produced by Tolman Collection; 1994, Japanese Prints: Then and Now, Wako Department Store Gallery, Tokyo, produced by Tolman Collection.

COLLECTIONS: Hokkaido Prefectural Museum; Hokkaido Prefectural Obihiro Museum; National Museum of International Art, Osaka; National Library, Paris; Cincinnati Art Museum.

品川　工
(plate 23)

SHINAGAWA Takumi

1908, born in Niigata; 1928, graduated from Tokyo School of Industrial Arts; 1935, studied with Onchi Koshiro; 1944, solo show, Mitsukoshi Department Store, Tokyo; 1940–90s, numerous solo shows in Japan and abroad; 1947, awarded prize at JPA show and became member; 1954, Lugano and São Paulo International Print Biennials; 1956, Modern Japanese Print Exhibition, Tokyo National Museum of

Modern Art; 1958, 60, 62, Tokyo International Print Biennial; 1958, Grenchen International Triennial, Switzerland; 1975, Krakow International Print Biennial; 1985, 87, Taiwan International Print Biennial; 1990, group show, Hara Museum ARC, Japan; 1991, group show Koshiro Onchi and His Circle, Okawa Museum, Gunma Prefecture; 1992, Woodblock Prints from the End of Meiji to Today, Nerima Ward Museum, Tokyo; honorary member of JPA; taught for more than 20 years at Tokyo Women's College of Fine Arts.

COLLECTIONS: Tokyo National Museum of Modern Art; Prefectural Museums of Niigata, Tochigi, and Miyagi; Newark Museum, New Jersey; Machida City Museum of Graphic Art, Tokyo; Oxford Library, England; Okawa Museum, Gunma, Japan.

篠田桃紅
(plates 34, 79)

SHINODA Tōkō

1913, born in Dairen, Manchuria; 1957, solo exhibition, Art Institute of Chicago; Galerie La Hune, Paris; and Taft Museum, Cincinnati; 1959, solo exhibition, Palais des Beaux Arts, Brussels; Matsuzakaya Department Store, Tokyo; group show, Ryksmuseum Kröller-Müller, Netherlands; 1965, 68, 77, solo exhibition, Betty Parsons Gallery, New York; 1971, group show (with Dubuffet, Hartung, De Kooning, Millares, Miro, Picasso, Soulages, Tapies, Zao Wou-ki), ROSC, Dublin; 1974, 28-meter commission by the Zojoji temple, Tokyo; 1976 to present, solo show, Tolman Collection; 1977, commission for Japanese ambassador's residence, Washington, D.C.; 1979–80, Three Pioneers of Abstract Painting in 20th Century Japan—Okada, Shinoda, Tsutaka, Phillips Collection, Washington, D.C., and throughout U.S.; 1980, solo show of prints and paintings, the Zojoji temple, Tokyo, produced by Tolman Collection; 1984, two-person show (with Ellen de Cuevas), Bruce Museum, Greenwich, Connecticut; 1989, solo show, Seibu Museum, Tokyo; 1990, traveling show Art Forum, Singapore; Galerie du Monde, Hong Kong; Honolulu Art Gallery; 1992, retrospective, Gifu Museum; 1993, solo show, Mitsukoshi Department Store, Tokyo, produced by Tolman Collection.

COLLECTIONS: Albright-Knox, New York; Art Institute of Chicago; Brooklyn Museum; Cincinnati Art Museum; Museum Folkwang, Essen; Museum of Fine Arts, Gifu; Tokyo National Museum of Modern Art; Guggenheim Museum, New York; Singapore National Museum; Rockefeller Collection, New York; Museum fur Ostasiatische Kunst, Berlin; Yale University Art Gallery, New Haven.

空 充秋
(plate 54)

SORA Mitsuaki

1933, born in Hiroshima; 1957, graduated from Tama University of Fine Arts, Tokyo; 1957–61, worked for Sears Roebuck, Tokyo; 1963–64, involved in constructing the Japanese pavilion for the New York World's Fair; visited Mexico; 1965–66, taught high school in Hiroshima; 1966–68, taught at Hiroshima Women's Cultural Education College; 1962–76, 1980, 89, solo show, Yoseido Gallery, Tokyo; 1964, made a stone sculpture for the Tokyo Olympic Village; 1965, began making woodblock prints; 1969, Contemporary Sculpture exhibition, Hakone Open Air Museum, prize; 1970, 71, CWAJ show; 1973, International Contemporary Sculpture Exhibition, Hakone Open Air Museum, grand prize; 1974, solo sculpture show, Hyatt Regency Hotel, Manila; 1977, solo sculpture show, Kauffman Fine Art Gallery, Houston; 1978, solo show, Suzuki Gallery, New York; Sogo Department Store, Hiroshima; 1980, group show, Space Museum, Seoul; 1981, solo show, Art Front Gallery, Tokyo; 1982, Suma Detached Palace Park Modern Sculpture Exhibition, Kobe, Tokyo National Museum of Art Prize; 1983, Modern Japanese Sculpture Exhibition, Ube, Yamaguchi; 1984, solo show, Modern Sculpture Center, Tokyo and Osaka; 1985, Modern Japanese Sculpture Exhibition, Yamaguchi, Kanagawa Museum Prize; 1986, Suma Detached Palace Park Modern Sculpture Exhibition, Kobe, grand prize; solo show, Sogo Department Store, Hiroshima; 1987, 89, Henry Moore Grand Prize Exhibition, Utsukushigahara Museum, Nagano, Excellent Work Prize; 1989, solo show, Mikimoto Plaza, Tokyo; 1991, Sora Family sculpture exhibition, Sogo Department Store, Hiroshima, and Gallery Mikimoto, Tokyo; 1992, Sora Family sculpture exhibition, Grand Hyatt Hotel, Hong Kong.

COLLECTIONS: Utsukushigahara Museum, Nagano; Tokyo National Museum of

Modern Art; Kure City Museum, Hiroshima; Kanagawa Prefectural Museum; Sapporo Open Air Museum; Ube City, Yamaguchi Prefecture; Setagaya Ward Office, Tokyo; Asahikawa City Museum; Hiroshima Museum of Contemporary Art.

菅井 汲
(plate 80)

SUGAI Kumi

1919, born in Kobe; 1933, studied briefly at Osaka University of Fine Arts; 1937–45, commercial designer for advertising department of Hankyu Railway Company; 1952 to present, has resided in Paris; 1954, solo show, Galerie Craven, Paris, and Palais des Beaux Arts, Brussels; 1959, 60, 61, 64, solo show, Kootz Gallery, New York; 1960, solo retrospective, Leverkusen State Museum, Germany; 1963, solo retrospective, Kestner Gesellschaft, Hanover, Germany; 1969, solo show, Minami Gallery and Tokyo Gallery, Tokyo; 1974, solo show, La Galerie Esplanade de la Défense, Paris; 1983, solo retrospective, Seibu Museum of Art, Tokyo; 1991, solo show, Ashiya City Museum, Kobe; 1992, solo show, Ohara Museum, Kurashiki; biennials include 1960, Tokyo International Print Biennial, Tokyo National Museum Prize; 1961, Grenchen International Triennial, Switzerland, grand prize; 1965, São Paulo International Print Biennial, prize; 1966, Krakow International Print Biennial, grand prize; 1972, Norway International Biennial, honorary prize.

COLLECTIONS: Art Institute of Chicago; Carnegie Institute, Pittsburgh; Cleveland Museum; Guggenheim Museum, New York; New York Museum of Modern Art; Fogg Art Museum, Harvard University; Rome National Museum of Modern Art; Grenchen Museum, Switzerland; Bern Museum; New York Metropolitan Museum; Stockholm Museum; Berlin National Museum; Oslo National Museum; Paris National Museum; Johannesburg Museum; Tokyo National Museum of Modern Art; Kyoto National Museum of Modern Art; Machida City Museum of Graphic Art, Tokyo; Prefectural Museums of Fukushima, Aichi, Toyama, and Wakayama.

杉浦和利
(plate 71)

SUGIURA Kazutoshi

1938, born in Kyoto; 1957, enrolled in painting course at Kyoto Municipal College of Fine Arts, graduating in 1963 with a major in *nihonga*, Japanese-style painting, then continued in graduate course; 1967, began studying Japanese classical painting, Kyoto National Museum; 1968–72, studied fine-art restoration, Kyoto National Museum; 1960 to present, solo show, Yamada Gallery, Kyoto; 1978, awarded prize by Kyoto Federation of Galleries for *nihonga* painting; 1979 to present, CWAJ show; 1988, solo show, Melbourne; 1989, exhibition, Portland, Maine Museum; 1986 to present, annual exhibition, Tolman Collection; presently teaches art at a Kyoto high school.

COLLECTIONS: Brooklyn Museum and numerous private collections.

高橋宏光
(plate 56)

TAKAHASHI Hiromitsu

1959, born in Tokyo; 1982, graduated from Nihon University, Tokyo; 1986, 87, 89, 91, 92, 93, group show, Salon d'Automne, Grand Palais, Paris; 1987–93, solo show, Tolman Collection; 1988, France-Japon show, Grand Palais, Paris, and Tokyo Metropolitan Museum; 1989–90, solo show, Columbia Arts Center, Vancouver; 1989–92, Salon des Artistes Francais, Grand Palais, Paris; 1989, solo show, Japan Art Center, Bellingham, Washington; 1990, group show, Retretti Art Centre, Finland, produced by Tolman Collection; 1991–93, CWAJ show; 1991–93, group show of Japanese contemporary art traveling to Ireland, Norway, Finland, Iceland, Greece, Italy, and Brazil; 1992, 2nd annual miniprint exhibition, Napa Art Center, California, purchase prize; 1993, solo show, Hankyu Department Store, Tokyo, produced by Tolman Collection; 1994, Japan Week '94, Cairo, Egypt, produced by Tolman Collection.

COLLECTIONS: Cincinnati Art Museum; Rockefeller Foundation, New York; Gallery of New South Wales, Australia; Museum of Arts and Crafts, Hamburg; Tikotin Museum of Japanese Art, Haifa, Israel; New Zealand Academy of Fine Arts, Wellington; Victoria Arts Centre Trust, Melbourne; Hotel New Otani, Hakata, Japan; Singapore National Museum.

高橋力雄 *(plate 26)*

TAKAHASHI Rikio

1917, born in Tokyo; 1947, studied under Onchi Koshiro; 1962, Tokyo International Print Biennial; 1962, two-person show (with Uchima Ansei), New York; solo show, Gima Gallery, Hawaii; 1963, solo show, Santa Barbara Museum; 1965, studied sculpture in Los Angeles and lectured on woodblock printing throughout California; solo show, Seattle Coliseum; 1966, group show of modern Japanese prints, Geneva Museum of History and Art; 1968, solo show, Tokyo American Club; 1978, solo show, Yamada Gallery, Kyoto; solo show, Asahikawa, Sendai, and Nagaoka; 1981, six-person show, Gallery 39, London; 1984, solo show, Funabashi Seibu Department Store, Chiba; Xylon International Print Triennial, Switzerland, first prize; 1985, Taiwan International Print Biennial; 1986, solo show, Mitsui Art Salon, Tokyo; 1987, solo show, Koto Japanese Arts Gallery, Hong Kong; 1993, solo show, Yoseido Reflections Gallery, Tokyo; 1994, solo show, Shiseido Gallery, Tokyo.

COLLECTIONS: New York Museum of Modern Art; Tokyo National Museum of Modern Art; Philadelphia Museum; British Museum, London; Oregon University Museum, Eugene; Art Institute of Chicago; University of Oklahoma Museum, Norman; Rockefeller Collection, New York; Cincinnati Art Museum.

高橋 潮 *(plate 87)*

TAKAHASHI Ushio

1944, born in Fukuoka; 1970, graduated from Musashino Art University; 1980, 82, solo show, Yoseido Gallery, Tokyo; 1981, 86, solo show, Chikugo Gallery, Fukuoka; 1984, solo show, Fujinoya Gallery, Tochigi Prefecture; 1985, inaugural exhibition of Nerima Ward Museum, Tokyo; 1986, college exchange exhibition between Musashino Art University and Dresden Art University, Germany; 1986–89, included in portfolio commissioned by the Nobel Prize Foundation, Sweden; 1989, Art in Nerima '89, Nerima Ward Museum, Tokyo; participated in Korea-China-Japan Art Exhibition; 1992, designed metrocard for *eidan* subway lines, Tokyo; 1993, 70th-anniversary exhibition of Shunyokai Art Association.

COLLECTIONS: Tobacco and Salt Museum, Tokyo; Musashino Art University, Tokyo; Korea Culture and Art Institute, Seoul; Eidan Subway Collection, Tokyo.

高松次郎 *(plate 45)*

TAKAMATSU Jirō

1936, born in Tokyo; 1958, graduated from the National University of Fine Arts and Music, Tokyo, specializing in oil painting; selected solo shows include 1966, 69, 71, 76, 78, 79, 82, Tokyo Gallery, Tokyo; 1976, 78, Kaneko Gallery, Tokyo; 1986, Seibu Department Store, Tokyo; 1989, 90, 92, Akira Ikeda Gallery, Tokyo; selected group shows include 1966, New Generation of Contemporary Artists, National Museum of Modern Art, Tokyo; 1966, Modern Art of Japan, Basilica San Marco, Venice; 1971, Guggenheim International, New York; 1972, 8th Tokyo International Print Biennial, prize; 1974, Bradford International Print Biennial, England, purchase prize; 1981, 25 Years of Contemporary Prints, Tokyo Metropolitan Museum; 1987, Icons in Contemporary Art, Museum of Modern Art, Saitama, Japan; 1989, Art of the Showa Period from the Museum Collection, National Museum of Modern Art, Tokyo; 1991, Words and Strokes, Niigata City Art Museum; 1992, Nagoya Contemporary Art Fair, Nagoya City Museum.

COLLECTIONS: National Museum of International Art, Osaka; Miyagi Prefectural Museum; Tokyo Metropolitan Museum; Tokyo National Museum of Modern Art.

田村文雄 *(plate 38)*

TAMURA Fumio

1941, born in Nagano Prefecture; 1968, graduated from Tokyo University of Art; 1969, solo show, Yoseido Gallery, Tokyo; 1970, Florence International Print Biennial, Grand Prix; 1973, 75, Ljubljana International Print Biennial; 1974, Petit Formes Gallery, Osaka; Heian Gallery, Kyoto; 1976, Norway International Print Biennial; 1977, solo show, Heian Gallery, Kyoto; 1980, group exhibition of Japanese prints, Paris; Tochigi Prefectural Museum; Tokyo Metropolitan Museum; 1984, solo show, Nichido Gallery, Tokyo; 1986, group show, Takashimaya Department Store, Tamagawa; 1989, Modern Japanese Prints, Tokyo Metropolitan Museum; 1990, two-person show (with Kato Kiyomi), Yoseido Reflections Gallery, Tokyo; 1991, Grand Prix show, Nichido Gallery, Tokyo; 1993, Modern Prints in Shinshu (Nagano), Suzaka Print Museum.

COLLECTIONS: Paris National Library; Tokyo National Museum of Modern Art; Kyoto National Museum of Modern Art; Tokyo Metropolitan Museum; Prefectural Museums of Oita and Tochigi.

田中良平
(plates 46, 47, 70)

TANAKA Ryōhei

1933, born in Takatsuki City, Osaka; 1963, studied etching with Professor Furuno Yoshio; 1966, started exhibiting with JPA and became regular member in 73; 1967 to present, CWAJ show; 1966 to present, intermittent solo shows, Yamada Gallery, Kyoto; 1971, Kansai Kokugakai show, New Talent Prize; 1972, Kokugakai show, top prize; 1971, 74, 81, 83, 88, 90, solo show, Yoseido Gallery, Tokyo; 1974, 77, solo show, Hendricks Gallery, Maryland; 1979, traveling exhibition of modern Japanese prints, Peking and Shanghai; 1980, 87, solo show, Azuma Gallery, Seattle; 1984, solo show, Gilbert Luber Gallery, Philadelphia; 1987 to present, solo show, Tolman Collection; 1990, group show, Retretti Art Centre, Finland, produced by Tolman Collection; 1992, traveling solo show, Azuma Gallery, Seattle; Ren Brown Collection, Bodega Bay, California; Verne Collection, Cleveland.

COLLECTIONS: Fogg Museum, Harvard University; Achenbach Foundation for the Graphic Arts, San Francisco; Cincinnati Art Museum; Boston Museum of Fine Arts; New York Metropolitan Museum of Art; Honolulu Academy of Arts; Cleveland Art Museum; Singapore National Museum; Joseph H. Hirshhorn collection.

谷口 茂
(plate 85)

TANIGUCHI Shigeru

1948, born in Fukuoka, Kyushu Prefecture; 1971–72, studied lithography at Japan Artists' Union, Tokyo; 1973, 74, JPA show; 1974, Graphic Images of Japan group show, Wako Department Store, Tokyo, produced by Tolman Collection; 1976, 82, Bradford International Print Biennial, England; 1977, 79, Ljubljana International Print Biennial; 1977, solo show, Nishi Ginza Gallery, Tokyo; 1978, solo show, Clarke Gallery, Sapporo; Seven Artists New Talent Show, AAA Gallery, New York; Robert Belknap Memorial Print Exhibition, New York, purchase prize; 1978, 82, solo show, Tolman Collection; 1976, 79, 81, special print commissions, Tolman Collection; 1979, Japan Art Festival, Osaka, prize; 1980, Krakow International Print Biennial, prize; Ibiza International Print Biennial, Spain, prize; 1982, Central Museum Gallery Print Exhibition, Tokyo, prize; 1985 to present, has been studying oil painting.

COLLECTIONS: Cincinnati Museum of Art; New York Museum of Modern Art, Study Collection; Prudential Insurance Company, Newark, New Jersey; Ibiza Museum of Modern Art, Spain; Honolulu Academy of Arts; Warsaw Museum of Modern Art; Osaka National Museum of International Art; Saitama Prefectural Museum of Modern Art, Japan.

とくだあきら
(plate 84)

TOKUDA Akira

1946, born in Dairen, China; 1968, graduated from Kuwazawa Design Institute, Tokyo; 1985, 87, 89, Ljubljana International Print Biennial; 1986, 10th International Exhibition of Original Drawings, Rijeka, Croatia, Zagreb National University Library Prize; 1988, 18th Works on Paper Annual, University of Texas, Austin, Award of Excellence; 1989, 5th Varuna International Print Biennial, Bulgaria, Bulgarian Government Offices Culture Department Prize; 1989, Franco-Japanese Art Exhibition, Tokyo and Paris; 1990, solo show, Tolman Collection; 1991, Greece International Contemporary Japanese Print Exhibition, Athens Graphic Art Center Prize; 1992, International Japanese Print Exhibition, Iceland, Reykjavik Art Museum Prize; 1992, group show, Hankyu Department Store, Tokyo, produced by Tolman Collection; 1992, 12th Mini Print International, Cadaques, Spain, Award of Excellence; 1972, 73, 89, Gallery Heian, Kyoto.

COLLECTIONS: Rijeka Modern Art Museum, Croatia; Varuna Modern Art Museum,

Bulgaria; Alberta Government Cultural Department, Canada; Krakow Modern Art Museum; Osaka City Contemporary Art Center.

利根山光人
(plate 17)

TONEYAMA Kōjin

(1921–94). Born in Tokyo; 1943, graduated from Waseda University in the department of literature; 1950, began making lithographs; 1951, Yomiuri Independent Exhibition, Tokyo; 1954, Asahi Exhibition of Excellent Works, Tokyo; 1959, São Paulo International Print Biennial; solo show, National Museum of Modern Art, Mexico; 1957, 59, 64, 67, Tokyo International Print Biennial; 1963, participated in archeological digs of Mayan ruins in Mexico; 1966, began making mosaic and ceramic paintings; 1967, Japan Art Festival, U.S., Mexico, and Paris; 1970, solo show, Misurake Gallery, Mexico; 1972, 87, awarded Order of Cultural Merit by the Mexican government; 1973, Japanese Prints of Today, Boston City Hall; awarded Blue Ribbon Medal by the Japanese government; 1979, solo show, Japan and Mexico; 1985, 17th Japan Art Exhibition, grand prize; 1991, Osaka Print Triennial, Bronze Prize.

COLLECTIONS: Kanagawa Prefecture Museum of Modern Art; Tokyo National Museum of Modern Art; National Museum of Australia, Canberra; Mexico City National Museum of Modern Art.

鍔本達朗
(plate 90)

TSUBAMOTO Tatsurō

1952, born in Aichi Prefecture; 1976, graduated from Musashino Art University, Tokyo; 1982, 84, Most Promising Artists Grand Prix Contest, Osaka, President's Prize in 82, Grand Prix in 84; 1984, 4th Mini Print International, Cadaques, Spain, prize; 1986, 88, Krakow International Print Biennial; 1983, 85, 87, Taiwan International Print Biennial; 1990, Interprint International Print Exhibition, Lvov, Ukraine, prize; 1993, International Print Biennial, Maastrict, Netherlands, prize; 1994–95, awarded one-year travel and study grant by Musashino Art University, Tokyo.

COLLECTIONS: Library of Congress, Washington, D.C.; Musashino Art University, Tokyo; Cincinnati Art Museum; Okazaki City Art Museum, Japan.

坪田政彦
(plate 69)

TSUBOTA Masahiko

1947, born in Himeji, Hyogo Prefecture; 1970, graduated from Osaka University of Fine Arts; 1970–71, solo show, Gallery Miyazaki, Osaka; 1972, 73, 74, 76, 79, solo show, Shinanobashi Gallery, Osaka; 1976, Bradford International Print Biennial, England; Art Now '76, Hyogo Prefectural Museum of Modern Art; 1977, 79, Ljubljana International Print Biennial; 1978, International Art Festival, Christchurch, New Zealand; Krakow International Print Biennial; 1981, 88, Contemporary Art Exhibition of Japan, Tokyo and Kyoto; 1986, Japan Art Fair, Central Museum Gallery, Tokyo; 1989, Taipei International Print Biennial; 1993, Gallery Vromena, Amsterdam; 1994, Seattle Art Fair.

内間安瑆
(plate 25)

UCHIMA Ansei

1921, born in Stockton, California; 1940–59, lived in Japan; 1944–52, majored in architecture at Waseda University, Tokyo, but left to study oil painting by himself; 1957, two-person show (with Nagare Masayuki), Yoseido Gallery, Tokyo; 1957, 60, Tokyo International Print Biennial; 1960 to present, has lived in New York; honorary professor at Sarah Lawrence College; assistant professor at Columbia University; 1958, 61, 70, Grenchen International Triennial, Switzerland; 1962, Guggenheim Fellowship; 1967, Vancouver International Print Exhibition; 1970, Venice International Print Biennial; Guggenheim Fellowship; 1973, Ljubljana International Print Biennial; 1985, retrospective, Sarah Lawrence College, New York; 1986, 89, 94, Ansei-Toshiko two-person show, Striped House Museum, Tokyo; 1988, retrospective of woodblocks, AAA Gallery, New York; 1992, Woodblock Prints from the End of Meiji to Today, Nerima Ward Museum, Tokyo.

COLLECTIONS: Art Institute of Chicago; Honolulu Academy of Arts; Library of

Congress, Washington, D.C.; Philadelphia Museum of Fine Art; National Gallery, Washington, D.C.; New York Metropolitan Museum; Whitney Museum, New York; British Museum, London; Brooklyn Museum; Striped House Museum, Tokyo; Tokyo National Museum of Modern Art.

若生秀二
(plate 99)

WAKŌ Shūji

1953, born in Sendai; 1977, graduated from Zokei University, Tokyo; 1978–87, Kanagawa Print Independent Exhibition; 1979–91, taught art at Zokei University; 1979 to present, JPA show, prizes in 80 and 83; 1980, Print Grand Prix, Nichido Salon, Tokyo; 1980, 83, Recommended Young Print Artists, Yoseido Gallery, Tokyo; 1980, 14th Exhibition of Selected Modern Artists, Cultural Affairs Agency, Tokyo; 1981, grant from Cultural Affairs Agency; 1983, Rockford Biennial, U.S.; 1983, 85, Pusan Biennial, Korea; 1980 to present, CWAJ show, Tokyo; 1982, CWAJ show cover artist for catalog; 1989, CWAJ poster artist; 1984 to present, solo show, Tolman Collection; 1987, traveled and studied throughout Europe; 1990, special commission by Tetrapak, Japan; 1991–92, group show, Galleria 25, Helsinki; 1990, group show, Retretti Art Centre, Finland, produced by Tolman Collection; 1992, Six Artists on the International Stage, Hankyu Department Store, Tokyo, produced by Tolman Collection; 1994, Japan Week '94, Cairo, Egypt, produced by Tolman Collection.

COLLECTIONS: British Museum, London; Cincinnati Art Museum; Rockefeller Foundation, New York; Gallery of New South Wales, Australia; Singapore National Museum; Hara Museum of Contemporary Art, Tokyo; University of Cairo, Egypt.

渡辺禎雄
(plate 55)

WATANABE Sadao

1913, born in Tokyo; 1941, began to specialize in the art of *katazome* (stencil) printing; studied under Serizawa Keisuke; 1947, first prize from Japan Folk Art Museum for *The Story of Ruth;* 1948, Kokugakai Prize; 1969, became member of Kokugakai Art Association; 1969–70, taught stencil printmaking, Linfield College, McMinnville, Oregon; 1976, taught in Minnesota and Ohio on invitation of Lutheran Church of America; 1981, honorary Doctor of Fine Arts from Linfield College; 1985, solo show, Honolulu Academy of Arts and Art Gallery of Greater Victoria, Canada.

COLLECTIONS: Japan Folk Art Museum, Tokyo; Kurashiki Folk Art Museum, Okayama; New York Museum of Modern Art; Art Institute of Chicago; Cincinnati Art Museum; Honolulu Academy of Arts; Vatican Museum of Modern Religious Art.

渡会純价
(plate 41)

WATARAI Junsuke

1936, born in Otaru, Hokkaido; 1957, studied etching with Komai Tetsuro; 1958, completed partial studies at Musashino Art University; 1962, first exhibited with JPA, becoming member in 1973; 1963, 73, exhibited with Shunyo-ten, prize in 73; 1974, became member of Shunyo-ten; 1971–72, 1983–84, visited Europe, studied in Paris; 1974, Exhibition of Young Modern Printmakers, Museum of Modern Art, Paris; 1978, Exhibition of Japanese Modern Prints, Mexico; 1987, Centennial of Hokkaido Art, Hokkaido Museum of Modern Art; 1991, Japan-Italy International Print Exhibition, Rome.

COLLECTIONS: Hokkaido Museum of Modern Art; British Museum, London; San Diego Museum; Cincinnati Art Museum.

山口　源
(plate 21)

YAMAGUCHI Gen

(1886–1976). Born in Shizuoka Prefecture; 1914, lived in Taipei; met Fujimori Shizuo, who introduced him to Onchi Koshiro in 1923; 1928, 8th exhibition of Japan Creative Print Association; 1939, joined Ichimokukai Art Association, headed by Onchi Koshiro; 1943, became member of JPA; 1944, moved from Tokyo to Numazu, Shizuoka Prefecture; 1949, became member of Kokugakai Art Association;

1956, first solo show, Yoseido Gallery, Tokyo; 1957, Ljubljana International Print Biennial, Excellence Award; 1958, Mostra Internazionale di Bianco e Nero exhibition, Lugano, Grand Prix; 1959, São Paulo International Print Biennial and Ljubljana International Print Biennial, prizes; 1963, honorary member of the Florence Art Academy, Italy; 1964, JPA show, special prize; 1966, became cochairman of Shizuoka Cultural Association; 1967, JPA show, Association Prize; 1968, solo show, Yoseido Gallery, Tokyo; 1972, became consultant to the Shizuoka Prefectural Print Association.

COLLECTIONS: Cincinnati Art Museum; Tokyo National Museum of Modern Art; Prefectural Museums of Wakayama and Fukushima.

矢柳　剛
(plate 77)

YAYANAGI Tsuyoshi (YAYANAGI Gō)

1933, born in Obihiro, Hokkaido; 1951, graduated from Obihiro Agricultural High School; 1951–53, attended Hoshi Pharmaceutical College, Tokyo; 1957–59, traveled in South America and Africa; 1965–68, studied graphic arts at S. W. Hayter's Atelier 17, Paris; selected solo shows, including 1957, São Paulo Museum of Modern Art; 1963, Nantenshi Gallery, Tokyo; 1967, 70, Gallery Solstice, Paris; 1969, Malmö Art Museum, Sweden; 1973, Pratt Graphics Center, New York, and Nichido Salon, Tokyo; 1974, 78, Tolman Collection; 1974, 75, Clark Gallery, Sapporo; Formes Gallery, Osaka; 1977, Wako Gallery, Tokyo; 1981, Ikeda 20th Century Museum of Art, Itoh; 1983, São Paulo Museum of Modern Art; 1991, Bunkamura Museum, Tokyo; selected international group shows and biennials, including 1966–74, Krakow; 1968–72, Paris; 1969, 71, Tokyo; 1969–76, Ljubljana; 1970–76, Bradford, England; 1972–77, Frechen, West Germany; 1983–91, Taiwan.

COLLECTIONS: Bibliothèque Nationale, Paris; Municipal Museum of Modern Art, Paris; New York Museum of Modern Art; Geneva Art Museum; Los Angeles County Museum of Art; Malmö Art Museum, Sweden; Cincinnati Art Museum; Rockefeller Foundation, New York.

吉田千鶴子
(plate 18)

YOSHIDA Chizuko

1924, born in Yokohama; 1941, graduated from Women's College of Fine Arts, Kanagawa Prefecture; 1953 to present, CWAJ show; 1953 to present, member of JPA; 1956, founding member of Women's Printmaker Group; 1970, Grenchen International Triennial, Switzerland, prize; 1973, Contemporary Japanese Prints, Los Angeles County Museum of Art; 1976, Xylon International Print Triennial, Switzerland.

COLLECTIONS: Art Institute of Chicago; Philadelphia Museum of Art; Tokyo National Museum of Modern Art; Los Angeles County Museum of Art; New York Museum of Modern Art.

吉田穂高
(plate 20)

YOSHIDA Hodaka

1926, born in Tokyo, the second son of Yoshida Hiroshi; 1949, graduated from Daiichi High School, Tokyo; 1951, began making woodblock prints; 1952, became member of JPA; 1955, visited U.S. and Mexico; 1957–66, Tokyo International Print Biennial; 1962, Lugano International Print Biennial, prize; 1963, 73, 81, Ljubljana International Print Biennial; 1967, São Paulo International Print Biennial; 1972, Seoul International Print Biennial, prize; 1973, U.S. World Print Competition, special edition purchase prize; 1974, 78, Ibiza International Print Biennial, Spain; 1977, on grant from Japan Foundation visited five Central American countries to introduce Japanese printmaking; 1981, visiting professor at University of Costa Rica; 1988, solo show, Machida City Museum of Graphic Arts, Tokyo; 1992, Woodblock Prints from the End of Meiji to Today, Nerima Ward Museum, Tokyo.

COLLECTIONS: British Museum, London; New York Museum of Modern Art; Art Institute of Chicago; Tokyo National Museum of Modern Art; Tokyo Metropolitan Museum; Hiroshima Contemporary Art Museum; Machida City Museum of Graphic Arts, Tokyo.

吉田克朗
(plate 66)

YOSHIDA Katsurō

1943, born in Saitama Prefecture; 1968, graduated from Tama University of Fine Arts, Tokyo, studying under Saito Yoshishige; 1970, Seoul International Print Biennial, grand prize; 1970, 72, 74, Tokyo International Print Biennial, Tokyo National Museum of Modern Art Prize in 72; 1971, solo show, Shirota Gallery, Tokyo; 1971, 75, 77, Ljubljana International Print Biennial; 1972, 74, Krakow International Print Biennial; 1973–74, studied in England on grant from Cultural Affairs Agency; 1978, Norway International Print Biennial; 1982, solo show, Art Front, Tokyo; 1983, solo show, CoCo Gallery, Kyoto; 1984, Prints of Today, Saitama Prefectural Museum; 1986, Japanese Avant-Garde show, Pompidou Centre, Paris; 1989, Hara Annual Exhibition, Hara Museum of Contemporary Art, Tokyo; Art Exciting '89, Saitama Prefectural Museum; 1990, Yokohama Art Exhibition; Odessa East-West Museum exhibition; 1994, Japanese Prints: Then and Now, Wako Department Store Gallery, Tokyo, produced by Tolman Collection.

COLLECTIONS: Tokyo National Museum of Modern Art; Kanagawa Prefectural Museum; Paris City Museum; New York Museum of Modern Art; Hyogo Prefectural Museum.

吉田政次
(plate 24)

YOSHIDA Masaji

(1917–71). Born in Wakayama Prefecture; 1935, studied at Kawabata Art School, Tokyo; 1941, graduated from Tokyo University of Fine Arts and finished postgraduate course in 1947; 1949, JPA show; elected member in 1952; 1955–64, taught printmaking every Sunday at own studio; 1956, Lugano International Print Biennial; 1956, 57, 58, 59, 62, Asahi Best Works exhibition; 1957–68, Tokyo International Print Biennial, prize in 57; 1957, Asahi's Today's New Faces exhibition, prize; 1957, 59, 61, Ljubljana International Print Biennial; 1959, São Paulo International Print Biennial; 1965, solo show, Yoseido Gallery, Tokyo; 1967, two-person show (with Fukita Fumiaki), Dainana Gallery, Tokyo; 1969, Joan Miro International Drawing Exhibition, Spain, grand prize; 1969, Barcelona International Print Exhibition, Silver Prize.

COLLECTIONS: Wakayama Prefectural Museum; Art Institute of Chicago; New York Museum of Modern Art; New York Public Library.

吉田遠志
(plate 19)

YOSHIDA Tōshi

1911, born in Tokyo, the eldest son of Yoshida Hiroshi; under father's influence began to learn painting at age 3 and woodblock printing at age 13; studied oil painting at Taiheiyo Art School; 1929, traveled with father to India and Southeast Asia; 1936, traveled in China and Korea; 1957–62, Tokyo International Print Biennial; 1951 to present, member of JPA; 1952–53, visited U.S. and Europe to exhibit works and lecture on woodblock prints; 1954, taught printmaking for one month at Art Institute of Chicago; since then, has often traveled to U.S., Canada, Mexico, Africa, Australia, and the South Pole for sketching, exhibitions, and lectures; after the war made abstract images, but current subject matter is mostly scenery and animals; 1980, opened the Miasa Cultural Center, Nagano Prefecture, to promote the learning of woodblock printmaking, dyeing techniques, and the making of glassware and pottery.

COLLECTIONS: Sydney Museum, Australia; New York Museum of Modern Art; Boston Museum of Fine Arts; Cincinnati Art Museum; Art Institute of Chicago; Tokyo National Museum of Modern Art; MOA Museum, Atami, Japan; British Museum, London; Portland Art Museum; Paris National Library; National Museum of Australia, Canberra; Seattle Museum of Art; Krakow National Museum.

吉原英雄
(plate 37)

YOSHIHARA Hideo

1931, born in Hiroshima; 1950–52, studied at Osaka Municipal Art Institute; 1954–55, member of the Gutai Group; studied oil painting under Yoshihara Jiro; 1955–57, belonged to Democrat Art Association, led by Izumi and Eikyu; 1957, 1962–72, 74, Tokyo International Print Biennial, prize in 68; 1959–69, member of JPA; 1967, 69,

71, 79, 81, 83, 85, 87, Ljubljana International Print Biennial; 1968, 70, 72, 74, Krakow International Print Biennial, prize in 72; 1970, 73, 77, 79, 81, 84, 89, solo show, Nantenshi Gallery, Tokyo and Osaka; 1983, Prints by Masuo Ikeda and Hideo Yoshihara, Fukuoka Municipal Museum of Art; 1988, Eikyu & Associates, Machida Museum of Graphic Arts, Tokyo; 1990, Space 11 Gallery, Tokyo, Democrat Group Artists from 1950 to 1960; shows over the years in Buenos Aires, India, Norway, Sweden, Finland, Dusseldorf, Manila, Basel, and Paris.

COLLECTIONS: Tokyo National Museum of Modern Art; Kyoto National Museum of Modern Art; New York Museum of Modern Art; Museums of Modern Art of Czechoslovakia; Posnan, Poland; Krakow, Poland; Warsaw, Poland; Queensland Art Gallery, Australia; Tokyo Metropolitan Art Museum; Prefectural Art Museums of Hyogo, Hiroshima, Hokkaido, Osaka.

由木 礼
(plate 32)

YUKI Rei

1928, born in Tokyo; 1952, graduated from Athénée-Français, Tokyo; studied printmaking under Shinagawa Takumi; 1954 to present, JPA show; 1963, 100 Japanese Prints exhibition, University of Oregon, Eugene; 1963 to present, CWAJ show; 1970, 90, Xylon International Print Triennial, Switzerland; 1974, 81, solo show, Denon Museum, Chalon-sur-Saone, France; 1975, Biennial of Paris; 1980, Premio International Print Biennial, Italy; 1991, solo show, Windmill Hole Studio, Berwick, England; 1992, Mexico-Japan Print Exhibition, Mexico City.

COLLECTIONS: British Museum, London; Osaka National Museum of International Art; Cincinnati Art Museum; Denon Museum, France; Yokohama Museum; University of Oregon, Eugene; Kanagawa and Yokohama Municipal Halls.

湯瀬義憲
(plate 94)

YUSE Yoshinori

1947, born in Akita Prefecture; 1971, graduated from Senshu University, Tokyo; 1979, began making silkscreen prints; 1980, solo show, Tolman Collection; 1980, 82, Ibiza International Print Biennial, Spain; 1980, solo show, Gallery Tak, Yokohama; 1980, 91, Krakow International Print Biennial; 1983, Taiwan International Print Biennial; 1984, Intergrafik, Berlin; 1984, solo show, Tolman Collection, Tokyo, 1992–93, CWAJ traveling show to Australia and New Zealand.

COLLECTIONS: British Museum, London; Ibiza Museum of Contemporary Art, Spain; Krakow National Museum; Gallery of New South Wales, Australia.

Suggested Readings

A reference library of works focusing on twentieth-century Japanese prints would ideally consist of the following nucleus:

Blakemore, Frances. *Who's Who in Modern Japanese Prints.* Tokyo and New York: John Weatherhill, 1975.

Johnson, Margaret K., and Dale K. Hilton. *Japanese Prints Today, Tradition with Innovation.* Tokyo: Shufunotomo Company, 1980.

Merritt, Helen. *Modern Japanese Woodblock Prints, the Early Years.* Honolulu: University of Hawaii Press, 1990.

Michener, James A. *The Modern Japanese Print: An Appreciation.* Tokyo and Rutland, Vermont: Charles E. Tuttle Company, 1968.

Petit, Gaston. *44 Modern Japanese Print Artists.* Tokyo: Kodansha International, 1973.

Smith, Lawrence. *Contemporary Japanese Prints: Symbols of a Society in Transition.* Organized by the British Museum, London, in association with the College Women's Association of Japan, Honolulu, Hawaii Loa College, and others. New York: Harper & Row, 1985.

Smith Lawrence. *The Japanese Print Since 1900: Old Dreams and New Visions.* London: the British Museum, 1983.

Statler, Oliver. *Modern Japanese Prints: An Art Reborn.* Tokyo and Rutland, Vermont: Charles E. Tuttle Company, 1959.

Tolman, Norman H., and Mary S. *People Who Make Japanese Prints: A Personal Glimpse.* Tokyo: Sobunsha, 1981.

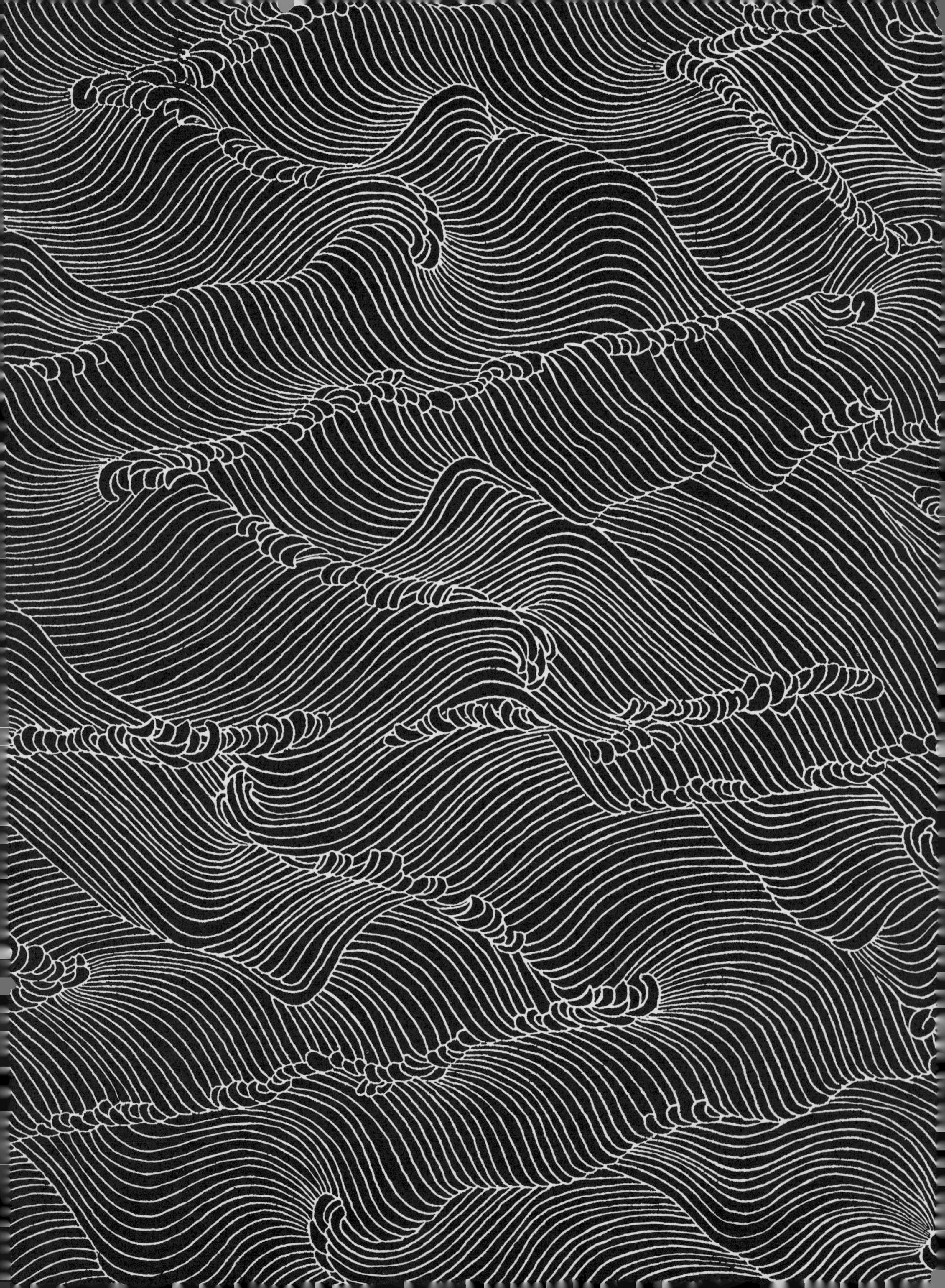